STRUCTURAL MODELING
BY EXAMPLE

STRUCTURAL MODELING BY EXAMPLE

APPLICATIONS IN EDUCATIONAL, SOCIOLOGICAL, AND BEHAVIORAL RESEARCH

Edited by

Peter Cuttance
University of Edinburgh

and

Russell Ecob
M. R. C. Medical Sociology Unit, Glasgow

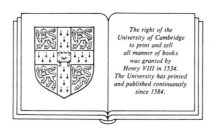

The right of the
University of Cambridge
to print and sell
all manner of books
was granted by
Henry VIII in 1534.
The University has printed
and published continuously
since 1584.

CAMBRIDGE UNIVERSITY PRESS

CAMBRIDGE

NEW YORK   NEW ROCHELLE   MELBOURNE   SYDNEY

Published by the Press Syndicate of the University of Cambridge
The Pitt Building, Trumpington Street, Cambridge CB2 1RP
32 East 57th Street, New York, NY 10022, USA
10 Stamford Road, Oakleigh, Melbourne 3166, Australia

© Cambridge University Press 1987

First published 1987

Printed in the United States of America

Library of Congress Cataloging-in-Publication Data
Structural modeling by example.
Includes index.
1. Social sciences–Mathematical models.
2. Social sciences–Research–Methodology.
I. Cuttance, Peter.   II. Ecob, Russell.
H61.25.S77   1987   300'.72   87–22419

ISBN 0 521 26195 3

British Library Cataloguing-in-Publication Data applied for

Contents

v

Contents

Preface

Since the development of structural equation models in the early 1970s, there has been a steady growth in their use in educational, social, and behavioral research. In the early period, two or three textbooks for researchers with a relatively advanced statistical knowledge were available, but it was not until the early 1980s that a basic introductory textbook (Saris & Stronkhorst 1983) became available. That volume, however, did not tackle the full range of issues in the application of structural modeling methods to the types of theories that most researchers work with in applied settings. Thus, the Saris and Stronkhorst text is best viewed only as a general introduction to the theory and methodology. There are also several introductory articles and short monographs that outline the basic methodology of structural modeling, but again they rarely describe in detail the process of applying the methodology to an applied research setting.

This volume attempts to fill that gap by providing several extended examples of the application of structural modeling to applied problems and by contrasting its strengths and weaknesses with the more naïve methods that are still the mainstay of applied research in these disciplines. These examples provide the reader with the rationale for, and a view of, the operational decisions that have to be made as the researcher works through an applied problem. In most publications, information is hidden from the view of the reader, since the focus is, rightly, on substantive issues rather than methodological issues.

This volume also reports a set of evaluations of the robustness of the method written from the point of view of the applied researcher rather than from the view of the statistician. The discussion is focused on the issues that emanate from a substantive perspective of the data, measurement, and modeling questions of most relevance to educational, social, and behavioral research. It is suggested that, although the statistical properties of estimators and of hypothesis testing are important, their salience in applied research is dependent on the properties of measurement and data generally available in these disciplines. Thus, the replication of findings, rather than a slavish adherence to hypothesis-testing method-ologies, is given prominence as the basic means of evaluating the validity of theories and of models based on them.

This does not mean, however, that hypothesis testing is in any sense irrelevant, because the other fundamental component of structural model-ing is the proposing of alternative models to explain the grid of relationships among the observed variables in the data. Models that do not adequately explain this pattern of relationships are rejected, and other model formulations developed from the literature and other sources of knowledge are put forward.

Although the volume does assume some basic familiarity with the fundamentals of structural modeling, it attempts to discuss the process of decision making as nontechnically as possible, although this is a tall order given the vocabulary surrounding the development of this methodology.

The authors are indebted to many colleagues in the research community for their generous contributions to the discussion of the issues that arose in the planning and development of this volume. The chapters benefited from the critical comments of colleagues too numerous to mention here, and the overall development of the volume owes much to the invisible college of researchers both in Edinburgh and in the international community.

We are particularly grateful for the support provided by the Centre for Educational Sociology at the University of Edinburgh. The program of research on the effectiveness of schooling initiated there in the early 1980s provided the impetus to reconsider the appropriateness of various statistical modeling techniques and to survey the applied modeling requirements of the wider social and behavioral science community. This work has recently led to the consideration of models for modeling multilevel processes, for which structural modeling, in its present stage of development, is not suitable.

We acknowledge the assistance provided by the U.K. Economic and Social Research Council through their support of workshops conducted by the editors and fellowships held by them during the production of the volume. The Centre for Educational Sociology at the University of Edinburgh provided generous secretarial and administrative support.

Contributors

ANNE BOOMSMA
Vakgroep Statistiek en Meettheorie, Faculteit der Sociale Wetenschappen, Rijksuniversiteit te Groningen, Oude Boteringestraat 23, 9712 GC Groningen, The Netherlands

JIM F. CASTEEL
Department of Educational Psychology, College of Education, University of South Carolina, Columbia, SC 29208

PETER CUTTANCE
Centre for Educational Sociology, University of Edinburgh, Edinburgh EH8 9LW, Scotland

RUSSELL ECOB
MRC Medical Sociology Unit, 6 Lilybank Gardens, Glasgow G12 8QQ, Scotland

JOAN K. GALLINI
Department of Educational Psychology, College of Education, University of South Carolina, Columbia, SC 29208

ROBERT M. HAUSER
Department of Sociology, University of Wisconsin–Madison, 1180 Observatory Drive, Madison, WI 53706

LESLIE HENDRICKSON
Center for Econometric Studies, P.O. Box 10925, Eugene, OR 97402

PETER W. HILL
Research Branch, Education Department of Western Australia, 151 Royal Street, East Perth, Western Australia 6000

BARNIE JONES
Motor Vehicles Division, Oregon Department of Transport, Salem, OR 97314

HENK KELDERMAN
Department of Education, Division of Educational Measurement and Data Analysis, Twent University of Technology, Postbus 217, 75000 EA Enschede, The Netherlands

PETER A. MOSSEL
560 Riverside Drive, Apt. 2F, New York, NY 10027

KATHARINE R. PARKES
Department of Experimental Psychology, University of Oxford, South Parks Road, Oxford OX1 3UD

J. DEN RONDEN
Department of Research Methods and Techniques, Vrije Universiteit, Valerinsplein 12–14, Amsterdam, The Netherlands

W. E. SARIS
Vakgroep Methodes en Technieken van Politicologisch Onderzoek, Universiteit van Amsterdam, Grimburgwal 10-gebouw 5, 1012GA Amsterdam, The Netherlands

A. SATORRA
Econometrics Department, Universidad Central, via Diagonal, Barcelona, Spain

LEE M. WOLFLE
College of Education, Virginia Polytechnic Institute and State University, Blacksburg, VA 24061

1

Introduction

PETER CUTTANCE AND RUSSELL ECOB

Structural modeling can be thought of as the marriage of two lines of methodological and statistical development in the social and behavioral sciences. These developments have their seminal roots in early attempts to apply statistical methods to economics and psychology, although similar developments can be observed in other disciplines also. The development of methods for the interpretation of data from widespread mental testing of adult populations in North America and Britain went hand in hand with the development of theories of mental ability. In order to test the efficacy of the various theories of mental ability put forward, the statistical model known today as factor analysis was developed. Since it was evident that a single test item could not tap the full extent of a person's ability in any given area, several items were employed jointly to measure ability. The variation that was common or shared among the items was interpreted as a measure of the underlying ability. Different sets of items were designed as measures of each of the mental abilities hypothesized by the alternative theories. The covariation among these underlying abilities (which were called factors or constructs) was then interpreted in terms of the evidence it provided for the alternative hierarchical and relational models of human abilities put forward in the research.

One aspect of these early models that has been carried over to structural modeling is the idea that a latent construct or factor can be *measured* by the responses to a set of items on a test. In later work this idea was carried forward as the concept of observable indicators for an unobservable construct or, in another context, as multiple measures of a *true score* in test score theory.

A second idea that has been carried forward into structural modeling is that of the correlation between unobservable constructs. This gives rise to the model of covariance structures among latent constructs in structural modeling. The essential feature of covariance structure models is that they deal not with the causal or predictive relationships between the substantive constructs of a theory, but rather with the covariation among latent constructs.

1

In contrast, developments in economics focused on the analysis of causal and predictive relationships between one set of variables (the dependent variables) and another set of variables (the independent variables). Economists were initially interested in simple single-equation models, but before long their attention turned to the modeling of systems of equations, representing several processes that theoretical models argued were interlinked and operating simultaneously.

The birth of the methodology known today as structural modeling was brought about by the recognition that many social and behavioral processes could be thought of as causal processes operating among unobserved constructs. This suggested the merging of the latent construct model from psychology with the causal models found in economics. Although the recognition of this model in the form of the path analysis model was useful, it was soon realized that this solution was inadequate, for two reasons. First, it did not allow the researcher to test how well the model explained the covariation in the data, and second, the parameter estimates for the model were apt to vary with the restrictions employed in identifying the model. In general, the substantive models that path models represented were often overidentified, because they posited that several of the causal relationships were zero, and this meant that the remaining relationships in the model could be estimated from different combinations of the correlations among the observed variables. These different combinations do not necessarily yield identical estimates of the parameters in the model. Hence, some method of obtaining estimates of parameters that in combination gave the best fit to the covariation among the observed variables was required, given the causal relationship specified by the model. This led to the development of maximum likelihood estimation methods for estimating and testing the fit of structural likelihood estimation methods for estimating and testing the fit of structural models. Other methods that make less restrictive distributional assumptions about the data have also been developed.

The major advance of structural modeling, then, has been that it has provided a means of testing the capacity of alternative substantive models to account for the pattern of covariation among the observed variables in the data and to do this in terms of latent constructs that parallel the underlying constructs of the substantive model.

Although this advance is in line with recent arguments about the nature of the relationship between theory and the measurement of social and behavioral phenomena, it obviously does not deal with the more radical critiques of the relationship between theory and observation/meaning emanating from phenomenological perspectives of the social world. It is useful for the researcher who uses structural modeling methods to keep in mind that there are alternative views of the appropriate methodology for studying social and behavioral phenomena, because it is unlikely that any one perspective or methodology for investigating and understanding the behavior under study will yield the *true* understanding of the behavior.

Chapter 2 provides an overview of structural modeling and presents the formal mathematical and statistical model employed to represent the substantive model the researcher wishes to investigate. Unless readers are already familiar with the basic statistical framework for the LISREL model, they are advised to acquaint themselves with the material in that chapter before going on to the other chapters. Chapter 2 is not intended, however, to be a detailed introduction to the model, for which the reader is referred to the text by Saris and Stronkhorst (1984) or the other material listed in the Reference section of Chapter 2.

Chapters 3–5 illustrate the application of structural modeling to situations that conform to psychologists' models of covariation among the latent constructs of a substantive model. In Chapter 3 Katharine Parkes examines the relationship between constructs represented in two widely used self-report inventories for measuring different aspects of neurotic disorders. The analysis compares the structure of disorders between two groups of subjects. The data had been analyzed previously by conventional correlational methods, and the structure of the relationships among the disorders found to differ between the two groups; however, the present simultaneous analysis of the data suggests that this earlier conclusion was unwarranted. The two main reasons for revising the conclusions are to be found in the fact that the structural modeling approach takes account of the fallibility of the measurement of the individual items in the model and formally tests the hypothesis that the structures differ in the two groups. The model that posits identical structures in the two groups can explain the pattern of covariation among the variables observed in the data just as well as the alternative model, which posits that the structure is different in the two groups. Thus, structural modeling analysis leads to a conclusion about the nature of neurotic disorders with respect to these groups that is substantially different from that arrived at by the earlier naïve analysis of the data.

Chapter 4 by Lee Wolfle illustrates a model of the structure of responses by high school seniors to a questionnaire inquiry about the level of education and the occupation of their parents. These responses are contrasted with those of the parents themselves. The social science survey literature indicates different subgroups in the population may respond with different degrees of accuracy and reliability on questionnaire items relating to parental background characteristics. In this study Wolfle models the responses of black and white children and their parents.

Measures of covariation and of the strength of causal relationships are attenuated by error introduced in the measurement of such characteristics, and differential attenuation across subgroups in the data could lead one astray when interpreting intergroup differences in such relationships. This chapter again illustrates the interplay between the substantive, methodological, and statistical aspects of the specification and fitting of structural models. The actual model presented is relatively simple, three factors among six observed variables, but because of the clarity of the methodology it yields significant information about the response reliability of the subgroups studied.

In Chapter 5 Peter Hill presents a structural model to test Bloom et al.'s (1956) taxonomy of cognitive learning structures. This taxonomy posits a hierarchical relationship among various learning behaviors and is modeled as an extension of Guttman's (1954) simplex design. This design specifies a hierarchical structure through an ordered multiplicative relationship among the constructs. Since the model takes into account the errors of measurement in each of the observed variables, the appropriate version of the design is that known as a quasi simplex. The analysis provides tests of certain specific substantive hypotheses that allow the researcher to refine issues of uncertainty sequentially in this field of empirical inquiry.

Chapters 6–8 illustrate how structural modeling can be applied in a causal framework. Here the factor and construct methodology of the psychologist is linked to the causal framework derived from that developed in economics. In Chapter 6 Leslie Hendrickson and Barnie Jones specify and estimate a model of the relationships between pupil achievement in the third and fourth grades. They contrast the modeling of this process in a causal framework with that of the usual gain score framework and show that the latter model is likely to yield misleading results in the presence of measurement error, because it omits relevant intervening variables from the model. They illustrate the use of sensitivity analysis to investigate key aspects of the specification of the model.

In Chapter 7 Robert Hauser and Peter Mossel model the relationship between educational attainment and occupational status attainment among siblings within families and among families. This allows them to estimate the variance components associated with families and hence to investigate the dynastic influences of families on the occupational careers of their offspring. They work with a relatively simple model containing only four observed variables, which again illustrates the point that one does not necessarily require highly complex models containing a large number of variables in order to make progress. Indeed, one of the lessons to be learned from successful applications of structural modeling methods is that models that are poorly thought out in terms of the substantive theory on which they are based rarely yield interpretable findings.

In Chapter 8 Russell Ecob employs a structural model to estimate and fit a longitudinal model of the relationship between learning difficulties and progress in learning to read. The model can be viewed as an extension of the conventional cross-lagged correlation model, but by incorporating it into a structural modeling framework he is able to take account of the fallibility of the observed measures and to control for aspects of pupils' social backgrounds that influence the process of learning. He shows that a model that fails to take account of these two dimensions of the research question is likely to provide a misleading account of the relationship between learning difficulties and progress in learning to read.

Chapters 9 and 10 report two studies of the robustness of structural modeling against the assumptions made in estimating and fitting the model. In Chapter 9 Anne Boomsma presents findings from a large-scale Monte Carlo study of the maximum likelihood method for estimating model parameters and tests of the fit of a model. She investigates the behavior of the method for a range of distributional features of data found in the social and behavioral sciences. This study is the most extensive investigation of the robustness of structural modeling conducted thus far and provides several benchmarks for the use of the method in various applied situations. In general, it suggests that the maximum likelihood estimator is relatively robust against modest departures from the skewness and kurtosis of the normal distribution for parameter estimates, but that the standard errors, confidence intervals, and likelihood ratio test of fit are somewhat more sensitive to such departures from the characteristics of the normal distribution. Joan Gallini and Jim Casteel investigate the structural modeling analogue of the issue of influential observations in the regression analysis model in Chapter 10. They compare estimates for a model based on a data set trimmed of outliers with those for the full data set. As in the regression analysis case, the influence of outliers is greatest in models estimated from small samples. They authors suggest that the effects of outlier observations on parameter estimates and standard errors are minor in moderately large samples.

In Chapter 11 Willem Saris, J. den Ronden, and Alberto Satorra present the statistical issues the researcher faces in assessing the fit of models through the use of the likelihood ratio test statistc. They demonstrate that many of the path models published in the literature do not fit the data and that the failure to test the fit of a model has often led to conclusions that are not warranted by the data. They argue that it is not sufficient to assess the fit of a model solely on the basis of the likelihood ratio test statistic, that the power of the test must also be taken into account before any conclusions about the adequacy of the model can be drawn. They show that tests of hypotheses associated with the parameters in a model are dependent both on sample size and on the structure and magnitude of parameters in the model. Some models can yield a relatively powerful test even if the samples are small, but others require much larger samples if the hypothesis tests are to yield informative results. The authors propose a formal testing procedure that also indicates the degree of power of the test. This procedure is to be incorporated into the LISREL program (version VII and later versions) so that it can be employed routinely in structural modeling applications.

In Chapter 12 Henk Kelderman shows how constraints on the relationships among the parameters in LISREL models can be incorporated into more advanced applications of structural modeling. Other parametrizations of structural models such as EQS in BMDP (Bentler 1984) and COSAN (McDonald 1985) deal with such constraints more directly because they employ a different basic parametrization of the model. A specific case of interest in many situations is the parametrization that can be used in LISREL to ensure that all estimates of error variances are positive, that is the avoidance of Heywood cases.

In the final chapter Peter Cuttance discusses a range of issues and problems that bear on the robustness and validity of the estimates from the various methods of estimation now available in structural modeling programs. He argues that the confirmatory aspect of structural modeling in conjunction with the replication of findings are at least as important in assessing the evidence about the robustness and validity of findings as are issues about the statistical robustness of the estimators and tests of model fit.

The chapter examines the role of replication in social and behavioral research before considering the methodological issues that influence the statistical robustness of parameter estimates, hypothesis tests, and tests of model fit. Given the imperfections of data collection, sample design, and sample administration in most social and behavioral research, we must evaluate the extent to which we emphasize the statistical robustness of the testing procedures and parameter estimates and the extent to which we focus on the replicability of the research findings. Structural modeling is, after all, only an intermediary between the observations of real social and behavioral processes and the theories or models through which we interpret and understand those processes. Hence, considerations of validity and interpretability require referents that are ultimately external to the model testing and estimation procedures themselves. It is these referents to which the methodology of replication and confirmation appeals for its veracity. The statistical robustness of models reduces the opportunity for disagreement among models that are true representations of the underlying processes when they are replicated using data collected from independent studies.

The characteristics of measurement in social and behavioral science underlie the basic concerns about the distributional properties of observed variables, which directly influence the choice of and characteristics of the measures employed to summarize the covariation in the data. The robustness of alternative estimators is discussed in terms of their susceptibility to departures from the distributional properties of the normal distribution. The class of estimators based on the maximum likelihood and generalized least squares estimation procedures are robust to moderate departures from normality. The findings from the chapter by Boomsma and from related studies provide a guide as to when more sophisticated distribution-free estimators should be employed. The distribution-free estimators are now more widely available, but they are still too computationally expensive to be employed as front line estimators to replace the maximum likelihood and generalized least squares procedures in the routine estimation of models.

The Appendix lists the LISREL model specifications required to estimate the main models in each of the chapters. It also illustrates the relationship between the mathematical model in its equation and matrix format, as well as the relationship between the latter and the LISREL matrix formulation of the model. The details of the model specification process shown in the Appendix should allow readers to check their own formulation of the models presented in the chapters and to run the models in order to check whether their estimates correspond to those presented in the text. The data for the analyses are also listed in the Appendix, and we suggest that readers make use of the material there to verify their understanding of the methodology and models presented in the book.

References

Bentler, P. M. (1984). *Theory and Implementation of EQS: A Structural Equations Program*. Los Angeles: BMDP Statistical Software.

Bloom, B. S., Englehart, M. D., Furst, E. J., Hill, W. H., & Krathwohl, D. R. (1956). *Taxonomy of Educational Objectives, Handbook 1: Cognitive Domain*. New York: McKay.

Guttman, L. (1954). A new approach to factor analysis: The radex. In P. Lazarsfeld (Ed.), *Mathematical Thinking in the Social Sciences*. Glencoe, IL: Free Press.

McDonald, R. P. (1985). *Factor Analysis and Related Methods*. Hillsdale, NJ: Erlbaum.
Saris, W. E., & Stronkhorst, L. H. (1984). *Introduction to Causal Modeling in Non Experimental Research*. Amsterdam: Sociometric Research Foundation.

2

An overview of structural equation modeling

RUSSELL ECOB and PETER CUTTANCE

Introduction

As indicated in Chapter 1, *structural equation modeling* can be conveniently viewed as a product of the merging of two approaches to model fitting: *multiple regression* and *factor analysis*. The multiple regression approach expresses the relationship of a dependent variable to a number of *regressor* variables, the partial relationship with each variable being expressed by the regression coefficient corresponding to that variable. In contrast, the factor analysis approach finds a number of underlying or latent variables (or factors) that account for the common relationship among a number of observed variables.

In this chapter we examine characteristics of the two approaches and illustrate the differences between them. We then show how the method of structural equation modeling arises from a merging of the two approaches. Finally, we list and explain the general conditions, or framework assumptions, of the models examined and the statistical assumptions required to make the estimation of the models tractable.

The regression (or structural) model

The regression model has four basic characteristics. First, it comprises one equation. Second, this equation specifies a directional relationship between two sets of variables, the dependent variable and a set of *regressor* variables. The variation in the dependent variable is explained by a weighted combination of the values of the regressor variables, the weights being the regression coefficients.[1] Third, the regressor variables are assumed to be measured without error. Fourth, each regressor variable is assumed to be linearly related to the dependent variable.

Of these four basic characteristics, only the second is fundamental to the regression model. All the others can be relaxed within the so-called general linear model. By considering more than one equation simultaneously, a variable that is a regressor variable in one equation can be

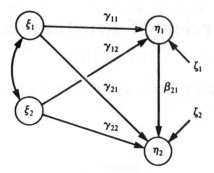

Figure 2.1. Structural model.

specified as a dependent variable in another. This system of equations is known to sociologists as *path analysis* and will be seen to represent the structural aspect of some of the applications in this volume. It also represents the basic form that many econometric models take.[2]

Unreliability, or measurement error, in the regressor variables, either when known by independent means or when estimated from the sample, can be dealt with in the regression approach. This is done by specifying the proportion of variance in the observed variable that is attributable to measurement error (Fuller & Hidiroglou 1978; Goldstein 1979).

Within the structural equation framework the regression model is specified in the *structural* model, and the factor analysis model is specified in the *measurement* model. Figure 2.1 shows a simplified version of the model employed in Chapter 6, which we use to illustrate the LISREL formulation of a structural model. We can think of the two latent constructs denoted by ξ_1 and ξ_2 as the regressor variables in the model and the two latent constructs denoted by η_1 and η_2 as the dependent variables in the model. The relationships between the dependent and regressor variables are then described by the following two equations:

$$\eta_1 = \gamma_{11}\xi_1 + \gamma_{12}\xi_2 + \zeta_1$$
$$\eta_2 = \beta_{21}\eta_1 + \gamma_{21}\xi_1 + \gamma_{22}\xi_2 + \zeta_2$$

How is this system related to the characteristics of the regression model introduced earlier?

There are now two equations, each involving a dependent variable. The regressor variable set is different in the two equations. The first equation includes the two constructs ξ_1 and ξ_2. The second equation includes, in addition, η_1. It is clear that a variable can serve in two roles, as a regressor variable in one equation and as a dependent variable in another.

In order to accommodate this, variables that function only as regressor variables in all equations in a system of equations, and are thus determined by factors outside the system, are called exogenous variables and are denoted by ξ (xi). The other variables are determined in part by variables within the system of equations; these are called endogenous variables and are denoted by η (eta). The regression coefficients of the endogenous variables on one another are denoted by β (beta), the subscripts corresponding, in order, to the dependent and regressor part of the relation. The regression coefficients relating the endogenous to the exogenous variables are denoted by γ (gamma). Since the dependent variable must be specified as an endogenous variable in the system, there are no regression relationships among exogenous variables (the ξ variables) in the system.

In the example above, the variables, both exogenous and endogenous, are measured according to a model specified by the measurement model. In the case of the exogenous variables this is equivalent to a simple factor analysis model, described in the next section.

The factor analysis (or measurement) model

Factor analysis has four basic characteristics.[3] First, relationships among observed variables are explained in terms of the relation of each observed variable to a number of latent or unobserved variables or constructs and in terms of the relations of the latent constructs to one another. The number of latent constructs is fewer than the number of observed variables. The factor analysis model should be distinguished from the *principal components analysis* model.[4] Second, all observed variables have an equivalent status: No distinction is made, as in regression, between dependent and regressor variables. Third, all variables and constructs are assumed to be continuous. Fourth, all relationships are assumed to be linear.

The first two characteristics are fundamental to the factor analysis method. However, nonlinear relationships can occur either among the latent constructs or between the latent constructs and observed variables. Nonlinear relationships among latent constructs can be modeled in some situations (Etezadi-Amoli & McDonald 1983), though such nonlinear models are rarely employed in the social and behavioral sciences because the theoretical formulation of most models is not sufficiently well developed to make such an approach feasible.

Factor analysis has been extended to deal with noncontinuous or categorical observed variables where the relationships with the latent constructs cannot be modeled directly in a linear sense. A particular case is that in which the observed variable is a binary variable, for example, a response to a questionnaire taking the values yes and no. In this case a continuous variable is assumed to underie the binary observed variable and is in turn linearly related to the latent construct.

Two common options for the creation of a proxy continuous variable are the logit function and the probit function, each giving rise to a continuous variable that can take any value. The logit function forms the value $\log[p/(1-p)]$ from the proportion p in one category of the observed variable. This is used by Bartholomew (1980) in his binary factor analysis model. The probit function forms the value of $\varphi^{-1}(p)$, where φ^{-1} is the value of a normally distributed variable whose cumulative probability is p. This approach is employed by Muthén (1978). Both probit and logit functions agree closely for values of p that are not extreme. Such models extend to observed variables in the form of a number of categories (polytomous variables) and to observed variables in which the categories can be ordered.[5]

Ordered categorical variables can be accommodated within the linear continuous framework of the LISREL model if they are represented as approximate measures of an underlying continuous variable. Thresholds are assigned to the values of this underlying variable corresponding to each value taken by the ordered categorical variable. By assuming that this variable has a normal distribution one obtains these thresholds from the inverse of the normal distribution function.

For any two observed categorical variables the polychoric correlation is calculated, representing the product–moment correlation between the underlying continuous variables. When one of the variables is continuous and the other is an ordered categorical variable, a polyserial correlation coefficient is calculated representing the product–moment correlation between the underlying and observed continuous variables. In this way, the correlation matrix is generated for observed variables with a mixture of scale types, which is then treated as equivalent to one generated by observed continuous variables.[6].

An alternative framework for incorporating categorical variables in the linear continuous framework is provided by the simultaneous analysis of multiple groups. The groups are defined by the values of the relevant categorical variable (e.g., gender – male/female groups), and factor models are estimated for each group. This allows for constraints to be applied across groups. For example, the factor loadings can be constrained to be equal across groups, thus allowing for a test of invariance in the factor structure across the groups. Chapters 3, 4, and 8 provide illustrations of the use of multiple-group models in the context of structural equation modeling.

An example of a factor analysis model is given in Figure 2.2. This forms

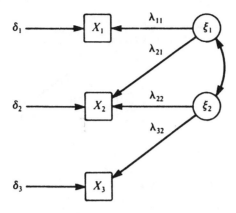

Figure 2.2. Measurement model (factor analysis).

part of the measurement model in Chapter 6 and shows the two latent constructs, or factors, denoted by ξ_1 and ξ_2. These are indicated, or measured, by three observed variables X_1, X_2, X_3.

The latent constructs are related to these observed indicator variables by the following equations:

$$X_1 = \lambda_{11}\xi_1 + \delta_1$$
$$X_2 = \lambda_{21}\xi_1 + \lambda_{22}\xi_2 + \delta_2$$
$$X_3 = \qquad\quad \lambda_{32}\xi_2 + \delta_3$$

By convention, observed variables are denoted by Latin symbols and latent variables by Greek symbols. These equations are similar in form to the equations in the structural part of the model. In this case the dependent variables are observed and the regressor variables are unobserved or latent. The coefficients relating the two sets of variables are called the loadings (of the indicator on the factor or latent construct).

It will be noted that some of the possible relationships between indicators and latent constructs do not appear in the model. This constraint is necessary in order that unique estimates for the loadings can be provided (in other words, so that the model can be "identified"). The particular relationships that do not appear, equivalent to constraining the relationships to be zero, are part of the specification of the model; hence, they derive from the theoretical model of which the mathematical model is the formal representation.

In order to provide estimates of the parameters of such models, certain distributional assumptions about the (indicator-specific) errors must be made. They are usually assumed to be independently normally distributed. The model then provides estimates of the loadings relating the

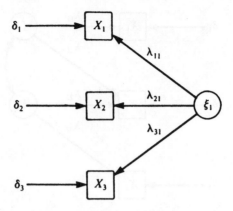

Figure 2.3. Measurement model (classical test score theory).

observed to the unobserved variables, the relationships (correlations, covariances) among the unobserved variables, and the variances and covariances for each of the errors.

A particular form of the factor analysis model occurs when there is only one latent construct on which a number of indicators load. This is shown in Figure 2.3. The models of classical test score theory are produced by varying the restrictions as to the equality of the loadings and the error variances. In Chapter 6, Hendrickson and Jones employ a particular form of this model to represent the measurement of reading attainment, using one indicator only on each occasion. For identification purposes it is usually necessary to specify either the construct loading or the measurement error variance when a construct is measured by only one observed variable. However, certain parts of a model may also be identified without the prior specification of one of these, as is the case for the endogenous constructs in that model.

The structural equation model

The integration of the structural and measurement models in Figures 2.1 and 2.2 into a structural model is shown in Figure 2.4. The structural model relates the latent constructs to one another, and the measurement model relates the latent constructs to the observed variables.

The version of the structural equation model[7] that we describe here is generally known as the Jöreskog–Keesling–Wiley model (Keesling 1972; Jöreskog 1973, 1981; Wiley 1973). Jöreskog was instrumental in making this model accessible to researchers through the computer program

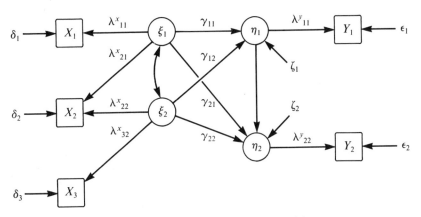

Figure 2.4. Structural equation model.

LISREL. Other versions, or parametrizations, of this model have been produced by McDonald (1978, 1980), Bentler and Weeks (1979), and McArdle and McDonald (1984). These have a number of attractive features, in particular a simple and economical representation. However, the LISREL version, with its separation of the measurement and structural aspects of the model, is convenient for researchers to conceptualize and is the one used in this volume.

One feature of the LISREL version of the structural equation model is the facility with which simple restrictions are imposed on the parameters. These allow for tests of the theoretical specification of the model. Any parameter in the model can be fixed either to zero or to another value, or can be fixed to be equal to another parameter or set of parameters. For example, constraining parameters in the structural part of the model to zero allows for a test of the hypothesis that latent constructs vary independently of one another.

Any two or more indicators can be constrained to have indicator-specific errors with equal variance or to have the same loadings on a common latent construct. Finally, in a multiple-group analysis, parameters can be constrained to be equal across groups in either the measurement or structural model, allowing tests of whether one or more parts of the model are equivalent across groups. One role for such analyses lies in determining the extent to which a model can be generalized across population groups, as in Chapters 3, 4, and 8.

The basic objective of structural modeling is to provide a means of estimating the relationships among the underlying constructs of a hypothesized substantive model. Here the method differs from others such as regression analysis and contingency table analysis in that it focuses not on the relationships among the observed variables but on those among the unobserved (latent) constructs of the substantive model. This requires a means of linking the observed variables to the latent constructs, which is specified in the *measurement model*. Thus, the observed variables are specified, on an a priori basis, to be *indicators* of a particular latent construct. Assuming linearity, the measurement model is written as

$$\mathbf{Y} = \Lambda_y \eta + \varepsilon$$
$$\mathbf{X} = \Lambda_x \xi + \delta$$

where $\mathbf{Y}$, $\mathbf{X}$ are, respectively, vectors of observed scores on the endogenous and exogenous variables, η and ξ are, respectively, vectors of endogenous and exogenous latent constructs, Λ_y and Λ_x are, respectively, matrices of construct loadings for η and ξ, and ε and δ are vectors of random measurement errors.

The relationships among the latent constructs are specified in the *structural model*, which, again assuming linearity, is written

$$\eta = \beta \eta + \Gamma \xi + \zeta$$

where the β (beta) is a matrix of structural parameters relating the endogenous constructs to one another, Γ (gamma) is a matrix of structural parameters relating the endogenous constructs to the exogenous constructs, and ζ (zeta) is a vector of disturbances representing the unexplained variation in the endogenous constructs.

Framework assumptions

Two types of assumption are required to estimate the parameters of the statistical model and to assess how well it accounts for the relationships in a given set of data. The first can be referred to as the *framework assumptions*, and they describe the general conditions embodied in the specification of the statistical model. The second are referred to as the *statistical assumptions* and are required in order to make the task of estimating and testing the model tractable.

There are five framework assumptions:
F1. The relationships among variables are linear.
F2. The effects of the latent explanatory variables on the latent outcome variables are additive.
F3. The relationship between latent explanatory and latent outcome variables is stochastic.
F4. The observed variables are continuous and measured on an interval scale.

F5. The data are represented by the means, variance, and covariances of the observed variables.

The assumption that the relationships between variables are linear (F1) is not as restrictive as it may appear at first sight. Many nonlinear relationships can also be approximated by or transformed into linear relationships by transforming with logarithms, exponentials, powers (the square or cube, square root, etc.) to give a relationship that is linear in the transformed metric. However, the main reason the relationships are often specified to be linear is that most social and behavioral science theories are not sufficiently well developed to specify the relationships among concepts in nonlinear forms. A linear form is thus assumed for reasons of parsimony, unless there are indications that a particular nonlinear form is more appropriate.

The assumption that the effects of variables are additive (F2) is also not as restrictive as it first appears. Additive models imply that the effect of each variable is independent of the values of other variables in the model. If the effect of one variable depends on the values of another variable, we say that there is an interaction between these variables. Two practical solutions are available in structural modeling when interactions are present. First, if the interaction involves a variable that takes few values (e.g., gender), then since the interaction implies that the relationships in the data differ for different subgroups (e.g., males and females) it makes sense to estimate the model for each subgroup separately. By using the facility to analyze several groups simultaneously in LISREL it is possible to allow for differences in these relationships across groups for those variables involved in the interactions. The second solution is to construct a new variable that captures the interaction (usually specified as a multiplicative composite of the variables) and to use this variable in addition to the original variables in the analysis. This second solution specifies an additive effect for the interaction, in addition to an additive effect for each of the original variables. A drawback of this second solution is that it may exacerbate the nonnormality of the multivariate distribution for the data.

Assumption F3, that the relationship between latent explanatory and latent outcome variables is stochastic, indicates that it is not fully deterministic. That is, the model specifies that not all of the variation in the latent outcome variables is accounted for ("explained") by the latent explanatory variables. The unexplained portion of the latent outcome variable is represented by a stochastic residual attached to each relationship. This residual is assumed to have certain statistical properties, which are introduced in the next section. The residual can be thought of as representing the net influence of potential explanatory variables, which are omitted from the model specified, usually because no measures of them are available in the data employed in the analysis. However, certain writers have suggested that human behavior contains an inherently random element; hence, it would be impossible *in principle* to account for all variation in an outcome measure in terms of systematic influences only. If this view is valid, the residual would also represent this random aspect of behavior for the outcome studied.

Assumption F4, that the observed variables are measured on a continuous scale with interval properties, implies that the underlying concept is continuous as opposed to categorical and that the distance between scale points is represented by their magnitude. We know that the actual measurement scales employed in the behavioral and social sciences often do not satisfy this assumption. In particular, they are often not interval but ordered polytomous scales. The magnitudes attached to points on the scales are assumed to reflect only approximately the underlying epistemology of the scale. The assumption that the variable could be represented by a continuous distribution is often less contentious. Variables that cannot be represented by a continuous distribution are referred to as categorical variables (e.g., gender, school identification numbers, a list of countries). Such variables, however, can also be represented as pseudocontinuous variables if each category is coded as a dummy variable (Fox 1984).

Assumption F5 indicates that the data are described by the means, variances, and covariances for the observed variables. This is satisfied if the variables are normally distributed but is not fully met if they have kurtosis or skewness that differs from that of the normal distribution.

Statistical assumptions

The statistical assumption made in order to estimate and test the model can be stated as follows:

S1. The disturbances in all equations have mean zero: $E(\zeta) = 0$.

S2. The disturbances are uncorrelated with the exogenous variables: $E(\zeta\xi) = 0$.

S3. The errors of measurement are uncorrelated with the constructs such that $E(\varepsilon\eta) = E(\delta\xi) = 0$.

S4. The measurement errors and the disturbances are all mutually uncorrelated: $E(\varepsilon\delta) = E(\varepsilon\zeta) = E(\delta\zeta) = 0$.

S5. The joint distribution of the observed variables is multivariate normal.

The first four assumptions are required for estimating the parameters of the model; the fifth is required to assess the fit of the model and to test hypotheses about the parameters. Assumption S1 is necessary, but not sufficient, for the estimates of the model to be unbiased.

Assumption S2 requires that the stochastic disturbances be uncorrelated with all explanatory variables in the model. Thus, the net variation of any potential explanatory variables that are omitted from the model is assumed to be orthogonal to that of the explanatory variables formally included. If this assumption is violated, the model is misspecified and the estimates of the parameters are biased. This is described in the econometrics literature under the rubric of specification bias.

Assumption S3 states that any errors of measurement in the observed variables are not systematically related to the constructs underlying those variables. The methodological impact of the assumption is to define the relationships in the measurement models such that the latent constructs are interpreted as measuring the common variation among the observed indicators and the error terms contain both random measurement error and variance that is unique to each indicator. Thus, the error terms in the measurement models conflate true measurement error and any unique variation in an observed indicator.

Assumption S4 is made in the LISREL specification of structural models, although it is partially relaxed in some other specifications of these models (e.g., McDonald 1978, 1980; Bentler & Weeks 1979). The assumption of independence between the measurement errors for the endogenous and exogenous variables [i.e., $E(\varepsilon\delta) = 0$] can be circumvented in the LISREL model by specifying all observed variables as Y variables and all latent constructs as η constructs (see Chapter 8 for an example). The assumption of independence between the measurement errors and the equation residuals is employed as a means of *identifying* the parameters of the model. In general, it is a relatively innocuous assumption in that it is probably satisfied in most data. Violation of the assumption would require that influences on the outcome variable due to variables omitted from the model also influence the errors of measurement on the observed variables, or that these omitted variables are correlated with the uniqueness attributable to the observed variables included in the model. As it turns out, only correlations between the errors on the explanatory variables and the residuals [$E(\zeta\delta) \neq 0$] will result in biased estimates of structural parameters. A nonzero correlation between the equation residuals and errors on the observed outcome variables will result in a confounding of these two sources of variation on the right (dependent variable) side of the model but will not bias the estimates of the structural parameters of the model. This confounding of variation on the right side of the model will, however, affect the calculation of variance explained by the equations in the model. The assumption that $E(\varepsilon\zeta) = 0$ is required in order to purge the latent construct representing outcomes of variance due to measurement error in the indicators of the construct. The explained variance of the equation is then calculated as the degree to which the explanatory latent constructs account for variation in the latent construct measuring outcomes.

Assumption S5, that the variables have a joint multivariate normal distribution is required for the maximum likelihood method of estimating the parameters in the model. This assumption is the statistical counterpart to assumption F5, that the means, variances, and covariances among variables fully describe the information in the data. The generalized least squares method of estimation (Jöreskog & Goldberger 1972; Browne 1982) allows the slightly weaker distributional assumption of nonnormal kurtosis. However, since most data with any degree of skewness will generally also have nonnormal kurtosis, this slightly weaker assumption is unlikely to be satisfied much more often than that of multivariate normality.

The assumption of multivariate normality is also required in order to assess the likelihood ratio test statistic, which has a chi-square distribution if the observed variables have a multivariate normal distribution. In the concluding chapter we discuss alternative ways of measuring the fit of models, but the likelihood ratio test statistic usually plays an important role in this process. Other estimation methods that require weaker distributional assumptions than those outlined are also discussed in the final chapter.

Notes

1. The regression coefficients are estimated by forming a model in which the dependent variable Y_i is expressed as a sum of products of the regressors X_i and regression coefficients β_i and, in addition, an error or disturbance term ε. Thus, $Y = \Sigma_{i=0}^{k}\beta_iX_i + \varepsilon$. The estimates of the regression coefficients using ordinary least squares are those that minimize the sum of squares of errors over the observations. This method is an optimum one in the sense of producing regression estimates that have minimum variance when the errors are independent across observations and have constant variance for different regressor values. Variation in the error variance with different regressor values is explicitly taken into account by the generalized least squares method (GLS) and the maximum likelihood method (ML). GLS and ML are the most efficient estimation methods possible for large samples and are more efficient than ordinary least squares when the errors are not independently and identically distributed.

2. An introduction to regression models is given by Zeller and Carmines (1978) and by Wonnacott and Wonnacott (1985). The extension to simultaneous

estimation in systems of more than one equation is provided in econometrics texts such as Wonnacott and Wonnacott (1979), and Van de Geer (1971) provides a path-analysis-orientated approach.

3. Overviews of factor analysis are provided by Van de Geer (1971), Gorsuch (1983), Long (1983), and McDonald (1985).

4. Factor analysis is distinguished from principal component analysis in the following way. Principal component analysis aims to express a set of observed variables in terms of a lower number of linear combinations so as to account for the maximum variation among them. In contrast to factor analysis it does not allow for unique variation in the observed variables other than that incorporated in their representation as linear combinations. Its statistical heritage is different from that of factor analysis, hence also from that of structural equation modeling. Comparisons are drawn between the two methods in Jöreskog and Wold (1981, chap. 12).

It is possible for structural equation methods to produce principal component analyses by constraining all measurement errors to be equal to zero and making the relations among the latent variables orthogonal by constraining the correlation among them to be zero. Estimation in factor analysis is carried out by maximizing the fit of the variance–covariance matrix of the observed variables to that derived through their modeled relations to the latent constructs, and of these to each other. The relationships between observed and latent variables can either be taken as known (confirmatory factor analysis) or estimated (exploratory factor analysis), the relationships among the latent variables usually being estimated. However, known or assumed relationships among these variables (e.g., that they vary independently of one another) can be introduced. In practice, the knowledge of the relationship between observed and latent variables may be partial, in that each observed variable is assumed to be related to a subset only of the latent variables. The particular form of relationship in this subset (in factor analysis terminology, the loadings on the factors) is generally unknown.

5. Other related methods for continuous and categorical variables are available. Wolfe (1970) describes model-based cluster analysis for continuous variables, and Clogg (1981) and Aitkin, Anderson, and Hinde (1981) apply methods that relate categorical latent constructs to ordered and unordered observed variables.

6. This method differs from those of Bartholomew (1980) and of Muthén (1978) in that the relationships between each pair of observed variables are summarized in terms of a (bivariate) correlation before they are input to the estimation procedures of structural modeling. The methods of Bartholomew and Muthén retain all of the information on the bivariate distributions of the observed categorical variables until the parameter estimation stage. This has the advantage of allowing for a more relaxed set of distributional assumptions, although at the expense of much more complex estimation procedures.

7. The term "covariance structure models" is used in the literature synonymously with "structural equation models." See, for example, Bielby and Hauser (1977), Bentler (1980), and Browne (1982).

References

Aitkin, M., Anderson, D., & Hinde, J. (1981). Statistical modeling of teaching styles (with discussion). *Journal of the Royal Statistical Society A, 144,* 419–61.

Bartholomew, D. J. (1980). Factor analysis for categorical data (with discussion). *Journal of the Royal Statistical Society B,* 42, 293–321.

Bentler, P. M. (1980). Multivariate analysis with latent variables: Causal modeling. *Annual review of Psychology, 31,* 419–56.

Bentler, P. M. & Weeks, P. G. (1979). Interrelations among models for the analysis of moment structures. *Multivariate Behavioral Research, 14,* 169–85.

Bielby, W. T., & Hauser, R. M. (1977). Structural equation models. In A. Inkles, J. Coleman, & N. Smelser (Eds.), *Annual Review of Sociology* (pp. 137–61). Palo Alto, CA: Annual Reviews.

Browne, M. W. (1982). Covariance structures. In R. M. Hawkins (Ed.), *Topics in Applied Multivariate Analysis* (pp. 71–141). Cambridge: Cambridge University Press.

Clogg, C. C. (1981). New developments in latent structure analysis. In D. M. Jackson & E. F. Borgotta (Eds.), *Factor Analysis and Measurement in Sociological Research* (pp. 215–46). Beverly Hills, CA: Sage.

Etezadi-Amoli, J., & McDonald, R. P. (1983). A second generation nonlinear factor analysis. *Psychometrika, 48,* 315–42.

Fox, J. (1984). *Linear Statistical Models and Related Methods with Applications to Social Research.* New York: Wiley.

Fuller, W. A., & Hidiroglou, M. A. (1978). Regression estimation after correcting for attenuation. *Journal of the American Statistical Association, 73,* 99–104.

Goldstein H. (1979). *The Design and Analysis of Longitudinal Studies.* New York: Academic Press.

Gorsuch, J. (1983). *Factor Analysis* (2nd ed.). Hillsdale, NJ: Erlbaum.

Jöreskog, K. G. (1973). A general method for estimating a linear structural equation system. In A. S. Goldberger & O. D. Duncan (Eds.), *Structural Equation Models in the Social Sciences* (pp. 85–112). New York: Academic Press.

——— (1981). Analysis of covariance structures. *Scandinavian Journal of Statistics, 8,* 65–92.

Jöreskog, K. G., & Goldberger, A. S. (1972). Factor analysis by generalised least squares. *Psychometrica, 37,* 243–60.

Jöreskog, K. G. & Wold, H. (Eds.). (1981). *Systems Under Indirect Observation.* Amsterdam: North Holland.

Keesling, W. (1972). *Maximum Likelihood Approaches to Causal Flow Analysis.* Unpublished doctoral dissertation. University of Chicago.

Long, J. Scott (1983). *Covariance Structure Models: An Introduction to LISREL.* Quantitative Applications in the Social Sciences. Beverly Hills, CA: Sage.

McArdle, J., & McDonald, R. P. (1984). Some algebraic properties of the reticular action model for moment structures. *British Journal of Mathematical and Statistical Psychology, 37,* 234–51.

McDonald, R. P. (1978). A simple comprehensive model for the analysis of covariance structures. *British Journal of Mathematical and Statistical Psychology*, *31*, 59–72.

(1980). A simple comprehensive model for the analysis of covariance structures: Some remarks on applications. *British Journal of Mathematical and Statistical Psychology*, *33*, 161–83.

(1985). *Factor Analysis and Related Methods*. Hillsdale, NJ: Erlbaum.

Muthén, B. (1978). Contributions to the factor analysis of dichotomous variables. *Psychometrika*, *43*, 155–60.

Van de Geer, J. P. (1971). *Introduction to Multivariate Analysis for the Social Sciences*. San Francisco: Freeman.

Wiley, D. E. (1973). The identification problem for structural equation models with unmeasured variables. In A. S. Goldberger & O. D. Duncan (Eds.), *Structural Equation Models in the Social Sciences* (pp. 69–83). New York: Academic Press.

Wolfe, J. H. (1970). Pattern clustering by multivariate mixture analysis. *Multivariate Behavioral Research*, *5*, 329–50.

Wonnacott, R. J., & Wonnacott, T. H. (1979). *Econometrics* (2nd ed.). New York: Wiley.

(1985). *Introductory Statistics for Economists* (4th ed.). New York: Wiley.

Zeller, R. A., & Carmines, E. G. (1978). *Statistical Analysis of Social Data*. Chicago: Rand McNally.

3

Field dependence and the differentiation of neurotic syndromes

KATHARINE R. PARKES

Introduction

Self-report scales are widely used in the fields of psychology and psychiatry to assess individual differences in personality and mental state. In psychometric theory, the scores obtained on psychological measures such as these are seen as the sum of two components. The first component represents the individual's true score on the characteristic of interest, and the second component is due to measurement error. True scores reflect real characteristics of the individual but they cannot be directly assessed, since observed scores are always to some extent contaminated by measurement error. Furthermore, because measurement error has an attenuating effect on measures of association, the magnitudes of the correlations among true scores tend to be underestimated by observed-score correlations. Structural modeling techniques, such as LISREL (Jöreskog & Sörbom 1981), provide a method of estimating correlations among latent unobservable variables free of this attenuation. This chapter illustrates the use of a LISREL measurement model to extend and refine a previous analysis carried out by conventional correlational methods.

Background of the study: the issue of symptom differentiation

The use of self-report questionnaires to assess severity of neurotic disturbance has been widely reported in the psychiatric literature (e.g., Howell & Crown 1971; Goldberg & Finnerty 1979; Haines, Imeson, & Meade 1980; Weise et al. 1980). In such research, it is often desirable to obtain separate scores for different neurotic syndromes. However, the aim of developing subscales that discriminate different aspects of neurotic disorder has not been fully achieved. In spite of extensive selection and validation of items, moderate to high correlations (between .35 and .75) have been consistently observed among scores on subscales that purport to assess different types of neurotic symptoms (e.g., Hoffman & Overall 1978; Crown & Crisp 1979; Goldberg & Hillier 1979). Consistent with this,

24

factor analyses of questionnaire responses reveal a large general factor (typically accounting for 30 to 50% of the variance). Thus, subjects appear to respond to symptom checklists not in a clear-cut manner reflecting the symptom patterns perceived by psychiatrists as characterizing particular disorders, but in a more global and undifferentiated way. In particular, anxiety and depression tend to show strongly overlapping symptom configurations, leading to controversy as to whether they should be regarded as two discrete disorders or variations within a single neurotic syndrome.

The general problem of distinguishing different aspects of neurotic disorder appears to be a common feature of all self-report symptom checklists, and not simply a deficiency of particular instruments. However, differences in discrimination do exist between different subject groups. For instance, greater differentiation is shown by psychiatrists than by patients (Leff 1978), and by patients of higher social class than by those of lower social class (Derogatis et al. 1971). Individual differences in cognitive style may also influence the extent to which subjects distinguish symptom configurations. Of particular relevance is the dimension of field dependence–independence (Witkin et al. 1974), which refers to the ability of individuals to perceive and categorize elements of their environment, whether internal or external, as discrete and separate from their contextual background. Field-independent (FI) subjects are able to separate and articulate their experience, whereas the perceptions of field-dependent (FD) subjects tend to be global and generalized.

Parkes (1982) reported that scores on the four subscales of the General Health Questionnaire (Goldberg & Hillier 1979), which assess anxiety, depression, somatic symptoms, and social dysfunction, were more highly correlated among FD subjects than among FI subjects. The differences between corresponding correlation coefficients in the FI and FD groups were statistically significant for all the subscale intercorrelations. The LISREL analysis described in this chapter reexamines these findings in the original data augmented by the addition of data from a further group of subjects, using scores from two measures of each syndrome instead of the single measures analyzed previously.

Use of LISREL modeling in the analysis of symptom differentiation

The major limitation of the approach outlined in the preceding section was that the analysis was based on correlations among observed scores from a single checklist, and the effects of measurement errors were disregarded, no information about the reliability of the measures being available at the time. Furthermore, the overall fit of the model to the data was not tested, correlations between each pair of subscales being examined independently. In the more sophisticated analysis presented here, a LISREL measurement model is applied to subscale scores from two symptom checklists, and the extent to which the responses of FD and FI subjects discriminate among different neurotic syndromes is examined by testing whether the correlations among the latent unobserved variables are the same in both groups. It should be noted that this LISREL analysis is based not on scores for individual questionnaire items, but on summed scores for subscales developed to assess specific neurotic syndromes. Thus, the analysis does not address the issue of the relationships of individual items within a subscale to the underlying latent construct, but is concerned rather with relationships of observed subscale scores to the corresponding true score for each construct and with relationship across true scores in the FI and FD groups.

This covariance structure analysis has several advantages over the previous correlational analysis:

1. Since there are two observed scores for each of the four neurotic syndromes, the reliabilities of the subscales concerned (i.e., the extent to which they assess their respective underlying constructs) can be estimated, and the correlations among the true scores disattentuated from the effects of measurement error.
2. The extent to which the pairs of measures for each construct are parallel across the two questionnaires, and across the FI and FD groups, can be examined.
3. The possibility that errors might be correlated across measures (e.g., as a result of generalized response tendencies) rather than randomly distributed can be taken into account.
4. The extent of symptom differentiation in FD and FI subject groups can be examined in terms of true-score correlations, free of measurement error distortions.
5. Specific hypotheses relating to symptom differentiation among FI and FD subjects can be tested by comparing the goodness-of-fit of competing models.

Method

Subjects

The data used in this study were collected from 221 female student nurses, almost all of whom were between the ages of 18 and 26 years and were of British or Irish nationality. The analyses reported here are based on data from 218 subjects, data from three subjects being incomplete.

Test materials

1. Middlesex Hospital Questionnaire (MHQ). [This was recently renamed the Crown–Crisp Experiential Index (Crown & Crisp 1966, 1979).] A modified form of this questionnaire, developed for use with nonclinical groups (D. E. Broadbent & D. Gath, pers. commun.), was used. Responses were scored on a three-point scale, 0-1-2, and separate scores for three seven-item subscales, assessing respectively anxiety (MHQ–ANX), depression (MHQ–DEP), and somatic symptoms (MHQ–SOM), were calculated.

2. General Health Questionnaire (Goldberg 1972). The 60-item version of this questionnaire was used, and it was scored on a four-point, 0-1-2-3, scale. For the present analysis, subscale scores were calculated for three of the four seven-item subscales derived by Goldberg and Hillier (1979). These subscales assessed anxiety (GHQ–ANX), depression (GHQ–DEP), and somatic symptoms (GHQ–SOM) and thus corresponded to the measures obtained from the MHQ. Since the MHQ did not include a measure of social dysfunction, the seven GHQ items that assessed this aspect of disturbance were randomly divided into two sets (GHQ–SD1 and GHQ–SD2), and separate subscale scores (one based on four items and one based on three items) calculated, so as to provide two measures of this construct.

3. Hidden Figures Test (Health Sciences Department, University of Toronto). This measure of field dependence is similar in concept to the Group Embedded Figures Test (Witkin et al. 1971). Details of test administration are given by Parkes (1982). Scores ranged from 0 to 16. A median split was used to divide subjects into two groups, an FD group with scores in the range 0–5 ($N = 98$), and an FI group with scores in the range 6–16 ($N = 120$).

Application of LISREL

Formulation of the LISREL model

The model that formed the basis of the LISREL analysis is shown in Figure 3.1. The true scores for anxiety, depression, somatic symptoms, and social dysfunction are represented by the four latent constructs. These latent constructs are seen as causal factors underlying the observed scores on each of the four pairs of MHQ and GHQ measures. It was assumed that the measured indicators loaded only on their respective constructs. In this diagram, the straight (single-arrow) lines represent the causal relation-

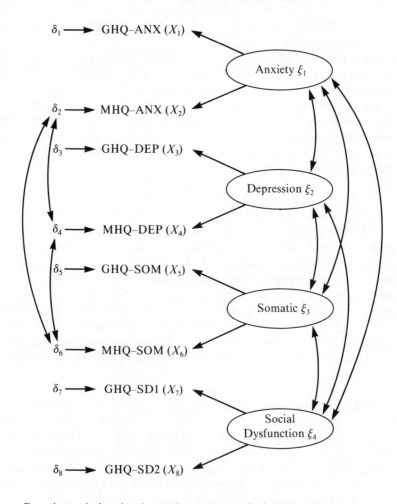

Equations relating the observed measures to the latent constructs:

$$X_1 = \lambda_{11}\xi_1 + \delta_1 \qquad X_5 = \lambda_{53}\xi_3 + \delta_5$$
$$X_2 = \lambda_{21}\xi_1 + \delta_2 \qquad X_6 = \lambda_{63}\xi_3 + \delta_6$$
$$X_3 = \lambda_{32}\xi_2 + \delta_3 \qquad X_7 = \lambda_{74}\xi_4 + \delta_7$$
$$X_4 = \lambda_{42}\xi_2 + \delta_4$$

Figure 3.1. Measurement model for symptom differentiation analysis, model 3.7.

ships between the latent constructs and their observed indicators. The curved (double-arrow) lines between the latent constructs represent the intercorrelations of the true scores; correlations among errors are also shown as curved lines. Errors were initially assumed to be random rather than systematically related. However, as discussed below, during the model-fitting process this constraint was relaxed for the three error correlations shown in Figure 3.1. The same pattern of eight observed scores underlying four latent constructs applied to both the FI and FD groups. The equations relating the observed measures to the latent constructs are also shown in Figure 3.1.

Analysis procedure

The LISREL analysis was carried out in two stages. Four questions were examined at the first stage:

1. Can the two observed indices (subscales) of each construct be regarded as parallel measures; that is, do they relate in the same way to the underlying construct and thus have equal construct loadings and equal measurement error variances?
2. Are the measurement models for each construct the same in the two groups?
3. Are the measurement models the same for all four constructs both within and across groups; that is, are the four pairs of observed measures equally reliable indicators of their respective underlying constructs?
4. Are there correlated errors across measures within the two questionnaires; that is, do systematic, nonrandom sources of error influence all measures derived from a particular questionnaire?

In specifying the LISREL models to address these questions, no constraints were placed on the intercorrelations among the latent constructs (the elements of the ϕ matrix); that is, they were allowed to take any value and to vary between the FI and FD groups. The LISREL matrices manipulated in this part of the analysis were the Λ_x matrix, for the construct loadings, and the Θ_δ matrix, for the measurement errors. Since the units of measurement for the GHQ and MHQ scales are arbitrary, the correlation matrices for the FI and FD groups (shown in Table 3.1) were used as the input to the LISREL analyses. As a means of identifying the measurement models, the variances of the latent constructs (the ξ variables) were set to 1.0 in both groups.

The second stage of the analysis examined the intercorrelations among the four latent constructs in the two groups. These latent constructs represent the "true" scores for the four syndromes, and the correlations among them are a measure of the extent to which the syndromes are interrelated after attenuation due to measurement error has been removed. The hypothesis that the relationships among the latent constructs,

Table 3.1 *Correlation matrix of observed measures for FI and FD groups*

	1	2	3	4	5	6	7	8
1. GHQ–ANX		.65	.48	.62	.38	.43	.30	.29
2. MHQ–ANX	.76		.49	.71	.33	.56	.19	.22
3. GHQ–DEP	.65	.63		.44	.27	.32	.18	.09
4. MHQ–DEP	.64	.76	.54		.31	.52	.22	.25
5. GHQ–SOM	.65	.56	.47	.42		.48	.23	.29
6. MHQ–SOM	.59	.64	.51	.59	.55		.10	.21
7. GHQ–SD1	.50	.52	.43	.46	.44	.49		.52
8. GHQ–SD2	.40	.39	.41	.36	.38	.34	.59	

Note: The correlation values for the FI group are shown above the diagonal, and the values for the FD group are shown below the diagonal.

specified in LISREL by the matrix of ϕ values, would be different in the FD and FI groups was examined by constraining the ϕ parameters to be the same in both groups. The goodness-of-fit of this constrained model was then tested against the fit of the model without this constraint.[1] In a further analysis the ϕ values in the FD group were constrained to be unity, thus allowing a test of the hypothesis that in the FD group there was no differentiation among the four syndromes. Other tests of specific ϕ parameters were also carried out.

Tests of model fit

The use of LISREL maximum likelihood techniques allows the significance of changes in goodness-of-fit resulting from alterations in the specification of model parameters to be assessed by calculating the significance of the change in the chi-square statistic. The approach adopted in the present work was to start by formulating a model with very few parameter constraints and subsequently to estimate a systematic series of models designed to test the effects of increasing or decreasing the constraints imposed on the model in accordance with specified hypotheses. The statistical significance of improvement or deterioration in goodness-of-fit resulting from changes in the extent to which the model was constrained was determined by examining the change in the chi-square statistic relative to the change in degrees of freedom. Models that resulted in a significant improvement in goodness-of-fit were accepted; models that resulted in a significant deterioration in goodness-of-fit were rejected. When the difference in goodness-of-fit between two models was found to be nonsignificant, the model that provided the more parsimonious solution, that is, the more constrained of the two models, was accepted.

In addition to the chi-square statistic for assessing the effects of changes in model fit, LISREL VI also provides other quantitative information that can be used to examine the overall goodness-of-fit of the model. The following two indices were used to assess the goodness-of-fit of the final model in the present analysis:

1. the root mean square residual, a measure of the average magnitude of the residual correlations, that is, an index of the extent to which the "fitted" matrix fails to reproduce the original correlation matrix and thus does not fully account for the observed data; and
2. the distribution of normalized residuals, which is output in the form of a graphic quantile–quantile (Q–Q) plot, thereby providing a visual representation of overall model fit.

Results

Estimation of measurement models

In the initial model to be tested the parameters shown in Figure 3.1 were estimated independently in both groups. Correlations between error terms were constrained to be zero; that is, uncorrelated errors were assumed. The model was standardized by fixing the diagonals of the ϕ matrix to 1.0, thus constraining the variance of each of the four latent variables to unity. The goodness-of-fit statistics for this model (Model 3.1) are shown in the first line of Table 3.2 (chi-square = 37.43, d.f. = 28, p = .11). These statistics indicated that the model was a sufficiently good fit to serve as a baseline against which to assess further models formulated in accordance with the hypotheses outlined above, although by conventional criteria .11 would not be an acceptable level of probability for a final model.

Since the pairs of GHQ and MHQ measures had been developed from clinical criteria to assess the same psychiatric disorder and had been carefully refined in the light of empirical validation, the hypothesis that the two measures within each pair related in the same way to the underlying true-score construct was substantively plausible. Therefore, the initial constraint imposed on Model 3.1 was to equate the construct loadings and the error terms within each pair of observed measures. This allowed a test of the hypothesis that the pairs of GHQ and MHQ measures were parallel. Initially, it was not assumed that the measurement models were identical across the FI and FD groups. The results for this model (Model 3.2 in Table 3.2) showed that the goodness-of-fit was not

Table 3.2. *Specification of successive measurement models: chi-square tests of goodness-of-fit*

	Model specification	Chi-square	d.f.	p	Change in Chi-square	Change in d.f.	Change in p	Decision
3.1	Unconstrained, except no correlated errors	37.43	28	.110				Initial measurement model
3.2	Corresponding MHQ and GHQ measures constrained to be parallel	59.44	44	.060	22.01	+16	>.10	ACCEPT – more parsimonious and not significantly worse fit than 3.1
3.3	As 3.2, plus parallel measures equated across groups	65.56	52	.098	6.12	+8	>.10	ACCEPT – more parsimonious and not significantly worse fit than 3.2
3.4	As 3.3, plus all four measurement models constrained to be identical	86.10	58	.010	20.54	+6	<.01	REJECT – significantly worse fit than 3.3
3.5	As 3.3, plus MHQ errors correlated in the FI group	45.20	49	.628	20.36	−3	<.001	ACCEPT – significantly better fit than 3.3
3.6	As 3.5, plus MHQ errors correlated within FI and FD groups	31.43	46	.950	13.77	−3	<.01	ACCEPT – significantly better fit than 3.5
3.7	As 3.6, plus correlated errors equated across groups	34.17	49	.947	2.74	+3	>.10	ACCEPT – more parsimonious and not significantly worse fit than 3.6

Note: Tests were carried out hierarchically; each model was tested against the last accepted model.

significantly worse than that of Model 3.1 (an increase in chi-square of 22.01 with 16 additional degrees of freedom, $p > .10$). Thus, the assumption of parallel measures within groups could be accepted.

Model 3.3 reexamined the parallel-measures assumption with the additional constraint that the measurement models were specified to be identical over the two groups; that is, corresponding construct loadings and measurement errors were equated over groups as well as within pairs of measures, giving an additional eight degrees of freedom as compared with the previous model. As shown in Table 3.2, the increase in chi-square associated with these additional constraints was nonsignificant. Thus, the assumption of parallel measures, and identical measurement models in the two groups, could be accepted.

Since questionnaire measures of different types of disorders are unlikely to be equally reliable indicators of the underlying true-score constructs, it was substantively not very likely that the measurement model parameters for the four constructs would be equal, that is, that the four pairs of observed measures would be equally reliable indicators of their respective underlying constructs. However, this possibility merited examination. To test for equal reliabilities across the constructs, all eight construct loadings were equated within and across groups, and all eight error terms similarly equated (Model 3.4). It can be seen from Table 3.2 that these constraints resulted in a significant increase in chi-square, indicating that the fit of the model was significantly worsened by specifying all the measurement models to be identical. This model was therefore rejected.

The models tested above assumed that measurement errors were uncorrelated, that is, that there were no common response tendencies that influenced the observed measures in a similar way within groups. However, in psychometrics, data obtained from self-report questionnaires are often liable to be systematically distorted by generalized response biases (e.g., tendency to agree with items regardless of content; tendency to respond consistently at either end of the scale rather than in the center or, conversely, the tendency to respond in the center of the scale; tendency to respond in a socially desirable manner; defensiveness, or tendency to deny all psychological difficulties). Thus, the validity of the assumption of uncorrelated errors was open to doubt.

Consistent with these psychometric arguments, examination of the LISREL "modification indices" showed that the largest values occurred among the off-diagonal elements of the measurement error (θ_δ) matrices, which suggested that allowing some correlations among errors would result in an improvement in model fit. The largest of the LISREL modification indices estimates the improvement in model fit if the parameter concerned were to be set free. Jöreskog and Sörbom (1981) recommend that only one parameter be freed at a time on the basis of modification index value, since a single change in the parameter specifications for the model changes all the modification indices. Provided that it accords with substantive considerations, the parameter with the largest index is usually chosen so as to bring about the maximum improvement in model fit.

In the present case, the parameter with the largest modification index (8.40) was that for element (6, 2) of the θ_δ matrix in the first group, that is, the correlation among errors for the measures of somatic symptoms and anxiety derived from the MHQ, in the FI group. This, therefore, was the most appropriate parameter to free. However, on psychometric grounds a single correlated error was implausible, since there were three MHQ symptom scales and all showed relatively high modification indices for the error correlations. All three θ_δ parameters representing correlations among measurement error terms for the measures of anxiety, depression, and somatic symptoms derived from the MHQ were therefore freed in the FI group, and the goodness-of-fit of the model reexamined.

The statistics for this model, Model 3.5, are shown in Table 3.2. It can be seen that Model 3.5 provides a good fit to the data and also represents a significant improvement in fit over Model 3.3. However, examination of the modification indices from Model 3.5 suggested that model fit could be improved further if the same three correlated errors were allowed in the FD group. Model 3.6, which specified these additional correlated errors, resulted in a further significant improvement in goodness-of-fit relative to Model 3.5. Model 3.7 tested the possibility that these correlated errors could be equated over groups, that is, that generalized tendencies influencing scores on the three MHQ symptom subscales were similar in the FI and FD groups. This represented a more parsimonious model than Model 3.6, and as is clear from Table 3.2, the goodness-of-fit did not deteriorate significantly when this constraint was added to the model specification. Model 3.7 was therefore accepted in preference to Model 3.6.

The same psychometric arguments underlying the rationale for allowing correlated errors in the MHQ measures also applied in principle to the GHQ measures. However, examination of the modification indices from Model 3.7 indicated that allowing the GHQ errors to intercorrelate within each group would not result in a further significant improvement in goodness-of-fit. Thus, it was unnecessary to test a further model to examine GHQ error intercorrelations. Indeed, since both the social dysfunction measures derived from the GHQ, a complete test of the GHQ correlated errors could not in any case be achieved by the method used above to model the MHQ correlated errors.[2] For present purposes, Model 3.7 was accepted as the optimum parameter specification for the construct loadings and measurement errors. This pattern of fixed, free, and equated parameters for the measurement model was kept constant in the second part of the analysis described in the next section.

Correlations among latent variables

The second part of the analysis was concerned with relationships among the four ξ variables (the true-score constructs) in the FI and FD groups. In LISREL, relationships among ξ variables are represented by the ϕ matrix. In developing the measurement model above, the values of the ϕ matrix had not been equated across groups or constrained in any other way. Thus, the relationships among the underlying true scores could take any values and vary between groups. The analyses carried out in this second stage were intended to test various hypotheses about relationships between the true scores in the FI and FD groups, specified on the basis of the substantive arguments outlined earlier. Several alternative models were compared by specifying constraints on the intercorrelations among the true scores, with the structure of the measurement model specified as in Model 3.7, which represented the optimum specification of the Λ_x and θ_δ parameters with no constraints on the matrix of ϕ values.

Tests of correlational structure across groups. In the first of these analyses, the values of the ϕ matrix were constrained to be equal across groups, that is, this specification tested the assumption that the true scores had the same correlational pattern in the FD and the FI groups. Table 3.3 shows the goodness-of-fit statistics for this model (Model 3.8). Although Model 3.8 provides an acceptable fit to the data, comparison with Model 3.7 shows that constraining the ξ variables to be equal across groups resulted in an increase in chi-square of 12.60 with six degrees of freedom. This represents a statistically significant ($p < .05$) deterioration in the goodness-of-fit, and therefore Model 3.8 was rejected in favor of the unconstrained model, Model 3.7. This finding implies that there is a significant difference in the degree to which the responses of FI and FD subjects to the GHQ and MHQ distinguish among different types of disorder.

Examination of the values of the ϕ matrix in each group indicated that the responses of FD subjects differentiate neurotic syndromes less clearly than those of FI subjects. For each pair of true scores, the correlation in the FI group was lower than the corresponding correlation in the FD group.

A significant difference between the FD and FI groups having been demonstrated (the responses of the FD subjects showing less discrimina-

Table 3.3. *Specification of the parameters of the φ matrix: chi-square tests of goodness-of-fit*

	Model specification	Chi-square	d.f.	p	Change in Chi-square	d.f.	p	Decision
3.7	Parallel measures, equated across groups; MHQ errors correlated within FI and FD groups and equated across groups; no constraints on φ parameters	34.17	49	.947				Initial structural model (from Table 3.2)
3.8	As in 3.7, but φ parameters equated across groups	46.77	55	.777	12.60	+6	<.05	REJECT – significantly worse fit than 3.7
3.9	As in 3.7, but φ parameters set to 1.0 throughout in the FD group	62.11	55	.238	27.94	+6	<.001	REJECT – highly significantly worse fit than 3.7
3.10	As in 3.7, but φ parameter for anxiety – depression set to 1.0 in both FD and FI groups	35.78	51	.948	1.61	+2	>.10	ACCEPT – more parsimonious than 3.7 and not significantly worse fit
3.11†	As in 3.10, but also with φ parameters for anxiety – somatic and somatic – depression correlations set to 1.0 in FD group only	40.92	53	.887	5.14	+2	<.10	BORDERLINE – goodness-of-fit less than that of 3.10, but difference only marginally significant
3.12	As in 3.11, but with specified φ parameters set to 1.0 in FI and FD groups	61.97	55	.241	21.05	+2	<.001	REJECT – highly significantly worse fit than 3.11

Note: Each model was tested against the last accepted model. Model 3.12 was tested against Model 3.11.

tion than those of the FI subjects), the further question arises as to whether the FD subjects respond in a totally undifferentiated manner. In LISREL, this question can be formulated as a test of whether, for the FD group, the intercorrelations among the true scores represented in the ϕ matrix can be constrained to unity (implying complete identity among the four latent constructs) without significantly impairing the goodness-of-fit of the overall model. This possibility was tested in Model 3.9, in which all the values in the ϕ matrix were set to 1.0 for the FD group but left unconstrained for the FI group. As shown in Table 3.3, this constraint resulted in a highly significant deterioration in the goodness-of-fit of the model, as compared with Model 3.7. Thus, the hypothesis that the FD subjects failed to make any differentiation among the four types of disorder is rejected.

In the models tested above the matrices of ϕ values in the two groups were specified in several different ways, but in each case all the ϕ parameters within each group were treated similarly; that is, they were all free, equated across groups, or constrained to 1.0. However, it may not be reasonable to assume that the extent of differentiation will be the same for different types of disorder. It was therefore of interest to examine models in which constraints were imposed selectively on some relationships among true scores but not others.

Anxiety–depression. Since the extent to which anxiety and depression are separate and distinguishable syndromes is an important and controversial issue in psychiatry, the values of the ϕ matrix representing relationships among the latent constructs for these two types of disorder was investigated first. Examination of the LISREL estimates in Model 3.7 showed that the values of the ϕ matrices representing the correlations between anxiety and depression in the FI and FD groups were both close to 1.0, whereas the other values of the ϕ matrices were considerably lower and differed between groups to a greater extent. This suggested the possibility that the responses of both groups of subjects might fail to differentiate between anxiety and depression, that is, that in practice these two disorders, as assessed by the GHQ and MHQ measures, can be regarded as a single entity. A further model (Model 3.10) was therefore tested in which the ϕ values for the anxiety–depression correlation in both groups were set to 1.0, whereas other ϕ values were unconstrained. As shown in Table 3.3, this model resulted in a small and nonsignificant increase in chi-square and was therefore accepted. This finding implies that in both the FI and FD groups, anxiety and depression should be regarded as a single construct, rather than as two syndromes with distinguishable configurations of symptoms.

Anxiety–depression–somatic symptoms. Once it was demonstrated that anxiety and depression were not differentiated in the responses of either FD or FI subjects, other interrelationships among the values of the ϕ matrix were examined to investigate further the extent of differentiation in the FD and FI groups. The estimates of the ϕ values in Model 3.10 suggested that, for FD subjects, somatic symptoms (which are a common element of many types of psychological disturbance) might also not be reliably distinguished from either anxiety or depression. Both the relevant values of ϕ were relatively high in the FD group (.909 and .841), but were considerably lower in the FI group. In Model 3.11 these paramaters were constrained to equal 1.0 in the FD group only. The reduction in the goodness-of-fit of the overall model was only of marginal significance ($p < .10$). Thus, the evidence that FD subjects are able to distinguish somatic disorders from anxiety or depression in their responses to the GHQ and MHQ subscales is weak. For comparison purposes, a further model was tested in which the same constraints were also imposed on the FI group; that is, the values of the ϕ matrix representing the intercorrelations of anxiety, depression, and somatic symptoms were set to 1.0 in the FI group in addition to the FD group. In this case (Model 3.12 in Table 3.3), a highly significant reduction in goodness-of-fit occurred, and this model could be clearly rejected.

In the light of these results the decision was made to accept Model 3.10 as the final model, taking note of the fact that the intercorrelations among the latent constructs for anxiety, depression, and somatics symptoms in the FD group were close to unity. Depending on the precise level of significance adopted for testing changes in the chi-square statistic, the values of the ϕ matrix for these three intercorrelations could be set to unity, thereby implying complete identity among the three constructs in the FD group, without substantially altering the fit of the model. Thus, overall, these results show that anxiety and depression, as measured by the GHQ and MHQ questionnaires, are not distinguished as separate psychological constructs by either FI or FD subjects; and the FD subjects' ability to distinguish either anxiety or depression from somatic symptoms is questionable. It appears, therefore, that the perceptions of FD subjects, as revealed by their responses to these questionnaires, are predominantly global and undifferentiated, and of the four syndromes assessed only social dysfunction is clearly perceived as a separate psychological construct. In contrast, FI subjects differentiate clearly among each of the four syndromes, with the exception of anxiety and depression, which are not distinguished by either the FD or the FI subjects.

Examination of the parameter estimates

The LISREL estimates of the parameters of the Λ_x, Θ_δ, and ϕ matrices in Model 3.10 were examined.

Measurement model parameters. The LISREL estimates for the parameters of the measurement model, as derived from Model 3.10, are shown in Table 3.4. Since pairs of GHQ and MHQ measures were shown to be parallel, the construct loadings and the measurement error variances are equal within each pair. The measures of anxiety have the highest construct loading and the lowest measurement error; thus, they have the highest reliability (.692). Conversely, the pair of measures that assess depression have the lowest construct loading and the highest measurement error and therefore the lowest reliability (.489). The measures of somatic symptoms and social dysfunction are intermediate in reliability. The total coefficient of determination for the observed measures was .921. This coefficient provides a generalized measure of the amount of variance in the observed measures accounted for by the measurement model. In this case the measurement model performs well, since it accounts for a high proportion of the variation in the observed scores.

The standard errors and the *t*-values for the construct loadings and the measurement errors were also examined. Significant *t*-values (> 2.00) can be regarded as indicative of parameter estimates significantly different from zero.[3] In the present case, the *t*-values for the construct loadings, the measurement errors, and the measurement error intercorrelations were all considerably greater than 2.0 and are thus statistically significant at better than the $p < .05$ level. Thus, the observed MHQ and GHQ scores in this sample were subject to measurement error, and the MHQ scores were also affected by generalized response tendencies, which resulted in nonrandom distributions of errors.

Intercorrelations of true-score estimates. The LISREL estimates for the correlations between the true scores, represented by the ξ-values, are shown in Table 3.5 for the FI and the FD groups. In Model 3.10, from which these data were obtained, the correlation between anxiety and depression was set to 1.0 in both the FI and FD groups, whereas the other intercorrelations were free to be estimated and not constrained to be equal across groups. The estimated correlation values are consistently higher in the FI group than in the FD group, as predicted, and all of the parameter estimates are highly significant. For both FI and FD subjects, the correlations of the true-score construct representing social dysfunction with the remaining true scores are lower than the intercorrelations among

Table 3.4. *Measurement model parameter values for Model 3.10*

Latent construct	Observed measure	Construct loadings Λ			Measurement error θ_δ			Estimate of subscale reliability
		Loading	S.E.	t-value	Loading	S.E.	t-value	
Anxiety	GHQ–ANX	0.827	0.048	17.066	0.308	0.029	10.756	.692
	MHQ–ANX							
Depression	GHQ–DEP	0.698	0.050	14.025	0.511	0.041	12.340	.489
	MHQ–DEP							
Somatic	GHQ–SOM	0.722	0.052	13.976	0.476	0.045	10.569	.524
	MHQ–SOM							
Social dysfunction	GHQ–SD1	0.742	0.052	14.323	0.444	0.043	10.392	.556
	GHQ–SD2							

Table 3.5. *LISREL estimates of the ϕ parameters in the FI and FD groups for Model 3.10*

		Anxiety	Depression	Somatic symptoms	Social dysfunction
Anxiety	FI	1.00*			
	FD	1.00*			
Depression	FI	1.00	1.00*		
	FD	1.00	1.00*		
Somatic symptoms	FI	0.690 (8.843)	0.687 (7.495)	1.00*	
	FD	0.909 (15.537)	0.841 (10.655)	1.00*	
Social dysfunction	FI	0.430 (4.176)	0.423 (3.616)	0.405 (3.498)	1.00*
	FD	0.682 (7.866)	0.746 (7.699)	0.719 (7.387)	1.00*

Note: The diagonals of the ϕ matrix (asterisked) were set to 1.00 in both the FD and the FI groups to standardize the model. The ϕ values for the intercorrelations of anxiety and depression were set to 1.00, because this constraint did not significantly reduce the goodness-of-fit of the model. The *t*-value shown in parentheses beneath each ϕ parameter estimate assesses the statistical significance of the correlation between the latent constructs.

the other true scores. Thus, social dysfunction appears to be a more clearly distinguishable psychological construct tan anxiety, depression, or somatic symptoms.

For comparison, the disattenuated correlations shown in Table 3.5 and the attentuated correlations shown in Table 3.1 are tabulated together in Table 3.6. It can be seen that, in both the FI and FD groups, each of the disattenuated correlations among true scores is larger than the four corresponding attenuated correlations, representing intercorrelations of the respective pairs of measured indicators. Thus, the observed-score correlations substantially underestimate the disattenuated correlations among the four constructs. This effect is greater for the more unreliable measures. Therefore, observed-score correlations involving the depression subscales (the least reliable measures) tend to be the most strongly attenuated. In the particular case of the relationship between anxiety and depression, for which the estimated true-score intercorrelation is 1.0 in both the FI and FD groups, it can be seen from Table 3.6 that two of the observed-score intercorrelations are less then .50. Thus, failing to take into account the effects of measurement error may give rise

Table 3.6. *Comparison of disattenuated and attenuated correlations among neurotic syndromes*

	Anxiety		Depression		Somatic symptoms		Social dysfunction	
	GHQ–ANX	MHQ–ANX	GHQ–DEP	MHQ–DEP	GHQ–SOM	MHQ–SOM	GHQ–SD1	GHQ–SD2
Anxiety			**1.0**		**.69**		**.43**	
GHQ–ANX			.48/.62		.38/.43		.30/.29	
MHQ–ANX			.49/.71		.33/.56		.19/.22	
Depression	**1.0**				**.69**		**.42**	
GHQ–DEP	.65/.63				.27/.32		.18/.09	
MHQ–DEP	.64/.76				.31/.52		.22/.25	
Somatic symptoms	**.91**		**.84**				**.41**	
GHQ–SOM	.65/.56		.47/.42				.23/.29	
MHQ–SOM	.59/.64		.51/.59				.10/.21	
Social dysfunction	**.68**		**.75**		**.72**			
GHQ–SD1	.50/.52		.43/.46		.44/.49			
GHQ–SD2	.40/.39		.41/.36		.38/.34			

Note: The values for the FI group are shown above the diagonal, and the values for the FD group are shown below the diagonal. The values of the disattenuated correlations among true scores are shown in bold type above the four values for the corresponding attenuated correlations between pairs of observed measures.

to serious distortions in the interpretation of MHQ and GHQ subscale scores.

Assessment of goodness-of-fit of Model 3.10

The root means square residual, which assesses the extent to which the estimated model fails to reproduce the original correlation matrix, was .051 for the FI group and d.050 for the FD group, both acceptably low values. The "Q–Q plot" shows the actual distribution of normalized residuals relative to the theoretical distribution of residuals with a mean of zero and a standard deviation of 1.0; this theoretical distribution is represented by the diagonal line in the Q–Q plot. The Q–Q plots for the FD and FI groups for Model 3.10 are shown in Figure 3.2. It can be seen that in both cases the line through the plotted points has a slope greater than the diagonal. This represents a good fit, in that it implies that most of the normalized residuals cluster closely around zero. However, Q–Q plot slope greater than the diagonal may be indicative of an "overfitted"

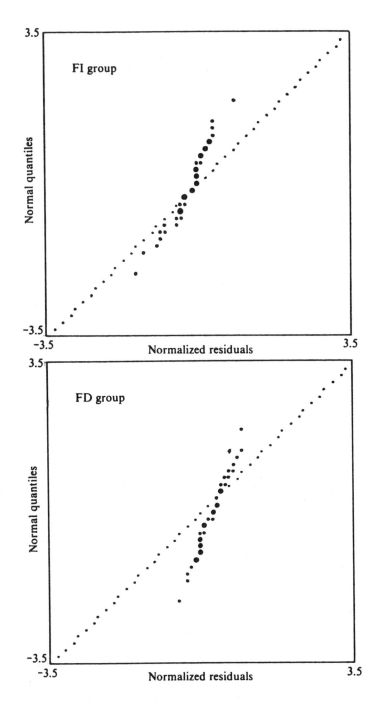

Figure 3.2. The Q–Q plots of normalized residuals in FI and FD groups.

model, that is, one in which the overall goodness-of-fit of the model is due partly to fitting chance variations in the data. In the present case, however, the slopes of the Q–Q plots are not markedly steeper than the diagonal, and the model can therefore be accepted. Thus, for this sample, both the root mean square residual and the Q–Q plot confirm the good fit of the estimated model to the data, but replication of the findings in other samples would clearly be desirable.

Discussion

The central issue addressed in this chapter, whether FD and FI subjects differ in the extent to which they distinguish among different neurotic syndromes in their responses to self-report scales such as the GHQ and the MHQ, is of both practical and theoretical relevance to psychiatry. Investigation of this question requires examination of the extent to which scores representing different neurotic syndromes, such as anxiety, depression, and somatic complaints, are intercorrelated in FD and FI groups of subjects. As discussed in the Introduction, conventional correlational techniques, based on observed subscale scores, do not provide an adequate methodology for this analysis. The results described above illustrate how the use of LISREL allows a more sophisticated approach in which intercorrelations among estimated true scores are examined (thus overcoming the limitations of observed-score analyses) and the goodness-of-fit of different models representing specific hypotheses about the correlational structure in the two groups are compared.

The first step of the LISREL analysis was concerned with determining the characteristics of the measuring instruments. The measurement model analyses demonstrated the parallel nature of the pairs of GHQ and MHQ measures, showed the important influence of generalized response tendencies on the MHQ subscale scores (but not those of the GHQ), and provided information about the reliability of the subscale measures, both individually and jointly, as measuring instruments for the underlying constructs. In all these respects, the LISREL analysis represented a methodological advance over the previous correlational analysis.

In addition to providing a basis for examining the intercorrelations of the true-score constructs, the measurement model provided some findings of substantive interest. In particular, it showed that the pairs of MHQ and GHQ subscales assessing anxiety, depression, and somatic symptoms and the two GHQ scales assessing social dysfunction could be regarded as parallel measures. Thus, although there are a number of differences in the content, wording, and initial instructions in the GHQ and the MHQ, corresponding subscale scores relate in the same way to the underlying true-score construct; that is, they have equal loadings and equal reliabilities. The parameters of the measurement model were also found to be identical across the FD and FI groups. The coefficient of determination for the measurement model as a whole showed that the observed measures performed well as indicators of the underlying constructs.

The measurement model was also of interest in that it provided information about the role of response bias in measurement errors. The problem of response bias is generally disregarded when scales such as the GHQ and MHQ are used in clinical settings, but the present findings suggest that, although both the GHQ and MHQ measures are equally reliable, they differ in the extent to which subscale scores are influenced by generalized response tendencies. Responses to the MHQ question-naire were found to be correlated across measures, which indicates that the errors are not random but systematically related. Thus, the MHQ appears to be influenced by generalized tendencies that affect all subscales in a similar way, whereas the GHQ is apparently not affected in this manner. The reason for this difference between the GHQ and the MHQ is not entirely clear, but it may be related to the greater variation in the wording of responses to different items in the GHQ as compared with those in the MHQ, the great majority of which are identically worded.

After the measurement model had been specified, the main part of the analysis was concerned with testing various hypotheses about relation-ships among the underlying true-score constructs in the FD and FI groups. In these analyses, the advantage of using LISREL was not only that the intercorrelations of true scores rather than observed scores could be examined, but also that it allowed the intercorrelations to be compared across FI and FD groups in the context of the entire model rather than for each syndrome separately, as in the previous analysis of these data. The following were points clear from the LISREL analysis:

1. The hypothesis that there was no difference in the extent to which the responses of FD and FI subjects discriminated among the four neurotic syndromes could be rejected.
2. Overall, the FI subjects showed better discrimination than the FD subjects.
3. In both the FD and FI groups, the anxiety and depression subscales did not differentiate between separate underlying constructs of anxiety and depression.
4. The responses of FD subjects (but not those of FI subjects)

distinguished somatic complaints from either anxiety or depression only to a marginal degree.

These findings raise two issues: First, to what extent does the more sophisticated analysis reported here produce findings in agreement with those of the previous correlational analysis (Parkes 1982)? Second, what are the substantive implications of the present findings?

The major difference between the results of the LISREL analysis and the previous correlational analysis is related to the discrimination of anxiety and depression. In the correlational analysis, the results showed that among FI subjects the intercorrelation of anxiety and depression (as assessed by the GHQ) was significantly lower than among FD subjects, although both values were moderately large (.43 and .64, respectively). In contrast, the LISREL analysis demonstrated that in both groups the correlation between the true-score constructs for anxiety and depression (derived from GHQ and MHQ measures) was unity. Thus, the GHQ and MHQ anxiety and depression subscales measure a common underlying construct. This difference in results illustrates the effect of failing to consider measurement errors in the previous analysis and the consequent attenuation of correlation values obtained. In other respects the results of the LISREL analysis were consistent with those of the correlational analysis, in that the responses of FD subjects differentiated less clearly between constructs (other than anxiety and depression) than did those of the FI subjects. However, as noted above, evidence that the responses of the FD group distinguished anxiety and depression from somatic symptoms was weak in that the true-score intercorrelations for these constructs were close to unity, and only a marginal reduction in goodness-of-fit occurred when they were set to 1.0. Again, these findings illustrate the potentially distorting effects of using observed scores without taking into account attenuation due to measurement error.

Substantively, the findings of the LISREL analysis provide support for the unitary model of anxiety and depression, that is, the view that these two aspects of neurotic disturbance represent a single syndrome rather than two distinct disorders. The fact that correlations among observed scores indicate that the symptom configurations are not identical can be attributed to measurement error effects rather than to a real distinction in the way the symptom patterns are perceived and reported. Whereas the previous correlational analysis suggested that the unitary model applied more closely to FD subjects, the results reported here imply that the unitary model is applicable to both groups. This result is in agreement with clinical findings that patients in various diagnostic categories covering anxiety and depressive disorders show extensive overlap in symptoms, and consequently a considerable proportion cannot be reliably assigned to their diagnostic groups on the basis of responses to symptom checklists (Prusoff & Klerman 1974; Snaith, Bridge, & Hamilton, 1976; Crisp, Jones, & Slater 1978). However, it should be noted that the conclusions of the present study are related to results obtained from two self-report checklists, specifically the GHQ and the MHQ, and do not necessarily imply that other diagnostic techniques (e.g, psychiatric interview ratings) would produce similar results. For instance, Roth et al. (1972) found that anxiety and depression were differentiated by symptom patterns when details of the symptoms were elicited by psychiatrists rather than self-reported.

Less research attention has been given to the differentiation of neurotic syndromes other than anxiety and depression. The present results imply that in this respect there are differences between the responses of FD and FI subjects to self-report symptom checklists. These differences are consistent with findings that FI subjects perceive the characteristic symptom configurations associated with different affective states to be more highly differentiated than do the FD group, whose perceptions are predominantly global and generalized (Parkes 1981). Thus, with the exception of the findings relating to anxiety and depression, the results of the present study are consistent with the view that perceptual style (as assessed by the measure of field dependence) may be an important underlying variable influencing the extent to which individuals are able to perceive and report discrete symptom patterns within a general context of affective disturbance.

Notes

1. Strictly speaking, this analysis tests the hypothesis that the matrix of ϕ values is the same for each group against the hypothesis that the ϕ values are different in the two groups. However, as shown in Table 3.5, all the correlations are larger in the FD group than in the FI group.
2. In the LISREL analysis above, correlations between error terms were modeled by freeing the appropriate elements of the matrix. For the three MHQ measures this allowed a complete representation of the correlated error terms; that is, each MHQ error term could be allowed to correlate with each other MHQ error term. However, if there are more than three measures (as in the case of the GHQ), a generalized response tendency is correctly modeled by nonzero error correlations, which obey certain functional relationships. In the present case, freeing all error correlations would result in a model with too few constraints.

There was the further complication that both the observed measures for the social dysfunction construct were derived from the GHQ, and therefore any correlation between error terms for these two measures was subsumed in the underlying construct and could not be modeled by allowing correlated error terms. In circumstances such as these, an alternative approach to modeling correlated errors, outlined below, could be adopted.

The alternative approach requires an additional latent construct to represent the generalized response tendencies. Thus, the model is based on five latent constructs, including the four true-score constructs for which the pattern of Λ_x and θ_δ loadings remained unchanged from the previous model. The additional latent construct represents the generalized response tendencies for the GHQ measures and is modeled as an underlying cause of the observed GHQ scores. This additional latent construct is constrained to be orthogonal to each of the four true-score constructs. All the GHQ measures load on the additional latent construct, and the loadings for the two social dysfunction subscales are constrained to be equal. This model allows a complete representation of GHQ correlated errors, while also taking into account the fact that the GHQ social dysfunction measures cannot be allowed to correlate directly. Corresponding loadings are equated across groups, and MHQ errors are allowed to correlate as previously by freeing the appropriate elements. Thus, the model is similar to Model 3.7 in Table 3.2 but allows the GHQ errors to intercorrelate by including an additional latent construct.

Chi-square for this model was 29.82 with 45 degrees of freedom. As tested against Model 3.7 (which allowed no GHQ correlated errors) the alternative model produced a decrease in chi-square of 4.35 with 4 degrees of freedom $(.30 < p < .50)$. Overall, therefore, the result of this approach to modeling the GHQ errors is consistent with the conclusion drawn previously; that is, no significant improvement in the fit of the model is obtained by allowing GHQ errors to intercorrelate.

3. The t-values produced in LISREL and most similar programs hold strictly only in the analysis of a covariance matrix. Their distribution properties do not conform to the normal distribution when a correlation matrix is analyzed (see Chapter 9, by Boomsma, this volume). However, t-values can be used as an approximate guide if the criterion value is set higher than that for the corresponding level of statistical significance in the normal distribution. For example, as a rule of thumb, the $p < .05$ level of significance, corresponding to $t = 1.96$ in the normal distribution, can be approximated by a t-value of 2.00.

References

Crisp, A. H., Jones, M. G., & Slater, P. (1978). The Middlesex Hospital Questionnaire: A validity study. *British Journal of Medical Psychology, 51,* 269–80.

Crown, S., & Crisp, A. H. (1966). A short diagnostic self-rating scale for psychoneurotic patients: The Middlesex Hospital Questionnaire (MHQ). *British Journal of Psychiatry, 112*, 917–23.

(1979). *Manual of the Crown–Crisp Experiential Index*. London: Hodder & Stoughton.

Derogatis, L. R., Lipman, R. S., Covi, L. & Rickels, K. (1971). Neurotic symptom dimensions: As perceived by psychiatrists and patients of various social classes. *Archives of General Psychiatry, 24*, 454–64.

Goldberg, D. P. (1972). *The detection of psychiatric illness by questionnaire*. New York: Oxford University Press.

Goldberg, D. P., & Hillier, V. F. (1979). A scaled version of the General Health Questionnaire. *Psychologial Medicine, 9*, 139–45.

Goldberg, H. L., & Finnerty, R. J. (1979). Comparative efficacy of tofisopam and placebo. *American Journal of Psychiatry, 136* (2), 196–9.

Haines, A. P., Imeson, J. D., & Meade, T. W. (1980). Psychoneurotic profiles of smokers and non-smokers. *British Medical Journal, 280* (6229), 1422.

Hoffmann, N. G., & Overall, P. B. (1978). Factor structure of the SCL-90 in a psychiatric population. *Journal of Consulting and Clinical Psychology, 46*(6), 1187–91.

Howell, R. W., & Crown, S. (1971). Sickness absence levels and personality inventory scores. *British Journal of Industrial Medicine, 28*, 126–30.

Jöreskog, K. G., & Sörbom, D. (1981). *LISREL VI: Analysis of Linear Structural Relationships by the Method of Maximum Likelihood*. Chicago: National Educational Resources.

Leff, J. P. (1978). Psychiatrists' versus patients' concepts of unpleasant emotions. *British Journal of Psychiatry, 133*, 306–13.

Parkes, K. R. (1981). Field dependence and the differentiation of affective states. *British Journal of Psychiatry, 139*, 52–8.

(1982). Field dependence and the factor structure of the General Health Questionnaire. *British Journal of Psychiatry, 140*, 392–400.

Prusoff, B., & Klerman, G. L. (1974). Differentiating depressed from anxious neurotic outpatients. *Archives of General Psychiatry, 30*, 302–9.

Roth, M., Gurney, C., Garside, R. F., & Kerr, T. A. (1972). Studies in the classification of affective disorders: 1. The relationship between anxiety states and depressive illnesses. *British Journal of Psychiatry, 121*, 147–61.

Snaith, R. P., Bridge, G. W. K., & Hamilton, M. (1976). The Leeds scales for the self-assessment of anxiety and depression. *British Journal of Psychiatry, 128*, 156–65.

Weise, C. C., Stein, M. K., Pereira-Ogan, J., Csanalosi, I., & Rickels, K. (1980). Amitriptyline once daily vs. three times dialy in depressed out-patients. *Archives of General Psychiatry, 37*, 555–60.

Witkin, H. A., Oltman, P. K., Raskin, E., & Karp, S. A. (1971). *A manual for*

the Embedded Figures Test. Palo Alto, CA: Consulting Psychologists Press.
Witkin, H. A., Dyk, R. B., Faterson, H. F., Goodenough, D. R., & Karp, S. A. (1974). *Psychological differentiation.* Hillsdale, NJ: Erlbaum.

4

High school seniors' reports of parental socioeconomic status: black–white differences

LEE M. WOLFLE

Introduction

Measurement error is insidious. It creeps into data collection and analysis in various ways, and its effect on substantive conclusions is more dangerous than is usually appreciated. This chapter investigates one aspect of measurement error – the structure of errors in high school seniors' reports of parental socioeconomic status – and compares the pattern of these reporting errors between blacks and whites.

Models of educational achievement often include measures of socioeconomic background in order to control for socioeconomic differences in assessing the effects of educational treatments. If, however, these background variables have been measured with substantial error, one's substantive conclusions will be affected. For example, if the background variables contain substantial random measurement error, the least squares estimates of their effects on measures of educational outcomes will be less than their true effects, and any assessment of the influence of educational treatments may be correspondingly inflated (Mason et al. 1976). The effects of intervening educational treatments will also be inflated in least squares analyses if the errors of measurement of socioeconomic background variables are correlated across different variables (Bowles 1972). As a result, the correlation among measured background variables will be artificially inflated, and the educational treatment variable will explain more of the variation in the outcome variable than warranted in actuality.

Moreover, when the effects of treatments are estimated across groups, such as blacks and whites, differential amounts and kinds of measurement error among background variables will have differential effects on estimates of the effects of both the background variables and the treatment. As a result, one could be led to the conclusion that an educational treatment worked differently for blacks and whites, not because it truly did, but because of different patterns of measurement error within these groups.

Many investigators of educational outcomes have collected data on the

51

socioeconomic characteristics of parents from students, not from the parents themselves. Nevertheless, students are often fallible informants of parental status. In the face of uncertainty, students may guess or reconcile their uncertainty by substituting known information about one parent for unknown information about the other.

A few studies have addressed the problem of students' reporting errors of parental status, but none have adequately compared the measurement properties of status variables as reported separately by students and parents using a common framework for estimating models for whites and blacks simultaneously. Mason et al. (1976) found that both white and black twelfth grade students reported parental status characteristics as accurately as did their parents but that neither black students nor their parents were as accurate in their reports as were whites. Unfortunately, the analysis was deficient to the extent that the authors estimated models independently for each group. Mare and Mason (1980) corrected this deficiency in their examination of students' reports in the sixth, ninth, and twelfth grades, but they restricted their analysis to the white subpopulation and did not compare whites and blacks with the more adequate methodology.

Wolfle and Robertshaw (1983) applied this methodology, Jöreskog's (1971) general framework for simultaneous covariance structure analyses of multiple populations, to a national sample of black and white high school seniors. They found that whites and blacks have an invariant construct pattern; that is, unit increases in true status characteristics led to the same increase in manifest measures tor blacks as for whites. However, they also found that reliability estimates for whites were significantly higher than for blacks, owing to differences in true-score variances and error variances. Their study, however, was restricted to multiple measures of parental status as reported by students, and they did not compare students' reports with those of the parents.

This chapter explores racial differences in high school seniors' reports of parental socioeconomic traits using a multiple-group measurement model suggested by Jöreskog (1971). The analysis begins by estimating the accuracy of reports of parental traits across races, for both parent and student reports. Next we consider the extent to which the students' reports matched those of their parents. Finally, and more restrictively, we compare the reliabilities of black and white parents and students.

Method

Data for this investigation were taken from "High School and Beyond" (HSB), a longitudinal study of U.S. high school sophomores and seniors[1] sponsored by the National Center for Education Statistics. The data are described in a user's guide prepared by the National Opinion Research Center (1980). In particular, these analyses are based on a sample of 3,197 HSB parents matched to their senior high school children. Both parents and children were asked to report the educational attainment of the mother and father, as well as the father's occupation. The analysis reported here was restricted to 1,502 white and 99 black respondents with complete records for the six variables included in the measurement model.

The questions used in the original survey, which are available in the user's guide (National Opinion Research Center, 1980), are summarized here. The seniors were first asked to categorize the job most recently held by their father by choosing one of 17 categories (clerical, craftsmen, farmer, etc.). These responses were then recoded to their Duncan (1961) Socio-Economic Index[2] equivalent scores as given in Levinsohn et al. (1978, App. O, p. 11). The seniors were next asked to indicate the highest level of education completed by their father. A similar question was asked about their mother's education. These responses were then recoded such that the categories reported by the parents and students were equivalent; the resulting scale ranged from 1 to 8, representing categories from less than high school ($=1$) to the receipt of a Ph.D., M.D., or other advanced degree ($=8$).

After the collection of the HSB base-year data from the high school students, 3,197 parents of the HSB seniors were contacted and additional data collected, which concentrated primarily on the parents' plans for financing their children's higher education. Included in the questionnaire, however, were items dealing with parental socioeconomic characteristics. In about 60 percent of the cases, it was the student's mother who completed the questionnaire; in the remaining cases, the student's father completed the questionnaire. (Students who had some other adult complete the questionnaire, such as an aunt or grandfather, were excluded from the analyses.) Parents completing the questionnaire were asked to report their occupation, their spouse's occupation, their education, and their spouse's education. These were recoded as appropriate to obtain a report of the father's education (as reported either by himself or by his spouse) and mother's education. Both education variables were recoded such that the scale used by students was equivalent to that used in the parents' reports. The occupation question in the parents' survey was coded according to the U.S. Census Bureau's detailed occupation code. In order to match these responses with the scale used by the high school seniors, the detailed occupational codes were collapsed into the identical categories used by the students and assigned the same Duncan (1961) Socio-Economic Index scores. The correlations among these six variables,

Table 4.1. *Correlations,[a] means, and standard deviations for measurement model of parental socioeconomic status*

	X_1	X_2	X_3	X_4	X_5	X_6
X_1		.678	.669	.559	.440	.451
X_2	.710		.625	.576	.434	.405
X_3	.580	.617		.830	.635	.593
X_4	.572	.614	.909		.560	.615
X_5	.411	.440	.604	.586		.828
X_6	.415	.452	.592	.599	.874	
Mean						
Blacks	38.630	40.167	3.162	3.192	3.071	3.212
Whites	45.260	43.916	3.626	3.558	3.073	3.073
Standard deviation						
Blacks	22.592	24.328	2.142	2.198	1.831	2.037
Whites	22.499	22.009	2.207	2.263	1.760	1.856

[a] Correlations for blacks are reported above the diagonal; correlations for whites are reported below the diagonal. The variable labels are defined as follows:

X_1 = parent's report of father's occupation
X_2 = student's report of father's occupation
X_3 = parent's report of father's education
X_4 = student's report of father's education
X_5 = parent's report of mother's eduction
X_6 = student's report of mother's education

Source: National Opinion Research Center (1980).

plus their means and standard deviations, are shown in Table 4.1 for both blacks and whites.

For each race, the basic measurement model used in these analyses can be described by a set of six equations in which both the parents' reports of their status and the children's reports of their parents' status are seen to be caused by the parents' true status (an unmeasured latent construct). That is, both the parent's report and the student's report of the father's occupation are considered to be dependent on the father's true occupational status. Similarly, for both the mother's and father's education, the parent's report and the student's report are considered to be dependent on the true underlying educational factor of the respective parent. The three true-score constructs are allowed to covary and are not necessarily constrained to have the same parameter estimates across racial groups (although this is a constraint to be applied in later models). Covariances among response errors were initially set at zero on the assumption that

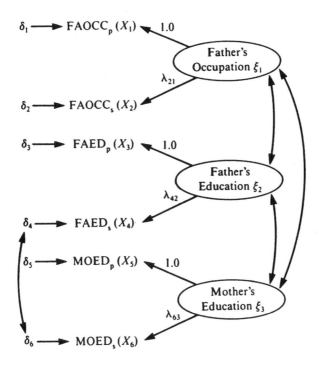

Figure 4.1. Measurement model of report of parental socioeconomic status, variables are described in Table 4.1.

response errors were random, but were subsequently allowed to covary on the assumption that specific components of measurement error in the measured variables exist and are correlated.

These equations are depicted in Figure 4.1. The straight, single-headed arrows represent assumed causal relationships among the latent constructs (shown in ellipses) and their measured indicators. The curved, double-headed arrows represent covariances; the covariation shown between response errors was not a part of the initial model specification, but was added during the analysis. The six equations represented in Figure 4.1 are, for each race,

$$X_1 = \lambda_{11}\xi_1 + \delta_1 \qquad X_4 = \lambda_{42}\xi_2 + \delta_4$$
$$X_2 = \lambda_{21}\xi_1 + \delta_2 \qquad X_5 = \lambda_{53}\xi_3 + \delta_5$$
$$X_3 = \lambda_{32}\xi_2 + \delta_3 \qquad X_6 = \lambda_{63}\xi_3 + \delta_6$$

where X_1 is the parent's report of father's occupation, X_2 the student's report of father's occupation, X_3 the parent's report of father's education,

X_4 the student's report of father's education, X_5 the parent's report of mother's education, and X_6 the student's report of mother's education; λ_{ij} are construct loadings from the jth latent construct to the ith measured variable; ξ_j are latent constructs; and the δ_i are response errors.

The statistical strategy employed in selecting a best-fitting model consisted of (1) estimating a model in which certain parameters are constrained to be equal, sometimes within one racial group and sometimes across groups; and (2) estimating a less constrained version of the same model. The test of model fit consisted of assessing the statistical significance of the improvement in fit between the constrained and the less constrained model. Such model-fitting techniques can be implemented in LISREL (Jöreskog and Sörbom 1981), which was used to estimate the parameters in the models being analyzed here.

In addition to the purely statistical criteria, substantive criteria were applied in the search for a best-fitting model. In particular, no model was accepted that implied children reported their parental socioeconomic characteristics with less error than the parents themselves. In the one case where this occurred the model was respecified such that the estimated parameters for parents and children were set equal to each other.

Results

This section presents a series of distinct hierarchical measurement models. The summary goodness-of-fit statistics are presented for these models, followed by a discussion of the parameter and reliability estimates for the model deemed to be best fitting for these data. In examining these estimates for blacks and whites, keep in mind that the sample size for blacks is quite small. Accordingly, misspecifications in the model for blacks are less likely to be detected than would statistically significant misspecifications of the same magnitude for whites.

In these analyses, the models for both blacks and whites were analyzed simultaneously, but in the initial model no constraints on the coefficients were imposed across groups. Model 4.1 contains 15 parameters to be estimated within each racial group. These parameters consisted of three true-score variances, three covariances among true scores, six error variances (one for each of the six measured variables), and three construct loadings that related one of the members of each pair of measured indicators to each latent construct. For each latent construct, one construct loading was set a priori to unity (i.e., $\lambda_{11} = \lambda_{32} = \lambda_{53} = 1.0$) in order to provide a metric for the latent construct and to identify the model. The goodness-of-fit chi-square statistic for this model (Model 4.1) is shown in Table 4.2. The chi-square statistic for Model 4.1 was 35.52

Table 4.2. *Goodness-of-fit statistics for measurement models of parental socioeconomic status*

Model	Chi-square statistic	d.f.	p	$\triangle\chi^2$	d.f.	p
4.1 No error covariances	35.52	12	.000			
4.2 Model 1 plus covariance among errors of father's and mother's education for white and black children	9.08	10	.524	26.44	2	.000
4.3 Model 2 plus equal λ coefficients for whites and blacks	11.39	13	.578	2.31	3	.511
4.4 Model 3 plus equal λ coefficients for whites and blacks, parents and children	17.18	16	.374	5.79	3	.122
4.5 Model 4 plus equal true-score variance–covariance matrix, error variances equal for black and white parents, and for whites equal error variance for father's occupation for parents and children	29.58	26	.285	12.40	10	.259

with 12 degrees of freedom ($p = .0004$), indicating that the model as initially specified did not adequately reproduce the observed covariance matrices.

Model 4.1 implicitly assumed that the reporting errors for parents and their children were randomly distributed and hence uncorrelated. Since the model did not provide an adequate fit to the data, it is necessary to consider an alternative model specification. For example, the reporting errors may have been nonrandom. Nonrandom errors in reporting would result in nonzero error covariances; for example, if a child knew one parent's education but not the other, he or she might guess the unknown with reference to the known.

The modification indices in the LISREL program provide a powerful tool for detecting misspecification within the general form of the model specified. In particular, they indicate which of the formal restrictions would improve the fit of a model if they were relaxed. An examination of

Table 4.3. *Model 4.2 parameter estimates*

Socioeconomic characteristic	Informant	True-score variance ϕ	Error variance θ_δ	Construct loading λ
Father's occupation	White parent	336.38	169.82	1.00[a]
	White child		116.77	1.04
	Black parent	365.48	144.91	1.00[a]
	Black child		212.08	1.02
Father's education	White parent	4.51	0.36	1.00[a]
	White child		0.56	1.01
	Black parent	4.38	0.20	1.00[a]
	Black child		1.34	0.89
Mother's education	White parent	2.74	0.35	1.00[a]
	White child		0.48	1.04
	Black parent	2.95	0.41	1.00[a]
	Black child		0.92	1.04

True-score covariance[b]

	1	2	3
1. Father's occupation	—	32.17	18.85
2. Father's education	28.82	—	2.49
3. Mother's education	16.54	2.33	—

Covariance between errors in children's report of mother's and father's education

Whites	0.093
Blacks	0.414

[a] Fixed parameter.
[b] Blacks above diagonal; whites below.

the modification indices for Model 4.1 indicated that the parameter for the error covariance between the children's reports of mother's and father's education should be relaxed (i.e., in this case, allowed to take on a nonzero value). Model 4.2 allowed this single error covariance to be a free, estimable parameter for both whites and blacks. The results are shown in Table 4.2. The difference in chi-square coefficients for Models 4.1 and 4.2 is itself distributed as chi-square. This value was 26.44 with 2 degrees of freedom and indicates that allowing these error terms to covary resulted in a significant improvement in the fit of the model. An examination of the modification indices for Model 4.2 indicated that the error covariance for the parent's report of mother's and father's education may also be nonzero, but when this restriction was relaxed the improvement in fit was not statistically significant. As a result, Model 4.2, with a chi-square statistic of 9.08 with 10 degrees of freedom (p = .524), was accepted on statistical grounds as producing a good fit for these data.

Nevertheless, Model 4.2 may not be the most parsimonious model for the data. An examination of the parameter estimates in Model 4.2, shown in Table 4.3, indicates that several of the construct loadings (λ coefficients) are nearly equal in value. This suggests that the construct pattern for whites may be the same as that for blacks. This hypothesis, if true, would indicate that unit increases in true scores led to the same increments in measured variables for blacks as for whites. This hypothesis was tested by constraining the construct loadings for whites and blacks to be equal; if these constraints do not significantly erode the fit of the model to the data, one may conclude that whites and blacks have a common construct pattern for these variables. The chi-square statistic for this model (Model 4.3 in Table 4.2) was 11.39 (d.f. = 13, p = .578), which can be compared with the chi-square statistic for Model 4.2. The difference in the chi-square statistics is 2.31 with three degrees of freedom (p = .511); thus, the additional restrictions do not lead to a significant deterioration in the fit of the model. We may conclude that black and white parents and high school senior children have a common construct pattern in their reports of parental status characteristics.

Having established that whites and blacks have a common construct pattern, we may now determine whether high school seniors report their parents' status characteristics as accurately as their parents do. To accomplish this, an additional set of constraints was added to the model; the construct loadings for the children's report of each status characteristic were constrained to be equal to those of the parents. This constraint implies that the construct loadings that relate the manifest measures to the latent true score for parents and children are equal. The chi-square statistic for this model (Model 4.4 in Table 4.2) was 17.18. The difference in the chi-square statistics between this model and that for Model 4.3 is 5.79 with three degrees of freedom (p = .122). We conclude that the construct loadings that relate the parents' reports to their socioeconomic characteristics are equal within the bounds of sampling error (at the .05 level) to the construct loadings that relate the children's reports to their parents' socioeconomic characteristics.

Although the construct loadings that relate manifest measures of background socioeconomic variables to their true scores are apparently the same for parents and their children, and apparently the same for blacks and whites, there may remain additional forms of invariance in the general measurement model. In particular, it is of substantive interest to examine whether the variances of the measurement errors are the same across racial groups and, within groups, whether they are the same for the reports of parents and children. We do not prsent all of the intermediate models that led to Model 4.5. The omitted models specified that, within each racial group and within each socioeconomic trait, the error variances are constrained to be equal for parents and children. After each successive constraint, the fit of the model was tested; if the fit did not deteriorate significantly, the constraint was retained; if the fit did deteriorate significantly, the constraint was rejected. Constraints were also placed across groups, in which the error variances for white parents were set equal to the error variances for black parents, and then those of white children were set equal to those of black children. One exception to these procedures developed when the error variance for the white parent's report of father's occupation was found to be significantly greater than that of the child. This result was substantively implausible, and the model was reestimated with the specification that these error variances are equal. Since the two variables concerned load on the same construct, setting their error variances equal implies that the reliability of the parent's report of the father's occupation was equal to the reliability of the child's report.

The parameter estimates for Model 4.5 are shown in Table 4.4. Comparing these coefficients with those in Table 4.3 reveals the differences in the specification between Model 4.2 and this final model. First, the true-score variances and covariances are equal for whites and blacks. Second, all λ coefficients in the model are found, within sampling error limits, equal to one another. Third, the error variances for white *parents* and black *parents* are equal.

The estimates of the reliabilities for thse variables are also shown in Table 4.4. The reliability of a variable is defined as the ratio of the true-score variance to the observed-score variance (Greene and Carmines 1980). In LISREL this is estimated by

$$r_{ii} = \lambda_{ij}^2 \phi_{jj}/(\lambda_{ij}^2 \phi_{jj} + \theta_{ii})$$

where r_{ii} is the estimated reliability of the ith measured variable, λ_{ij} the construct loading from the jth latent construct to the ith measured variable, ϕ_{jj} the variance of the jth latent construct, and θ_{ii} the error variance for the ith variable. Because all of the construct loadings in the present model are unity, this equation reduces to

$$r_{ii} = \phi_{jj}/(\phi_{jj} + \theta_{ii})$$

The reliability estimates shown in Table 4.4 indicate that both black and white parents report their eductional achievements with nearly equal reliability. The father's occupation is not reported as reliably as education, but both black and white parents report occupational status with equal reliability.

Table 4.4. *Model 4.5 parameter estimates*

Socioeconomic characteristic	Informant	True-score variance ϕ	Error variance θ_δ	Construct loading[a] λ	Reliability $\lambda^2\phi/(\lambda^2\phi + \theta_\delta)$
Father's occupation	White parent		143.72	1.0	.71
	White child	352.84	143.72	1.0	.71
	Black parent		143.72	1.0	.71
	Black child		208.97	1.0	.63
Father's education	White parent		0.35	1.0	.93
	White child	4.50	0.57	1.0	.89
	Black parent		0.35	1.0	.93
	Black child		1.23	1.0	.79
Mother's education	White parent		0.29	1.0	.91
	White child	2.86	0.54	1.0	.84
	Black parent		0.29	1.0	.91
	Black child		1.03	1.0	.74

True-score covariance[b]

	1	2	3
1. Father's occupation	—	29.62	17.21
2. Father's education	29.62	—	2.37
3. Mother's education	17.21	2.37	—

Covariance between errors in children's report of mother's and father's education
Whites	0.100
Blacks	0.398

[a] All fixed parameters.
[b] Blacks above diagonal; whites below.

The finding of equal error variances among parents does *not* extend to the reports of high school seniors; the errors with which black high school seniors report their parents' socioeconomic characteristics were consistently larger than those of white high school seniors. Correspondingly, the estimated reliability coefficients for black children are lower than those for whites. Moreover, save for the white children reporting their father's occupation, children reported their parents' socioeconomic traits with greater error than their parents, and hence their reliability coefficients were lower.

Conclusion

Models of educational achievement usually include measures of socioeconomic background. Manifest measures of these variables are often obtained retrospectively from children, and not from the parents themselves. If, however, the children report these variables with substantial error, substantive conclusions about the effects of such variables will be affected.

Previous investigations indicated for the most part that children report parental status almost as accurately as parents do. Bielby, Hauser, and Featherman (1977) found that men reported their own status as reliably as they reported their father's education and occupation. Corcoran (1980) reached the same conclusion about the reports of women. Mason et al. (1976) concluded for both whites and blacks that the reports of twelfth grade children were as reliable as the reports of their parents, and Mare and Mason (1980) concluded that for whites the reports of parents and twelfth grade children were equally reliable.

The findings of the present investigation vary somewhat from those of the previous studies. First, although the construct loadings that relate manifest measures to their true scores are the same for parents and children, the residual error variances are not equal for parents' and children's reports. Hence, in the present investigation the reliability of reports by children are significantly lower than that of reports by parents.

Second, whereas previous studies have, in general, not found significant covariances among reporting errors of background variables, the present investigation found a relatively large covariance between children's reporting errors of mother's and father's education. In the HSB survey the high school seniors may thus have reported their parents' educational attainment with a common bias. Wolfle and Robertshaw (1983) also found correlated errors in high school seniors' reports of parental eduction but attributed the correlation to the parallel-form question used in the National Longitudinal Study questionnaire (see Levinsohn et al., 1978). Moreover, Mare and Mason (1980) reported correlated errors between mother's and father's education for sixth and ninth graders, but not for twelfth graders; and Bielby et al. (1977) reported correlated errors for blacks between father's education and respondent's education. The evidence therefore seems to suggest that students tend to report the education of their parents with a common bias. Judging by the means shown in Table 4.1, students tend to overestimate the amount of schooling received by their parents.

The present investigation also found that parental education was reported more reliably than the father's occupation. This result parallels similar findings by Bielby et al. (1977) and Wolfle and Robertshaw (1983) but disagrees with the results of Mason et al. (1976) and Mare and Mason (1980), who found that father's education, mother's education, and father's occupation were reported with equal reliability.

Bowles (1972) argued that using respondents' reports of parental socioeconomic status underestimates to a serious degree the influence of origin variables. In contrast, Jencks et al. (1972) argued that random measurement error is of relatively little importance. It would seem, in conclusion, that neither of these positions is correct. Random measurement error among children's reports of parental status is neither trivial nor as serious as some have believed. Yet caution is indeed warranted, for the usual assumption about measurement error is that it is random; but significant covariances were found here between reporting errors of father's and mother's education.

Notes

An earlier version of this chapter was delivered at the annual meetings of the American Educational Research Association, Montréal, April 11–15, 1983. I am indebted to Bunty Ethington for comments and discussions in the course of preparing the chapter.
1. High school seniors in the United States are in their twelfth year of school; their modal age is 18.
2. The Socio-Economic Index was constructed to predict the prestige rating of U.S. occupations (Duncan 1961, p. 145). There is substantial evidence that the structure of the index is fundamentally socioeconomic (see Hauser & Featherman 1977); for example, Duncan (1961, p. 124) reports that 83% of the variation in the prestige of 90 occupational titles can be explained by income and education.

References

Bielby, W. T., Hauser, R. M., & Featherman, D. L. (1977). Response errors of black and nonblack males in models of the intergenerational transmission of socioeconomic status. *American Journal of Sociology, 82,* 1242–88.

Bowles, S. (1972). Schooling and inequality from generation to generation. *Journal of Political Economy, 80,* S219–51.

Corcoran, M. (1980). Sex differences in measurement error in status attainment models. *Sociological Methods & Research, 9,* 199–217.

Duncan, O. D. (1961). A socioeconomic index for all occupations. In *Occupations and Social Status*, ed. A. J. Reiss, pp. 109–38. New York: Free Press.

Greene, V. L., & Carmines, E. G. (1980). Assessing the reliability of linear composites. In *Sociological Methodology 1980*, ed. K. F. Schuessler, pp. 160–75. San Francisco: Jossey-Bass.

Hauser, R. M., & Featherman, D. L. (1977). *The Process of Stratification: Trends and Analyses.* New York: Academic Press.

Jencks, C., Smith, M., Acland, H., Bane, M. J., Cohen, D., Gintis, H., Heyns, B.,

& Michelson, S. (1972). *Inequality: A Reassessment of the Effects of Family and Schooling in America.* New York: Basic Books.

Jöreskog, K. G. (1971). Simultaneous factor analysis in several populations. *Psychometrika, 36,* 409–26.

Jöreskog, K. G., & Sörbom, D. (1981). *LISREL V: Analysis of Linear Structural Relationships by Maximum Likelihood and Least Squares Methods.* Chicago: National Educational Resources.

Levinsohn, J. R., Henderson, L. B., Riccobono, J. A., & Moore, R. P. (1978). *National Longitudinal Study: Base Year, First, Second and Third Follow-Up Data File Users Manual,* Vols. 1 and 2. Washington, D.C.: National Center for Education Statistics.

Mare, R. D., & Mason, W. M. (1980). Children's reports of parental socioeconomic status: A multiple group measurement model. *Sociological Methods & Research, 9,* 178–98.

Mason, W. M., Hauser, R. M., Kerckhoff, A. C., Poss, S. S., & Manton, K. (1976). Models of response error in student reports of parental socioeconomic characteristics. In *Schooling and Achievement in American Society,* ed. W. H. Sewell, R. M. Hauser, & D. L. Featherman, pp. 443–94. New York: Academic Press.

National Opinion Research Center. (1980). *High School and Beyond, Information for Users: Base Year (1980) Data.* Chicago.

Wolfle, L. M., & Robertshaw, D. (1983). Racial differences in measurement error in educational achievement models. *Journal of Educational Measurement, 20,* 39–49.

5

Modeling the hierarchical structure of learning

PETER W. HILL

Introduction

In the social and behavioral sciences, theories abound that view phenomena as hierarchically organized and decomposable into entities that can be ordered in terms of their complexity. For example, learning has frequently been conceptualized as a hierarchy of processes or outcomes of increasing complexity. Of particular importance to educators because of the impact they have had on curriculum and test development are a number of educational taxonomies – taxonomies being, of course, a type of theory – that embody the notion of a hierarchy of processes or outcomes (Bloom et al. 1956; Gagné 1975; Ausubel & Robinson 1969; Merrill 1971; Biggs & Collis 1981).

This chapter illustrates how theories involving the notion of a hierarchy of variables of increasing complexity can be expressed in mathematical form as a series of structural models and how the analysis of empirical data using these models can be employed to reformulate the original theories.

Modeling hierarchical structure: the Guttman simplex model

One of the most significant attempts to express the concept of a hierarchy of variables of increasing complexity in mathematical form was that of Guttman (1954), who proposed a theory to explain the pattern of intercorrelations to be observed among mental test scores. Guttman proposed (pp. 260–1) that, if content is held constant, a set of tests will differ only in terms of their complexity and are said to belong to a "simplex," since they can be arranged in rank order from least to most complex.

In translating the concept of the simplex into mathematical terms, Guttman considered the case of continuous variables. Furthermore, he expressed his theory not in terms of the "difficulties" or means of the variables – these he considered arbitrary – but in terms of the pattern of

Table 5.1. *Hypothetical correlation matrix exhibiting a perfect simplex structure*

	X_1	X_2	X_3	X_4
X_1	1.000			
X_2	.900	1.000		
x_3	.630	.700	1.000	
x_4	.504	.560	.800	1.000

$r_{31} = r_{21}r_{32} = .9 \times .7 = .63$
$r_{42} = r_{32}r_{43} = .7 \times .8 = .56$
$r_{41} = r_{21}r_{32} = .9 \times .7 \times .8 = .504$

correlations among variables. According to Guttman, a perfect simplex structure is indicated when the correlation between two variables (i and j) is equal to the product of the correlations between all adjacent pairs of intervening variables:

$$r_{ij} = (r_{i,i+1})(r_{i+1,i+2}) \ldots (r_{j-1,j}), \qquad i < j \qquad (5.1)$$

This implies that the partial correlation between any two variables $i - 1$ and $i + 1$ on either side of a third variable i is equal to zero when the third variable is controlled:

$$r_{i-1,i+1.i} = 0 \qquad (5.2)$$

The perfect simplex pattern is illustrated by the hypothetical correlations of Table 5.1. As this table illustrates, when a simplex structure applies, the correlations of largest magnitude will be adjacent to the main diagonal; the magnitude of correlations will decrease with distance from the main diagonal, and the correlations of smallest magnitude will be in the lower left and upper right corners. Interpreting the Guttman simplex model in terms of various stochastic processes, Jöreskog (1970a,b) has shown how the estimation and testing of simplexes incorporating various assumptions concerning errors of measurement can be carried out in the context of structural equation modeling with latent variables. Jöreskog's (1973) LISREL model and its computer program implementation (Jöreskog & Sörbom 1981) considerably extend the flexibility and scope of this approach.

Examples of the application of LISREL to the analysis of simplex models are given by Werts, Linn, and Jöreskog (1977, 1978); more complex models are considered by Jöreskog and Sörbom (1977). In fact, the data used in these applications are longitudinal growth data rather than data for variables ordered in terms of their complexity. Although several

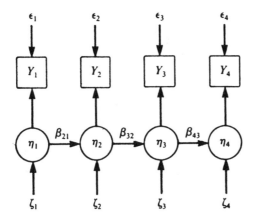

Figure 5.1. Four-variable quasi-simplex model.

writers have drawn attention to the applicability of LISREL to the analysis of hierarchical test data (Keesling 1972; Kerlinger 1977; Bergan 1980), for actual examples the reader is referred to Hill and McGaw (1981) and Hill (1982).

Figure 5.1 depicts a four-variable "quasi-" (or nonperfect) Guttman simplex model. A perfect simplex is indicated when the score η_i on any variable i is related to the score on the preceding variable $i-1$ by the linear regression equation

$$\eta_i = \beta_i \eta_{i-1} \tag{5.3}$$

With disturbances to allow for lack of fit, the structural model can then be expressed as

$$\eta_i = \beta_i \eta_{i-1} + \zeta_i \tag{5.4}$$

Further, this model can be expressed in terms of true scores by specifying the relation between true score η_i and observed score y_i as

$$y_i = \eta_i + \varepsilon_i \tag{5.5}$$

For example, suppose that measures are obtained on four variables, y_i to y_4, which are taken to be indicators of four latent variables η_1 to η_4, where η_1 is the least complex variable and η_4 the most complex variable.

As a set of equations, the measurement model can be written as

$$\begin{aligned} y_1 &= \eta_1 + \varepsilon_1 \\ y_2 &= \eta_2 + \varepsilon_2 \\ y_3 &= \eta_3 + \varepsilon_3 \\ y_4 &= \eta_4 + \varepsilon_4 \end{aligned} \tag{5.6}$$

and the structural model as

$$
\begin{aligned}
\eta_1 &= && + \zeta_1 \\
\eta_2 &= \beta_{21}\eta_1 && + \zeta_2 \\
\eta_3 &= && \beta_{32}\eta_2 && + \zeta_3 \\
\eta_4 &= && && \beta_{43}\eta_3 + \zeta_4
\end{aligned}
\tag{5.7}
$$

In addition to the specification in (5.6) and (5.7) we make the further assumption that the errors of measurement ε_i are uncorrelated with one another and with all the latent variables η_i. It is also assumed that ζ_{i+1} is uncorrelated with $\eta_i (i = 2, 3)$. As a LISREL model, this model has 11 parameters ($\varepsilon_1, \ldots, \varepsilon_4, \beta_{21}, \beta_{32}, \beta_{43}, \zeta_1, \ldots, \zeta_4$) and is not identified. This is apparent from the fact that there are only 10 unique elements in the covariance matrix for y_1 to y_4. Jöreskog and Sörbom (1977, pp. 302–3) show that there are indeterminacies associated with the outer variables y_1 and y_4. A convenient way of eliminating these indeterminacies is to fix $\varepsilon_1 = \varepsilon_4 = 0$. This reduces to nine the number of independent parameters, and the model can then be shown to be identified with $10 - 9 = 1$ degree of freedom.

The quasi-simplex model of (5.6) and (5.7) provides a test of the hypothesis of hierarchical ordering among the four latent variables ordered in terms of their complexity. Other more complex models incorporating multiple indicators of the latent variables are possible. In addition, such models can be fitted simultaneously to data from several groups and any degree of invariance of the parameters for each group can be tested.

Illustration

The Kropp and Stoker data

The notion of a hierarchy of variables ordered by complexity is at the heart of what has been one of the most influential ideas in education, namely, that detailed in the *Taxonomy of Educational Objectives, Handbook 1: Cognitive Domain* of Bloom et al. (1956). The Bloom taxonomy arranges cognitive behaviors in terms of their complexity into six major classes: Knowledge, Comprehension, Application, Analysis, Synthesis, and Evaluation. The taxonomy is both hierarchical and cumulative. It is hierarchical in that each successive class of behaviors is considered to be more complex than preceding classes, the most complex class being Evaluation. It is cumulative in that each successive class of behaviors contains those of preceding classes, with Evaluation including all the behaviors represented by Knowledge, Comprehension, Application, Anal-

Table 5.2. *Observed subtest correlations for "Atomic Structure":*
combined grades (N = 5,057)

	Kn	Co	Ap	An	Sy	Ev
Knowledge (Kn)	1.000					
Comprehension (Co)	.514	1.000				
Application (Ap)	.496	.712	1.000			
Analysis (An)	.358	.648	.632	1.000		
Synthesis (Sy)	.412	.415	.450	.371	1.000	
Evaluation (Ev)	.386	.355	.348	.294	.426	1.000

ysis, and Synthesis, in addition to a unique component with respect to the behaviors in the lower classes. Another feature of the taxonomy is that the behaviors of the various classes are assumed to apply irrespective of subject matter, age, or type of instruction.

To investigate the validity of the claimed psychological properties of the Bloom taxonomy, Kropp & Stoker (1966) designed four tests in two content areas (science and social studies). Each test involved a reading passage of 600 to 900 words. The passages were entitled "Atomic Structure," "Glaciers," "Lisbon Earthquake," and "Stages of Economic Growth." The four tests contained six subtests, one for each of the major classes of the taxonomy, and were administered to large samples of students in grades 9–12 in 10 Florida schools.

The data reported by Kropp and Stoker include the four 24-variable correlation matrices formed by intercorrelating subtest scores over all four tests each of the four grades and a fifth 24-variable combined-grades matrix.

Single-variable simplex models

To illustrate how structural modeling can be used to test the hypothesis of a cumulative hierarchy of variables, we begin by considering part of the 24-variable combined-grades matrix. Table 5.2 gives the correlation matrix for the six subtests comprising the first of the four taxonomic tests, entitled "Atomic Structure."

It is evident from a visual inspection that the matrix does not exhibit the perfect simplex form. Not all of the largest correlations are adjacent to the main diagonal, and not all correlations decrease steadily as one moves out to the lower left corner. It therefore remains to be seen whether a quasi-simplex model fits these data within the bounds of sampling error.

Table 5.3 indicates the sequence of hypotheses investigated in testing

Table 5.3. *Goodness-of-fit for six models: "Atomic Structure," combined grades (N = 5,057)*

Model	χ^2	d.f.	Critical N
5.1.1 One-factor	725.25	9	117
5.2.1 Quasi-simplex	380.35	6	165
5.2.2 5.2.2 with β_{51} free	124.77	5	439
5.3.1 One-factor	405.02	5	136
5.4.1 Quasi-simplex	23.10	3	1,654
5.4.2 5.4.1 with var$\zeta_3 = 0$	29.17	4	1,620

the final model. Given the positive correlations of Table 5.2, the most parsimonious explanation of the data is not that they conform to a simplex structure, but rather that they can be accounted for by a single underlying factor. We therefore begin by fitting a one-factor model of the form

$$\begin{bmatrix} y_1 \\ y_2 \\ y_3 \\ y_4 \\ y_5 \\ y_6 \end{bmatrix} = \begin{bmatrix} \lambda_1 \\ \lambda_2 \\ \lambda_3 \\ \lambda_4 \\ \lambda_5 \\ \lambda_6 \end{bmatrix} \eta_1 + \begin{bmatrix} \varepsilon_1 \\ \varepsilon_2 \\ \varepsilon_3 \\ \varepsilon_4 \\ \varepsilon_5 \\ \varepsilon_6 \end{bmatrix} \tag{5.8}$$

to the data. This model (Model 5.1.1), which is shown diagrammatically in Figure 5.2, serves as a null model with which to compare various hypothesized models.[1] Model 5.1.1 yields $\chi^2(9) = 725.24$, $p < .05$, indicating, from a statistical point of view, poor fit to the data. Actually, with a sample size in excess of 5,000 cases, the likelihood ratio chi-square statistic is likely to reject almost any hypothesized model, so we turn to another indicator of fit, Hoelter's (1983) "critical N" (CN), to decide whether to reject the one-factor model as an adequate explanation of the data of Table 5.2. Critical N is an estimate of the size that a sample must reach in order to accept the fit of a given model on a statistical basis. The index is most conveniently computed as

$$CN = \frac{(z_{\text{crit}} + \sqrt{2\,\text{d.f.} - 1})^2}{2\chi^2/(N - G)} + G \tag{5.9}$$

where z_{crit} is the critical value of the normal variate z for a selected probability level and G the number of groups analyzed simultaneously. Hoelter proposes that values exceeding $200G$ may be taken as indicating that a particular model adequately reproduces an observed covariance structure. Thus, for Model 5.1.1

$$CN = \frac{(1.65 + \sqrt{(2 \times 9) - 1})^2}{(2 \times 725.25)/(5,057 - 1)} + 1 = 117$$

indicating a lack of fit between the estimated correlation matrix $\hat{\Sigma}$ and the observed correlation matrix S.

The next step is to fit our hypothesized quasi-simplex model (Model 5.2.1) to the data. We therefore specify a quasi-simplex model in which the measurement model is

$$\begin{bmatrix} y_1 \\ y_2 \\ y_3 \\ y_4 \\ y_5 \\ y_6 \end{bmatrix} = \begin{bmatrix} 1 & 0 & 0 & 0 & 0 & 0 \\ 0 & 1 & 0 & 0 & 0 & 0 \\ 0 & 0 & 1 & 0 & 0 & 0 \\ 0 & 0 & 0 & 1 & 0 & 0 \\ 0 & 0 & 0 & 0 & 1 & 0 \\ 0 & 0 & 0 & 0 & 0 & 1 \end{bmatrix} \begin{bmatrix} \eta_1 \\ \eta_2 \\ \eta_3 \\ \eta_4 \\ \eta_5 \\ \eta_6 \end{bmatrix} + \begin{bmatrix} \varepsilon_1 \\ \varepsilon_2 \\ \varepsilon_3 \\ \varepsilon_4 \\ \varepsilon_5 \\ \varepsilon_6 \end{bmatrix} \quad (5.10)$$

and the structural model is

$$\begin{bmatrix} \eta_1 \\ \eta_2 \\ \eta_3 \\ \eta_4 \\ \eta_5 \\ \eta_6 \end{bmatrix} = \begin{bmatrix} 0 & 0 & 0 & 0 & 0 & 0 \\ \beta_{21} & 0 & 0 & 0 & 0 & 0 \\ 0 & \beta_{32} & 0 & 0 & 0 & 0 \\ 0 & 0 & \beta_{43} & 0 & 0 & 0 \\ 0 & 0 & 0 & \beta_{54} & 0 & 0 \\ 0 & 0 & 0 & 0 & \beta_{65} & 0 \end{bmatrix} \begin{bmatrix} \eta_1 \\ \eta_2 \\ \eta_3 \\ \eta_4 \\ \eta_5 \\ \eta_6 \end{bmatrix} + \begin{bmatrix} \zeta_1 \\ \zeta_2 \\ \zeta_3 \\ \zeta_4 \\ \zeta_5 \\ \zeta_6 \end{bmatrix} \quad (5.11)$$

This model is shown diagrammatically in Figure 5.2.

Note that, because there are no X variables in the model, the full LISREL model, $\eta = B\eta + \Gamma\xi + \zeta$ is reduced to $\eta = B\eta + \zeta$ in (5.11). As noted earlier, the model of (5.10) and (5.11) is not identified since there are indeterminacies associated with the "outer" variables y_1 and y_6. Following Jöreskog and Sörbom (1977, p. 303), we eliminate these indeterminacies by fixing $\varepsilon_1 = \varepsilon_6 = 0$; that is, we treat η_1 and η_6 as though they were perfectly measured. Model 5.2.1 results in $\chi^2(6) = 380.35, p < .05$, and $CN = 165$. Although Model 5.2.1 is statistically a better fitting model than our one-factor null model, with the difference in $\chi^2(9 - 6) = (725.25 - 380.34)$, $p < .05$, as indicated by critical N, it is still an ill-fitting model.

Inspection of the modification indices suggests that fit can be improved by postulating a path (β_{51}) between Knowledge and Synthesis. We incorporate this link into Model 5.2.2 (Figure 5.2) by freeing β_{51} and obtain

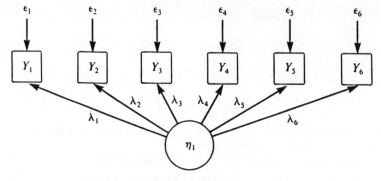

Model 5.1.1. $\chi^2(9) = 725.25$, $CN = 117$

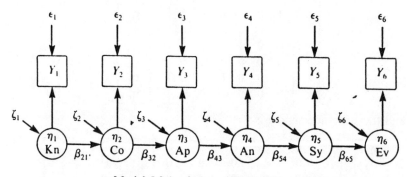

Model 5.2.1. $\chi^2(6) = 380.35$, $CN = 165$

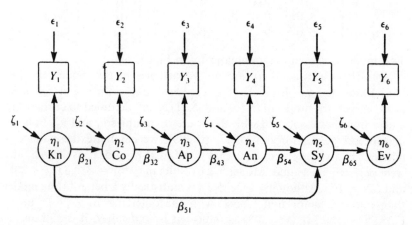

Model 5.2.2. $\chi^2(5) = 124.77$, $CN = 439$

Figure 5.2 Models 5.1.1, 5.2.1, and 5.2.2 as fitted to the Kropp and Stoker data for atomic structure. Kn, Knowledge; Co, Comprehension; Ap. Application; An, Analysis; Sy, Synthesis; Ev, Evaluation.

Table 5.4. *Normalized residuals for Model 5.2.2: "Atomic Structure"*
(N = 5,057)

	Kn	Co	Ap	An	Sy	Ev
Knowledge (Kn)	0.000					
Comprehension (Co)	0.000	0.000				
Application (Ap)	1.908	0.348	0.000			
Analysis (An)	−3.489	0.911	−0.245	0.000		
Synthesis (Sy)	−0.942	−0.676	2.219	−0.084	−0.015	
Evaluation (Ev)	1.305	−0.703	−0.648	−1.755	−0.017	−0.011

an improvement of 255.57 in the value of chi-square for the loss of one degree of freedom. In addition, critical N is now 439 and well above the critical value of 200, suggesting that we might accept Model 5.2.2 as providing an adequate fit to the data.

Before accepting Model 5.2.2, however, it is important to probe further. The chi-square statistic and critical N index are overall indicators of fit that do not reveal localized problems within a model. A more detailed assessment of fit can be obtained by direct inspection of the matrix of residuals $S = \hat{\Sigma}$ or, more conveniently, of normalized residuals (residuals divided by their standard deviation). Normalized residuals larger than 2 are indicative of specification errors in the model.

The matrix of normalized residuals for Model 5.2.2 is given in Table 5.4. Two of the elements of this matrix exceed 2 in value. Inspection of Table 5.4 and of the modification indices for the B matrix suggests a further modification incorporating an additional path between Knowledge and Analysis. It is now evident that the fit of our models to these data is highly dependent on paths linking Knowledge and the more complex classes of behaviors in the taxonomy. That is, Knowledge does not appear to be hierarchically related to the other five variables.

We therefore consider the effects of deleting Knowledge from the hierarchical structure of the taxonomy, beginning again with a one-factor null model fitted to the five variables Comprehension, Application, Analysis, Synthesis, and Evaluation. As can be seen from Table 5.3, this model (Model 5.3.1) does not fit the data. Next, we fit our hypothesized model, Model 5.4.1, which is a quasi-simplex model for a five-variable simplex. This results in a very good fit to the data considering the very large sample size ($N = 5,057$), with $\chi^4(3) = 23,10$, $p < .05$, and this is reflected in $CN = 1,654$. The maximum likelihood estimates for all identified parameters in Model 5.4.1 are given in the left side of Table 5.5 and standard errors are shown in parentheses.[2] Unstandardized

Table 5.5. *Maximum likelihood estimates and standard errors[a] for all identified parameters in Models 5.4.1 and 5.4.2: "Atomic Structure"* (N = 5,507)

Parameter	Model 5.4.1		Model 5.4.2	
	Unscaled solution	Standardized solution	Unscaled solution	Standardized solution
λ_2		0.841		0.842
λ_3		0.738		0.755
λ_4		0.725		0.726
β_{32}	0.902 (.016)	1.028	0.896 (.106)	1.000
β_{43}	0.676 (.020)	0.688	0.672 (.020)	0.699
β_{54}	0.810 (.029)	0.588	0.809 (.029)	0.587
var ζ_3	−0.031 (.012)	−0.056	0.000[b]	0.000
var ζ_4	0.277 (.019)	0.526	0.269 (.018)	0.512
var ζ_2	0.292 (.010)		0.291 (.010)	
var ζ_3	0.455 (.015)		0.430 (.011)	
var ζ_4	0.474 (0.20)		0.474 (.020)	

[a]   Standard errors in parentheses.
[b]   Fixed parameter.

coefficients are all greater than twice their respective standard errors.

All is not well with Model 5.4.1, however: An examination of the parameter estimates of Table 5.5 indicates that a "Heywood case" has been obtained. The estimate for the residual variance (var ζ_3) for Analysis has a negative value. The notion of a negative variance clearly is meaningless, and so we are unable to accept such an estimate. To eliminate this problem, we modify the model and reestimate it with var ζ_3 fixed at zero to provide an estimate that is logically interpretable (i.e., a "proper" solution). Because the magnitude of the negative variance estimate is small, the new parameter estimates, which are given in the right side of Table 5.5, closely resemble those shown in the left side of the table. Referring back to Table 5.3, it will be seen that the fit of our final model (Model 5.4.2), in which we fix var ζ_3 to zero to deal with the Heywood case, is little different from that of Model 5.4.1.

Now the fixing of var ζ_3 to zero in Model 5.4.2 is more than simply a convenient way of overcoming the problem of a negative variance estimate. The interpretation changes as well, since var $\zeta_3 = 0$ implies that the standardized path (β_{32}) linking Application and Analysis is unity, indicating a perfect correlation between these two latent variables. In fact, Model 5.4.2 can be reparametrized as a four-factor quasi-simplex model

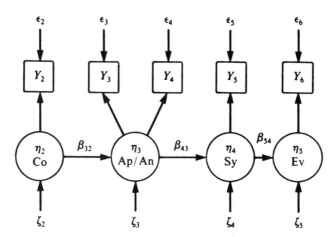

Figure 5.3. Reparametrization of Model 5.4.2 as a four-factor quasi-simplex model. Co, Comprehension; Ap, Application; An, Analysis; Sy, Synthesis; Ev, Evaluation.

with the observed variables for Application and Analysis measuring a single latent construct, as indicated in Figure 5.3.

In choosing between a five- or four-factor interpretation, the issue is whether we regard Application and Analysis as a single process or as two processes that are indistinguishable as measured by the Kropp and Stoker tests. In other words, our model fitting may have exposed conceptual or theoretical problems with the taxonomy, or it may have revealed technical problems with the measures used.

The problems of retaining the variable Knowledge in the taxonomic flow are of a similar kind. In a paper that reported a preliminary LISREL reanalysis of the Kropp and Stoker data to test the simplex assumption in Bloom's taxonomy, Hill and McGaw (1981) discussed the misplacement of the Knowledge category from a theoretical viewpoint. They noted that the authors of the Bloom taxonomy had themselves been aware of difficulties with the Knowledge category, distinguishing it from the other categories they referred to collectively as "arts and skills." They further noted that others had found it necessary to make a similar distinction. Ryle's (1949) classic attack on the intellectualist doctrine of "the ghost in the machine" in his chapter "Knowing How and Knowing That" was quoted as a good example. There are clear parallels between Ryle's propositional knowledge and Bloom's Knowledge category, and Ryle's procedural knowledge and Bloom's higher-order categories. On the basis of this parallelism, it was suggested that although no hierarchical

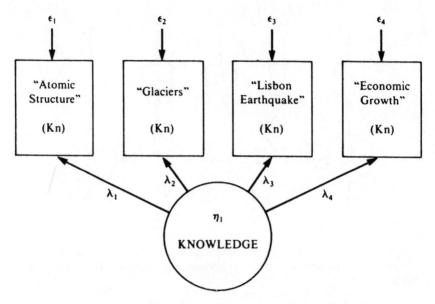

Figure 5.4. One-factor model for Knowledge (Kn).

relationship exists between the two forms of knowing, there is a hierarchical structure among the five higher-order categories.

Multivariable simplex models

It will be recalled that Kropp and Stoker designed not one but four
taxonomic tests, two in science and two in social studies. We now illustrate
how structural models can be used to test the hypothesis of a cumulative
hierarchy of variables making use of all the data contained in the 24-
variable combined-grades matrix referred to earlier.

The first step is to determine whether the four tests do in fact belong to
two distinct content areas (science and social studies). Expressing this in
terms of a structural model, the question is whether, at each level of the
taxonomy, the relationships among the four tests can be explained in
terms of a two-factor model.

We investigate this empirically by considering the six variables (Knowledge through Evaluation) separetely and fitting a one-factor null model
to each of the six four-variable submatrices for each latent variable. Thus,
beginning with the variable Knowledge, we fit the model shown diagrammatically in Figure 5.4 to the correlations among the Knowledge subtests
of the four Kropp and Stoker taxonomic tests and proceed to fit a similar

Table 5.6. *Goodness-of-fit for one-factor model: combined grades*
(N = 3,850)

Variable	$\chi^2(2)$	Critical N
Knowledge	40.22[a]	448
Comprehension	4.32	5,097
Application	23.05[a]	956
Analysis	4.50	4,893
Synthesis	6.73[a]	3,272
Evaluation	4.35	5,061

[a] $p < .05$.

model to the other five four-variable submatrices (Comprehension through Evaluation). The results are given in Table 5.6. Clearly a one-factor model fits these data very well indeed as judged by critical N (CN = 448 − 5,097).

In Table 5.7, the first two columns present parameter estimates obtained from fitting a one-factor model to the six four-variable submatrices for each latent variable. In the third column are the factor model reliability coefficients for the observed variables in measuring the six latent variables and analogous reliability coefficients reported by Kropp and Stoker (1966, p. 71). The reliability coefficients computed from the factor model are simply the squares of the factor loadings given in the first column of Table 5.7. The reliabilities reported by Kropp and Stoker are Kuder–Richardson 20-item analysis internal consistency coefficients for Knowledge through Analysis and inter judge reliability coefficients for Synthesis and Evaluation. In every case the coefficients reported by Kropp and Stoker are considerably larger than the corresponding factor model estimates.

These results point to two conclusions. First, the good fit of the one-factor model to the data indicates that the hypothesis of two content factors should be rejected. Had the two science tests ("Atomic Structure" and "Glaciers") and the two social studies tests ("Lisbon Earthquake" and "Stages of Economic Growth") defined two content areas, the one-factor model would have been rejected and the matrix of residuals would have revealed significant residual correlations between pairs of subtests at each level of the taxonomy. This, however, is not the case. Second, the discrepancies between the Kropp and Stoker internal consistency estimates and the factor model estimates of reliability suggest that each subtest is associated with a significant amount of test-specific variance. The relatively higher values of KR-20 are due to test-specific variance,

Table 5.7. *Parameter estimates and reliabilities: combined grades*
(N = 3,850)

Variable/test	λ_i	var ε_i	Factor model reliability estimates	Reliabilities reported by Kropp & Stoker KR-20
Knowledge				
"Atomic Structure"	0.741	0.451	.549	.810
"Glaciers"	0.811	0.343	.658	.816
"Lisbon Earthquake"	0.718	0.485	.516	.758
"Economic Growth"	0.734	0.461	.539	.824
Comprehension				
"Atomic Structure"	0.668	0.553	.446	.693
"Glaciers"	0.770	0.407	.593	.677
"Lisbon Earthquake"	0.753	0.432	.557	.743
"Economic Growth"	0.793	0.372	.629	.745
Application				
"Atomic Structure"	0.670	0.551	.449	.694
"Glaciers"	0.785	0.384	.616	.731
"Lisbon Earthquake"	0.758	0.426	.575	.689
"Economic Growth"	0.766	0.413	.587	.731
Analysis				
"Atomic Structure"	0.599	0.641	.359	.632
"Glaciers"	0.598	0.642	.358	.539
"Lisbon Earthquake"	0.706	0.501	.498	.684
"Economic Growth"	0.718	0.485	.516	.614
Synthesis				Interjudge
"Atomic Structure"	0.678	0.540	.460	.89
"Glaciers"	0.502	0.748	.252	.72
"Lisbon Earthquake"	0.792	0.372	.627	.71
"Economic Growth"	0.685	0.531	.469	.79
Evaluation				
"Atomic Structure"	0.653	0.574	.426	.83
"Glaciers"	0.702	0.507	.493	.75
"Lisbon Earthquake"	0.649	0.579	.421	.81
"Economic Growth"	0.591	0.651	.349	.72

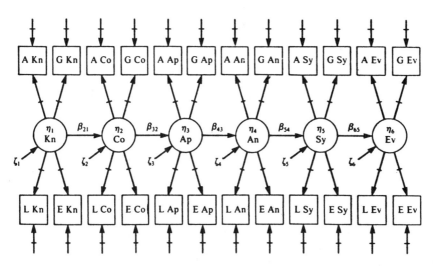

Figure 5.5. Model 5.5.1 as fitted to the Kropp and Stoker combined-grades data. A, "Atomic Structure"; G, "Glaciers"; L, "Lisbon Earthquake'; E, "Economic Growth"; Kn, Knowledge; Co, Comprehension; Ap, Application; An, Analysis; Sy, Synthesis; Ev, Evaluation; ↔, fixed parameter.

which in the factor model is treated as a component of error variance. This test-specific variance could reflect detailed content differences between subtests as well as other differences, such as time of testing or other sources of variance peculiar to each subtest. Because of the difficulty of ascribing any meaningful interpretation to the notion of distinct content differences among the four subtests at each level of the taxonomy, we take the view that this test-specific variance should be regarded as measurement error only.

From this decision, we proceed to fit various quasi-simplex models to the full 24-variable correlation matrix on the assumption that at each level of the taxonomy all four of the Kropp and Stoker taxonomic tests measure a single latent variable. The first model to be fitted (Model 5.5.1) is shown diagrammatically in Figure 5.5. A second model (Model 5.6.1) is essentially the same model applied to the 20-variable correlation matrix for all subtests after deleting those relating to Knowledge. In both Models 5.5.1 and 5.6.1, the values of λ_i and var ε_i are fixed equal to the parameter estimates obtained from first fitting a one-factor model to the subtests measuring each of the six latent variables. These are the values shown in the first two columns of Table 5.7. By fixing the measurement model component of the full structural model represented by Figure 5.5, a considerable saving in computer processing time is obtained, but more

Table 5.8. *Goodness-of-fit for five models: combined grades*
(N = 3,850)

Model	χ^2	d.f.	Critical N
5.5.1	6692.30[a]	289	190
5.6.1	5064.15	201	178
5.5.2	1280.57	229	798
5.6.2	659.44	161	1,118
5.7.1	662.14	146	1,018

[a] $p < .05$ for all values in this column.

important, the possibility of "interpretational confounding" of the latent variables is avoided.[3]

As is evident from the high chi-squares and the low critical N of Table 5.8, both Models 5.5.1 and 5.6.1 result in a poor fit to the observed data. Inspection of the matrices of normalized residuals revealed that this was due to correlated errors of measurement between subtests within tests. This is not surprising: As noted earlier, each of the four taxonomic tests is based on a single topic and involves an extended reading passage. We may therefore anticipate a significant amount of common factor variance among subtests within tests. Thus, we modify Models 5.5.1 and 5.6.1 to allow correlations among the errors for all subtests with each test by specifying the covariance matrix of the errors of measurement ε as

$$
\theta_\varepsilon = \begin{matrix}
\theta_{\varepsilon_{AA}} & 0 & 0 & 0 \\
0 & \theta_{\varepsilon_{GG}} & 0 & 0 \\
0 & 0 & \theta_{\varepsilon_{LL}} & 0 \\
0 & 0 & 0 & \theta_{\varepsilon_{FE}}
\end{matrix} \tag{5.12}
$$

in which $\theta_{\varepsilon_{AA}}$ to $\theta_{\varepsilon_{EE}}$ are submatrices of correlations among errors, and the subscripts A, G, L, and E refer to the four tests ("Atomic Structure," "Glaciers," "Lisbon Earthquake," and "Economic Growth," respectively). Tests of fit for these modified models (Models 5.5.2 and 5.6.2) are given in Table 5.8, and parameter estimates for the structural component of the modified models are shown in Table 5.9.

Tables 5.8 and 5.9 also give results for a third model (Model 5.7.1), which is fitted to the 20-variable matrix in order to investigate and illustrate an alternative approach to modeling these data. In Model 5.7.1, which is shown diagrammatically in Figure 5.6, the values of λ_i and var ε_i are allowed to be free, and the correlations among errors of measurement

Table 5.9. *Standardized parameter estimates for three models: combined grades ($N = 3,850$)*

Parameter	Model		
	5.5.2	5.6.2	5.7.1
$\beta_{Kn.Co}(\beta_{21})$	0.798	—	—
$\beta_{Co.Ap}(\beta_{32})$	0.996	0.997	0.997
$\beta_{Ap.An}(\beta_{43})$	0.988	0.992	0.993
$\beta_{An.Sy}(\beta_{54})$	0.866	0.854	0.858
$\beta_{Sy.Ev}(\beta_{65})$	0.849	0.846	0.868
var $\zeta_{Kn}(\zeta_1)$	1.000	—	—
var $\zeta_{Co}(\zeta_2)$	0.363	1.000	1.000
var $\zeta_{Ap}(\zeta_3)$	0.008	0.006	0.006
var $\zeta_{An}(\zeta_4)$	0.025	0.016	0.013
var $\zeta_{Sy}(\zeta_5)$	0.251	0.272	0.264
var $\zeta_{Ev}(\zeta_6)$	0.279	0.284	0.246

within tests are assumed to be accounted for by four test-specific factors. Both the fit and the parameter estimates for the structural component of this model closely resemble those of Model 5.6.2.

As can be seen from Table 5.8, the modified models (5.5.2, 5.6.2, and 5.7.1) fit the data much better than do the initial models (5.5.1 and 5.6.1), and judging by the values for critical N all three of the modified models can be regarded as providing a good fit to the data. Two important features of the modified models are that they result in "proper" solutions (i.e., positive estimates of residual variances) and have all their structural parameters uniquely identified. These two features tend to favor the present models over the single-variable quasi-simplex models described earlier. A further critical feature of the results for the modified models is the relatively small improvement in fit resulting from deleting the Knowledge subtests from the analysis. Whereas a dramatic improvement in fit is achieved between Models 5.2.1 and 5.4.1 (or 5.4.2), only a modest improvement is obtained between Models 5.5.2 and 5.6.2 (or 5.7.1). Although the critical N fit index for Model 5.2 suggests that Knowledge could be retained in the model, it should nevertheless be noted that the path coefficient Kn → Co has the smallest value of the path coefficients linking the five process factors. We therefore conclude that our structural analyses of the Kropp and Stoker data generally support the psychological assumptions underlying Bloom's taxonomy, although on both theoretical and empirical grounds doubts remain regarding the status of Knowledge in the taxonomic flow and also regarding Application and Analysis as separate processes.

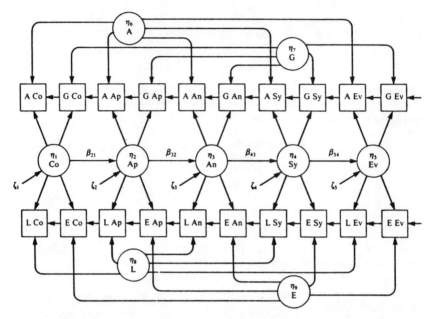

Figure 5.6. Model 5.7.1 as fitted to the Kropp and Stoker combined-grades data. For abbreviations, see begins to Figure 5.5.

This is not to say that a quasi-simplex model is the most parsimonious explanation of the Kropp and Stoker data. Indeed, the parameter estimates are strongly suggestive of a two-factor model. However, the goal of the theory-confirming process in structural modeling is not to identify the most parsimonious model, but to test an a priori theoretical structure. Therefore, in view of the degree of support for the initially hypothesized structure, we resist the temptation to pursue other models with fewer parameters and better fit, but for which there may be little or no theoretical support.

In stating that our results generally support the Bloom assumptions, we must make a further qualification. The models have been estimated with the maximum likelihood procedures in LISREL, which assume that the observed variables have a multinormal distribution. Multinormal data represent an ideal that is seldom, if ever, realized in practice and is particularly unlikely in the case of taxonomic test data. Furthermore, if subtest means follow the hypothesized ordering of the corresponding taxonomic categories, higher-order subtests are likely to exhibit positive skewness and lower-order tests are likely to be associated with negative skewness. Such score distributions will result in estimated intercorrelations of reduced magnitude, which, though not necessarily producing a simplex structure, may nevertheless reinforce and exaggerate any tendency toward such a structure. It would seem possible that aspects of the distribution of the observed variables may in part be responsible for the observed pattern of intercorrelations among the Kropp and Stoker tests, although the available data published as a correlation matrix do not allow an investigation of their effects. In the absence of such information it is necessary to acknowledge that a degree of uncertainty is associated with the analyses and interpretation of results presented above.

For a more detailed analysis of the Kropp and Stoker data and discussion of the influence of distribution factors in taxonomic test data, the reader is referred to Hill (1982).

Conclusion

Our analyses of Kropp and Stoker's data for Bloom's taxonomy illustrate the power and flexibility of a structural modeling approach to the testing of theories involving a hierarchy of variables of increasing complexity. By making successive adjustments to obtain models that accord with the observed data, we are able to identify possible problems with the original theory or with the measurement of variables in the models and to obtain clues as to the directions further empirical research might take.

Notes

This study is based on work done as part of the author's doctoral studies at Murdoch University under the supervision of Professor Barry McGaw, for whose support the author is especially grateful.

1. For a discussion of indices for comparing the fit of a hypothesized model with a zero- or one-factor null model, the reader is referred to Tucker and Lewis (1973) and Bentler and Bonett (1980).
2. Strictly speaking, standard errors in LISREL are applicable only to analyses based on covariance matrices. The analysis of correlation matrices is justified in the present instance on the basis of their greater interpretability and because the variables in the data have no inherent metric; thus, a standardized covariance (correlation) matrix is as meaningful as any other arbitrary scaling.
3. The problem of "interpretational confounding" is explained by Burt (1973) as follows: "Because the confirmatory factor-analytic model of estimation will consider all ... observed variables simultaneously, it will take advantage of the covariance of the indicants of separate concepts to improve the fit of the model to the data set by allowing the covariance of the indicants of different concepts to influence the extraction of the unobserved variables.... What this means to the theorist is that the unobserved variables will not only be a function of the

covariance of their constituent indicants, but will also be a function of their constituent indicants with the indicants of other unobserved variables in a proposed structure. In this fashion, the confirmatory factor model can confound the interpretability of the unobserved variables it extracts" (p. 159).

References

Ausubel, D. P., & Robinson, F. G. (1969). *School Learning: An Introduction to Educational Psychology*. New York: Holt, Rinehart & Winston.

Bentler, P. M., & Bonett, D. G. (1980). Significance tests and goodness of fit in the analysis of covariance structures. *Psychological Bulletin, 88*, 588–606.

Bergan, J. R. (1980). The structural analysis of behavior: An alternative to the learning-hierarchy model. *Review of Educational Research, 50*, 625–46.

Biggs, J. B., & Collis, K. F. (1981). *Evaluating the Quality of Learning: The SOLO Taxonomy*. Academic Press: New York.

Bloom, B. S., Englehart, M. D., Furst, E. J., Hill, W. H., & Krathwohl, D. R. (1956). *Taxonomy of Educational Objectives, Handbook 1: Cognitive Domain*. New York: McKay.

Burt, R. S. (1973). Confirmatory factor-analytic structures and the theory construction process. *Sociological Methods and Research, 2*, 131–90.

Gagne, R. M. (1965). *The Conditions of Learning*. New York: Holt, Rinehart & Winston.

Guttman, L. (1954). A new approach to factor analysis: The Radex. In P. Lazarsfeld (Ed.), *Mathematical Thinking in the Social Sciences*. Glencoe, IL: The Free Press.

Hill, P. W. (1982). *Process Hierarchy Theory: A Holistic Approach to Theory Building in Education*. Unpublished Ph.D. thesis, Murdoch University.

Hill, P. W., & McGaw, B. (1981). Testing the simplex assumption underlying Bloom's taxonomy. *American Educational Research Journal, 18*, 93–101.

Hoelter, J. W. (1983). The analysis of covariance structures: Goodness-of-fit indices. *Sociological Methods and Research, 11*, 325–44.

Jöreskog, K. G. (1970a). A general method for analysis of covariance structures. *Biometrika, 57*, 239–51.

(1970b). Estimation and testing of simplex models. British Journal of Mathematical and Statistical Psychology, 23, 121–45.

(1973). A general method for estimating a linear structural equation system. In A. S. Goldberger & O. D. Duncan (Eds.), *Structural Equation Models in the Social Sciences* (pp. 85–112). New York: Seminar Press.

Jöreskog, K. G., & Sörbom, D. (1977). Statistical models and methods for analysis of longitudinal data. In D. J. Aigner & A. S. Goldberger (eds.), *Latent Variables in Socioeconomic Models* (pp. 285–326). Amsterdam: North Holland.

(1981). *LISREL VI: Analysis of Linear Structural Relationships by the Method of Maximum Likelihood*. Chicago: National Educational Resources.

Keesling, W. (1972). *Maximum Likelihood Approaches to Causal Flow Analysis.* Unpublished doctoral dissertation, University of Chicago.

Kerlinger, F. N. (1977). The influence of research in education practice. *Educational Researcher, 6*(8), 5–11.

Kropp, R. P., & Stoker, H. W. (1966). *The Construction and Validation of Tests of the Cognitive Processes as Described in the Taxonomy of Educational Objectives.* Tallahassee: Florida State University, Institute of Human Learning and Department of Educational Research and Testing (ERIC ED 010 044).

Merrill, M. D. (1971). Necessary psychological conditions for defining instructional outcomes. *Educational Technology, 11,* 34–9.

Ryle, G. (1949). *The Concept of Mind.* London: Hutchinson.

Tucker, L. R., & Lewis, C. (1973). A reliability coefficient for maximum likelihood factor analysis. *Psychometrika, 38,* 1–10.

Werts, C. E., Linn, R. L., & Jöreskog, K. G. (1977). A simplex model for analyzing academic growth. *Educational and Psychological Measurement, 37,* 745–56.

(1978). Reliability of college grades from longitudinal data. *Educational and Psychological Measurement, 38,* 89–95.

6

A study of longitudinal causal models comparing gain score analysis with structural equation approaches

LESLIE HENDRICKSON AND BARNIE JONES

Introduction

Current trends in applied research have witnessed the widespread adaptation of multiple regression techniques to research projects and program evaluations. Although regression analysis is a powerful technique, it owes much of its power to highly restrictive and often unrealistic assumptions. The interpretation of regression results, especially the assessment of the relative impact or importance of independent variables, can be difficult.

This chapter compares methodological procedures for analyzing longitudinal data. It critically compares regression analysis of gain scores with structural equation approaches. The analytic techniques discussed here are applicable to any longitudinal analysis. These general techniques are exemplified by the secondary analysis of data from the *What Works in Reading?* study conducted by the School District of Philadelphia (Kean et al. 1979a,b).

Following an introduction to the data, the analysis proceeds in three steps. First, specification of the dependent variable is examined. The original report (Kean et al. 1979a) treated reading improvement as a net change or gain score. Gain scores are widely used in American schools. Results of using the gain score as a dependent variable are compared with results obtained when reading at time 1 (T_1) and reading time 2 (T_2) are treated as separate dependent variables in a longitudinal model (see Models 1 and 2 in Figures 6.1 and 6.2, respectively). Second, the model is reformulated as a latent variable structural model to relieve problems due to collinearity among the independent variables. Third, the latent variable model is subjected to a sensitivity analysis (Land & Felson 1978) with regard to random measurement error in the dependent variables and to specification error due to the omission of theoretically important independent variables. This analysis demonstrates how small changes in model specification and residual assumptions can modify results.

Sample and data collection

The original sample consisted of 1,800 fourth grade students in 25 schools drawn from a population of 190 schools. Schools were stratified on the basis of average scores in 1974 and 1975, for grades 1–4, on reading portions of the California Achievement Test (CAT). The sample excluded schools that showed major shifts in average reading score level from 1974 to 1975, selecting 10 with high, 10 with low, and 5 with medium scores in both years. Schools were selected from all eight administrative subdistricts of the city. The resulting sample is representative of the range of average school achievement levels in the district, but it purposely screens out schools in which the average ability level is changing. Student-level data were gathered from school records. In all, data on 245 variables were gathered and analyzed.

Selection of variables

Using regression analysis, the researchers (Kean et al. 1979a,b) narrowed the field from 245 to 18 variables that had statistically significant regression coefficients when predicting change in reading achievement. The selection process by which these variables were identified was evidently statistical significance alone.[1] Our secondary analysis began with these 18 variables. Seven were quickly eliminated because they accounted for less than 1 percent of the variance in the dependent variable and appeared to contribute nothing to the analysis.

Table 6.1 lists definitions, means, and standard deviations for 11 of the independent variables and for the 3 dependent variables: the gain score and the third and fourth grade reading scores. The 11 independent variables include measures of student, teacher, and school organization. These variables were selected because the Philadelphia researchers found that they had a statistically significant β weight in predicting the gain score.

Table 6.2 shows the correlation matrix of the variables listed in Table 6.1. The impression obtained from Table 6.2 is that the matrix is thin. Of the 90 correlations in it, only 19 percent are greater than .15, and only 13 percent are greater than .25. Among pairs of the 11 independent variables only 9 percent of the correlations are greater than .25. The highest correlation of any variable with CATGAIN, the gain score, is .08.

Gain score model

The regression analysis used the difference between the third and fourth grade reading achievement scores as a single dependent variable. The use

Table 6.1. *Code names, definitions, means, and standard deviations for 11 independent variables and 3 dependent variables*

Code name	Definitions	Mean	S.D.
X_1	Days students were present in grade 4	130.51	10.41
X_2	Student attended kindergarten, 1 = NO, 2 = YES	1.80	0.40
X_3	Number of nonteaching support staff per school, grade 4	—[a]	11.02
X_4	Percentage of students scoring above 84th percentile in California Achievement Test 1976 – Total Reading, measured at grade 4; the grade 3 proportion is assumed to be similar to grade 4	0.20	0.13
X_5	Percentage of classroom teachers with less than two years of experience; measured at grade 4; the grade 3 proportion is assumed to be similar to grade 4	0.20	0.14
X_6	Number of teacher pay periods with no absence	13.89	3.79
X_7	Teacher attends outside professional conference meetings, 1 = NO, 2 = YES	1.17	0.39
X_8	First year teaching grade 4, 1 = NO, 2 = YES	1.17	0.35
X_9	Minutes per week of individual independent reading	73.35	60.31
X_{10}	Teacher would select the same reading program again	1.54	0.50
X_{11}	Times per week aide in room during reading	2.55	2.31
$T_1 - T_2$	Difference between grade 3 and grade 4 scale score	28.43	52.50
T_1	California Achievement Test – Reading Comprehension Scale Score for grade 3, 1975	385.06	67.74
T_2	California Achievement Test – Reading Comprehension Scale Score for grade 4, 1976	412.50	72.56

[a] The mean for X_3 was not shown in the November 1979 technical report of *What Works in Reading?* (Kean et al. 1979b). If not indicated, variable is measured at grade 4.

of "difference," "change," or "gain" scores has been thoroughly examined (Thorndike & Hagen 1955; McNemar 1958; Thorndike 1966; Bohrnstedt 1969; Cronbach & Furby 1970; Alwin & Sullivan 1975; Kim & Mueller 1976; Kessler 1977; Pendleton, Warren & Chang 1979). As a result of these examinations the use of gain scores has been discouraged, because the difference between the two measures has lower reliability than the

Table 6.2. *Correlation matrix for 14 variables in Philadelphia achievement study (N = 1,363)*

	Days stud. present X_1	Stud. attended X_2	No. of non-teaching support staff X_3	% Studs. above 84th percentile CAT – 1976 X_4	% Classrm. teachers with less than 2 yr. exper. X_5	No. of teacher pay periods with no absence X_6	Teacher attends outside conf. X_7	1st yr. teaching gr. 4 X_8	Min./wk. individ. independ. reading X_9	Teacher select same reading program X_{10}	Aide time during reading each wk. X_{11}	Diff. betw. gr. 3 & gr. 4 scale score $T_2 - T_1$	CAT – Read. Comp. Scale Score, gr. 3–1975 T_1	CAT – Read. Comp. Scale Score, gr. 4–1976 T_2
X_1	1.000													
X_2	.115	1.000												
X_3	-.134	-.145	1.000											
X_4	.141	.141	-.626	1.000										
X_5	-.056	-.095	.327	-.154	1.000									
X_6	-.017	-.006	.135	-.040	.078	1.000								
X_7	-.033	.004	-.027	-.082	.118	.005	1.000							
X_8	-.061	.013	.104	.007	.021	.021	.021	1.000						
X_9	.086	.034	-.143	.113	.005	-.004	-.125	-.011	1.000					
X_{10}	-.029	-.006	-.142	.030	-.033	.080	.023	-.012	-.119	1.000				
X_{11}	-.116	-.110	.527	-.427	.074	.010	.254	-.002	-.069	-.106	1.000			
$T_2 - T_1$	.074	.020	-.004	-.051	.071	.042	-.037	-.139	.083	-.007	.004	1.000		
T_1	.161	.123	-.290	.386	-.118	.076	-.112	-.139	.090	.187	-.362	-.292	1.000	
T_2	.197	.129	-.273	.382	-.065	.101	-.132	-.132	.144	.169	.335	N.A.	.722	1.000

measures considered separately. Consequently, their use requires low error variance and high reliability of measurement. Also, calculations of the gain score reliability tend to be untrustworthy because the calculations depend on five estimates: three correlations and two variances. Finally, the analysis of gain scores is complicated by the effects of regression toward the mean.

However, in addition to the problem of poor reliability, there is another, perhaps more serious problem with the gain score model. To illustrate, consider the following two models:

$$T_2 = \beta T_1 + \sum \lambda_i' X_i + e_1 \tag{6.1}$$

$$T_2 - T_1 = \sum \lambda_i X_i + e_2 \tag{6.2}$$

Equation (6.1), which we call the conditional model, is derived from Figure 6.2. Equation (6.2) represents the gain score model described in Figure 6.1. If T_1 is added to both sides of (6.2), the result is

$$T_2 = T_1 + \sum \lambda_i X_i + e_2 \tag{6.3}$$

Comparing (6.3) with (6.1), it can be concluded that, unless $\beta = 1$,

$$\sum \lambda_i' X_i + e_1 \neq \sum \lambda_i X_i + e_2 \tag{6.4}$$

One could say that the gain score model produces biased estimates of the effects of the independent variables by unnecessarily constraining β to equal 1.

A structural equation model

Model 6.1, a gain score model, is shown in Figure 6.1. All independent variables are assumed to influence the gain score and are assumed to be measured without error. One alternative to the gain score analysis is one that uses data from both time points rather than the difference score. The analyses reported in this chapter used the maximum likelihood exploratory factor analysis (EFAP) and structural equation programs (LISREL V) of Jöreskog and Sörbom (1981).

Figure 6.2 shows one alternative model (Model 6.2) for analyzing the Philadelphia data using both dependent variables, T_1 and T_2, together instead of analyzing their difference. Two structural equations were estimated using the 11 variables; first the third grade achievement variable was used as the dependent variable, then the fourth grade variable was used. Three of the 11 variables are hypothesized to influence both the third and fourth grade scores, whereas the other eight are hypothesized to influence only the fourth grade score. The three variables influencing scores at both times were the student's attendance in kindergarten (X_2),

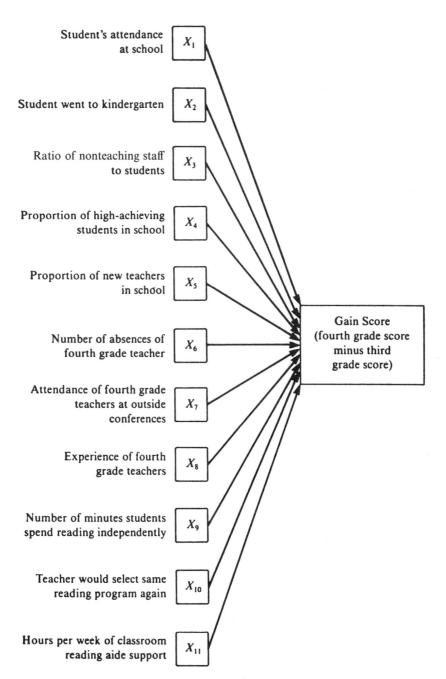

Figure 6.1. Model 6.1: a gain score model. No time assumptions are made; all independent variables are assumed to affect a single dependent variable. All error terms are assumed to be zero.

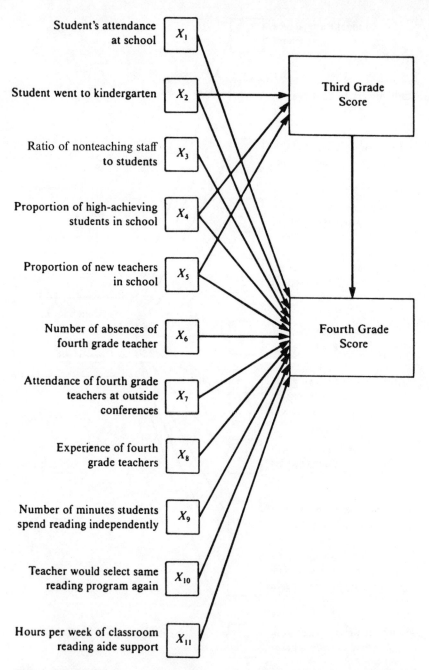

Figure 6.2. Model 6.2: a longitudinal model. Three independent variables are assumed to affect T_2, the third grade score. All variables and the third grade score are assumed to affect T_2, the fourth grade score. All error terms are assumed to be zero.

the proportion of students in the school scoring well on the achievement test (X_4), and the proportion of new teachers (X_5).

This model is recursive in that the fourth grade score is assumed to have no effect on the third grade score. The identification of recursive models is usually obtained by making particular assumptions about error terms. A common procedure for identifying Model 6.2 is to assume that the disturbance terms (residuals) are uncorrelated and that the independent variables are measured without error. Two additional modeling strategies might be proposed. One is simply to include T_1 among the X_i in the following single-equation model:

$$T_2 = \sum \beta_{i+1} X_{i+1} + e_3 \qquad (6.5)$$

The difficulty here is that autocorrelation in the residuals of the serially measured variables T_1 and T_2 will affect all the estimates of the b_i.

Bornstedt (1969) has proposed a method using residualized scores that avoids this problem. The first step is to calculate the regression of T_1 on T_2, as in (6.6):

$$T_2 = \beta T_1 + e_4 \qquad (6.6)$$

Although estimates of β and e_4 may be inefficient because of autocorrelation, they are unbiased (Johnston 1972, p. 246; Neter & Wasserman 1974, p. 352). Estimates for the remaining independent variables are then obtained by solving for β in (6.7):

$$e_4 = \sum \beta_i X_i + e_5 \qquad (6.7)$$

However, rearranging (6.6), we see that

$$e_4 = T_2 - \beta T_1 \qquad (6.8)$$

And substituting for e_4 in (6.7) it is evident that (6.9) and (6.10) are formally equivalent to (6.1); that is, the longitudinal model is formally equivalent to Bornstedt's (1969, p. 118) model for residualized scores:

$$T_2 - \beta T_1 = \sum \beta_i X_i + e_5 \qquad (6.9)$$

$$T_2 = \beta T_1 + \sum \beta_i X_i + e_5 \qquad (6.10)$$

This method does not resolve doubts about estimates of β when autocorrelation is present. However, it does isolate β so that more satisfactory estimates of the other slope coefficients in the equation can be obtained. To a limited extent, additional steps are taken to address autocorrelation in the sensitivity analysis presented later in this chapter.

Table 6.3. *Estimates of Model 6.1 and Model 6.2*[a]

Independent variable	Gain Score Model	Longitudinal Model	
	$T_2 - T_1$	T_1	T_2
X_1	0.373* (0.074)		0.579* (0.083)
X_2	2.587 (0.020)	10.445* (.062)	4.183 (0.024)
X_3	−0.407* (−0.085)		0.434* (0.066)
X_4	−44.753* (−0.111)	190.846* (.366)	63.114* (0.113)
X_5	31.111* (0.081)	−24.782* (−.050)	3.733 (0.007)
X_6	0.635 (0.046)		1.064* (0.056)
X_7	−3.829 (0.028)		−4.075 (−0.022)
X_8	1.803 (0.012)		14.180* (−0.068)
X_9	0.062* (0.071)		0.123* (0.102)
X_{10}	−0.625 (−0.006)		12.267* (0.085)
X_{11}	0.010 (0.000)		−3.642* (−0.116)
T_1			0.653* (0.610)
R^2	.03	.20	.47
χ^2/d.f.		278/8	

[a] Asterisked values are significant at less than .05; values in parentheses are standardized estimates.

Analysis of Models 6.1 and 6.2

Estimates were obtained for all 11 independent variables. These estimates are presented in Table 6.3. The gain score model yields quite a different picture than the longitudinal model. First, $\beta = 0.65$ in the conditional model; we demonstrated earlier that in order for the gain score model to be unbiased it is necessary for β to equal unity. This suggests substantial misspecification in the gain score model. The variables X_2 and X_7 are not significant in Model 6.1 or in equation (6.2) of Model 6.2. Teacher's attendance at outside conferences, X_7, is an ambiguous measure. It may measure level of professional interest and awareness, but it may also measure teacher absence from the classroom or a desire for upward professional mobility, that is, to get out of the classroom.

Student attendance at kindergarten, X_2, is an interesting variable since it is insignificant in Model 6.1 and in the equation involving dependent variable T_2 of Model 6.2, but significant in the equation involving dependent variable T_2 in Model 6.2. Kindergarten experience has an indirect effect on achievement, which is omitted in the specification of the gain score model.

The variable for teacher experience, X_5, is significant in Model 6.1 but not in Model 6.2. This suggests that students of experienced teachers show more improvement than students of inexperienced teachers, but when we control for reading competence at T_1, teacher experience makes no difference in reading competence at T_2. The effect found in Model 6.1 could represent a difference in assignment, since Model 6.2 suggests that the assumption that experienced teachers are more effective is false.

Four teacher and classroom variables, X_6, X_8, X_{10}, and X_{11}, are non-significant in Model 6.1 but are significant in Model 6.2. Again this may reflect patterns of assigning pupils with low achievement to classrooms with more available resources.

Three remaining variables, X_1, X_4, and X_9, are significant in both models. However, X_4 changes sign. It is interesting that X_1 and X_9, along with X_2, are the only independent variables measured at the student level. All others are observed at the classroom and school levels. The interpretation of X_1, student attendance, and X_9, time in the classroom spent reading independently, is straightforward. Students who come to school more often and spend more time reading while at school can read better at the end of the year.

The variables X_3 and X_4, supplementary staff and proportion of high-achieving students, have a positive sign in Model 6.2 and a negative sign in Model 6.1. Model 6.2 provides more plausible results, indicating that supplemental staff contribute to, rather than detract from, a student's ability to read.

This is a complex association. The variables X_3 and X_4 are highly correlated negatively, $-.626$. Considering just Model 6.2, they have opposite signed correlations with the dependent variable, but their effects in Model 6.2 have the same sign. Substantively, it seems that X_4 is measuring the level of general reading achievement in the school. It is also possible that what is being measured is the socioeconomic level of the school. Middle- and upper-middle-class students tend to have higher levels of scholastic success than working and lower-class students.[2]

In either case, Model 6.2 suggests that since supplemental staff persons are assigned on the basis of need, schools with low general levels of competence will receive more staffing resources, accounting for the high negative correlation between X_3 and X_4. Consequently, X_3 has a negative correlation with T_2, because of this allocation effect; but when X_3 and X_4 are entered in the same equation, the partial effect of X_3 is positive, suggesting that, when the allocation effect of staffing is controlled, the effect of supplement staffing on reading levels is positive.

In Model 6.1 the effects of both X_4 and X_3 on the gain score are negative, which has led users of the earlier study to conclude that supplementary staffing has a detrimental influence (Rankin 1980). However, it is likely that this is due instead to the negative association between gain and initial competence level. Low-achieving students make higher gains, perhaps because there is more room for improvement and perhaps also because of supplementary staff, that is, more concentrated instruction.

The foregoing interpretation seems satisfactory except that it is contradicted by the behavior of X_{11} (classroom aide time) in the model. Support staff (X_3) and aide time (X_{11}) are positively correlated (.527), and it should be reasonable to expect each to measure the same underlying attribute. However, the effect of X_{11} on reading achievement is negative. One or both of the following may account for this apparent anomaly. First, since X_3 and X_{11} are correlated at a moderately high level, the effect of each may be distorted when both are included in the same equation. Second, since X_{11} is measured at the classroom level and X_3 at the school level, X_{11} may be sensitive to within-school effects that are not picked up by X_3. It seems reasonable to assume that similar considerations that lead to allocation of more staff to low-achieving schools will lead to a similar allocation among classrooms within a school. Once again, however, whatever compensatory results aides may accomplish, these may be offset by the circumstances that led to their assignment in the first place.

In any case, it seems quite clear that three correlated variables X_3, X_4, and X_{11} have both common and unique effects on reading achievement. In the next section we describe a measurement model that is intended to simplify this complex structure.

In summary, Model 6.2 tends to produce a pattern of effects that comes closer than the pattern of Model 6.1 to matching reasonable expectations about reading achievement. Reversals in signs of effects suggest that the performance of a particular student depends largely on that student's achievement at T_1. When a student's initial achievement level is taken into account, a clearer picture of the factors contributing to his or her progress is obtained.

Model 6.2 accounts for approximately 20 percent of the T_1 variance and 45 percent of the T_2 variance. This is a substantial improvement over the small (2.5%) amount of gain score variance accounted for by Model 6.1. At the same time it must be emphasized that effects are small in both models and, although statistically significant, may be substantively trivial. For example, Model 6.2 indicates that each day of absence from the classroom results in an expected loss of half a point on the CAT – Total Reading when the mean and standard deviation of that test are 412.50 and 72.56, respectively. Model 6.2 also indicates that each additional hour per week spent reading independently results in an increase of 6.12 points on the CAT, perhaps a small return for the increase in effort.

These findings must be viewed in the context of model specification. We have seen how readily the sign and magnitude of effects can be altered when new information is added. The addition of other variables would probably alter the estimates, because the low percentage of variance explained suggests that there are other major influences on reading abilities that have not been taken into consideration.

The results demonstrate the principal advantage of a two-equation longitudinal model over the more conventional gain score model. The gain score model incorporates the assumption that the third grade score has no effect on achievement, except to define a starting point relative to which gain is measured. We have argued that decisions about the use of educational resources are based partly on the child's past performance. Consequently, the effect of past achievement on present and future achievement is much more complex than what the gain score assumes, and it is therefore advisable to estimate the effect of past on present achievement directly from data. We have shown that differences in estimates that were found between the gain score and longitudinal models could plausibly be accounted for in terms of decisions to allocate resources, based on a child's past performance and current needs, and that the gain score model presents a remarkably distorted view of the effects of school resources on reading achievement.

A measurement model with correlated errors

Model 6.2 leaves the issue of the effects of X_4 and X_{11} unresolved. Along with X_3, which we temporarily treat as a proxy measure of staff allocation, these two variables were analyzed using confirmatory factor analysis to explore a range of factor structures. The two-factor structure shown in Model 6.3 (Figure 6.3) produced the most satisfactory fit.

The measurement model was identified by fixing λ_{33} at 1. The final fit was very good ($\chi^2 = 20.79$ with 15 degrees of freedom and $p = .143$). Substantial improvement in the indicators of goodness-of-fit were obtained by allowing the indicated error terms to be correlated.

Note that variables specified to have errors correlated to that of X_4 are variables relating to the teacher's training, confidence, and experience. We suggest that these correlations may indicate that teachers in schools that have been identified as low-achieving schools may feel more pressure to exaggerate their qualifications. Not having participated in the data collection process, we undertake this discussion of measurement error with some hesitation, but we venture to say that this would not be the first time that subjects in an evaluation study felt threatened.

The Model 3 structure suggests that X_3 and X_{11} have different but overlapping structures with X_4. The correlation between the two factors is $-.75$. If the lack of similarity of effects of X_3 and X_{11} had been due to a

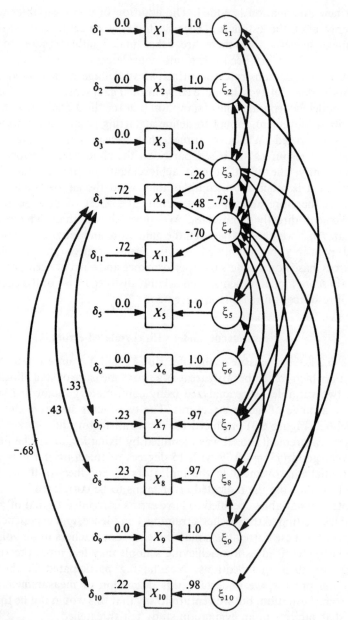

Figure 6.3. Model 6.3: independent measurement model, showing detail of factor structure. Estimates have been standardized.

distortion from collinearity, it should have been possible to load all three variables on one factor. That a single-factor structure did not fit is empirical evidence that the effect of X_{11} is indeed partly different from that of X_3.

A modified structural model

Model 6.4, shown in Figure 6.4, includes Model 6.3, the measurement model. To simplify presentation, links among the factors shown in Model 6.3 are not shown in Model 6.4. The full model links the measurement model for the independent variables to that for the dependent variables.

Model 6.4 is like Model 6.2 except that it incorporates a measurement model (Model 6.3) on the independent side. In Model 6.2, X_4 is hypothesized to influence both T_1 T_2, but X_3 and X_{11} influence only T_2. This results in a dilemma concerning the place of the two factors that replace these three variables in Model 6.4. Empirical underidentification is a possible problem here (Rindskopf 1984). Since X_4 loads on both factors, it was decided that both factors should be allowed to influence T_1.

As mentioned χ^2 for the fit of the measurement model was low (20.79 with 15 d.f.). For the full structural model, the fit was not as good ($\chi^2 = 212.34$ with 74 d.f.). The fit improved when six Γ parameter estimates, Γ_{11}, Γ_{16}, Γ_{17}, Γ_{18}, Γ_{19}, Γ_{10}, were freed ($\chi^2 = 43.73$ with 80 d.f.). However, it is not theoretically sensible to free these Γ elements, because they represent events in 1976, which can have no causal impact on a 1975 test score.

Comparison of Models 6.2 and 6.4

Table 6.4 compares estimates obtained from Model 6.2 with those obtained from Model 6.4. The more complex factor structure has increased the proportion of variance explained in the T_1 and T_2 variables, T_1 from .20 to .31, T_2 from .47 to .55. Of major interest are the effects of the two factors associated with X_3, X_4, and X_{11}. Factor 3, which is influenced by X_3 but not X_{11}, has a positive effect greater than the effect of either X_3 or X_4 in Model 6.2. Factor 4, influenced by X_{11} but not X_3, has a very large effect, which is considerably larger than the negative effect of X_{11} in Model 6.2. Recalling that X_{11} (aide time) loads negatively ($-.698$) on Factor 4, it appears that specification of a latent structure did not eliminate the negative effect of aide time on reading achievement. Indeed, that negative effect is stronger and more evident.

There are other notable changes in estimates. Teacher attendance, X_6,

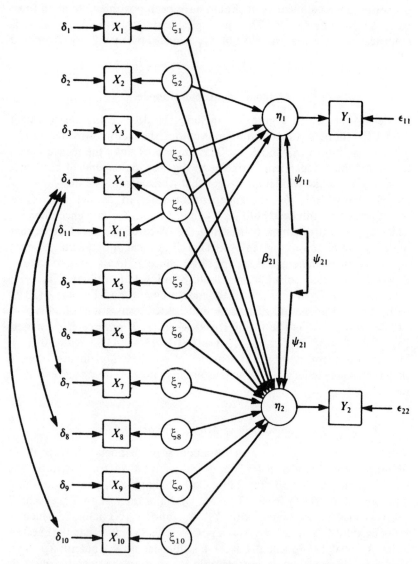

Figure 6.4. Model 6.4: the full model, detailing effects between independent factors omitted for clarity. See Model 6.3 for details.

has a small but significant effect in Model 6.2 but an insignificant effect in Model 6.4. Teacher attendance at outside conferences, X_7, is not significant in Model 2 but has a small significant effect in Model 6.4. Teacher approval of the reading program, X_{10}, is significant in Model 6.2 but not

Table 6.4. *Comparison of Model 6.2 with Model 6.4*[a]

Independent variable	Model 6.2		Model 6.4	
	T_1	T_2	T_1	T_2
X_1		0.58* (0.08)		0.30* (0.04)
X_2	10.45* (0.06)	4.183 (0.02)	3.81* (0.02)	2.13 (0.01)
X_3		0.43* (0.07)		
Factor 3			1.91* (0.31)	1.46* (0.22)
X_4	190.85* (0.37)	63.11* (0.11)		
Factor 4			−30.94* (0.74)	−17.81* (0.40)
X_{11}		−3.64* (0.12)		
X_5	−24.78 (−0.05)	3.77 (0.01)	−63.19* (−0.13)	−6.50 (−0.01)
X_6		1.06* (0.06)		0.38 (0.02)
X_7		4.07 (0.02)		12.80* (0.06)
X_8		14.18* (0.07)		−9.18* (−0.04)
X_9		0.12* (0.10)		0.13* (0.11)
X_{10}		12.27* (0.09)		3.72 (0.02)
T_1		0.65* (0.61)		0.59* (0.55)
R^2	.20	.47	.31	.55
$\chi^2/\text{d.f.}$		277/8		212/18

[a] Asterisked values are significant at less than .05; values in parentheses are standardized estimates.

in Model 6.4. Since the magnitude of these effects is of minor substantive importance, one hesitates to draw conclusions, but they are consistent with the suggestion that a teacher's performance is related to his or her effectiveness in the use of aides. The process of separating out the effect of a possible overreliance on aides caused the effects of other teacher and classroom variables to shift.

The analysis of measurement and specification error

To this point we have considered three different models. Regardless of which is considered best, our modifications have resulted in changes in the magnitudes of estimated effects, leading to changes in interpretation as well. However, investigation need not, and often should not, end with a model with an acceptable fit. Variables in education and social science research are usually measured with more than negligible error. Also, it is never possible to be sure that all relevant variables have been included in a given model.

Given strong theory and excellent research design, it is sometimes possible to obtain direct estimates of error by constructing a measurement model based on multiple indicators, as suggested by Hauser and Goldberger (1971). However, although we have neither strong theory nor a particularly good design, all is not lost. Sensitivity analysis (Land & Felson 1978; Kim 1984) is a general method by which specific estimates obtained from a particular model can be scrutinized in terms of "sensitivity" to alterations of assumptions.

The sensitivity analysis described here uses alternative combinations of fixed values and compares their results. This procedure is discussed by Kim (1984, pp. 276). The LISREL framework makes it very convenient to perform sensitivity analysis. To specify assumed error in a dependent variable, for example, one need only specify a fixed value for the appropriate error term. To specify errors in equations, appropriate values are entered as fixed parameters in the Ψ matrix and, for errors in the measurement of variables, in the θ matrix.

Thirty-six alternative models were specified. Each of the two dependent variables was assumed to contain zero, 5 or 10 percent measurement error, resulting in nine possible combinations. In addition, for each combination of measurement assumptions, four levels of specification error in equations were tested (0%, 5%, 10%, 15%).

The level of specification error was to reflect variables not in the model, which should be expected to have some impact on both η_1 and η_2. Specification error may also be reflected in a correlation between the residuals $(\varepsilon_1, \varepsilon_2)$ for each equation explaining η_1 and η_2, respectively. A correlation between ε_1 and ε_2 reflects influences on both equations, which can be attributed to omitted variables. In Model 6.4, there are no measures of student background characteristics, and we would expect this omission to be reflected in such a correlation. Thus, the direct effect of η_1 and η_2 and (β_{21}) may be spuriously high.

The error assumptions investigated are, even in the worst case, fairly optimistic about Model 6.4, assuming that the test scores (dependent variables) are 90 percent reliable and that all relevant unmeasured independent variables would explain only 15 percent of additional variance in η_2.

Results of the sensitivity analysis are presented in Table 6.5. Several expected but interesting conclusions can be drawn from this analysis. First, β_{21} is not sensitive to error in Y_2.[3] Unstandardized slope estimates will be affected only when measurement error is in the independent variable. Of more interest is the impact of specification error ψ_{21}, which has a dramatic impact on the magnitude of β_{21} and its standard error. Note that, as β_{21} decreases, its standard error increases. One of the insidious aspects of this kind of autocorrelation is this double bias toward rejection of a true null hypothesis with respect to β_{21} because of underestimation of mean squared error (Neter & Wasserman 1974).[4]

Concluding comments

The original report (Kean et al. 1979a) bases conclusions on methodological practices that may be inappropriate. Among these are the procedure by which 18 "significant" independent variables (out of 245) were selected, the uncritical use of gain scores, and disregard for problems of measurement error.

Important methodological lessons can be drawn from the secondary analysis described in this chapter. The procedure by which independent variables were selected reflected a lack of theoretical guidance about the substantive model of interest, although this is essential in multivariate analysis. With a large number of variables, statistical significance is not a particularly useful criterion. With 245 variables, 12 correlations can be expected to be "significant" by chance (at the .05 level), to say nothing of the even larger number of partial regression coefficients that can be expected to be significant.

The secondary analysis reported here entailed successive refinements. This is not to say that other approaches would not be equally appropriate. For example, the gain score model could also be refined by "residualizing" the gain score variable, as recommended by Bohrnstedt (1969).

The gain score model (Model 6.1) yields results that are virtually uninterpretable. Effects contradict long-standing principles of educational practice. The longitudinal model (Model 6.2) results in large changes in the magnitude and sign of effects compared with findings in Model 6.1. Effects in Model 6.2 are also more in agreement with expectations (see Rankin 1980). Subsequent refinements, including the introduction of a measurement model among the independent variables (Model 6.3), and

Table 6.5. *Resulting parameter estimates given error assumptions in Y_1, Y_2, and ψ_{21}*

Percentage of error in:			Estimates[a] of:			Percentage of error in:			Estimates of:			Percentage of error in:			Estimates of:		
Y_1	Y_2	ψ_{21}	β_{21}	S_β	R^2	Y_1	Y_2	ψ_{21}	β_{21}	S_β	R^2	Y_1	Y_2	ψ_{21}	β_{21}	S_β	R^2
0	0	0	0.592	0.029	.581	5	0	0	0.639	0.029	.597	10	0	0	0.694	0.031	.617
0	0	5	0.515	0.029	.577	5	0	5	0.557	0.030	.594	10	0	5	0.607	0.031	.613
0	0	10	0.437	0.031	.566	5	0	10	0.476	0.031	.582	10	0	10	0.520	0.032	.601
0	0	15	0.359	0.032	.548	5	0	15	0.393	0.033	.564	10	0	15	0.434	0.034	.582
0	5	0	0.593	0.029	.611	5	5	0	0.639	0.030	.629	10	5	0	0.694	0.032	.649
0	5	5	0.516	0.030	.608	5	5	5	0.559	0.031	.625	10	5	5	0.609	0.032	.645
0	5	10	0.440	0.031	.597	5	5	10	0.479	0.032	.614	10	5	10	0.524	0.033	.634
0	5	15	0.364	0.033	.579	5	5	15	0.399	0.034	.595	10	5	15	0.440	0.035	.615
0	10	0	0.592	0.030	.645	5	10	0	0.639	0.031	.664	10	10	0	0.694	0.032	.685
0	10	5	0.519	0.031	.642	5	10	5	0.561	0.032	.660	10	10	5	0.611	0.033	.681
0	10	10	0.445	0.032	.631	5	10	10	0.483	0.033	.649	10	10	10	0.529	0.034	.670
0	10	15	0.371	0.034	.613	5	10	15	0.405	0.035	.630	10	10	15	0.447	0.036	.651

[a] S_β is the standard error of β_{21}.

an analysis of the sensitivity of the estimates to measuremenι error (Model 6.4), do not suggest large shifts in parameter estimates from the unrefined model, but they do illustrate techniques that can be applied as new generations of software make them not only practical but accessible.

Notes

1. This kind of analysis may clearly capitalize on chance, and if the analysis was in fact conducted as we have suggested, by an undisciplined romp through a correlation matrix, it might be said that there is no point in further consideration of variables selected in this manner. However, our point of view is that, like too much policy research, its methodological limitations have not hindered the adoption of the study's recommendations by practitioners in education who may lack sophistication in research methodology.

   We did not have the option of going back and replicating the analysis. Instead, we chose to make those refinements in method that were available to us. In this way, we showed that, by introducing a more appropriate specification of the model, support for some of the more important and controversial policy recommendations of the original study disappeared or was reversed.

2. This variable, it might be logically concluded, should have been based on data from 1975 (T_1) instead of 1976 (T_2). However, data from 1975 were not available. Conversations with School District of Philadelphia staff indicated that year-to-year changes in such school wide measures of achievement could be assumed to be negligible. Also, the sampling method described above (see also Kean et al. 1979a,b) helps to ensure that 1975–6 changes in schoolwide reading achievement are trivial.

3. Changes in β_{21} over levels of error in Y_2 occur whenever $\psi_{21} > 0$. Parameter ψ_{21} is specified as a percentage of η_{21}, whereas ε_2 is specified to be a percentage of Y_2. When ε_2 changes, so does η_2 and, therefore, the quantity $(\psi_{21})(\eta_2)$. The changes in β_{21} result from this level of specification error.

4. It is tempting to be reassured by the observation that $t = \beta/S_\beta$ is relatively constant, but in a multivariate model it is possible to have upward bias in one or more β_{21} estimates with downward bias in corresponding standard errors, resulting from poor reliability of one or more variables. It is only in the bivariate case that measurement error can be relied on to result only in simple attenuation (Won, 1982).

References

Alwin, D. F., & Sullivan, M. J. (1975). "Issues of Design and Analysis in Evaluation Research," *Sociological Methods and Research* 4 (August): 77–100.

Bohrnstedt, G. W. (1969). "Observations on the Measurement of Change," pp. 113–33 in E. F. Borgatta & G. W. Bohrnstedt (eds.), *Sociological Methodology 1969*. San Francisco: Jossey-Bass.

Cronbach, L. J., and Furby, L. (1970). "How We Should Measure 'Change' – or Should We?" *Psychological Bulletin* 74: 68–80.

Hauser, R. M., & Goldberger, A. (1971). "The Treatment of Unobservable Variables in Path Analysis," pp. 81–117 in H. Costner (ed.), *Sociological Methodology 1971*. San Francisco: Jossey-Bass.

Johnston, J. (1972). *Econometric Methods*. New York: McGraw-Hill.

Jöreskog, K. G., & Sörbom, D. (1981). *LISREL V: Analysis of Linear Structural Relationships by Maximum Likelihood and Least Squares Methods*, University of Uppsala, Department of Statistics.

Kean, M. H., Summers, A. S., Raivetz, M. J., & Farber, I. J. (1979a). *What Works in Reading? The Results of a Joint School District/Federal Reserve Bank Empirical Study in Philadelphia*. Office of Research and Evaluation, School District of Philadelphia (May).

(1979b) *What Works in Reading? Technical Supplement of a Joint School District/Federal Reserve Bank Empirical Study in Philadelphia*. Office of Research and Evaluation. School District of Philadelphia (November).

Kessler, R. C. (1977). "The Use of Change Scores as Criteria in Longitudinal Survey Research." *Quality and Quantity* 11: 43–66.

Kim, J. (1984). "An Approach to Sensitivity Analysis in Sociological Research," *American Sociological Review*, 49 (April): 272–82.

Kim, J., & Mueller, C. W. (1976). "Standardized and Unstandardized Coefficients in Causal Analysis: An Expository Note," *Sociological Methods and Research* 4 (May): 423–37.

Land, K. C., and Felson, M. (1978). "Sensitivity Analysis of Arbitrarily Identified Simultaneous-Equation Models," *Sociological Methods and Research* 6 (February): 283–307.

McNemar, Q. (1958). "On Growth Measurement," *Educational and Psychological Measurement*, 18: 47–55.

Neter, John, and Wasserman, William. (1974). *Applied Linear Statistical Models*. Homewood, IL: Irwin.

Pendleton, B. F., Warren, R. D., & Chang, H. C. (1979). "Correlated Denominators in Multiple Regression and Change Analysis," *Sociological Methods and Research* 7 (May): 451–74.

Rankin, R. (1980). *What Works in Reading*. Unpublished manuscript, University of Oregon, College of Education.

Rindskopf, D. (1984). "Using Phantom and Imaginary Latent Variables to Parameterize Constraints in Linear Structural Models," *Psychometrika*, 49 (1): 37–47.

Thorndike, R. L. (1966). "Intellectual Status and Intellectual Growth," *Journal of Educational Psychology* 57: 121–7.

Thorndike, R. L., and Hagen, E. (1955). *Measurement and Evaluation in Psychology and Education*. New York: Wiley.

Won, E. (1982). "Incomplete Corrections for Regression Unreliabilities: Effects on the Coefficient Estimates," *Sociological Methods and Research* 10 (February): 271–84.

7

Some structural equation models of sibling resemblance in educational attainment and occupational status

ROBERT M. HAUSER AND PETER A. MOSSEL

Introduction

Sociologists and economists have long recognized the importance of measuring the effects of schooling. Its influence on such measures of success as occupational status and earnings serves, on the one hand, as an indicator of the role of educational institutions in fostering (or hampering) social mobility and, on the other hand, as an indicator of the productivity of personal and public investments in schooling. At the same time, it is well known that social and economic success may depend directly on personal characteristics and conditions of upbringing that also affect the length and quality of schooling.[1] For these reasons, it is by no means obvious that an association of schooling with social or economic success can be interpreted in causal terms, and many studies have attempted to determine the degree to which such causal inferences are warranted.

The effects of background, broadly conceived, on achievement can be taken into account by modeling the similarity of siblings. That is, a research design based on sibling pairs (or *n*-tuples) permits a statistical decomposition of variances and of covariances into "between-family" and "within-family" components. If fraternal differences in schooling lead to differences in adult success, we can be confident that the association of schooling with success is not merely an artifact of the tendency of school success to run in families that are also economically successful. This has helped to motivate a number of studies of the stratification process that are based on samples of siblings, rather than of the general population, perhaps most notably in the two major studies by Jencks and associates (1972, 1979).

Griliches (1977, 1979) noted a potentially significant methodological twist in the use of sibling-based research designs. In a regression, say, of occupational status on schooling, random response error (unreliability of measurement) in schooling will lead to more (downward) bias in the within-family estimator than in a naïve regression that ignores family effects. This occurs because response error will affect the validity of individual responses, but not of family effects, when the latter have been specified as latent variables. Consequently, a given component of unreliable variance in schooling is larger relative to within-family variance than to total variance. The biases attributable to omitted background variables and to response error are probably opposite in effect, and it is necessary to correct both at the same time.

In the late 1960s, little was known about the sensitivity of estimated parameters to response error in models of the stratification process. Since then, there have been a number of efforts to measure the reliability and validity of survey reports of socioeconomic variables, and contrary to some expectations (Bowles 1972), they have not led to massive downward revisions in estimates of the effects of schooling on occupational or economic success (Hauser, Tsai, & Sewell 1983). At the same time, Griliches's (1977, 1979) argument shows that it is important to correct for response error in within-family regressions of adult success on schooling. Jencks et al. (1972, App. B) and Olneck (1976; pp. 166–98) made pioneering efforts to do this.

The present analysis uses multiple measurements of educational attainment and occupational status for 518 male, Wisconsin high school graduates and a random sample of their brothers to develop and interpret skeletal models of the regression of occupational status on schooling that correct for response error and incorporate a family variance component structure. Hauser (1984) cross-validated our findings in Wisconsin sister pairs and sister–brother pairs and in Olneck's (1976) Kalamazoo brother sample. We call our models "skeletal" because they do not include explicit socioeconomic background variables, mental ability and other social psychological variables, or outcomes of schooling other than occupational status. Methodological complications arise because the sample consists of sibling pairs; primary respondents rather than families are the sampling units; and primary respondents served in some cases as informants about their brothers.

The methodological issues addressed here occur also in larger models and are closely paralleled in other areas of social scientific research. For example, in analyses of neighborhood effects (Bielby 1981), husband–wife interaction (Thomson & Williams 1982), fertility (Clarridge 1983), political identification (Jennings & Niemi 1981, Chap. 4), and, more generally, in the analysis of change over time (Jöreskog & Sörbom 1977, Kenny 1979, Kessler & Greenberg 1981). It could even be argued that models of the present form should supplant the analysis of covariance as the standard model for analyses of contextual effects (Boyd & Iversen 1979); one practical advantage is that many models are identified with only two observations per family, organization, or other unit of aggregation.

Following a brief description of the Wisconsin data, the first part of the analysis compares the simple regressions of occupational status on schooling between brothers without correcting for response error. Next, we specify a structural model with separate regressions of occupational status on schooling for families, primary respondents, and brothers, but without any correction for response error. Following this, we develop a measurement model for the regressions of status on schooling and compare the corrected regressions of primary respondents and their brothers. We combine the measurement model with the family variance component structure and compare within- and between-family structural regressions. We then compare these estimates with the naïve estimates that fail to compensate for response error or for family effects. Finally, we briefly discuss models with cross-sibling effects and close with a discussion of some possible extensions of this work.

The Wisconsin sibling data

The Wisconsin Longitudinal Study has followed a random sample of more than ten thousand men and women who were seniors in the state's public, private, and parochial high schools in 1957 (Sewell & Hauser 1980). Late in the senior year, detailed information was collected on the social origins, the academic ability and performance, and the educational aspirations of the students. There were successful follow-up surveys of the total sample (with ~90% response rates) in 1964 and in 1975. The first follow-up, a mail survey of the parents of the primary respondents, yielded education histories and reports of marital status, occupation, and military service. The 1975 telephone survey yielded additional firsthand reports of social background, educational and occupational experiences, marital and fertility histories, and formal and informal social participation.

From the 1975 survey we obtained a roster of the siblings of the primary respondent, including date of birth, sex, and educational attainment. For a randomly selected sibling, current address and occupation were ascertained. In 1977, telephone interviews were conducted with a stratified sample of the selected siblings. Of 879 brothers of male primary respondents in this sample, telephone interviews were completed with 749, a response rate of 85.2 percent (Hauser, Sewell, & Clarridge 1982, pp. 7–13). For the present analysis, we further restricted the sample to those 518 pairs of brothers aged 20 to 50 for whom the nine variables listed in Table 7.1 had been ascertained. Only 19 pairs were lost because of the age restriction, but an additional 212 pairs were dropped because they lacked complete data. In many cases the missing data were due to school

Table 7.1. *Names and descriptions of variables: 518 brother pairs in the Wisconsin sample with complete data*

Variable	Label	Description (source, date of survey)
Y_1	EDEQYR	Respondent's years of schooling (R, 1975)
Y_2	EDAT64	Respondent's years of schooling (P, 1964)
Y_3	XEDEQYR	Brother's years of schooling (B, 1977)
Y_4	SSBED	Brother's years of schooling (R, 1975)
Y_5	OCSXCR	Respondent's current occupation (R, 1975)
Y_6	OCSX70	Respondent's 1970 occupation (R, 1975)
Y_7	XOCSXCR	Brother's current occupation (B, 1977)
Y_8	OCSSIB	Brother's 1975 occupation (R, 1975)
Y_9	XOCSX70	Brother's 1970 occupation (B, 1977)

Note: Educational attainment is scaled in years of schooling. Occupational status is scaled on Duncan's Socio-Economic Index. R, Respondent; P, Parent; B, brother.

enrollment or absence from the labor force rather than to item nonresponse.

As shown in Table 7.1, there are two indicators of the educational attainment of the primary respondent (EDEQYR, EDAT64) and of his brother (XEDEQYR, SSBED). The first member of each pair is a self-report and the second is a proxy report. In the case of the primary respondent, the proxy report (EDAT64) was coded from the educational history in the 1964 follow-up, and in that of the brother, the proxy report (SSBED) was given by the primary respondent in the 1975 survey. In both cases there is some slippage in time between the self-report and proxy report, and consequently some true educational mobility may appear as response variability in later models. To minimize this problem, as well as that of classifying postgraduate education in years, we followed the U.S. Census Bureau practice of collapsing schooling at or beyond 17 years.

All of the occupation reports have been classified using materials from the U.S. Census Bureau and coded in the Duncan Socio-Economic Index (Duncan 1961; Hauser & Featherman 1977, App. B). There are self-reports of the primary respondent's occupational status in 1970 (OCSX70) and in 1975 (OCSXCR), there are self-reports of the brother's occupational status in 1970 (XOCSX70) and in 1977 (XOCSXCR), and there is a proxy report (by the primary respondent) of the brother's occupational status in 1975 (OCSSIB).

As in the case of educational attainment, there is some spread in the temporal referents of these measurements, and some true status mobility may appear to be response variability. There are two reasons for our decision to treat the indicators for each brother as measures of the same occupational status construct. First, even over a period of several years, unreliability looms large relative to mobility as a component of observed change in occupational status (Bielby, Hauser, & Featherman 1977). Second, our intention is not to depict the true status of the individual at an instant in time, but to highlight a relatively stable feature of his placement in the occupational hierarchy. Thus, our concept of response variability in occupational status is inclusive of true short-run changes in status.

Table 7.2 reports the means and standard deviations of the nine status variables and their intercorrelations. Note that brothers have slightly less schooling than primary respondents but are more variable in schooling. There is a similar pattern in the case of occupational status. This reflects basic differences between the populations of primary respondents and of brothers. There is a floor on the schooling of primary respondents but not of their brothers; because they were selected as high school seniors, none of the former obtained less than 12 years of regular schooling. Moreover, nearly all of the primary respondents were born in 1939, whereas the ages of their brothers varied widely over the range from 20 to 50. These cohort and age differences between the primary respondents and their brothers may also have affected the joint distributions of educational attainment and occupational status.

In modeling sibling resemblance, the usual procedure is to treat the members of a given sibling pair as unordered or indistinguishable (Jencks et al. 1972, 1979; Olneck 1977; Olneck & Bills 1980). Common family factors affect each member of the pair in the same way, so there is only one within-family regression. Families, rather than individuals, are the units of analysis. This greatly simplifies data analysis. In particular, regressions of intrapair differences yield unbiased estimates of within-family regressions, regardless of the pattern of common (family) causation. Because the Wisconsin brothers are sampled through a narrowly defined cohort of primary respondents, symmetry between brothers in the joint distributions of variables cannot be assumed, but must be demonstrated empirically.

Simple regressions of status on schooling

The first step in our analysis is to estimate and compare the simple regressions of occupational status on schooling for primary respondents and their brothers without correcting for response error. We anticipate that there may be differences between the regressions for primary respondents and their brothers because there is a floor on the schooling of primary respondents and because the brothers (but not the primary

Table 7.2. *Product–moment correlation coefficients, means, and standard deviations: Wisconsin brothers* $(N = 518)$

Variable	Label	Y_1	Y_2	Y_3	Y_4	Y_5	Y_6	Y_7	Y_8	Y_9
Y_1	EDEQYR	1.000								
Y_2	EDAT64	.906	1.000							
Y_3	XEDEQYR	.404	.437	1.000						
Y_4	SSBED	.419	.450	.926	1.000					
Y_5	OCSXCR	.552	.525	.251	.252	1.000				
Y_6	OCSX70	.590	.562	.300	.295	.818	1.000			
Y_7	XOCSXCR	.217	.243	.622	.568	.264	.315	1.000		
Y_8	OCSSIB	.217	.245	.627	.593	.265	.307	.815	1.000	
Y_9	XOCSX70	.228	.257	.628	.575	.247	.275	.819	.780	1.000
Mean		13.60	13.38	13.37	13.29	4.91	4.88	4.80	4.72	4.49
S.D.		2.09	1.83	2.27	2.22	2.44	2.41	2.57	2.51	2.54

Note: Correlations are based on 518 pairs of brothers for whom complete data were available. For an explanation of labels, see Table 7.1. For convenience in the scaling of coefficients, values of the Duncan Socio-Economic Index have been divided by 10.

Table 7.3. *Least squares regressions of occupational status on educational attainment for primary respondents and their brothers: Wisconsin brothers (N = 518)*

Dependent variable	Independent variable	Parameter	Estimate	Standard error
OCSXCR	EDEQYR	ψ_{51}	.643	.058
OCSXCR	EDAT64	ψ_{52}	.701	.066
OCSX70	EDEQYR	ψ_{61}	.678	.059
OCSX70	EDAT64	ψ_{62}	.739	.066
XOCSXCR	XEDEQYR	ψ_{73}	.702	.058
XOCSXCR	SSBED	ψ_{74}	.656	.058
OCSSIB	XEDEQYR	ψ_{83}	.691	.057
OCSSIB	SSBED	ψ_{84}	.669	.058
XOCSX70	XEDEQYR	ψ_{93}	.701	.058
XOCSX70	SSBED	ψ_{94}	.657	.058

Note: Duncan Socio-Economic Index scale values have been divided by a factor of 10. Standard errors are estimated to take account of the clustering of observations within families and persons. Parameters ψ_{ij} are labeled as in Figure 7.1.

respondents) vary widely in age. Table 7.3 displays the 10 zero-order regressions of own occupational status on won schooling, four among primary respondents and six among their brothers. Considering the heterogeneity of populations, informants, and temporal referents, these regressions are remarkably similar. The two extreme estimates, both pertaining to the primary respondent, are .643 and .739, and the remaining estimates cluster in the range from .65 to .70.

To establish a baseline for later comparisons, we want to obtain pooled estimates of the zero-order regressions for primary respondents, for their brothers, and for all persons regardless of response status. We want to know whether these several estimates are significantly different from one another. Furthermore, we want to learn the sources of differences, if any, among the estimates. These appear to be straightforward problems, but they are complicated by two facts: (1) There are two measurements of educational attainment for each brother, and (2) the brother's equation and the primary respondent's equation are not independent of one another because of the family linkage.

The general form of the regression is

$$Y_R = \beta_1 X_R + \varepsilon_R \tag{7.1}$$
$$Y_S = \beta_2 X_R + \varepsilon_S \tag{7.2}$$

where Y_R and Y_S are measurements of socioeconomic status of respondent and sibling, respectively, X_R and X_S are the respective measurements of educational attainment, and ε_R and ε_S are disturbances $\text{cov}(\varepsilon_R, \varepsilon_S) \neq 0$. Furthermore, there may also be cross-sibling covariances $\text{cov}(X_R, \varepsilon_S) \neq 0$ and $\text{cov}(X_S, \varepsilon_R) \neq 0$. The first complication is that we have multiple observations of X_R and X_S, but we want a single estimate of β_1 and a single estimate of β_2. The second complication is related to the fact that

$$\text{cov}(Y_R, Y_S) = \beta_1\beta_2 \text{cov}(X_R, X_S) + \text{cov}(\varepsilon_R, \varepsilon_S)$$
$$+ \beta_1 \text{cov}(X_R, \varepsilon_S) + \beta_2 \text{cov}(X_S, \varepsilon_R) \quad (7.3)$$

where $\text{cov}(X_R, X_S)$ is, in general, not equal to zero. The implication of $\text{cov}(Y_R, Y_S) \neq 0$ is thus that β_1 and β_2 have to be estimated jointly subject to $\text{cov}(\varepsilon_R, \varepsilon_S) \neq 0$, $\text{cov}(X_R, \varepsilon_S) \neq 0$, and $\text{cov}(X_S, \varepsilon_R) \neq 0$.

A simple rescaling model permits us to specify several hypotheses about β_1 and β_2 and, at the same time, allows multiple measures of X_R and X_S. Figure 7.1 is a symbolic representation of this model in the LISREL notation (Jöreskog & Sörbom 1978). To illustrate this model, we present the simple regression of status on schooling among primary respondents. Let Y_R be measured by $\text{OCSXCR} = \eta_5$ and X_R by $\text{EDEQYR} = \lambda_1\eta_1$, and note that $\text{cov}(\eta_5, \eta_1) = \psi_{51}$ by construction. Then by the definition of the zero-order regression coefficient,

$$b_{\text{OCSXCR, EDEQYR}} = \beta_1 = \frac{\text{cov}(\text{EDEQYR}, \text{OCSXCR})}{\text{var}(\text{EDEQYR})}$$
$$= \text{cov}(\lambda_1\eta_1, \eta_5)/\text{var}(\text{EDEQYR}) = \lambda_1\psi_{51}/\text{var}(\text{EDEQYR}) \quad (7.4)$$

It follows that, if we choose $\lambda_1 = \text{var}(\text{EDEQYR})$, the variances cancel in the numerator and denominator of (7.4) and $\hat{\beta}_1 = \hat{\psi}_{51}$. More generally, under the following choice of scalar transformations, namely,

$$\lambda_1 = \text{var}(\text{EDEQYR}) \quad (7.5)$$
$$\lambda_2 = \text{var}(\text{EDAT64}) \quad (7.6)$$
$$\lambda_3 = \text{var}(\text{XEDEQYR}) \quad (7.7)$$
$$\lambda_4 = \text{var}(\text{SSBED}) \quad (7.8)$$

the covariances (elements of Ψ) between the four education indicators and the five indicators of occupational status are rescaled as zero-order regression coefficients, and it becomes possible to test the desired equality restrictions on the β's by imposing them on corresponding ψ's in the LISREL model.

Table 7.4 shows goodness-of-fit and restricted estimates of slopes under four versions of the model of Figure 7.1. In Model 7.1.1 the four regressions pertaining to primary respondents have been restricted to be

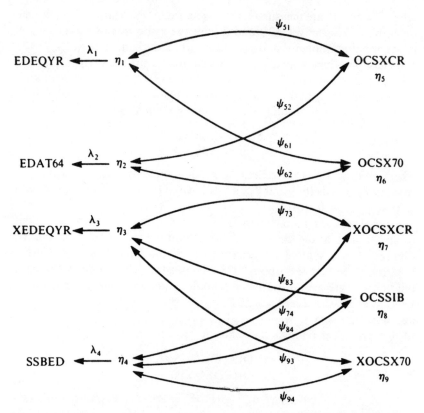

Figure 7.1. Structural equation model for testing homogeneity within and between siblings in regressions of occupational status on educational attainment. The model includes all covariances among $\eta_1 \ldots \eta_9$, but only those subject to constraints are shown and labeled. See text for explanation.

equal, yielding a pooled slope estimate of .662. Under this specification, the inequalities among slopes are not statistically significant at the .05 level; that is, the fit of the model is acceptable. In Model 7.1.2, the six regressions pertaining to brothers of primary respondents have been pooled, yielding a common slope estimate of .690; again, heterogeneity is not statistically significant. In Model 7.1.3, the two preceding sets of constraints are imposed simultaneously; that is, there is one pooled slope for primary respondents and another slope for their brothers. Here, heterogeneity is of borderline statistical significance ($p = .03$), and the common slope estimates are .666 for primary respondents and .679 for brothers. In Model 7.1.4, a single common slope across alternate measures

Table 7.4. *Constrained estimates of the regression of occupational status on educational attainment for primary respondents and their brothers: Wisconsin brothers (N = 518)*

Model of homogeneity	L^2	d.f.	p	Slope (standard error) Respondent	Brother
7.1.1. Primary respondents	7.71	3	.052	.662 (.057)	—
7.1.2. Brothers	8.93	5	.112	—	.690 (.055)
7.1.3. Within siblings	16.73	8	.033	.666 (.057)	.679 (.054)
7.1.4. Complete	16.76	9	.053	.673 (.042)	.673 (.042)

Note: Line numbers refer to alternative specifications of the model of Figure 7.1.

and across primary respondents and their brothers is estimated to be .673, and the fit is negligibly worse than that of Model 7.1.3.

We conclude that there is very little evidence of heterogeneity in the zero-order regressions of occupational status on schooling between primary respondents and their brothers; indeed, there is more evidence of heterogeneity in the estimates for the same brother than between brothers. We take the common slope estimates of Model 7.1.3 and Model 7.1.4 as the desired bases for comparison with estimates under models with response error and/or a common family factor.

Within- and between-family regressions

Figure 7.2 shows a simple path model of sibling resemblance in educational attainment and occupational status. Here X_1 and X_2 are measures of the educational attainment of the primary respondent and his brother, respectively; Y_1 and Y_2 are the corresponding measures of occupational status. Both X_1 and X_2 load on a between-family education factor ξ_2, and each also loads on a unique, within-family component of education ξ_1 or ξ_3,

$$X_1 = \xi_2 + \xi_1 \qquad (7.9)$$
$$X_2 = \lambda_{22}^x \xi_2 + \xi_3 \qquad (7.10)$$

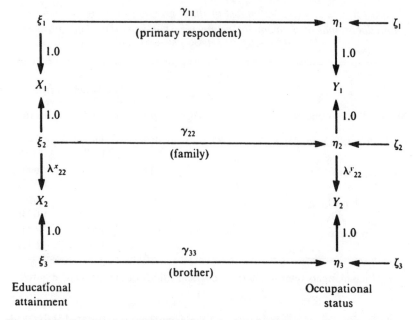

Figure 7.2. Structural equation model of sibling resemblance in educational attainment and occupational status.

where $\mathrm{cov}[\xi_i, \xi_j] = \phi_{ij} = 0$ for $i \neq j$. Similar equations define between- and within-family components of occupational status:

$$Y_1 = \eta_2 + \eta_1 \tag{7.11}$$
$$Y_2 = \lambda_{22}^y \eta_2 + \eta_3 \tag{7.12}$$

Last, the model specifies regressions of occupational status on educational attainment for primary respondents, families, and brothers, respectively,

$$\eta_1 = \gamma_{11}\xi_1 + \varsigma_1 \tag{7.13}$$
$$\eta_2 = \gamma_{22}\xi_2 + \varsigma_2 \tag{7.14}$$
$$\eta_3 = \gamma_{33}\xi_3 + \varsigma_3 \tag{7.15}$$

where ς_i is defined as the disturbance of η_i, and $\mathrm{cov}[\xi_i, \varsigma_i] = \mathrm{cov}[\xi_i, \varsigma_i] = \mathrm{cov}[\varsigma_i, \varsigma_i] = 0$ for $i \neq j$.

The path diagram in Figure 7.2 gives the appearance that each of the parameters of the model may differ between the primary respondent and his brother. In fact, we cannot make this assumption because the model would not be identified. As shown, the model has 11 parameters: 3 variances of ξ's (in Φ), 3 variances of disturbances in η's (in Ψ), 3 structural regressions (γ's), and 2 scale factors (λ_{22}^x and λ_{22}^x). However, there are only 10 sample moments: 4 variances and 6 covariances among the 4 observable indicators. In order to identify the model, it is necessary to impose at least one restriction on the parameters. We chose to impose two restrictions $\lambda_{22}^x = \lambda_{22}^y = 1$; this implies that both pairs of within-family variables are in the same metric as the family factors, which justifies comparisons of slopes among the three regressions.

We experimented with other identifying restrictions, for example, $\psi_{11} = \psi_{33}$, which says that disturbance variances are equal in the two within-family regressions. However, this restriction does not equate the metrics of the two within-family slopes. It is interesting that in this one-population model, where observations are clustered within families, we find exactly the same problem of normalizing the metrics of unobserved variables that is usually discussed in connection with interpopulation comparisons. Fortunately, to anticipate our empirical findings, the data for primary respondents and their brothers are so nearly symmetric that in retrospect the choice of initial identifying restrictions does not seem as serious a matter as we first thought.

The model of Figure 7.2 differs from some other models of sibling resemblance in its expression of the within-family regressions (Olneck 1976, pp. 139–49, 1977; Corcoran & Datcher 1981, pp. 195–7). That is, in the present model, the within-family regressions are written in disturbances of the family factor model, and in the alternative model, the within-family regressions are written directly in the individual educational and occupational variables. Critics have suggested either that the alternative is superior to our model or that the two models are equivalent. Hauser (1988) has compared the two models and shown that they are algebraically equivalent when the two within-family regressions are homogeneous. Otherwise, they are not equivalent, and the alternative model has undesirable logical implications. Moreover, when the within- and between-family regressions are nearly homogeneous in slope, as we have found in the present case (Hauser 1984), the second model exhibits symptoms of "empirical underidentification."

Table 7.5 shows goodness-of-fit and selected parameter estimates for one version of the model of Figure 7.2. The model uses only one indicator of educational attainment and of occupational status for each member of the fraternal pair, and we have selected the self-reports of educational attainment and occupational status at the survey dates. We begin with a model that imposes equivalent scales on all of the variables, and we then test whether the parameters for primary respondents, their brothers, and families are similar in other respects. In line 7.2.1 the baseline model yields seemingly disparate slope estimates for primary respondents, brothers, and families. Indeed, the within-family slope estimate for primary

Table 7.5. *Maximum likelihood estimates of models of sibling resemblance in educational attainment and occupational status with latent family variables but no correction for response variability: Wisconsin brothers (N = 518)*

Model	Slope (standard error)			L^2	d.f.	p
	Respondent	Brother	Family			
7.2.1. $\lambda^x_{22} = \lambda^y_{22} = 1$	.620 (.074)	.735 (.059)	.659 (.074)	0.73	1	.39
7.2.2. Add $\gamma_{11} = \gamma_{33}$	.691 (.047)	.691 (.047)	.650 (.074)	2.28	2	.32
7.2.3. Add $\gamma_{11} = \gamma_{22} = \gamma_{33}$	.676 (.029)	.676 (.029)	.676 (.029)	2.44	3	.49
7.2.4. Add $\psi_{11} = \psi_{33}$	.676 (.029)	.676 (.029)	.676 (.029)	2.52	4	.64
7.2.5. Add $\phi_{11} = \phi_{33}$	.676 (.029)	.676 (.029)	.676 (.029)	6.65	5	.25

Note: Estimates are based on self-reports of education and current occupation (EDEQYR, OCSXCR, XEDEQYR, XOCSXCR). Line numbers refer to alternative specifications of the model of Figure 7.2.

respondents is quite low, whereas the estimate for brothers exceeds that for families. We shall see that this initial, equivocal finding on bias in the schooling–occupation relationship recurs throughout the analysis.

The within-family slope estimates for primary respondents and their brothers do not differ significantly.[2] The common, within-family slope estimate shown in line 7.2.2 of Table 7.5, $\gamma_{11} = \gamma_{33} = .691$, is actually larger than the common slope that we estimated without correction for measurement error or family bias ($\beta = .673$). Again, there is little evidence that the omission of common family variables significantly affects these estimates.

Because of the common influence of families on schooling and occupation, we expected to find steeper between-family than within-family regressions of occupational status on schooling, but this proved not to be the case. In the model of line 2.2, the within-family slope estimate is larger than the between-family slope. Moreover, as shown in line 7.2.3 of Table 7.5, there is virtually no deterioration in the fit of the model when all three regressions are constrained to share a common slope. Sociologically, this is a remarkable finding, for it says that there is no family bias in the relationship between educational attainment and occupational success; that relationship is just what we would expect from the differential rewards of schooling across individuals. Again, the common slope estimate is virtually the same as that estimated under the model of Figure 7.1 (.676 vs. .673).

In lines 7.2.4 and 7.2.5 of Table 7.5, two more restrictions are added to the model; neither affects the slope estimates or their standard errors. First, we specify that $\psi_{11} = \psi_{33}$; this says that the unexplained variance in the two within-family regressions, that is, for primary respondents and for brothers, is the same. Under this additional restriction, there is virtually no change in fit. Second, we specify that $\phi_{11} = \phi_{33}$; this says that the within-family variances in educational attainment are the same for primary respondents and their brothers. Congruent with our observations about selection into the sample, the data do not meet the latter restriction.[3] Thus, with this one exception, the data do not depart significantly from the usual assumption of symmetry between siblings.

Measurement models

Figure 7.3 shows a LISREL model that corrects the regressions of occupational status on schooling for response error. In the structural portion of the model, there is a corrected regression for each brother,

$$\eta_3 = \beta_{31}\eta_1 + \varsigma_1 \tag{7.16}$$
$$\eta_4 = \beta_{42}\eta_2 + \varsigma_4 \tag{7.17}$$

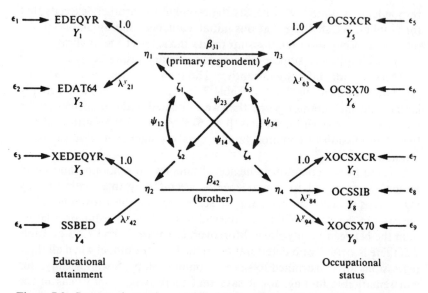

Figure 7.3. Structural equation model of distinct fraternal regressions of occupational status on educational attainment with errors in variables but no family factors. See Table 7.6 for specification of error covariances.

and the four cross-sibling covariances (ψ_{12}, ψ_{14}, ψ_{23}, and ψ_{34}) are free parameters. The measurement model incorporates response error in each of the indicators of educational attainment ($Y_1, \ldots, Y_4$) and occupational status ($Y_5, \ldots, Y_9$).[4] We specify the scale of the latent constructs by fixing the loadings (λ's) of the self-reports of educational attainment (Y_1 and Y_3) on the education constructs (η_1 and η_2) and the loadings of the self-reports of current occupational status (Y_5 and Y_7) on the occupational status constructs (η_3 and η_4) at 1.0 for primary respondents and brothers, respectively. This implies that the constructs are in the metrics of the reference indicators and that the variances of the constructs are the true variances of the respective indicators. This is a convenient normalizing constraint, because each of the reference indicators is a self-report and because the same methods were used to ascertain and to code these variables for the primary respondent and his brother.

The measurement model also includes selected covariances among response errors, which are not shown in Figure 7.3. The initial specification of these error covariances is shown in Table 7.6. Covariances were permitted between the errors in any pair of variables that had been ascertained on the same occasion or from the same informant. Thus, the model permits all possible error covariances among reports by primary

Table 7.6. *Specification of nonzero error covariances in the model of Figure 7.3*

Variable	1	2	3	4	5	6	7	8	9
1. EDEQYR	θ^ϵ_{11}								
2. EDAT64	—	θ^ϵ_{22}							
3. XEDEQYR	—	—	θ^ϵ_{33}						
4. SSBED	$\theta^{\epsilon*}_{41}$	—	—	θ^ϵ_{44}					
5. OCSXCR	θ^ϵ_{51}	—	—	$\theta^{\epsilon*}_{54}$	θ^ϵ_{55}				
6. OCSX70	θ^ϵ_{61}	—	—	$\theta^{\epsilon*}_{64}$	θ^ϵ_{65}	θ^ϵ_{66}			
7. XOCSXCR	—	—	θ^ϵ_{73}	—	—	—	θ^ϵ_{77}		
8. OCSSIB	$\theta^{\epsilon*}_{81}$	—	—	θ^ϵ_{84}	$\theta^{\epsilon*}_{85}$	$\theta^{\epsilon*}_{86}$	—	θ^ϵ_{88}	
9. XOCSX70	—	—	θ^ϵ_{93}	—	—	—	θ^ϵ_{97}	—	θ^ϵ_{99}

Note: θ^ϵ_{65} is not separately identified and is estimated by $\theta^\epsilon_{65} = \theta^\epsilon_{97}$. Covariances marked with an asterisk were not statistically significant in the baseline model of Table 7.7 and were dropped from all subsequent models.

respondents and among reports by their brothers, but it permits no error covariances between reports by primary respondents and brothers, by primary respondents and parents, or by brothers and parents.[5]

Table 7.7 shows measures of fit and estimates of the corrected regressions of occupational status on educational attainment in several versions of the model of Figure 7.3. The rows of Table 7.7 described various restrictions on the measurement model. For each version of the measurement model, panel A (left) pertains to a model with distinct regressions for each brother (β_{31} and β_{42}), whereas panel B (right) pertains to an otherwise similar model, but with a common slope for the two brothers ($\beta_{31} = \beta_{42}$). Under every measurement model in Table 7.7, the two regressions are homogeneous; the contrast between β_{31} and β_{42} yields test statistics of the order of 0.5 with one degree of freedom. Thus, our discussion focuses on comparisons among the rows of the table, which are virtually unaffected by the slope restriction anyway, and for the most part we ignore the distinction between versions A and B of each model.

The baseline, Model 7.3.1, incorporates all of the error covariances in Table 7.6, and it specifies only normalizing restrictions on the loadings of indicators on constructs.[6] That model fits well, but it is possible to specify a more parsimonious (and statistically more powerful) model by restricting selected parameters. In the baseline model, six error covariances were statistically insignificant, and these were dropped from Model 7.3.2: θ^ϵ_{54}, θ^ϵ_{64}, θ^ϵ_{81}, θ^ϵ_{85}, and θ^ϵ_{86}. Interestingly, these exhaust the possible terms

Table 7.7. *Selected models of the regression of brothers' occupational status on educational attainment with errors in variables: Wisconsin brothers (N = 518)*

Model	A. Distinct slopes					B. Common slope ($\beta_{31} = \beta_{42}$)			
	β_{31}	β_{42}	L^2	d.f.	p	$\beta_{31} - \beta_{42}$	L^2	d.f.	p
7.3.1. Baseline model	.672 (.047)	.708 (.041)	10.51	9	.31	.693 (.032)	10.88	10	.37
7.3.2. $\theta^\epsilon_{41} = \theta^\epsilon_{81} = \theta^\epsilon_{54} = \theta^\epsilon_{64} = \theta^\epsilon_{85} = \theta^\epsilon_{86} = 0$	.672 (.047)	.709 (.040)	11.72	15	.70	.694 (.032)	12.13	16	.74
7.3.3. $\theta^\epsilon_{15} = \theta^\epsilon_{16} = \theta^\epsilon_{37} = \theta^\epsilon_{39}$	.672 (.047)	.709 (.040)	11.83	18	.86	.694 (.032)	12.23	19	.88
7.3.4. 3.3 plus all $\lambda^y_{ij} = 1$	.703 (.044)	.719 (.036)	24.51	23	.38	.713 (.029)	24.60	24	.43
7.3.5. 3.3 plus $\lambda^y_{42} = \lambda^y_{63} = \lambda^y_{84} = \lambda^y_{94} = 1$	.698 (.043)	.719 (.036)	19.86	22	.59	.710 (.029)	20.02	23	.64
7.3.6. 3.5 plus $\theta^\epsilon_{11} = \theta^\epsilon_{33}, \theta^\epsilon_{55} = \theta^\epsilon_{77}, \theta^\epsilon_{66} = \theta^\epsilon_{99}$	.687 (.042)	.720 (.036)	29.58	25	.24	.706 (.029)	29.96	26	.27
7.3.7. 3.5 plus $\theta^\epsilon_{11} = \theta^\epsilon_{33}, \theta^\epsilon_{55} = \theta^\epsilon_{77}$	.689 (.042)	.720 (.036)	24.39	24	.44	.707 (.029)	24.72	25	.48
7.3.8. 3.7 plus $\psi_{33} = \psi_{44}$	.689 (.042)	.720 (.037)	24.44	25	.49	.707 (.029)	24.77	26	.53
7.3.9. 3.8 plus $\psi_{11} = \psi_{22}$	.685 (.040)	.720 (.038)	29.28	26	.30	.705 (.029)	29.73	27	.33

Note: Line numbers and parameter restrictions refer to alternative specifications of the model of Figure 7.3 and Table 7.6. Parenthetic entries are standard errors.

pertaining to confounding between the primary respondent's reports of his own and of his brother's status characteristics. All of the remaining, statistically significant error covariances occur between reports about the same person. There is little difference in fit between Model 7.3.1 and Model 7.3.2. The preceding models yielded similar estimates of the four covariances between errors in self-reports of educational attainment and of occupational status. In Model 7.3.3 these parameters were constrained to be equal with no significant deterioration in fit.

In Model 7.3.4 all of the loadings of observables on constructs were fixed at unity. This says that the true variance in every indicator of the same construct is equal; that is, every indicator of the same construct can serve equivalently to normalize the scale of the construct. Fit deteriorates under this specification.[7] We determined that the violation of these scale restrictions was due primarily to differences in the scales of the two reports of education of the primary respondent, EDEQYR and EDAT64. Thus, in Model 7.3.5 we relaxed the equivalence between the scales of these two indicators while retaining the other four scale restrictions.[8]

To the restrictions of Model 7.3.5, Model 7.3.6 adds three equalities between error variances in pairs of indicators that were similar in content, that were self-reported, and that were ascertained and coded in the same way: EDEQYR and XEDEQYR, OCSXCR and XOCSXCR, and OCSX70 and XOCSX70. Not all of these restrictions fit the data.[9] The estimation of common error variances for reports of 1970 occupation accounted for the significant lack of fit, and in Model 7.3.7 we dropped this constraint.[10]

Model 7.3.8 adds to Model 7.3.7 the restriction that the variances of the disturbances are the same in the regressions for the primary respondent and his brother. There is virtually no change in fit under this restriction. However, Model 7.3.9 adds the restriction that the variances in educational constructs are equal for primary respondents and brothers, and this leads to a statistically significant deterioration in fit.[11]

It is instructive to compare the slope estimates (β_{31} and β_{42}) in Models 7.3.7A and 7.3.7B with the common slope estimates in the naïve regressions, reported in lines 7.1.3 and 7.1.4 of Table 7.4. The corrected estimate for primary respondents ($\beta_1 = .689$) is only 3.5 percent larger than the common, uncorrected estimate (.666); the corrected estimate for brothers ($\hat{\beta}^2 = .720$) is only 6.0 percent larger than the common, uncorrected estimate (.679). The corrected, common estimate for primary respondents and brothers ($\hat{\beta} = .707$) is only 5.1 percent larger than the common, uncorrected estimate (.673). Because all of the indicators of educational attainment are highly reliable, these corrections in slope are minimal. Table 7.8 reports the reliabilities of the indicators and the

Table 7.8. *Reliabilities and error correlations in a measurement model of sibling resemblance in educational attainment and occupational status*

Variable	1	2	3	4	5	6	7	8	9
1. EDEQYR	.887	—	—	—	.093	.088	—	—	—
2. EDAT64	—	.929	—	—	—	—	—	—	—
3. XEDEQYR	—	—	.904	—	—	—	.073	—	.073
4. SSBED	—	—	—	.948	—	—	—	−0.44	—
5. OCSXCR	.304	—	—	—	.746	.078	—	—	—
6. OCSX70	.327	—	—	—	.267	.775	—	—	—
7. XOCSXCR	—	—	.304	—	—	—	.770	—	.070
8. OCSSIB	—	—	—	−.284	—	—	—	.835	—
9. XOCSX70	—	—	.289	—	—	—	.235	—	.741

Note: Estimates are from Model 7.3.8B in Table 7.7. Entries on the main diagonal are reliabilities. Entries below the main diagonal are correlations between errors in variables. Entries above the main diagonal are error covariances, expressed as proportions of the respective observed covariances. All of the error covariances are significantly different from zero at the .05 level.

correlations between response errors under Model 7.3.8B. The reliabilities of the indicators of educational attainment range from .89 to .95; since slope corrections are inverse to the square root of reliability, the corrections are quite small.

The reliabilities of the indicators of occupational status are lower than those of educational attainment, but unreliability in indicators of the ultimate endogenous variable (occupational status) has no effect on the slope estimates. Four of the five estimates are close to .75, and only the reliability of OCSSIB is as large as .84. The lower reliabilities of the indicators of occupational status may reflect temporal spread as well as errors in reporting and processing the data. Of course, the unreliabilities in all of the indicators affect the estimated correlations between status variables. The observed correlations between educational attainment and occupational status range from .525 to .590 for primary respondents and from .568 to .628 for brothers. In Model 3.8B the correlation between true educational attainment and true occupational status is .653 for primary respondents and .689 for their brothers.

Correlated errors of measurement also affect the regressions and correlations between the educational and occupational constructs. The entries below the main diagonal of Table 7.8 are correlations between errors in Model 7.3.8B. There are positive correlations of approximately .3 between errors in self-reports of educational attainment and of occupational status. These tend to compensate for random response error by increasing the regressions (and correlations) between observed indicators of schooling and occupational status. At the same time, there is a negative correlation of about the same size between errors in the primary respondent's reports of his brother's educational attainment and occupational status, and this adds to the effect of random response error by decreasing the observed correlation between those two variables. Last, there are positive correlations of approximately .25 between response errors in the various self-reports of occupational status; these positive, within-construct error correlations add to the effect of random response error by decreasing the observed correlations between educational and occupational indicators.

As a practical matter, none of the correlated errors has a very large effect on slope estimates in the model. The error correlations are relatively large because the response error variances are relatively small. The entries above the main diagonal of Table 7.8 express the estimated error covariances as proportions of the respective observed covariances, and none of these is as large as 10 percent of an observed covariance.

A family factor model with response variability

Figure 7.4 displays a structural equation model of fraternal resemblance that combines the latent family structure of Figure 7.2 with the measurement model of Figure 7.3. The structural model of Figure 7.4 is identical, except for changes in notation, to the model in Figure 7.2, whereas the measurement model of Figure 7.4 is identical to that in Figure 7.3. Table 7.9 shows goodness-of-fit statistics and slope estimates for several versions of the model in Figure 7.4.[12] Again, the unrestricted slope estimate for primary respondents is less than that for families, which is in turn less than that for the brothers. Model 4.2 adds the restriction of equal, within-family slopes for primary respondents and brothers, and this does not significantly affect fit. As in the uncorrected model, the common, within-family slope estimate ($\hat{\gamma}_1 = \hat{\gamma}_2 = .728$) is actually larger than the between-family slope estimate ($\hat{\gamma}_3 = .678$). Moreover, the common, within-family slope estimate under Model 7.4.2 is also larger than the total slope ($\hat{\beta} = .707$) estimated for primary respondents and brothers in the constrained measurement model (line 7.3.7B in Table 7.7).

Model 7.4.3 adds the restriction that all three slopes are homogeneous; again, there is no deterioration in fit. The common slope estimate $\hat{\gamma}_1 = \hat{\gamma}_2 = \hat{\gamma}_3 = .708$ is virtually the same here as in the measurement model without the family factors, $\hat{\beta} = .707$ (see Model 7.3.7B of Table 7.7). The common slope estimate in Model 7.4.3 is only 4.7 percent larger than the

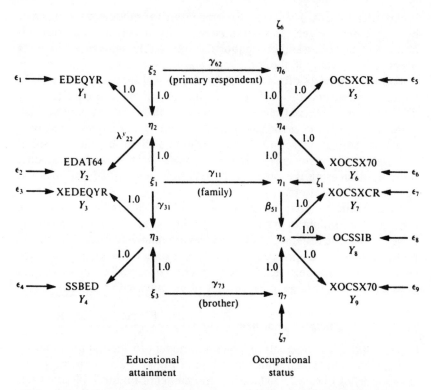

Figure 7.4. Structural equation model of sibling resemblance in educational attainment and occupational status with errors in variables and latent family factors.

uncorrected common slope in Model 7.2.3 of Table 7.5 ($\hat{\gamma}$ = .676); it is 1.051 times larger than the common slope estimate in the naïve regressions ($\hat{\beta}$ = .673). We are left with the strong impression that neither family factors nor response error have substantial effects on our estimates of the occupational effects of schooling.[13]

Model 7.4.4 of Table 7.9 adds the constraint that disturbance variances are the same in the within-family regression of primary respondents and brothers ($\psi_{66} = \psi_{77}$), and the fit is virtually unaffected by this. However, the data are not consistent with the addition of the restriction in Model 7.4.5 that true within-family variances in educational attainment are equal for primary respondents and their brothers ($\psi_{66} = \psi_{77}$); L^2 = 4.97 with 1 degree of freedom. Model 7.4.4 is our preferred measurement and structural model, and Table 7.10 gives additional structural parameters of that model.

Table 7.9. *Maximum likelihood estimates of models of sibling resemblance in educational attainment and occupational status with errors in variables and latent family factors: Wisconsin brothers (N = 518)*

Model	Slope (standard error)			L^2	d.f.	p
	Respondent	Brother	Family			
7.4.1. $\gamma_{31} = \beta_{51} = 1$	.674 (.081)	.756 (.057)	.684 (.062)	26.07	25	.40
7.4.2. Add $\gamma_{62} = \gamma_{73}$	.728 (.047)	.728 (.047)	.678 (.062)	26.74	26	.42
7.4.3. Add $\gamma_{62} = \gamma_{73} = \gamma_{11}$	.708 (.029)	.708 (.029)	.708 (.029)	27.03	27	.46
7.4.4. Add $\psi_{66} = \psi_{77}$	.708 (.029)	.708 (.029)	.708 (.029)	27.07	28	.51
7.4.5. Add $\phi_{22} = \phi_{33}$	.708 (.029)	.708 (.029)	.708 (.029)	32.04	29	.32

Note: Line numbers refer to alternative specifications of the model of Figure 7.4. These results are based on the measurement model of line 7.3.4A in Table 7.7.

Table 7.10. *Estimates of structural parameters in a model of sibling resemblance in educational attainment and occupational status with errors in variables and latent family factors: Wisconsin brothers (N = 518)*

Parameter	Estimate	Standard error
$\gamma_{62} = \gamma_{73} = \gamma_{11}$	0.708	0.029
$\psi_{66} = \psi_{77}$	1.823	0.169
ψ_{11}	0.793	0.147
ϕ_{11}	1.991	0.217
ϕ_{22}	1.885	0.234
ϕ_{33}	2.730	0.256

Note: Estimates are based on Figure 7.4 and Model 7.4.4 in Table 7.9.

If regressions of occupational status on schooling are homogeneous across persons and families, this by no means denies the importance and visibility of families in the stratification process. For example, for primary respondents, 51.4 percent of the variance in schooling lies between families, and for their brothers 42.2 percent of the variance in schooling lies between families. Thus, there is just about as much variance in schooling between as within families.[14]

Of the total variance in occupational status, whether or not it is attributable to differences in schooling, 39.3 percent lies between families in the case of primary respondents, and 35.9 percent lies between families in the case of their brothers. Similarly, there is much less unexplained variance in occupational status between than within families: 30.3 percent occurs between families, and the remaining 69.7 percent lies between individuals within families. Thus, the unexplained within-family and between-family variances in occupational status are by no means equal.[15] The within- and between-family variances of schooling are not very different from one another, and the slopes of occupational status on schooling are also homogeneous across families and persons; thus, the low unexplained between-family variance in occupational status implies that the correlation between occupational status and schooling will be larger between than within families. Under Model 7.4.4 of Table 7.9, the within-family correlations are .584 for primary respondents and .655 for their brothers; the between-family correlation is .746.

An extension: cross-sibling effects

Siblings' achievements may be similar by virtue of modeling, tutoring, financing, or other directly facilitating roles and activities, as well as common upbringing. Nonetheless, most models of sibling resemblance have specified common factor causation and neglected intersibling influences. In other cases, age or ordinal position of siblings has been invoked to specify the direction of causality (from older to younger), thus sidestepping the issue of reciprocal influence (Benin & Johnson 1984). For example, Olneck (1976, pp. 198–214) showed that, with one minor exception, intersibling differences in achievement among Kalamazoo brothers were not related to age differences between them; he concluded that models of common family causation were at least as plausible as any of his own efforts to specify effects of older upon younger brothers. Where age differentials in sibling resemblance have been observed, these have alternatively, and in statistically equivalent ways, been explained by variations in the strength of common factor causation (Jencks et al. 1979, pp. 68–70) or in the influence of older upon younger siblings (Benin & Johnson 1984). Whatever the theoretical basis of the assumption that older siblings affect younger siblings, we are doubtful about its wholesale application in studies of sibling resemblance that extend throughout the life cycle. Successful younger as well as older siblings may serve as role models, tutors, or social contacts. Even in the case of schooling, it is not clear whether age is a valid indicator of temporal or causal precedence, and there is even less reason to invoke it in the cases of occupational or economic standing.

Cross-sibling effects are not identified when families are the sampling units (so the data are symmetric), and there is a common factor for each pair of observations on siblings (Olneck 1976), Benin & Johnson 1984). In the structural portion of the model of Figure 7.4, this corresponds to the specification that $\lambda_{31} = \beta_{51} = 1.0$, $\gamma_{62} = \gamma_{73}$, $\psi_{66} = \psi_{77}$, and $\phi_{22} = \phi_{33}$, where β_{67} and/or β_{76} are the cross-sibling effects that we want to estimate.

Nonetheless, some of the models developed here may be modified to include direct unidirectional or reciprocal effects of the characteristics of one sibling on the other. We offer an illustrative, but by no means exhaustive list of these possibilities. In the model just described, either of the specifications $\gamma_{11} = \gamma_{62} = \gamma_{73}$ or $\psi_{11} = 0$ is sufficient to identify β_{76} or $\beta_{67} = \beta_{76}$ is identified without further restrictions. That is, one regressions or specification of a single family factor identifies equal cross-sib effects. In the baseline structural model of line 4.1 in Table 7.9, β_{67}, β_{76}, or $\beta_{67} = \beta_{76}$ are identified without further restrictions. That is, one may postulate an effect of the primary respondent on the brother or vice versa, but not of each on the other, unless the reciprocal effects are equated. Since the baseline model postulates no equality restriction between the two within-family regressions, the equality restriction on cross-brother effects appears unattractive in this case.

In the model of line 4.2 in Table 7.9, where the constraint of equal within-family regressions ($\gamma_{62} = \gamma_{73}$) is added to the baseline model, equal across-brother effects ($\beta_{67} = \beta_{76}$) are also identified. Also, in the baseline model of line 4.1 in Table 7.9, the specification that $\psi_{11} = 0$, that is, that there is a single family factor, identifies distinct cross-brother effects ($\beta_{67} \neq \beta_{76}$). In fact, a good fit and plausible parameter estimates are obtained with the present data when both of these identifying restrictions are imposed simultaneously, that is, $\gamma_{62} = \gamma_{73}$ and $\psi_{11} = 0$. Under this specification, the likelihood ratio statistic of the model is $L^2 = 25.17$ with 26 degrees of freedom. The cross-brother effects of occupational status are $\hat{\beta}_{67} = \hat{\beta}_{76} = .140$ with a standard error of .024, and the within-family regressions of occupational status on schooling are $\hat{\gamma}_1 = \hat{\gamma}_2 = .823$ with a standard error of .051. Thus, the within-family regressions are actually larger here than in the two-factor models without cross-brother effects.

Discussion

We have expressed a model of sibling resemblance in the LISREL framework, thus facilitating the process of model specification, estimation, and testing. A useful innovation in this model has been our specification of distinct within- and between-family regressions. Conventionally, the latter have not been made explicit (Olneck 1976, pp. 139–49, 1977; Corcoran & Datcher 1981, pp. 195–7). We believe that the between-family slopes and, especially, their contrasts with the within-family slopes are of real sociological importance. They show whether families enter the stratification system as relatively homogeneous, but neutral aggregates of persons or whether they affect returns to the attributes and resources of their members (see Chamberlain & Griliches 1977, p. 111). Furthermore, we have incorporated random (and certain types of correlated) response errors in the model by obtaining multiple measurements of schooling and occupational status.

Within this framework, we have estimated regressions of occupational status on educational attainment among primary respondents and among their brothers, with and without response error and common family factors. Paralleling Chamberlain and Griliches's (1975, pp. 428–32) analyses of schooling and income in the Gorse-line data, we find little evidence that the omission of common family variables leads to bias in our estimates of the effect of schooling on occupational status. The between-family variance in schooling is about as large as the within-family variance, and there is substantial between-family variance in occupational status as well. Nonetheless, the regression of occupational status on schooling is homogeneous within and between families in the simple models we have estimated.

This does not at all imply an absence of omitted-variable bias in the relationship between schooling and occupational status. As shown by Sewell & Hauser (1975), Sewell, Hauser, and Wolf (1980), and Hauser et al. (1983), among others, the bias is substantial, but our finding suggests that intrafamily differences in such variables as ability and motivation are its sources, rather than common family influences. The relationship between schooling and occupational status across families is just what we would expect from the differential rewards of schooling across individuals.

The present model lends itself to elaboration in a number of ways. First, it is possible to add more variables that have been observed (possibly with error) for respondent and sibling and to specify their corresponding within- and between-family components and regressions. Perhaps the two most obvious constructs to be added in this fashion are mental ability and earnings, of which the former is an antecedent of schooling and the latter is a consequence of schooling and occupational status. Second, it is possible to add constructs to the model that are common to primary respondents and their brothers and that have no "within-family" components. Here the most obvious variables are shared characteristics of the family or community of orientation: parents' education, occupations, and earnings; family size, ethnicity, and religious preference; community size and location. In most cases these variables will be specified as antecedent to other "between-family" variables. Third, other elaborations of the model may exploit the multiple-group feature of LISREL (Hauser 1984). For example, the full Wisconsin sibling sample is based on a design that crosses sex by response status, so primary respondents of each sex are paired with randomly selected siblings of each sex. Thus, we can increase the statistical power of our analyses by fitting models within the multiple-group framework and pooling estimates where similar populations occur in different pairings, for example, male primary respondents paired with sisters as well as with brothers. Moreover, within this framework it will be possible to contrast parameters of the model between men and women.

Notes

This research was carried out with support from the Spencer Foundation, the National Science Foundation (SES-80-10640), National Institute of Mental Health (MH-06275), and the Graduate School of the University of Wisconsin–Madison. Computations were performed using facilities of the Center for Demography and Ecology at the University of Wisconsin–Madison, which are

supported by the Center for Population Research of the National Institute for Child Health and Human Development (HD-5876). Part of this work was carried out while the senior author was Visiting Professor at the University of Bergen, Norway. We thank William T. Bielby, Richard T. Campbell, Brian R. Clarridge, Robert D. Mare, Christopher S. Jencks, Michael R. Olneck, and William H. Sewell for helpful advice. The opinions expressed herein are those of the authors.
1. For example, Sewell & Hauser (1975, pp. 72, 81, 93, 98) and Sewell et al. (1980, pp. 571, 581) have found substantial biases in effects of postsecondary schooling on the occupational success of Wisconsin youth when such factors are omitted from the model. However, Jencks et al. (1979, pp. 169–75) and Olneck (1976, 1977) have found much smaller biases in effects of postsecondary schooling than in effects of primary or secondary schooling.
2. When this equality restriction is imposed, the fit deteriorates by only $L^2 = 2.28 - 0.73 = 1.55$ with 1 d.f.
3. The fit of the model deteriorates significantly ($L^2 = 4.13$ with 1 d.f.).
4. Because of the hypothesized pattern of correlation between errors in indicators, we have specified that all of the observed variables are Y's in the LISREL model.
5. One potential error covariance was not identified within the model, that between errors in the respondent's reports of his current occupation (OCSXCR) and his occupation in 1970 (OCSX70). We specified that error covariance to be equal to the corresponding error covariance for brothers, between XOCSXCR and XOCSX70, which is identified.
6. One critic has proposed that we start with a model without correlated error and add error covariances to it as needed. We chose to be as generous as possible to published suggestions that correlated errors are pervasive in reports of socioeconomic variables. In fact, correlated errors are of little importance here.
7. For example, in the contrast between Model 7.3.4A and Model 7.3.3A, $L^2 = 12.68$ with 5 d.f., which is statistically significant with $p = .027$.
8. There is a significant difference in fit between Model 7.3.5A and Model 7.3.4A ($L^2 = 4.65$ with 1 d.f., $p = .031$), but not between Model 7.3.5A and Model 7.3.3A ($L^2 = 8.03$ with 4 d.f., $p = .091$).
9. For example, the contrast between Models 7.3.6A and 7.3.5A yields $L^2 = 9.72$ with 3 d.f., which is statistically significant with $p = .021$.
10. The fit of Model 7.3.7A is significantly better than that of Model 7.3.6A ($L^2 = 5.19$ with 1 d.f.), but it is not significantly worse than the fit of Model 7.3.5A ($L^2 = 4.53$ with 2 d.f.).
11. The contrast between Model 7.3.9A and Model 7.3.8A yields $L^2 = 4.84$ with 1 d.f., $p = .028$.
12. Whereas Figure 7.4 shows distinct, nonunit loadings for five of the observable variables, Table 7.9 pertains to models in which the measurement constraints of Model 7.3.7A in Table 7.7 have been imposed. Also, whereas the path diagram in Figure 7.4 shows distinct scale factors, γ_{31} and β_{51}, for the effects of the family factors on the true educational attainment and occupational

status of the brothers, Table 7.9 pertains to models in which these two coefficients have been fixed at unity in order to identify the model and normalize slope estimates. For this reason, Model 7.4.1 of Table 7.9 incorporates one more restriction than Model 7.3.7A of Table 7.7, but the fit is not significantly affected.

13. This finding was quite unexpected, and at the suggestion of Christopher Jencks, Hauser (1984) validated it in other, larger subsamples of siblings drawn from the Wisconsin Longitudinal Study and in comparisons with the Kalamazoo study. The evidence of family bias in these samples was weak, and observed biases disappeared when corrections were made for response error in schooling. All of these findings apply mainly to high school graduates, and it is important to test them again in populations that are more variable in levels of completed schooling.

14. In a contrast with Model 7.4.4 of Table 7.9, there is no significant difference between the family variance component of schooling (ϕ_{11}) and the within-family variance component (ϕ_{22}) for primary respondents ($L^2 = 0.13$ with 1 d.f.). For brothers, the corresponding contrast (between ϕ_{11} and ϕ_{33}) is marginally significant ($L^2 = 4.2$ with 1 d.f., p = .04).

15. If we add the restriction $\psi_{11} = \psi_{66} = \psi_{77}$ to Model 4.4 of Table 7.9, the test statistic increases significantly by $L^2 = 15.98$ with 1 d.f.

References

Benin, M. H., & Johnson, D. R. (1984). Sibling similarities in educational attainment: A comparison of like-sex and cross-sex sibling pairs. *Sociology of Education*, *57*, 11–21.

Bielby, W. T. (1981). Neighborhood effects: A LISREL model for clustered samples. *Sociological Methods and Research*, *10*, 82–111.

Bielby, W. T., Hauser, R. M., & Featherman, D. L. (1977). Response errors of black and nonblack males in models of the intergenerational transmission of socioeconomic status. *American Journal of Sociology*, *82*, 1242–88.

Bowles, S. (1972). Schooling and inequality from generation to generation. *Journal of Political Economy*, *80*, S219–51.

Boyd, L. H., Jr., & Iversen, G. R. (1979). *Contextual Analysis: Concepts and Statistical Techniques*. Belmont, CA: Wadsworth.

Chamberlain, G., & Griliches, Z. (1975). Unobservables with a variance-components structure: Ability, schooling, and the economic success of brothers. *International Economic Review*, *16*, 422–49.

   (1977). More on brothers. In *Kinometrics: Determinants of Socioeconomic Success Within and Between Families*, ed. Paul Taubman, pp. 97–107. Amsterdam: North Holland.

Clarridge, B. R. (1983). *Sibling Fertility: From Family of Orientation to Family of Procreation*. Unpublished doctoral diss., University of Wisconsin–Madison.

Corcoran, M., & Datcher, L. P. (1981). Intergenerational status transmission and the process of individual attainment. In *Five Thousand American Families: Patterns of Economic Progress*, Vol. 9, ed. M. S. Hill, D. H. Hill, & J. N. Morgan, pp. 169–206. Ann Arbor: University of Michigan, Institute for Social Research.

Duncan, O. D. (1961). A socioeconomic index for all occupations. In *Occupations and Social Status*, ed. A. J. Reiss, Jr., pp. 109–38. New York: Free Press.

Griliches, Z. (1977). Estimating the returns to schooling: Some econometric problems. *Econometrica, 45*, 1–22.

  (1979). Sibling models and data in economics: Beginnings of a survey. *Journal of Political Economy, 87*, S37–64.

Hauser, R. M. (1984). Some cross-population comparisons of family bias in the effects of schooling on occupational status. *Social Science Research, 13*, 159–87.

  (1988). A note on two models of sibling resemblance. *American Journal of Sociology, 93*, in press.

Hauser, R. M., & Featherman, D. L. (1977). *The Process of Stratification*. New York: Academic Press.

Hauser, R. M., Sewell, W. H., & Clarridge, B. R. (1982). *The Influence of Family Structure on Socioeconomic Achievement: A Progress Report*, Working Paper 82–59. Madison: University of Wisconsin, Center for Demography and Ecology.

Hauser, R. M., Tsai, S., & Sewell, W. H. (1983). A model of stratification with response error in social and psychological variables. *Sociology of Education, 56*, 20–46.

Jencks, C., Bartlett, S., Corcoran, M., Crouse, J., Eaglesfield, D., Jackson, G., McClelland, K., Mueser, P., Olneck, M., Schwartz, J., Ward, S., & Williams, J. (1979). *Who Gets Ahead? The Determinants of Economic Success in America*. New York: Basic Books.

Jencks, C., Smith, M., Acland, H., Bane, M. J., Cohen, D., Gintis, H., Heyns, B., & Michelson, S. (1972). *Inequality*. New York: Basic Books.

Jennings, M. K., & Niemi, R. G. (1981). *Generations and Politics: A Panel Study of Young Adults and Their Parents*. Princeton, NJ: Princeton University Press.

Jöreskog, K. G., & Sörbom, D. (1977). Statistical models and methods for analysis of longitudinal data. In *Latent Variables in Socioeconomic Models*, ed. D. J. Aigner & A. S. Goldberger, pp. 285–325. Amsterdam: North Holland.

  (1978). *LISREL IV: Analysis of Linear Structural Relationships by the Method of Maximum Likelihood. User's Guide*. University of Uppsala.

Kenny, O. A. (1979). *Correlation and Causality*. New York: Wiley.

Kessler, R. C., & Greenberg, D. F. (1981). *Linear Panel Analysis: Models of Quantitative Change*. New York: Academic Press.

Olneck, M. R. (1976). *The Determinants of Educational Attainment and Adult Status Among Brothers: The Kalamazoo Study*. Unpublished doctoral diss., Harvard University.

  (1977). On the use of sibling data to estimate the effects of family background, cognitive skills, and schooling: Results from the Kalamazoo brothers study.

In *Kinometrics: Determinants of Socioeconomic Success Within and Between Families*, ed. Paul Taubman, pp. 125–62. Amsterdam: North Holland.

Olneck, M. R., & Bills, D. B. (1980). What makes Sammy run? An empirical assessment of the Bowles–Gintis correspondence theory. *American Journal of Education*, *89*, 27–61.

Sewell, W. H., & Hauser, R. M. (1975). *Education, Occupation, and Earnings*. New York: Academic Press.

   (1980). The Wisconsin Longitudinal Study of Social and Psychological Factors in Aspirations and Achievements. *Research in Sociology of Education and Socialization*, *1*, 59–99.

Sewell, W. H., Hauser, R. M., & Wolf, W. C. (1980). Sex, schooling, and occupational status. *American Journal of Sociology*, *86*, 551–83.

Thomson, E., & Williams, R. (1982). Beyond wives' family sociology: A method for analyzing couple data. *Journal of Marriage and the Family*, *44*, 999–1008.

8

Applications of structural equation modeling to longitudinal educational data

RUSSELL ECOB

Introduction

My objectives in this chapter are the following:

1. To analyze data on learning difficulties and reading collected over a period of two years using the so-called two-wave model (Rogosa 1979; Plewis 1985) and to test a number of hypotheses concerning the relation of learning difficulties to progress in reading the relation of reading attainment to changes in learning difficulties from one year to the next.

2. To investigate the effect of different estimates of the reliability (or, equivalently, measurement error variance) of the reading test, given in the first year, on the relationships between reading and learning difficulties over time.

3. To analyze data collected during a three-year period by means of a "three-wave" model to investigate systematically the stability over the years of the measurement properties of the scales and of the structural aspects of the model, as well as to test various forms of restrictions on the model that are determined by particular substantive questions.

4. To examine the influence of the child's gender and of the father's social class on the relationships in the two-wave model. Both gender and social class have been shown to be important determinants of learning difficulties, both in these data and in other studies.

In the multiple-group model of LISREL the influences of the child's gender and father's social class, which are exogenous variables in the model, are partialed out in order to ensure that the relationship between attainment and learning difficulties is not an artifact of their common dependence on gender and social class. In addition, I test whether the relationships in the model are the same within each combination of gender and social class categories. If the relationships are found to be the same within each category, the explanatory power of the model is strengthened. Coefficients in the multiple-group model can be compared with those in the original two-wave model, which does not control for these exogenous variables.

My general aim in this chapter is to show how the structural equation framework allows a modeling of the following aspects of the data: the longitudinal structure, the multidirectional relationships,[1] the relationships between indicator or test-specific errors over occasions of measurement, and, finally, the variation in relationships between the endogenous variables in the model according to the values of additional exogenous variables.

The conceptualization of models in terms of latent constructs makes it possible to examine theories independently of the indicators used. Within the confirmatory framework, models can be tested against one another in a predetermined sequence in order to arrive at the most concise model, within a given specification of alternatives, that is consistent with the data.

A conceptual framework for examining relationships between attainments and behavior

Research on children's behavior in school has tended to view the behavior of the child as dependent on other school-based variables. For example, Rutter et al. (1979), using observation measures of behavior at class level, found behavior to be dependent on the social class balance of intake to the secondary school. Similarly, Hughes, Pinkerton, & Plewis (1979) found teacher ratings of individual children to be dependent on the date of entry to infant school and in particular to the proportion of children in the class who entered school in the January after the September start of the school year.

The child's behavior in school, and in particular the child's learning difficulties with which this chapter is concerned, are dependent on gender and socioeconomic variables, such as parent's social class, and education. However, behavior has rarely been viewed as mediating the relationships between these variables and particular cognitive attainments. I investigate this issue here.

An alternative conceptual framework views learning difficulties as the product of low attainment. From this view, interest lies in the conditions required for a reduction in learning difficulties over time. Two possible conditions that I investigate are the reading attainment at the first occasion and the improvement in reading attainment between occasions. An interesting parallel to the relationship between learning difficulties and attainment is the relationship between self-concept and attainment (Calsyn & Kenny 1977; Shavelson & Bolus 1982). Here the self-enhancement model (Shavelson & Bolus 1982) predicts that evaluation of others

Table 8.1. *"Child-at-school" teacher-rated behavior schedule: items measuring learning difficulties*

	1	2	3	4	5	
Cannot concentrate on any particular task; easily distracted	–	–	–	–	–	Can concentrate on any task; not easily distracted
Eager to learn; curious and inquiring	–	–	–	–	–	Shows little interest, curiosity, or motivation in learning
Perseveres in the face of difficult or challenging work	–	–	–	–	–	Lacks perseverance; is impatient with difficult or challenging work

Note: The first item is reversed in the analysis.

influences self-concept, which in turn influences academic attainment. In contrast, a skill development model (Calsyn & Kenny 1977) supposes that academic attainment influences both self-concept and perceived evaluation of others. The two sets of authors come to contrary conclusions.[2]

The data

A cohort of children was followed through junior school[3] from year 1 to year 3. This includes all children in one year group in a random sample of 49 schools in Inner London Education Authority (Mortimore et al. 1986). The following variables are examined in this chapter:

1. Reading attainment. Scores on the Edinburgh Reading Test (Stage 1 in years 1–2 and Stage 2 in year 3) were used as measures of reading attainment. Testing was carried out by the class teacher near the beginning of the school year, in the autumn term.

2. Learning difficulties. Every child's learning difficulties were rated by the class teacher each year (at a time close to the corresponding reading test) on three 5-point scales assessing, respectively, concentration on work, keenness to learn new things, and perseverance with work. A high score on each of these scales represents a high degree of difficulty. These scales, shown in Table 8.1, comprise part of a more general assessment of behavior in the classroom (Kysel et al., 1983).

3. Social class. Information about father's social class was collected at the beginning of the junior school. Using the registrar general's measure of father's social class (Office of Population Censuses and Surveys 1980), these data were grouped into the following four categories: Nonmanual (registrar general's classes I, II, III nonmanual), Manual (registrar general's classes III manual, IV, V), Other (long-term unemployed, economically inactive, father absent), and, finally, No information/Nonresponse.

Eight groups formed by combinations of the two gender and the four social class categories constituted the groups in the multiple-group analyses. All analyses were then carried out on the covariance matrix. For multiple-group analyses, in particular, the use of the covariance matrix with unstandardized coefficients avoids some of the problems of interpretation of standardized coefficients (Kim & Ferree 1981). There are number of alternative methods of standardizing the data in multiple-group analyses. Either the whole sample or any one of the subgroups can be used as a reference point. Here the pooled sample is standarized to a unit variance; as a result, within each subgroup the variances of the observed variables are generally less than 1 owing to the degree of clustering within subgroups.

For the two-wave analyses, data from the first two years were used. All observations, 1,487, that had nonmissing values for all the learning difficulties indicators and reading test scores were included. The sample containing information on all variables in all 3 years was smaller, having 1,317 observations. This was used for the three-wave analyses.

Two-wave analyses: three models for the relationship between reading attainment and learning difficulties over occasions

These models relate reading attainment and learning difficulties over the first two years. Gender and social class are not represented in these models. Four hypotheses are tested over the whole sample. The first two hypotheses are concerned, respectively, with the relation of progress in reading over a year to the assessment of the extent of learning difficulties at the beginning of the year and to the change in the assessment of learning difficulties over the year.

Hypothesis 1 is concerned with children who have a high degree of learning difficulty in relation to their reading test score and concerns their relative progress in reading over the year. It takes the following form:

(H1) Learning difficulties in year 1 influence reading attainment in year 2, given reading attainment in year 1.

Hypothesis 2 tests whether a change in learning difficulties causes a change, with a time lag, in reading. The time lag is assumed to have an unknown period of less than a year. This hypothesis takes the following form:

(H2) Learning difficulties in year 2 influence reading attainment in
year 2, given learning difficulties and reading attainment in year 1.

The third and fourth hypotheses are the mirror images of the first two
and reverse the explanatory roles of reading attainment and learning
difficulties. They are concerned with causes or explanations of change in
learning difficulties over the year and examine, respectively, the dependency on the reading attainment at the beginning of the year and the
extent of progress in reading over the year. Hypothesis 3 takes the
following form:

(H3) Reading attainment in year 1 influences learning difficulties in
year 2, given learning difficulties in year 1.

Hypothesis 4 investigates the realtionship between progress in reading
attainment over a year and the change in learning difficulties over the year.
It tests whether progress in reading causes, with an unknown time lag of
less than a year, a change in learning difficulties. It takes the following
form:

(H4) Reading attainment in year 2 influences learning difficulties in
year 2, given reading attainment and learning difficulties in year 1.

The four hypotheses are illustrated in Figure 8.1, which shows the
structural part of the models used as tests. Let us consider why paths
$L2R2$ and $R2L2$ are the appropriate ones for testing hypotheses 2 and 4,
respectively, and consider hypothesis 4 first. For these purposes, we
measure progress in reading by the expression $RP = R2 - \gamma(R1)$, where γ
is an unknown parameter (estimated by a regression coefficient) that
measures the degree of relationship between reading scores on each
occasion and takes account of any differences in scale between the two
tests. Regressing learning difficulties at the end of the year ($L2$) on learning
difficulties at the beginning of the year ($L1$), progress in reading over the
year (RP), and reading at the beginning of the year ($R1$), we obtain the
following equations:

$$L2 = \alpha + \beta_1 L1 + \beta_2(R2 - \gamma R1) + \beta_3 R1 + \varepsilon_1 \qquad (8.1)$$
$$L2 = \alpha + \beta_1 L1 + \beta_2 R2 + (\beta_3 - \beta_2\gamma)R1 + \varepsilon_2 \qquad (8.2)$$

In (8.1), the parameter β_2 represents the relation of progress in reading
to learning difficulties at the end of the year, and from (8.2) it can be seen
that this represents the path $R2L2$ in the bottom right diagram in Figure
8.1. It is independent of the unknown scaling parameter γ. A similar
argument applies to hypothesis 2. These models include no further
explanatory variables. Later, I will examine models that allow for the
influence of further variables in the model.

I now construct a LISREL model (Model 8.1) to provide tests of
hypotheses 1 and 3. This is shown in Figure 8.2. Hypothesis 1 is specified

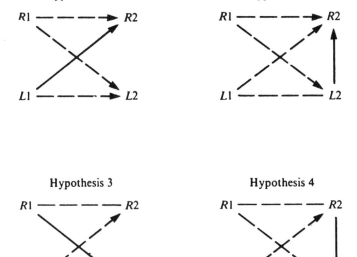

Figure 8.1. Structural models for two-wave analysis for investigation of hypotheses: *L*1, learning difficulties, Year 1; *L*2, learning difficulties, year 2; *R*1, reading attainment, year 1; *R*2, reading attainment, year 2. The dashed and solid lines represent the paths in the model, each bold line representing the path that tests the hypothesis.

via the path β_{14} and hypothesis 3 via path β_{23}. In this model the measurement errors for the observed measures of learning difficulties are allowed to covary over occasions (represented by curved lines in Figure 8.2). Empirically, this has been found to be a common feature of such models (Wheaton et al. 1977) and probably arises from the fact that each indicator has some indicator-specific variation[4] as well as measurement error. The former, and possibly the latter, is likely to be correlated over occasions. This model was arrived at after testing against the more restrictive model, which assumed that the measurement errors in the observed measures were independent over occasions. A reduction of chi-square of 70.37 with 3 degrees of freedom led to acceptance of the model that allows correlated errors. For this model the variance of the measurement error of the (now standardized) reading test was fixed at .054, corresponding to a reliability of .946 given in the test manual (Carroll 1977).[5]

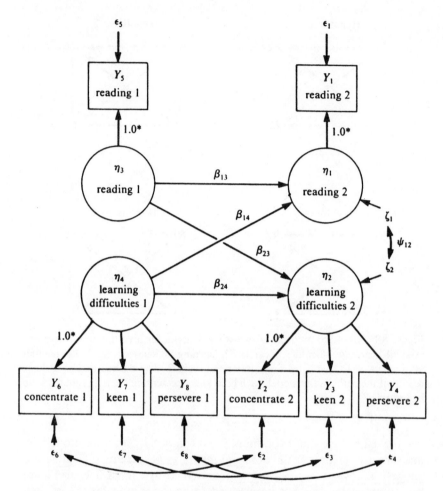

Figure 8.2. Two-wave anaylsis: testing hypotheses 1 and 3 (Model 8.1). Asterisk indicates fixed parameter value.

The regression coefficients within the structural part of Model 8.1 are shown in Table 8.2. Both β_{14} and β_{23} are highly significantly different from zero and so provide support for both hypotheses 1 and 3.[6] The signs of the coefficients lead me to conclude that, after controlling for the assessment of learning difficulties at the beginning of the year, low reading attainment results in a higher assessment of learning difficulties at the end of the year. Similarly, after controlling for reading attainment at the

Table 8.2. *Estimates of regression coefficients among latent constructs for three models of the relationship between reading and behavior in years 1 and 2*

Parameter	Model 8.1[a]	Model 8.2	Model 8.3
β_{12}	—	—	$-0.13\ (.03)^{b}$
β_{21}	—	$-0.19\ (.04)$	
β_{13}	$0.80\ (.02)$	$0.80\ (.02)$	$0.78\ (.02)$
β_{24}	$0.50\ (.03)$	$0.49\ (.03)$	$0.52\ (.03)$
β_{14}	$-0.12\ (.03)$	$-0.12\ (.03)$	$-0.05\ (.03)$
β_{23}	$-0.19\ (.02)$	$-0.02\ (.04)$	$-0.17\ (.02)$
Goodness-of-fit index (χ^2_{13})	86.16	86.16	86.16

Note: All models show the same statistically significant lack of fit to the data. However, the sample size ($N = 1,487$) is so large as to render the significance of the chi-square of test of fit of little value as a diagnostic of goodness-of-fit. A better diagnostic is the normed fit index of Bentler and Bonnet (1980), which takes the value of .958 in comparison with the null model, chosen as the one-factor model with the same measurement properties as Model 8.1. This is within the range considered acceptable by Bentler and Bonnet and is higher than that found in any of the examples given in that paper.
[a] Standard errors are given in parentheses.
[b] Model 8.1 includes the parameter ψ_{12}, the covariance between errors in the two equations. This has to be fixed to zero in Models 8.2 and 8.3.

beginning of the year, higher assessment of learning difficulties leads to lower reading attainment at the end of the year.

The LISREL model used to test hypothesis 4 is shown in Figure 8.3. The structural coefficient β_{21} provides a test of this hypothesis.[7] Hypothesis 2 is tested with a similar model, which reverses the structural coefficient β_{21} to β_{12}. The estimates of these coefficients are given in Table 8.2. They provide support for both hypotheses.

The strengths of these relationships are assessed by the absolute values of the coefficients, which represent the relation of a unit change in one variable to change in another. Thus, reading in year 1 has a greater influence on change in learning difficulties ($b_{23} = -0.185$) than do learning difficulties in year 1 on progress in reading ($b_{14} = -0.119$). Moreover, the estimate of the coefficient relating change in reading to change in learning difficulties is higher in absolute terms ($b_{21} = -0.19$) than that of the coefficient expressing the opposite relationship ($b_{12} = -0.13$). The probability of rejecting the null hypothesis of zero relationship is similar in both cases.

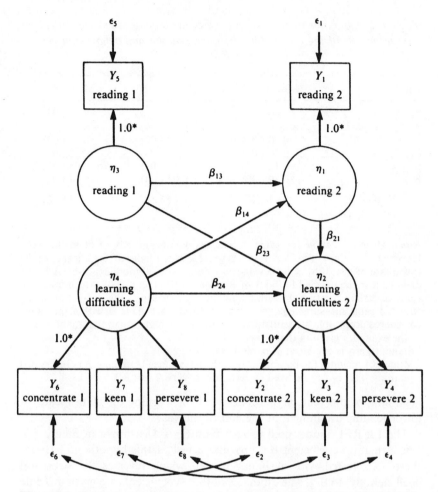

Figure 8.3. Two-wave analysis: testing hypothesis 2 (Model 8.2). Asterisk indicates fixed parameter value.

Two-wave analyses: sensitivity to the reliability of the reading test in year 1

I now investigate the sensitivity of the parameter estimates in a particular model (Model 8.1) to the reliability of the reading test in year 1. Five values were chosen at equal intervals of .04 in range from 1.00 to .84, respectively. Three of these values are lower than the test manual estimate of .946. Only the reliability of the reading test in year 1 was allowed to

Table 8.3. *Effects of differing degrees of reliability of reading (year 1) on the parameter estimates in the structural model*

Parameter	Reliability				
	1.00	.96	.92	.88	.84
	Parameter estimates				
β_{13}	0.74 (.02)	0.78 (.02)	0.84 (.02)	0.90 (.03)	0.97 (.03)
β_{24}	0.53 (.03)	0.52 (.03)	0.51 (.03)	0.50 (.03)	0.49 (.03)
β_{14}	−0.17 (.02)	−0.13 (.02)	−0.10 (.03)	−0.05 (.03)	0.00 (.03)
β_{23}	−0.16 (.22)	−0.17 (.02)	−0.18 (.03)	−0.19 (.03)	−0.21 (.03)
λ_{42}	0.99 (.03)	0.99	0.99	0.99	0.99
λ_{43}	1.12 (.03)	1.12	1.12	1.12	1.12
λ_{22}	0.95 (.03)	0.95	0.95	0.95	0.95
λ_{23}	1.07 (.03)	1.07	1.07	1.07	1.07

Note: Standard errors are given in parentheses. Standard errors of loadings do not vary with the reliability and so are given only for the perfect reliability condition.

vary, that of the reading test in year 2 being fixed at a common value of .946 in all analyses.[8]

In the simple bivariate regression, unreliability in the explanatory variable attenuates the regression coefficient. The disattenuated regression coefficient, this being the coefficient relating to the true or underlying scores, is obtained by dividing the estimated regression coefficient by the reliability estimate. In a structural equation model the effect of changes in the reliability of explanatory variables on the paths in the model is more complex. This is in part due to the larger number of explanatory variables and to the existence of measurement errors, or more generally indicator-specific errors, in more than one explanatory variable.

Table 8.3 shows the effects on the paths in the two-wave model (Model 8.1) of different reliabilities of the reading test in year 1. The structural coefficient β_{13} of reading attainment in year 1 on reading attainment in year 2 increases with decreasing reliability for reading in year 1. The structural coefficient β_{24} of learning difficulties in year 1 on learning difficulties in year 2 decreases slightly with decreasing reliability of reading. Table 8.4 shows the estimates under the two possible models, the simple regression model (where the true regression coefficient is obtained by dividing the observed regression coefficient by the reliability estimate of reading in year 1) and the given structural model, and shows that the degree of disattenuation in the structural model is

Table 8.4. *Comparison of the relationships among latent constructs in the simple regression model for reading and the two-wave structural model*

Reliability, reading year 1	1.00	.96	.92	.88	.84
Estimate of β_{13} by applying simple disattenuation formula	0.74	0.77	0.80	0.84	0.88
Estimate of β_{13} in two-wave model	0.74	0.79	0.84	0.90	0.97
Increase of β_{13} in two-wave model relative to simple disattenuation prediction	—	1.55	1.60	1.62	1.67

greater at each level of reliability than is predicted from the simple regression model.

The other structural coefficients are also substantially affected by changes in the reliability of the test in year 1. From Table 8.3 it is seen that, as reliability decreases, the size of the path β_{14} between learning difficulties in year 1 and reading in year 2 is reduced and becomes zero at the lowest value of reliability examined. In contrast, the structural coefficient β_{23} between reading in year 1 and learning difficulties in year 2 increases with decreasing reliability. The estimated loadings of the indicators of learning difficulties are unaffected by the reliability of the tests.

Decreasing the reliability, assumed known, does not alter the total information extracted from the model, because the number of free or estimated parameters is not altered. It is convenient to view the incorporation of measurement error variance or unreliability in the year 1 reading score as simply correcting the variance–covariance matrix of the observations by subtracting the variance of the measurement error from the variance of the year 1 reading score. In this view, the models themselves are not altered, only the data. All models, moreover, have the same goodness-of-fit to the data as judged by the chi-square measure, although with increases in measurement error the *t*-values of all coefficients are reduced. This is true even when the structural coefficient itself increases, as in the relation of reading at the beginning of the year to learning difficulties at the end of the year.

An important conclusion to draw from this sensitivity analysis is that, once reading attainment in year 1 is controlled, the influence of learning difficulties in year 1 on reading attainment in year 2 (tested in hypothesis 1) is crucially dependent on the reliability of the measure of reading attainment in year 1.

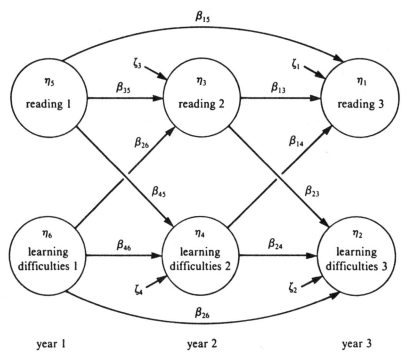

Figure 8.4. Three-wave analysis: basic structural model.

Three-wave analyses: testing restrictions on the model

The extension from two to three occasions allows, in particular, the consistency of the relationships observed over occasions to be examined. It also allows a test of whether the direct relationships between the first and third occasions are zero, in other words whether, for both reading attainment and learning diffculties, the measure in year 2 mediates all of the influence of year 1 on year 3. For these analyses additional measurements on all variables were obtained in the autumn term in the third year of junior school. These and a number of other questions can be investigated by successive modifications of the basic structural model shown in Figure 8.4 by imposing restrictions on the parameter matrix.

First, however, I ascertain the measurement properties of the model.[9] These analyses show that, in almost every respect, the measurement properties of the learning difficulties indicators are different across occasions.

The first restrictions on the structural model are concerned with the disturbance terms $\zeta_i (i = 1, 2, 3, 4)$. Covariation among disturbance terms indicates that variables omitted from the model may have a common effect on more than one variable in the model. Table 8.5 shows four forms of restrictions I examine on the basic model with the measurement properties I have arrived at.

The first restriction is that the covariation among disturbance terms across the second and third occasions is constrained to be zero. This hypothesis results in a nonsignificant increase in chi-square and so is accepted (Model 8.1). This implies that there are no variables exogenous to the model that have common effects, independent of other variables in the model, on endogenous variables at different occasions. The second restriction tests whether the covariances among disturbances corresponding to reading and behavior difficulties within the second and third occasions are equal. This is accepted (Model 8.2). The third restriction tests this common value against zero (Model 8.3). This is rejected. The fourth restriction on the disturbance terms (Model 8.4) is that, for both reading and learning difficulties separately, the variance of the disturbance terms is the same in years 2 and 3. In conjunction with Model 8.2 this means that the correlations among the disturbances at each occasion are equal. This model is accepted.

The importance of imposing these last three restrictions is in producing models with fewer parameters. They have no particular substantive rationale.

The next series of restrictions operates on the structural part of the model, the **B** matrix. I first examine the joint hypothesis that the structural coefficients between reading in year 1 and learning difficulties in year 3 and between learning difficulties in year 1 and reading in year 3 are zero. This model (Model 8.5) is accepted, showing that the relationships between these two variables have a lag period of at most one year.

Next I examine whether the lagged relationships over a one-year period have the same values between year 1 and year 2 as between year 2 and year 3. This is accepted for relationships between learning difficulties and reading attainment in both directions (Models 8.6 and 8.7), showing that the relationships between the two constructs are constant and stable across the two time periods.

The structural component of the final model, Model 8.7 is shown in Figure 8.5. This model shows that, for both reading attainment and learning difficulties, a child's score in year 3 is positively related to the score in year 1 independently of the score in year 2 (i.e., $\beta_{15}, \beta_{26} > 0$). This means that in predicting reading attainment a year ahead in junior school,

Table 8.5. *Goodness-of-fit of models with various restrictions on structural parameters for three-wave data*

Description of model	Chi-square	Increase in chi-square from the basic model	Accept model?
Basic model	$\chi^2_{33} = 86.73$	—	—
Model 8.1: Disturbance terms covary only within occasion	$\chi^2_{37} = 86.73$	$\chi^2_4 = 0.00$	Yes
Model 8.2: Covariance between disturbances for reading and learning difficulties at occasions 2 and 3 are equal	$\chi^2_{38} = 87.20$	$\chi^2_1 = 0.47$	Yes
Model 8.3: Covariance between disturbances for reading and learning difficulties at occasions 2 and 3 are zero	$\chi^2_{39} = 120.73$	$\chi^2_1 = 33.53$	No
Model 8.4: Variances of disturbances are equal at years 2 and 3 for reading and learning difficulties	$\chi^2_{40} = 92.46$	$\chi^2_2 = 5.26$	Yes
Model 8.5: Structural coefficients from reading year 1 to learning difficulties year 3 and from learning difficulties year 1 to reading year 3 are zero	$\chi^2_{42} = 94.75$	$\chi^2_2 = 2.29$	Yes
Model 8.6: Structural coefficients from reading year 2 to learning difficulties year 3 and from reading year 1 to learning difficulties year 2 are equal	$\chi^2_{43} = 96.60$	$\chi^2_1 = 1.85$	Yes
Model 8.7: Structural coefficients from learning difficulties year 2 to reading year 3 and from learning difficulties year 1 to reading year 2 are equal	$\chi^2_{44} = 97.13$	$\chi^2_1 = 0.53$	Yes

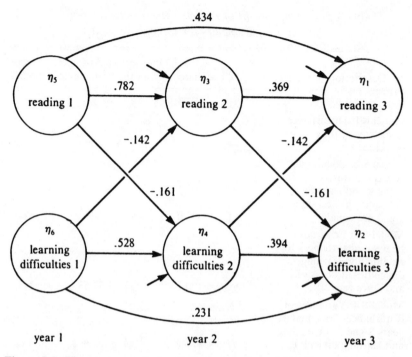

Figure 8.5. Three-wave analysis: final structural model, with structural coefficients among the latent variables.

account should be taken not only of the present reading attainment but
also of attainment in previous years. But another way, a child's potential
for progress in reading is related to the progress the child has made in the
previous year. For example, differential effectiveness of different teachers
may result in transitory relative gains or losses in the relation of reading
attainment at the end of the year to the child's potential progress over that
year.[10]

   The changes between years in reading and learning difficulties are also
related, this being indicated by the correlation between the disturbance
terms for both variables, which takes the same nonzero value in both years
2 and 3. Such a result may be due to the common effect on both reading
attainment and learning difficulties of experience in the classroom over the
previous year, an effective teacher raising a child's reading attainment
while reducing the child's experience of learning difficulties.

Table 8.6. *Goodness-of-fit for multiple-group models for two-wave data*

Description of model	Chi-square	Increase in chi-square	Accept model?
Basic model	$\chi^2_{104} = 183.25$	—	—
Measurement error structure and values identical between groups	$\chi^2_{167} = 221.99$	$\chi^2_{63} = 38.74$	Yes
Matrix of disturbance terms identical between groups	$\chi^2_{209} = 283.26$	$\chi^2_{42} = 61.27$	No
Matrix of structural coefficients identical between groups	$\chi^2_{195} = 240.19$	$\chi^2_{38} = 18.20$	Yes

Multiple-group analyses on two waves: testing for differences between groups defined by gender and father's social class

The combination of the four social class categories described earlier and the two gender categories forms eight groups. In each of the two years, reading attainment was found to be higher and learning difficulties lower for girls than for boys and for nonmanual than for all other groupings of social classes. Such differences may result in biased estimates in the structural models so far examined, the relationship between reading attainment and learning difficulties being in part a reflection of a common dependance on these grouping variables. In order to test this hypothesis, the two-occasion model (model 8.1, Figure 8.2) is fitted simultaneously within each group.

The complete sequence of tests on the measurement and structural parts of the multiple-group model is summarized in Table 8.6. A model having identical measurement structure and parameter values in each group is accepted. However, the disturbance terms are found to have different variances and covariances in the different groups.

Finally, the matrix of structural coefficients, the structural part of the model, is found to be identical across groups. This allows one to draw the strong conclusion that the relationships between learning difficulties and reading attainment over the two occasions are identical in each of the eight groups and a fortiori are the same for each gender and for each social class group.

However, I still wish to ascertain whether the relationships within the groups are the same as those over the whole sample. This is illustrated in

Table 8.7. *Estimates of structural coefficients for the multiple-group model for two-wave data: comparison with single-group model*

Structural coefficient	Multiple-group model	Single-group model
β_{13}	0.64 (.02)	0.80 (.02)
β_{24}	0.53 (.03)	0.50 (.03)
β_{14}	−0.12 (.02)	−0.12 (.03)
β_{23}	−0.15 (.02)	−0.18 (.02)

Table 8.7, which compares the structural coefficients in the multiple-group model with the comparable two-wave single-group model (Model 8.1, Figure 8.2). Three conclusions emerge from these analyses:

1. The structural coefficient from reading in year 1 to learning difficulties in year 2 is lower, by 20.5 percent, in the multiple-group model than in the single-group model. However, there is no change in the structural coefficient from learning difficulties in year 1 to reading in year 2.

2. The relationship between reading attainment over the two years is lower in the multiple-group model, the relationship over years between learning difficulties being little changed.

3. There is a tendency overall for the standard errors to be lower in relation to the coefficients in the multiple-group model. This is a reflection of the greater number of degrees of freedom obtained by imposing the measurement and structural restrictions in the multiple-group model. The fit of the multiple-group model to the data as judged by the ratio of chi-square to the degrees of freedom is better (1.24) than in the single-group model (6.62).

This comparison has shown that some of the relationships between reading and learning difficulties, when considered within the groups defined by gender and social class, differ from the relationships over the whole sample. This, in turn, implies that the relationships between the mean values of these variables between groups (shown in a between-group model) are therefore different from the within-group relationships (shown in a within-group or multiple-group model).

In summary, the main conclusions drawn from the single-group model, of a lagged relationship between reading attainment and learning difficulties at a later occasion and between learning difficulties and reading attainment at a later occasion, hold up when the common relationships to social class and gender are controlled for.

Discussion and conclusions

I have examined a number of structural models on a longitudinal educational data set comprising two latent variables measured on three occasions. I have illustrated how the values of the structural coefficients in the models, particularly those between reading and learning difficulties on different occasions, are in some cases crucially dependent on the estimated reliability of the reading test at the earlier occasion.[11] They are also affected by conditioning on exogenous variables related to both reading and learning difficulties.

A reasonable interpretation of the path in the multiple-group analysis from learning difficulties in year 1 to reading attainment in year 2 is that learning difficulties in year 1 (or indeed a combination of some other variables related within gender and social class groups to learning difficulties in year 1 independently of reading in year 1) is related to progress in reading between years 1 and 2 in a similar way within each gender and social class group. The educational importance of such a result depends on whether learning difficulties are considered to be a variable open to educational influence independently of reading attainment.

Conclusions from such analyses can be dependent on the choice of variables analyzed or even collected and, in this example, on the particular variables used to define the groups in the multiple-group analysis. For a grouping variable to influence a regression coefficient between two variables in the model it is necessary, though not sufficient, that it be related to more than one variable in the model over one or more occasions. The variables that form the groups in our analysis are those that are most highly related in the data to both variables simultaneously. However, in principle, the conclusions may be altered by conditioning on other socioeconomic variables.

A further limitation on inferences that can be drawn arises from the particular occasions at which the variables are measured. The absence of paths between variables in years 1 and 3 provides evidence that no causative link is operating with a lag period of more than one year. However, the relationships found with a lag period of one year may be the result of causative links having lag periods of less than one year and could, for example, be generated by a process that distributes the lags continuously over a period of up to a maximum of one year.

Finally, the following caveats should be borne in mind when interpreting the results of the models fitted in this chapter.

1. The teacher's rating of the child, being the outcome of a particular relationship between the teacher and the child, is affected by the characteristics of both parties. The teacher's characteristics – for

example, personality, teaching methods, and perception of children in general – will affect the rating of a particular child over and above the child's characteristics.

2. If relationships among the endogenous variables in the model were to vary across the groups defined by variables at a higher level of aggregation (e.g., the social class and gender groups), further modeling could relate the variation in these relationships between groups to the values of the higher-level variables. Analyses of this type cannot be performed with the structural equation models described here, although they can be if multilevel models are used (e.g., Goldstein 1986; Longford 1986). However, these models do not at present allow for the use of latent constructs in structural modeling.

3. The sample is a clustered sample at the pupil level, the data being obtained from a whole year group of children from a random sample of schools. The standard errors reported will therefore generally underestimate the true standard errors.

Notes

This research was supported by the Inner London Education Authority. The analyses and conclusions do not necessarily reflect the views or policies of this or any other organization. The author thanks Pamela Sammons, Doug Willms, Kathy Parkes, Peter Cuttance, and John Bynner for their comments on earlier drafts of this chapter.

1. We are not confined to the dependent versus explanatory convention of multiple regression: One of the endogenous variables may explain variation in another and its variation in turn be explained by a third variable.

2. This may be in part due to their different methodologies, Shavelson and Bolus using a structural equation model and Calsyn and Kenny using cross-lagged correlations, a method with proved methodological deficiencies (see Rogosa 1979).

3. In the English education system, the junior school takes children for four years, from age 7 to age 11. Compulsory schooling begins at age 5 at the infant school.

4. Indicator-specific variation is variation in an indicator that is not shared by the other indicators of the same latent construct.

5. The reliability estimates obtained from the test manual are not necessarily appropriate for this sample. They are calculated on a different population, assessed 8 years earlier on a population containing both urban and rural elements, and in addition do not allow for the different ages of children in the standardizing sample, which will inflate the variance of both the observed and the true scores. Nor do they allow for the multifaceted nature of the reading test. This test comprises five subtests measuring vocabulary, sequences, syntax,

comprehension, and extraction of relevant details from text. I am at present investigating methods of estimating reliability that take these factors into account. This may modify the substantive conclusions presented here. (Later in this chapter I investigate the sensitivity of the parameter estimates to variations in the reliability estimates.) An empirical investigation (Ecob & Goldstein 1983) has suggested that the Kuder–Richardson internal consistency estimates probably suffer from unknown biases. In structural equation modeling, a test with a given reliability or measurement error variance can be modeled by fixing the variance of the measurement error in relation to the variance of the observed variable. Alternatively, the loading of observed test score on the true test score can be fixed at the value $\lambda = \sqrt{r}$, where r is reliability.

6. There are two alternative methods for testing for a zero value of a parameter. One method is to refit the model with the parameter constrained to be zero and evaluate the increase in the chi-square measures of goodness-of-fit in relation to one degree of freedom gained. This method is a special case of the general method used when imposing any number of simultaneous constraints on a model and is used elsewhere in this chapter, for example, when evaluating constraints on the measurement models. In this case a more straightforward method is to compare the parameter estimate with its standard error. The parameter estimates are assumed to have normal sampling distributions. If the parameter estimate is found not to be significantly different from zero, a further run with the new constraint is then necessary to obtain correct estimates for other parameters in the model.

7. This model differs from Model 8.1 both in the introduction of the extra structural coefficient β_{21} and in the constraint that the disturbance terms are uncorrelated, which is necessary for identification of the model. It has the same degrees of freedom as Model 8.1 and will give the same goodness-of-fit to the data, being simply a reparametrization of the model.

8. The coefficients in the model are also dependent on this value. However, we do not investigate the relationship in this chapter, the value chosen being that in the test manual.

9. A measurement model is first constructed in which covariance is allowed between indicator-specific errors across occasions (as in the two-wave Model 8.1), but in which the loading of each indicator of learning difficulties on the appropriate latent variable is the same on each occasion. (This restriction gives a nonsignificant increase in the chi-square goodness-of-fit of the model to the data and so is accepted.) Further restrictions are rejected. These are that the indicator-specific variances are equal over all occasions, that the covariances of all indicator-specific errors on a given occasion are equal, and that the covariances of indicator-specific errors between any two occasions are equal.

10. Such a result could also arise from a heterogeneity of within-class regression coefficients for reading attainment on reading attainment in the previous years. To examine this question within a structural equation modeling framework, it is necessary to consider each class as a group in a multiple-group LISREL model. There is another possible explanation for the effect of the year 1 score on the year 3 score, given the year 2 score for learning difficulties. A

child is usually rated by a different teacher in each year. The rating of the child's learning difficulties by a given teacher is dependent to some extent on the terms of reference, different teachers using different criteria. Such results could arise if different teachers view a child in different ways, interpret the behavior scales in different ways, or simply operate on different absolute standards when judging behavior. This is not likely to apply to the reading attainments because the tests were administered by the teacher under specific instructions regarding the timing of the test and the use of practice items and the tests were marked by external markers.

11. The range of values examined is within that commonly found in educational practice, and I have obtained reliability estimates near the lower extreme of the range when the possibility that different components of reading attainment are assessed by the different subtests has been taken into account. In contrast, the estimate from the test manual is near the upper extreme of the range. These models can be alternatively estimated by dividing the test at each occasion into a number of replicates. In this case the reliability of the test is estimated within the model.

References

Bentler, P., & Bonett, D. G. (1980). Significance tests and goodness of fit in the analysis of covariance structures. *Psychological Bulletin, 88*, No. 3, 588–606.

Calsyn, R. J., & Kenny, D. A. (1977). Self-concept of ability and perceived evaluation of others: Cause or effect of academic achievement? *Journal of Education Psychology, 69*, 136–45.

Carroll, N. J. (1977). *Edinburgh Reading Tests: Manual of Instructions.* University of Edinburgh, Godfrey Thompson Unit.

Ecob, R., & Goldstein, H. (1983). Instrumental variable methods for the estimation of test score reliability. *Journal of Educational Statistics, 8*, 223–41.

Goldstein, H. (1986). Multilevel mixed linear model analysis using iterative generalised least squares. *Biometrika, 73*, 43–56.

Hughes, M., Pinkerton, G., & Plewis, I. (1979). Children's difficulties in starting infant school. *Journal of Child Psychology and Psychiatry, 20*, 187–96.

Kim, J., & Ferree, G. D. (1981). Standardisation in causal analysis. *Sociological Methods and Research, 10*, 187–210.

Kysel, F., Varlaam, A., Stoll, L., & Sammons, P. (1983). *The Child at School: A new behaviour schedule*, Internal Report RS 907/83. London: Inner London Education Authority, Research and Statistics Branch.

Longford, N. (1986). *A Fast Scoring Algorithm for Maximum Likelihood Estimation in Unbalanced Mixed Models with Nested Random Effects.* University of Lancaster, Centre for Applied Statistics.

Mortimore, P., Sammons, P., Ecob, R., Lewis, D., & Stoll, R. (1986). *The ILEA Junior School Study: Final Report.* London: Inner London Education Authority, Research and Statistics Branch.

Office of Population Censuses and Surveys (1980). *Classification of Occupations.* London: HMSO.

Plewis, I. (1985). *Analysing Change: Methods for the Measurement and Explanation of Change in the Social and Behavioural Sciences.* New York: Wiley.

Rogosa, D. (1979). Causal models in longitudinal research: Rationale, formulation and interpretation. In J. R. Nesselroade & P. B. Baltes (Eds.), *Longitudinal Research in the Study of Behavior and Development.* New York: Academic Press.

Rutter, M., Mortimore, P., Maughan, B., Ouston, J., & Smith, A. (1979). *Fifteen Thousand Hours: Secondary Schools and Their Effects on Children.* London: Open Books.

Shavelson, R. J., & Bolus, R. (1982). Self-concept: The interplay of theory and methods. *Journal of Educational Psychology, 74,* 3–17.

Wheaton, B., Muthén, B., Alwin, D., & Summers, G. (1977). Specification and estimation of panel models incorporating reliability and stability parameters. In D. R. Heise (Ed.), *Sociological Methodology* (pp. 84–136). San Francisco: Jossey-Bass.

9

The robustness of maximum likelihood estimation in structural equation models

ANNE BOOMSMA

1. Introduction

General methods for the analysis of covariance structures were introduced by Jöreskog (1970, 1973). Within the general theoretical framework it is possible to estimate parameters and their corresponding standard errors and to test the goodness-of-fit of a linear structural equation system by means of *maximum likelihood methods*. Although other methods of estimating such models (least squares procedures, instrumental variable methods) are available, we do not discuss them here.

For an introduction to the general model the reader is referred to Chapter 2 and for more detailed statistical discussions to Jöreskog (1978, 1982a,b). The LISREL model considers a data matrix $\mathbf{Z}(N \times k)$ of N observations on k random variables. It is assumed that the rows of $\mathbf{Z}$ are *independently* distributed, each having a *multivariate normal distribution* with the same mean vector $\boldsymbol{\mu}$ and the same covariance matrix $\boldsymbol{\Sigma}$; that is, each case in the data is independently sampled from the same population. In a specified model there are s independent model parameters ω_i to be estimated. For *large* samples the sampling distribution of the estimated parameters $\hat{\omega}_i$ and the sampling distribution of the likelihood ratio estimate for goodness-of-fit are approximately known, provided that the preceding assumptions hold. Under the same conditions the standard errors of the estimated parameters $se_{\hat{\omega}_i}$ are also known asymptotically. In the following, standardized parameter estimates are defined by $\hat{\omega}_i^* = (\hat{\omega}_i - \omega_i)/se_{\hat{\omega}_i}$. For large samples the sampling distribution of $\hat{\omega}_i^*$ is approximately standard normal, and the goodness-of-fit estimate has an approximate chi-square distribution with $k(k + 1)/2 - s$ degrees of freedom.

Since the distributional properties of maximum likelihood estimates are based on asymptotic (large sample) statistical theory and on the assumption of multivariate normality, it is of prime interest to know how the estimates of parameters, standard errors, and goodness-of-fit behave under specific violations of these assumptions.

160

The importance of this issue should be evident from the fact that in the social sciences and in economics the sample size is often small. Moreover, in applications, the observed variables frequently have nonnormal univariate distributional properties (e.g., discrete or categorical variables with skewed and kurtotic distributions).

This chapter reports findings from a research project (Boomsma 1983) in which the following two robustness questions were investigated: Using maximum likelihood procedures, how robust is LISREL (1) against small sample size and (2) against nonnormality?

The basic investigative tools were *Monte Carlo procedures*, employed to produce sample covariance matrices $S(k \times k)$ of known properties, which were then used as sample input for LISREL analyses. For the two research problems addressed, these matrices are based on small samples (with multivariate normality of the observed variables) and on samples of size 400 from nonnormally distributed variables, respectively.

We present a summary of the results of the Monte Carlo study, emphasizing what the regular user of LISREL can expect under specific violations of assumptions and recommending ways to avoid making incorrect statistical inferences.

2. Design of the study, Monte Carlo methods, and model choice

This section provides an overview of the most important aspects of the design of the study (variations in sample size and nonnormality), the Monte Carlo procedures, and the covariance models for which robustness was studied. For illustrative purposes one of these models is presented in detail in section 2F.

A. Sample size

The robustness against small samples was investigated for samples of sizes 25, 50, 100, 200, and 400. However, in the study of nonnormally distributed variables, sample size N was not varied. In order to avoid interaction of sample size and nonnormality effects, it was kept at a constant size of 400.

B. Number of replications

The number of replications NR (i.e., the number of Monte Carlo samples S that were analyzed) is important for the accuracy of estimating the sampling distributions of parameters, standard errors, and the goodness-of-fit statistic. For each model, 300 samples were analyzed. Thus, for all violations of assumptions under study each conclusion is based on the results obtained after analyzing 300 covariance matrices.

C. Monte Carlo procedures

(i) Models with normally distributed variables Given a LISREL population model with a specified covariance structure Σ, $N \times k$ pseudorandom "observations" were generated from a multivariate normal distribution with covariance matrix Σ using IMSL subroutine GGNMS (International Mathematical and Statistical libraries 1982). From these N vectors of k "observations" a sample covariance matrix $S(k \times k)$ was computed. This sampling process was performed a large number of times, after which LISREL analyses of particular models were undertaken. (For our Monte Carlo purposes an adapted version of LISREL III was used on a CDC Cyber 74/18 and 170/760 computer.) The models were estimated for each of the 300 replicated samples. Thus, 300 *estimates* of each parameter, along with its standard error, and the chi-square goodness-of-fit statistic for each model were computed. A statistical evaluation of robustness was made by comparing the empirical sampling distributions of the estimates based on these 300 replications with their theoretical (asymptotic) distributions.

(ii) Models with nonnormally distributed variables Nonnormality was defined by the *skewness* and the *number of categories* of the observed variables, which were assumed to be discrete variables. Boomsma (1980) presented a numerical solution for generating sample covariance matrices S of such discrete and skew variables given their *known* population covariance structure Σ. This sampling procedure is basically the same as for the normal case, except that here samples are taken from a multivariate normal distribution with a covariance matrix $\Sigma^* \neq \Sigma$, followed by specific transformations of the continuous pseudorandom "observations" into categorical variables. The specific choice of Σ^*, which depends on the number of categories and the skewnesses, has the following effect: *After* the transformations, the samples S of the nonnormal variables can be regarded as samples from their nonnormal population with covariance structure Σ. See Boomsma (1983, chap. 6) for further details.

D. Standardization

The statistical theory for analyzing covariance structures with maximum likelihood methods assumes a Wishart distribution of the samples S. Therefore, population covariance matrices Σ are employed as the basic population models for the study; in sample terminology this implies that samples **S** are analyzed, while diag($\hat{\mathbf{\Sigma}}$) $\neq$ **I**. However, researchers often analyze sample correlation matrices $\mathbf{R} = \mathbf{V}^{-\frac{1}{2}}\mathbf{S}\mathbf{V}^{-\frac{1}{2}}$, where $\mathbf{V}^{\frac{1}{2}}(k \times k)$ is a diagonal matrix with the sample standard deviations of the observed variables as elements (i.e., the variances of the observed variables are standardized to 1); for most model specifications this implies that diag ($\hat{\mathbf{\Sigma}}$) = **I**. For example, this is the case in many applications of factor analysis models, where the units of measurement are often arbitrary and where a strong tradition of standardization exists. Correlation samples **R** do not have a Wishart distribution; thus, the decision to analyze sample correlation matrices instead of covariance matrices is not without complication. Therefore, we compare results from both approaches for some models.

E. Model choice and design variations within models

The effects of small sample size and departures from normality were investigated for specific structural equation models. Two substantive models, extensively discussed in the literature, and a number of theoretical factor analysis models were chosen for study. The substantive models are a recursive one for the stability of alienation (Wheaton et al. 1977) and a nonrecursive one for peer influence on aspiration (Duncan, Haller, & Portes 1968). These models are discussed by Jöreskog & Sörbom (1984) as examples 5 and 7, respectively. The 12 theoretical factor analysis models (each with two factors) studied are described in detail by Boomsma (1982, 1983). Also, a separate one-factor model with six observed variables reported by Olsson (1979a, p. 493, second case) was studied under nonnormality conditions. Figure 9.1 presents details of the four main models referred to in this chapter: Model 9.1 (the stability of alienation), Model 9.2 (peer influence on aspiration), Model 9.3 (an oblique factor analysis model), and Model 9.4 (Olsson's one-factor model).

As indicated earlier, for the normal small-sample case, five sample sizes were chosen: 25, 50, 100, 200, and 400. It is beyond the scope of this chapter to give the variations in the number of categories and in skewnesses for each of the models studied for nonnormality. Table 9.1 provides a summary of some of the characteristics of four main models, from which it can be seen that in Models 9.2 and 9.3 the most extreme deviations from nonnormality are about twice as large as in Models 9.1 and 9.4.

In studying the effects of nonnormality, symmetric (all k observed, discrete variables having a skewness of zero) and nonsymmetric variations of the models are constrasted (see Table 9.2 for an example). It should be

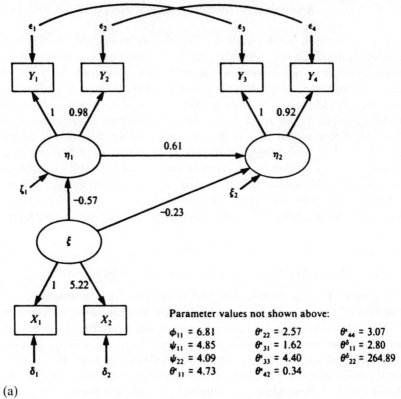

Parameter values not shown above:

$\phi_{11} = 6.81$ $\theta^{\epsilon}_{22} = 2.57$ $\theta^{\epsilon}_{44} = 3.07$
$\psi_{11} = 4.85$ $\theta^{\epsilon}_{31} = 1.62$ $\theta^{\delta}_{11} = 2.80$
$\psi_{22} = 4.09$ $\theta^{\epsilon}_{33} = 4.40$ $\theta^{\delta}_{22} = 264.89$
$\theta^{\epsilon}_{11} = 4.73$ $\theta^{\epsilon}_{42} = 0.34$

(a)

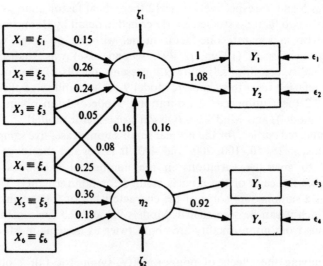

Parameter values not shown above:

$\psi_{11} = 0.28$ $\theta^{\epsilon}_{11} = 0.42$ $\theta^{\epsilon}_{33} = 0.30$
$\psi_{22} = 0.27$ $\theta^{\epsilon}_{22} = 0.33$ $\theta^{\epsilon}_{44} = 0.41$

(b)

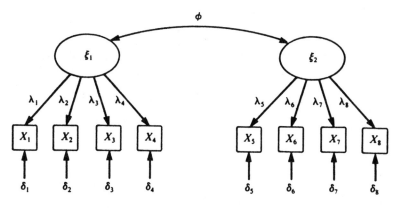

Parameter	Population value	Standard error N = 50	Standard error N = 400
$\lambda_1, \lambda_2, \lambda_5, \lambda_6$	0.60	0.142	0.050
$\lambda_3, \lambda_4, \lambda_7, \lambda_8$	0.80	0.134	0.047
ϕ	0.30	0.161	0.056
$\theta_1, \theta_2, \theta_5, \theta_6$	0.64	0.147	0.052
$\theta_3, \theta_4, \theta_7, \theta_8$	0.36	0.125	0.044

(c)

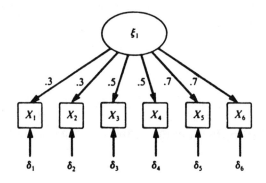

Parameter values not shown above:

$\theta^\delta_{11} = 0.91$ $\theta^\delta_{33} = 0.75$ $\theta^\delta_{55} = 0.51$
$\theta^\delta_{22} = 0.91$ $\theta^\delta_{44} = 0.75$ $\theta^\delta_{66} = 0.51$

(d)

Figure 9.1. Four models for covariance structure analysis:
(a) Model 9.1, the stability of alienation;
(b) Model 9.2, peer influence on aspiration;
(c) Model 9.3 factor analysis model with two correlated factors and four observed variables for each factor;
(d) Model 9.4, Olsson's one-factor model.

165

Table 9.1. *Characteristics of models studied for nonnormality*

		Model 9.1	Model 9.2	Model 9.3	Model 9.4
No. of observed variables k		6	10	8	6
No. of estimated model parameters		17	17	17	12
No. of categories[a]	min	2	2	2	2
	max	5	7	5	5
Absolute skewness	min	0.00	0.00	0.00	0.00
	max	2.00	4.00	4.00	1.50
Median of absolute skewness[b]	min	0.63	1.25	0.56	0.38
	max	1.25	2.50	2.25	1.13

[a] The range of the number of categories and of the absolute skewness among the k observed variables is calculated across all variations of a model, including the symmetric ones.
[b] The range of median of the absolute skewnesses among the k observed variables is calculated across all nonsymmetric variations.

stressed that, when the number of categories and the skewnesses of the marginal discrete variables are varied, the *kurtosis* of these variables is implicitly varied, as shown in the following section.

F. An example: Model 9.3

As an illustration of the type of models that were studied, a *two-factor measurement model* is chosen, which is also used to exemplify some characteristic results in later sections. In LISREL notation (see Figure 9.1) the model is defined by $\mathbf{X} = \boldsymbol{\Lambda}\boldsymbol{\xi} + \boldsymbol{\delta}$, where $\mathbf{X}(8 \times 1)$ is a vector of observed variables, $\boldsymbol{\Lambda}(8 \times 2)$ is a matrix of factor loadings (simple structure) on the latent variables ξ_1 and ξ_2, and $\boldsymbol{\delta}(8 \times 1)$ is a vector of measurement errors. The population covariance matrix can now be written $\boldsymbol{\Sigma} = \boldsymbol{\Lambda}\boldsymbol{\Phi}\boldsymbol{\Lambda}^1 + \boldsymbol{\Theta}$, where $\boldsymbol{\Phi} = E(\xi\xi)$ is a (2×2) correlation matrix of the latent factors and $\boldsymbol{\Theta} = (\boldsymbol{\delta}\boldsymbol{\delta}')$ an (8×8) diagonal matrix with the variances of the measurement errors (uniquenesses) as elements. In the population these elements are defined by $\theta_i = \theta_i^\delta = 1 - \lambda_i^2 \ (i = 1, \ldots, 8)$, which implies that the variances of the observed variables in the population are equal to 1. In Model 9.3 the population values λ_i were chosen as

Table 9.2. *Number of categories C and variations in degrees of skewness for the observed variables X_i in the nonnormal robustness design for Model 9.3*

Variable	C	Degree of skewness			
		SK0	SK1	SK2	SK3
X_1	5	0	0.375	0.75	1.5
X_2	2	0	0.750	1.50	3.0
X_3	3	0	0.500	1.00	2.0
X_4	2	0	0.250	0.50	1.0
X_5	5	0	1.000	2.00	4.0
X_6	2	0	0.375	0.75	1.5
X_7	3	0	1.000	2.00	4.0
X_8	2	0	0.750	1.50	3.0

follows: $\lambda_1 = \lambda_2 = \lambda_5 = \lambda_6 = 0.6$, and $\lambda_3 = \lambda_4 = \lambda_7 = \lambda_8 = 0.8$; thus, by definition $\theta_1 = \theta_2 = \theta_5 = \theta_6 = 0.64$ and $\theta_3 = \theta_4 = \theta_7 = \theta_8 = 0.36$. The population correlation ϕ between the two factors was chosen as .3. For this model Figure 9.1 gives all population parameter values and their corresponding standard errors for $N = 50$ and $N = 400$.

Model 9.5 (no picture shown; referred to in Tables 9.6 and 9.7 only) is also a two-factor measurement model, but with only three observed variables per factor. Its population factor loadings are specified as follows: $\lambda_1 = \lambda_2 = \lambda_4 = \lambda_5 = 0.4$ and $\lambda_3 = \lambda_6 = 0.6$. The size of the population values of the uniquenessess are thus the same as in Model 9.3, and the correlation ϕ between the factors is again .3.

In studying nonnormality for Model 9.3 only the skewness of the eight observed variables was varied; the number of categories was kept constant across variations in degrees of skewness. Table 9.2 gives details of the research design employed for this model. In variation SK0 the univariate distributions of the discrete variables are symmetric; in variation SK3 these distributions are extremely skewed. Figure 9.2 shows the population distributions of variable X_1 in Model 9.3: the symmetric case and three positively skewed cases. It can be seen how the kurtosis of these discrete variables varies with their skewness; note that the skewness and the kurtosis of a variable having a standard normal distribution equal 0 and 3, respectively. By comparing the results obtained in variation SK0 with those from the corresponding normal case ($N = 400$), a pure effect of categorization can be measured; by comparing the same normal case and variations SK0 through SK3, the additional effect of varying skewness can be assessed.

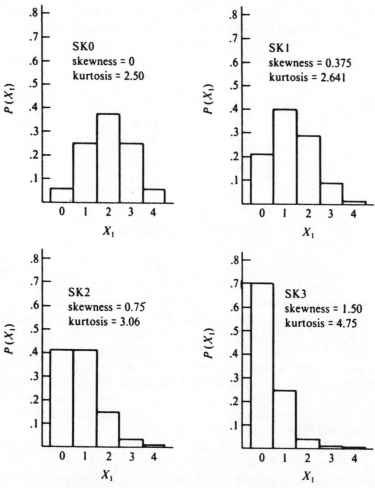

Figure 9.2. Probability distribution of discrete variable X_1 in Model 9.3, having five categories and a skewness of 0, 0.375, 0.75, and 1.5, respectively.

3. Robustness against small sample sizes

A. Bias and variance

Generally, for $N \geqslant 100$ there is little evidence of bias in estimating parameters and standard errors, even when correlation matrices are analyzed. Negative as well as positive biases occur in small samples. For $N < 100$ "outlier estimates" can be expected, which may have serious

Table 9.3. *Standard deviation of standardized parameter estimates*[a]

Parameter	N = 100		N = 200		N = 400	
	S	R	S	R	S	R
λ_1	.05	−.19	.06	−.20	.01	−.21
λ_2	−.00	−.23	.04	−.22	.01	−.21
λ_3	−.00	−.38	.10	−.35	.08	−.35
λ_4	.03	−.35	−.01	−.37	.01	−.43
λ_5	.05	−.21	−.00	−.24	−.05	−.25
λ_6	−.02	−.25	−.00	−.23	−.05	−.29
λ_7	−.03	−.40	.03	−.35	.05	−.40
λ_8	.01	−.38	−.00	−.36	−.00	−.40
ϕ	.17	.17	.01	.01	.03	.03
θ_1	.10	−.07	−.00	−.04	−.05	−.09
θ_2	.05	−.09	.04	−.06	.08	−.10
θ_3	.05	.09	−.01	.12	.04	.12
θ_4	.03	.10	.07	.10	−.02	−.02
θ_5	.03	−.07	−.01	−.11	.01	−.13
θ_6	.15	−.10	.01	−.11	−.01	−.17
θ_7	.06	.04	.06	.11	−.06	.04
θ_8	.01	.10	.06	.09	−.02	.03

[a] The observed standard deviation of $\omega_{ij}^* = (\hat{\omega}_{ij} - \omega_i)/se_{\hat{\omega}_{ij}}$, minus the expected (theoretical) value of 1. A value of .00 thus indicates no bias, whereas a positive value indicates an underestimate and a negative value an overestimate of the expected value of the standard deviation of ω_{ij}^*. Here **S** means analysis of covariance matrices, **R** analysis of corresponding correlation matrices. Model 9.3 $NR = 300$.

effects on other results as well, for example, on confidence intervals for parameters. Frequently such outlier estimates occur when variances are estimated to be negative. In practice it is very difficult to recognize "extreme" estimates in small samples without replication or cross validation.

These outlier estimates provide a clue to why the observed variance of the parameter estimates is regularly underestimated, compared with the expected squared standard error $se_{\omega_i}^2$. However, when correlation matrices are analyzed, severe overestimation of these empirical variances occurs for several parameters owing to the uncorrected estimation of standard errors, as can be seen from Table 9.3. This finding merits special attention.

A decision to base an analysis on the *correlation matrix* rather than the covariance *matrix* has implications for inference to the population model: Using a correlation matrix means that diag(Σ) is standardized to an identity matrix (see Section 2D for further discussion). This affects the accuracy of the estimation of the variances and covariances of the parameter estimates and hence of the estimation of the standard errors and the correlations among parameter estimates. This holds regardless of whether a sample covariance matrix S or a correlation matrix R is used as *input* for the analyses, since it depends on the matrix *analyzed.*

When correlation matrices are analyzed, LISREL overestimates the standard errors for many parameters. Table 9.3 indicates that, when covariance matrices S are analyzed, the observed standard deviations of standardized parameter estimates $\omega_{ij}^* = (\hat{\omega}_{ij} - \omega_i)/se_{\hat{\omega}_{ij}} (j = 1, \ldots, 300)$ are close to the expected theoretical value of 1, whereas when correlation matrices R are analyzed, the observed standard deviations of the estimated factor loadings are clearly smaller than 1. Apart from sampling fluctuations such effects on the parameter covariances do not depend on the sample size; even for much larger samples (e.g., $N = 1,000$) similar differences between the analyses of S and R can be expected. These findings have serious consequences for the estimated confidence intervals for population parameters, which are discussed in the next section.

Lawley and Maxwell (1971) discuss the effects of standardization in maximum likelihood factor analysis. They give (approximate) formulas for the sampling (co)variances of the rescaled parameter estimates. Browne (1982, p. 94) gives general (approximate) formulas for the variances of such estimates. Under certain conditions of invariance, standardization does not affect the chi-square estimate for goodness-of-fit (cf. Krane & McDonald 1978; Browne 1982). Given the same sample of observations, and apart from small "rounding errors," the goodness-of-fit estimate is then the same for analyses based on either the covariance or correlation matrix.

In summary, we conclude that in analyzing covariance matrices a sample size of $\geqslant 200$ seems to offer a reasonable protection against bias and unacceptable deviations in sampling variances. In analyzing correlation matrices the LISREL program does *not* make the necessary *corrections* for the (co)variances of parameter estimates.

B. Confidence intervals for parameters

For model parameters ω_i, approximate 95 percent two-sided confidence intervals $\hat{\omega}_{ij} \pm 1.96se_{\hat{\omega}_{ij}}$ were calculated, where $se_{\hat{\omega}_{ij}}$ is the standard error estimated from replication $j = 1, \ldots, 300$. For $N > 100$ such intervals were close to theoretical expectations when covariance matrices were analyzed. For $N < 100$, the number of 95 percent intervals covering the population values was often too high or too low, depending on the type of parameter and the model under study.

Table 9.4. *Results from approximate 95% confidence intervals for parameters (correlation matrices analyzed)*[a]

Parameter	Sample size					Population value of ω_i
	25	50	100	200	400	
λ_1	3%	3%	2%	3%	4%	0.60
λ_2	2	4	5	4	3	0.60
λ_3	4	5	5	5	5	0.80
λ_4	4	5	5	5	5	0.80
λ_5	1	3	3	4	5	0.60
λ_6	1	3	4	4	4	0.60
λ_7	4	5	5	5	5	0.80
λ_8	4	5	5	5	5	0.80
ϕ	-5	-1	-3	0	-2	0.30
θ_1	0	-2	1	1	1	0.64
θ_2	-3	2	1	1	0	0.64
θ_3	-5	-4	1	-3	-4	0.36
θ_4	-4	-4	-1	-4	1	0.36
θ_5	-2	1	1	1	3	0.64
θ_6	-6	-2	1	2	3	0.64
θ_7	-3	-3	0	-2	-1	0.36
θ_8	-5	-3	-2	-4	-1	0.36

[a] The percentage across 300 replications in which the population value ω_i is included in the estimated interval $\hat{\omega}_{ij}^* \pm 1.96se_{\hat{\omega}_{ij}}$, minus the expected 95%. A positive value indicates that the population value is included in the estimated 95% confidence interval too often; a negative value indicates that it is excluded too often. Model 9.3.

In analyzing correlation matrices the construction of such confidence intervals is not recommended (nor are hypothesis tests for the parameters), because the intervals frequently cover too high a proportion of the population values. For Model 9.3 this is illustrated by the results presented in Table 9.4. For factor loadings λ_i, the percentage of confidence intervals covering the population value ω_i systematically exceeded the expected 95 percent.

For all parameters symmetric intervals were constructed. If, however, ω_i is contained in some bounded range (e.g., variances > 0, absolute factor loadings $\leqslant 1$) such a strategy can be criticized. An alternative procedure would have been to construct confidence intervals for these parameters in the model restricted by such bounds (see Browne 1982).

When the results for many independent confidence intervals are considered, the correct estimates will usually be obtained in analyzing covariance matrices when $N \geqslant 200$. For samples of $\leqslant 100$, however, there is a substantial chance that estimates may vary considerably, which in many instances may lead to incorrect inferences. This can be especially serious for those model parameters that estimate variances.

Even if these variances are not the parameters of most interest to the rsearcher, it must be realized that all parameters are estimated simultaneously and that they are not independent of one another. Therefore, estimates of other parameters may also be affected by the estimates of variances.

C. Estimating goodness-of-fit

In general, for $N < 100$ the chi-square statistic for goodness-of-fit cannot be completely trusted. Depending on the model under study, the right tail of its sampling distribution is either too heavy or too light. With increased sample size the results did not always improve systematically, probably owing to sampling fluctuations. For samples of 100, 200, or 400 there appeared to be no striking differences in the observed chi-square statistic. Therefore, the findings indicate that for $N \geqslant 100$ the estimated goodness-of-fit statistic is reasonably well behaved.

Small-sample results for Model 9.3 are presented in Table 9.5. For $N = 25$ it appears that the right tail of the observed sampling distribution is too heavy: The observed percentage of chi-square values that are larger than the theoretical 95th quantile of 30.1 is 17 percent instead of the expected 5 percent. In practice this means that the true population model is rejected too often.

For a number of factor analysis models Anderson and Gerbing (1984) discuss effects of small sample size on three additional goodness-of-fit indices.

D. Other effects of sample size

In this section a number of issues are mentioned that are affected by sample size and hence may indirectly affect parameter bias, standard errors, confidence intervals, and goodness-of-fit. Therefore, they are of importance both for the interpretation of the results discussed so far and for practical recommendations.

(i) Problems of convergence As is sometimes the case in applications of structural modeling, a specific sample **S** may not give a convergent maximum likelihood solution within 250 iterations for a particular model specification. This frequently occurred with samples of $\leqslant 50$, and with

Table 9.5. *Characteristics of the sampling distribution of the chi-square statistics for goodness-of-fit*[a]

(a) Observed minus expected values of statistics from the chi-square sampling distribution with 19 degrees of freedom

Sample size	Observed minus expected value				
	Mean	S.D.	Skewness	Kurtosis	% $\chi^2_{19} < 30.1$[b]
25	4.2	.14	−0.2	−0.4	12
50	1.7	0.1	−0.0	−0.5	2
100	0.4	0.3	−0.1	−0.9	3
200	0.3	−0.0	0.2	0.7	1
400	−0.2	0.3	−0.0	−0.2	1

(b) Expected values of statistics from the chi-square distribution with 19 degrees of freedom and the standard error of their observed values, given NR = 300

	Mean	S.D	Skewness	Kurtosis	% $\chi^2_{19} < 30.1$
Expected value	19.0	6.2	0.6	3.6	5
Standard error of observed value; $NE = 300$	0.4	0.3	0.2	0.8	1

[a] Model 9.3; $NR = 300$.
[b] The value 30.1 is the theoretical 95th quantile of the distribution.

$N = 25$ up to half the replications failed to converge given the sample covariance matrices and the particular model specification studied. As sample size increased, thus giving smaller sampling fluctuations in the **S** matrix, the frequency of nonconvergence diminished. The sample size required to avoid problems of convergence depends strongly on the population structure Σ (Table 9.6).

In general, we conclude that, when the sample fluctuations of the covariances are relatively large (i.e., when sample size is small), convergence problems may well occur. In most circumstances a sample size of 200 will not lead to such difficulties.

It should be noted that it is always possible to restart the iteration process by using the estimated parameter values attained after the first 250 iterations as starting values in a continued analysis. However, the failure to converge within 250 iterations may indicate that there are fundamental problems in the data with respect to the model being estimated. Indeed, the discrepancy between the data and a specified model may be so large

Table 9.6. *Percentage of nonconverging solutions*[a]

Model	Sample size				
	25	50	100	200	400
9.1	22.1%	5.7%	0.7%		
9.2	6.5	0.7			
9.3	1.6				
9.5	55.0	35.3	16.4	2.9%	

[a] The percentage is expressed as $100x/(300 + x)$, where x is the number of nonconverging replication before the 300th convergent solution is found. A blank means 0%.

that the convergence criterion will not be met; sometimes convergence cannot be obtained even if no limit on the maximum number of iterations is set.

(ii) Negative estimates of variances A serious problem in parameter estimation is that of negative estimates of variances. In factor analysis, such estimates are known as "Heywood cases," and they correspond to estimates of the variances of measurement errors θ_i that are nonpositive. The LISREL algorithm does not automatically constrain estimates of variances to be equal to or greater than zero. Lee (1980) suggests that inequality constraints in estimating parameters can easily be implemented in programs for covariance structure analysis. In Chapter 12 Kelderman discusses how to handle the problem for LISREL models, as does Rindskopf (1983, 1984). In our study, samples resulting in negative estimates were included in the total set of 300 replications. (For a comparison between the strategies of including and excluding replications with improper variance estimates, see Boomsma 1983, 1985.)

It was found that the problem of negative variance estimates frequently occurs when $N \leqslant 50$. As sample size increases the percentage of improper solutions diminishes (Table 9.7). The percentage depends on the model under study: The closer the population value of an error variance to zero, the higher is the chance of obtaining inadmissible estimates. For example, in Model 9.3 with $N = 25$ the percentage of negative estimates for $\theta_1 = 0.64$ was very low, whereas for $\theta_3 = 0.36$ it was about 8 percent.

The practice of fixing some or all of the negatively estimated variances in a model to a positive value close to zero is disputable, particularly

Table 9.7. *Percentage of replications (NR = 3000) for which negative estimates of variances occur*[a]

Model	Sample size				
	25	50	100	200	400
9.1	64.0%	40.0%	19.7%	4.3%	
9.2	46.3	8.7	0.3		
9.3	27.3	1.0			
9.5	47.3	32.7	18.3	6.3	2.7%

[a] A blank means 0%.

because of the dependencies among parameters in the model. If more than one parameter has a negative estimate, one strategy would be to fix the single variance with the largest negative estimate and see what happens. Another would be to make a decision after inspecting the correlations among parameter estimates. Thus, if initially two negative variance estimates were found to be positively correlated, it would make sense to fix one of them to a positive value in subsequent analyses.

We conclude that using a sample of medium (say, $N = 200$) or large size is probably the best way to avoid improper solutions and the problems they pose for interpretation. Extensive results and discussion of both nonconvergence and improper solutions are given in Boomsma (1985).

(iii) Correlations among parameter estimates For $N < 200$ the Pearson product–moment correlations among parameter estimates can substantially deviate from their asymptotic values. The empirical correlations $\rho(\hat{\omega}_{ij}, \hat{\omega}_{i'j})$, $i \neq i'$, based on 300 replications were often too large or too small. In practice, inspection of the estimated correlations among the parameter estimates may often be of assistance in understanding the estimates.

When correlation matrices are analyzed in LISREL, the correlations among parameter estimates are based on uncorrected estimates of parameter (co)variances; hence, they should be ignored.

(iv) Correlations between parameters and standard errors It is well known that there are interdependencies between parameter estimates and their corresponding estimated standard errors, though there remains a lack of theoretical knowledge because the distribution of the standard errors is unknown. In our study it was found that the (Pearson product–moment)

Table 9.8. *Overview of categorization C and skewness SK effects on assessment criteria (covariance matrices analyzed)*[a]

	Model 9.1		Model 9.2		Model 9.3		Model 9.4	
Assessment criterion	C	SK	C	SK	C	SK	C	SK
1. Convergence problems	0	0	0	0	0	0	0	0
2. Improper solutions	0	*	0	0	0	0	0	0
3. Bias of $\hat{\omega}_{ij}$	0	0	0	0	0	0	0	0
4. Bias of $se_{\hat{\omega}_{ij}}$	0	0	0	0	0	0	0	0
5. Variance of ω_{ij} or ω_{ij}^*	0	*	*	**	*	***	**	**
6. Confidence intervals for $\hat{\omega}_i$	0	*	0	***	*	***	*	*
7. Normality test for $\hat{\omega}_{ij}$	0	0	*	*	0	***	*	*
8. Correlations $\rho(\hat{\omega}_{ij}, \hat{\omega}_{i'j})$	0	*	*	**	***	***	***	***
9. Correlations $\rho(\hat{\omega}_{ij}, se_{\hat{\omega}_{ij}})$	0	0	0	0	***	***	***	***
10. Chi-square goodness-of-fit	0	0	*	***	0	***	0	0

[a] Effects: zero or minor (0), small (*), moderate (**), and strong (***). $N = 400$.

correlations between parameter estimates and their standard errors $\rho(\hat{\omega}_{ij}, se_{\hat{\omega}_{ij}})$ vary substantially with sample size and that they appear to converge toward some unknown value as sample size increases.

E. Conclusions

The results of the small-sample study lead to the qualitative conclusion that maximum likelihood estimation with LISREL is robust against small samples if $N \geqslant 200$. Depending on the model under study it might even be robust for $N \geqslant 100$. In general, samples of a size smaller than 100 have clear effects on parameter estimates, on approximate confidence intervals, and on estimates for goodness-of-fit.

Table 9.9. *Standard deviation of standardized parameter estimates (covariance matrices analyzed)[a]*

Parameter	Normal case	Nonnormal case degree of skewness				Population value of ω_i
		SK0	SK1	SK2	SK3	
λ_1	.01	−0.04	0.00	−0.01	0.32	0.60
λ_2	.06	−0.16	−0.08	0.11	0.73	0.60
λ_3	.06	−0.07	−0.01	0.08	0.50	0.80
λ_4	.06	−0.37	−0.33	−0.29	−0.13	0.80
λ_5	.02	−0.01	0.18	0.53	1.52	0.60
λ_6	.04	−0.14	−0.15	−0.08	0.00	0.60
λ_7	.01	−0.12	0.05	0.39	1.74	0.80
λ_8	.00	−0.41	−0.24	0.13	0.89	0.80
ϕ	.00	0.04	0.10	0.16	0.39	0.30
θ_1	.05	−0.03	0.04	0.03	0.36	0.64
θ_2	.02	−0.03	0.02	0.10	0.59	0.64
θ_3	−.02	0.02	0.09	0.17	0.53	0.36
θ_4	.08	0.09	0.16	0.20	0.46	0.36
θ_5	.01	−0.04	0.11	0.63	1.95	0.64
θ_6	.02	0.00	0.03	0.23	0.59	0.64
θ_7	−.01	−0.02	0.21	0.57	1.33	0.36
θ_8	.02	0.01	0.20	0.49	2.50	0.36

[a] The observed standard deviation of $\omega_{ij}^* = (\hat{\omega}_{ij} - \omega_i)/se_{\hat{\omega}_{ij}}$, minus the expected (theoretical) value of 1. A value of 0.00 thus indicates no bias, whereas a positive value indicates an underestimate and a negative value an overestimate of the expected value of the standard deviation of ω_{ij}^*. Model 9.3; $NR = 300$; $N = 400$.

4. Robustness against nonnormality

Table 9.8 gives an overview of the effects of nonnormality for each of the four main models discussed in section 1, all with $N = 400$. The overview is meant to be a rough quantification of the results. Because differences in findings across models may be due either to dissimilarities in the model structures or to differences in the degree of deviation from univariate normality among the variables within those models, or both, Table 9.8 should be interpreted with care.

A. Bias and variance

No substantial bias in estimates of parameters or their standard errors was found. This implies that *on average*, across repeated sampling, the user of

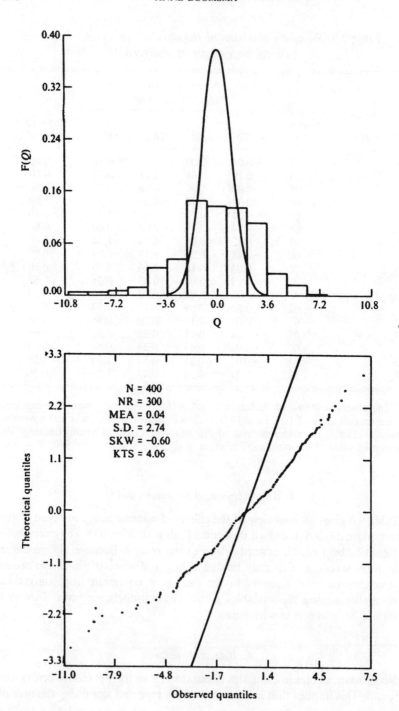

LISREL is not too far off from the population values when univariate distributions are of the form investigated here.

However, the standard deviation of these parameter estimates across the 300 replications is not what would be expected on theoretical grounds. The observed values may be either too small (mainly for variations with zero or small skewnesses) or too large (variations with moderate and large skewnesses). Here, small categorization and moderate to strong skewness effects were observed. This finding also applies to the empirical standard deviation of the standardized parameter estimates, defined as $\omega_{ij}^* = (\hat{\omega}_{ij} - \omega_i)/se_{\hat{\omega}_{ij}}$. Results for Model 9.3 are presented in Table 9.9. Figure 9.3 shows the effect of the skewed univariate distributions in Model 9.3 on the variance of a standardized parameter: It does not behave as it should if normality assumptions were not violated. The histogram is "flatter" than it should be, indicating more large deviations from the mean than one would expect. As to the quantile–quantile (Q–Q) plot, if no distributional distortions occurred the empirical (dotted curve) and theoretical (straight line) distributions would coincide. Here, the Q–Q plot clearly shows that there are more parameter estimates in the left and right tails than expected. (For a more detailed discussion of Q–Q plots the reader is referred to Gnanadesikan 1977.)

These results on the variance of (standardized) parameter estimates are of practical importance. An enlarged variance of an almost unbiased parameter estimate implies that its mean square error is overestimated; it is underestimated when the estimated variance is too small. In practice, this means that in a single sample the estimated parameters may be either too far away from their expected values or too close to them. Because estimates are often correlated, this result may hold for several parameters in the same model. Such findings support the general proposition that the cross validation of statistical inferences is an important aspect of any research methodology that employs structural modeling methods.

Figure 9.3 (*facing page*). Histogram (upper) and corresponding Q–Q plot (lower) of the standardized parameter estimate λ_7. The plotted curve in the upper graph is the standard normal density function. In the lower graph this normal distribution is drawn as a cumulative distribution (straight line); the dotted graph represents the cumulative distribution of the parameter estimates across all 300 replications. Model 9.3; nonnormal variation SK3. N denotes sample size; NR, number of replications; MEA, S.D., SKW, and KUR indicate the mean, standard deviation, skewness, and kurtosis, respectively, of the standardized parameter estimates across 300 replications.

Table 9.10. *Results from approximate 95% confidence intervals for parameters (covariance matrices analyzed)*[a]

Parameter	Normal case	Nonnormal case degree of skewness				Population value of ω_i
		SK0	SK1	SK2	SK3	
λ_1	0%	2%	2%	0%	−9%	0.60
λ_2	−2	4	1	−2	−20	0.60
λ_3	−1	1	−1	−3	−14	0.80
λ_4	−1	5	5	4	2	0.80
λ_5	0	−1	−5	−16	−35	0.60
λ_6	−1	3	3	2	0	0.60
λ_7	1	4	−2	−10	−41	0.80
λ_8	0	5	4	−3	−25	0.80
ϕ	−1	−1	−3	−5	−11	0.30
θ_1	−1	1	−1	0	−10	0.64
θ_2	−1	1	−2	−4	−17	0.64
θ_3	−1	1	2	−5	−15	0.36
θ_4	0	−4	−2	−7	−11	0.36
θ_5	0	2	−3	−18	−45	0.64
θ_6	−1	1	0	−7	−16	0.64
θ_7	0	0	−5	−16	−34	0.36
θ_8	0	0	−5	−13	−40	0.36

[a] The percentage across 300 replications in which the population value ω_i is included in the estimated interval $\hat{\omega}_{ij} \pm 1.96se_{\hat{\omega}_{ij}}$, minus the expected 95%. A positive value indicates that the population value is included in the estimated 95% confidence interval too often; a negative value indicates that it is excluded too often. Model 9.3; $N = 400$.

B. Confidence intervals for parameters

As discussed in the previous section, the effect of an increased or decreased variance on the approximate 95 percent confidence interval for parameters, $\hat{\omega}_{ij} \pm 1.96se_{\hat{\omega}_{ij}}$ (see also Section 2B), is substantial. The population value ω_i will be included in such intervals either too infrequently or too often. The effect of skewness is particularly strong, whereas the categorization effect is less clear. These effects are illustrated in Table 9.10, where it is evident that for Model 3, with the largest degrees of skewness, the width of the confidence intervals is severely overestimated.

If researchers employ such confidence intervals regularly in covariance modeling, they should be careful not to overinterpret them when data are substantially skewed. The findings above imply that the researcher would conclude that the parameters fall within given intervals more often than

Table 9.11. *Characteristics of the sampling distribution of the chi-square statistics for goodness-of-fit*[a]

(a) Observed minus expected values of statistics from the chi-square sampling distribution with 19 degrees of freedom

	Observed minus expected value				
	Mean	S.D.	Skewness	Kurtosis	% $\chi^2_{19} < 30.1$[b]
Normal case	0.4	0.5	0.3	1.2	0
Nonnormal case[c]					
SK0	0.6	0.5	−0.0	−0.2	3
SK1	1.3	0.5	0.4	1.0	4
SK2	4.9	1.4	0.1	0.5	14
SK3	15.4	6.1	0.1	0.1	49

(b) Expected values of statistics from the chi-square distribution with 19 degrees of freedom and the standard error of their observed values, given NR = 300

	Mean	S.D	Skewness	Kurtosis	% $\chi^2_{19} < 30.1$
Expected value	19.0	6.2	0.6	3.6	5
Standard error of observed value; $NR = 300$	0.4	0.3	0.2	0.8	1

[a] Model 3; $NR = 300$; $N = 400$.
[b] The value 30.1 is the theoretical 95th quantile of the distribution.
[c] SK0 through SK3 indicate the degree of skewness; see Table 9.2.

they should. The researcher is urged to be aware of the uniqueness of a one-sample result and to be very careful about generalizing to population values when the data are clearly nonnormally distributed.

C. Estimating goodness-of-fit

With the chi-square statistic for goodness-of-fit we are dealing with one outcome per replication; hence, its robustness can be summarized more easily in quantitative terms. From Table 9.8 (line 10) it is evident that a minor effect of categorization was found. For models with only a moderate degree of skewness in variable distributions (Models 1 and 4, where the median absolute value of skewness for the k observed variables is ≤ 1.25 and ≤ 1.13, respectively) there were only minor deviations from the asymptotic theory. However, in Models 9.2 and 9.3, which contain

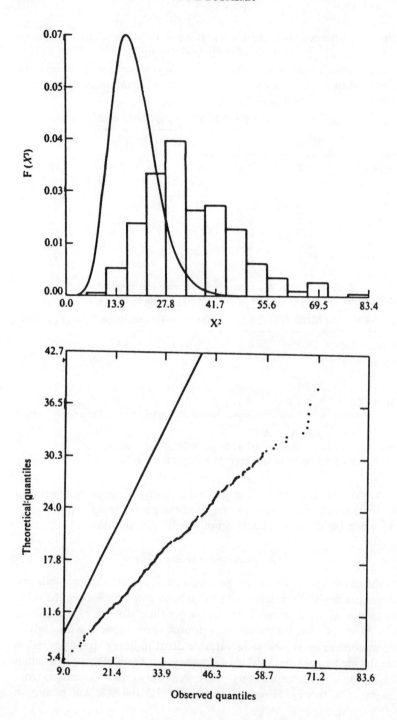

variables of more extreme skewness (in nonsymmetric variations, median absolute skewness ≥ 1.25; see Table 9.1), there was evidence that the goodness-of-fit of the population model would be rejected too often if we relied solely on assessing it against the chi-square distribution.

The results for Model 9.3 are summarized in Table 9.11, and the effects for skewness variation SK3 are illustrated in Figure 9.4. We conclude that the chi-square statistic is a poor guide for testing the hypothesis that a particular model is the population model when the observed variables have long-tailed, skewed distributions.

D. Other effects of nonnormality

(i) Convergence problems and improper solutions. With a sample size of 400 the models with discrete and skewed variables did not encounter convergence problems. Also, only a few occurrences of negative estimates of variances were found (Model 9.1).

(ii) Normality test for standardized parameter estimates. The distribution of standardized parameter estimates ω_{ij}^* was inspected by a *scale-invariant test* proposed by Shapiro and Francia (1972). In our study it was generally found that the shape of this distribution was not dramatically different from a normal distribution, although a strong skewness effect for Model 9.3 was detected (see Table 9.8, line 7). Few systematic changes were detected across different degrees of nonnormality. It should be noted that, although we reported earlier that the standard deviation of parameter estimates gave incorrect confidence intervals, we now find that the distributions of the standardized parameter estimates do not depart significantly from normality. This is not a contradiction of the earlier finding: Standardized parameter estimates are expected to have a standard normal distribution; however, for skewed data the variances of these distributions are often too large, though their shape is still approximately normal. Apart from a few very small values in the left tail of the observed sampling distribution, this is also indicated by Figure 9.3.

(iii) Correlations among estimates. Table 9.8 summarizes the effect of categorization and skewness on the product–moment correlations among parameter estimates (line 8) and on the correlations between parameter

Figure 9.4 (*facing page*). Histogram (upper) and corresponding Q–Q plot (lower) of the chi-square estimate for goodness-of-fit. The plotted curve in the upper graph is the chi-square density function with 19 degrees of freedom. In the lower graph this chi-square distribution is drawn as a cumulative distribution (straight line); the dotted graph represents the cumulative distribution of the estimated model fit across all 300 replications. Model 9.3; nonnormal variation SK3. N denotes sample size; NR, number of replications; d.f., degrees of freedom.

estimates and their corresponding standard errors (line 9). Both sets of estimates are substantially affected by nonnormality.

The findings suggest that, under conditions of nonnormality, the advice given earlier that inspection of estimated correlations among parameters be a standard rather than an optional practice, has to be followed cautiously.

E. Conclusions

On the basis of all the nonnormality findings, our general qualitative conclusion is that maximum likelihood estimation with LISREL is rather robust against the categorization of symmetrically distributed observed variables with normal kurtosis, but not against skewed (kurtotic) distributions of those variables. More specifically, we do not recommend that this estimation procedure be used when the median (or mean) absolute skewness of the observed variables is larger than 1.0 (approximately), because it can be expected to affect crucial elements of statistical estimation and testing.

5. Discussion

One of the goals of science is to offer *stable explanations* for the relations among empirical phenomena, with the ultimate aim of generalization and prediction of results in future samples from the same domain of interest. In line with this position we suggest that the estimation of structural equation models by maximum likelihood methods be used only when sample sizes are at least 200. Studies based on samples smaller than 100 may well lead to false inferences, and the models then have a high probability of encountering problems of convergence and improper solutions. The validity of findings based on small samples should always be investigated by replication of the work.

In dealing with the effect of nonnormality, we emphasized the effect of skewness because of the design of the study. In Section 2E, it was stressed that skewness and kurtosis are linked: High skewness is always accompanied by high kurtosis (see, e.g., Figure 9.2). Therefore, it is difficult to decide whether a distortion of distributional properties of the statistics under consideration is due to skewness or to kurtosis. Asymptotic theory (Browne 1982) shows, however, that the effect of kurtosis on the chi-square likelihood ratio test statistic is $O(N^{-1})$, whereas the effect of skewness is $o(N^{-1})$. This at least suggests that the effect of kurtosis is more important than that of skewness, though it does not imply that skewness is unimportant. The conclusions regarding symmetric distributions in the preceding section are based on our findings that for the models under study kurtosis had no effect in symmetric distributions. (For these distributions the kurtosis was in the range 0.00–2.67.) The effects of kurtosis outside this range, in the absence of skewness, must be investigated further. It can be expected that distortions will increase with kurtosis. The class of elliptical distributions serves as an example of symmetric distributions that distort the distribution of the normal theory likelihood ratio test statistic and lead to incorrect estimates of standard errors for parameter estimators, purely because of kurtosis (Browne 1982, 1984). It seems plausible that distributions of variables that are both skew and kurtotic will result in greater distortions of the distributions of parameter estimates and of the chi-square test statistic than will distributions with no skewness but high kurtosis. Given these considerations, it is recommended that in practice one always examine *both* skewness and kurtosis before deciding whether it seems appropriate to apply normal theory procedures.

In discussing the effects of skewness we have employed the median absolute value of skewnesses as an indicator of the degree of nonnormality in a model, although we do not consider it to be the one and only guideline in deciding to what extent departures from normality might affect the inferences. For example, one or two extremely skewed variables among several other variables having symmetric distributions may well lead to nonrobust results.

The present study has considered skewed, discrete variables with two to seven categories. It is plausible that maximum likelihood estimation is also robust when variables have nonsymmetric but continuous distributions, provided that the degree of skewness is approximately the same as or smaller than that studied for Models 9.2 and 9.3.

With the latest versions of LISREL one can compute polychoric (including tetrachoric) and polyserial correlations from the raw data and analyze matrices of such sample correlations (see Olsson 1979b; Olsson, Drasgow, & Dorans 1982). In principle, one can thus handle discrete (ordinal) variables as well as continuous variables together. (Some of the effects found in this study when analyzing correlation matrices might also apply when these approaches are used, since they are correlations rather than covariances.) The latent variable analysis of dichotomous, ordered categorical, and continuous indicators with a generalized least squares procedure, as developed by Muthén (1983, 1984), also employs polychoric and polyserial correlations. The use of both types of correlation coefficients assumes that the observed variables are discrete (ordered) realizations of latent variables that have *normal distributions*. In using these methods the researcher must consider how realistic such assumptions might be for the variables to be analyzed. At the same time more research is needed to determine the effect of analyzing polychoric and polyserial correlations rather than analyzing raw covariance matrices.

Since stronger deviations from the asymptotic theory were found when the observed variables had extreme skewnesses, we must consider what the researcher might do in practice with such distributions. Before that, one could ask how often such nonnormal distributions are encountered. Bradley (1977) mentions some examples of long-tailed, skewed distributions in the behavioral sciences and makes a general plea to study the robustness of "nonfamiliar" distribution shapes. In four empirical data sets from the social sciences, Boomsma (1983, chap. 5) found that the degree of skewness was quite moderate and that kurtosis most often was in the range 0.5–3.5.

However, the common practice of regrouping discrete categories with few observations undoubtedly gives the impression that skew distributions occur less often than they actually do. After such regrouping and recoding, discrete variables have fewer categories and are usually more symmetrically distributed. Whether such procedures should be used routinely can be questioned. The researcher might be tempted to transform discrete or continuous variables to approximately symmetric distributions. From our Monte Carlo results it is clear that such procedures would reduce the effects of skewness and would thus give statistical estimates that were "closer to theory" than those obtained in a situation where no transformations were employed. But is it possible to talk of the same theoretical domain of a variable before and after transforming it? And is it methodologically acceptable to transform the data after inspection of the observations in the sample? One prediction can be safely made: The sample covariances of the transformed variables will differ from the covariances of the untransformed variables. Given the same theoretical model under study, the researcher should consider the possibility that the transformed variables could lead to inferences different than those obtained from the raw variables.

We have two general recommendations. First, given the results of our robustness study, the researcher should avoid analyzing covariance structures by maximum likelihood methods when observed variables are both discrete and strongly skewed. Second, rather than performing transformations it might be useful to develop instruments of measurement that have attractive distributional properties and are linked directly to a substantive theory of what they are intended to measure.

References

Anderson, J. C., & Gerbing, D. W. (1984). The effect of sampling error on convergence, improper solutions, and goodness-of-fit indices for maximum likelihood factor analysis. *Psychometrika, 49*, 155–73.

Boomsma, A. (1980). The robustness of LISREL against non-normality. In *COMPSTAT 1980, Proceedings in Computational Statistics*, M. M. Barritt & D. Wishart (Eds.), pp. 174–80. Vienna: Physica-Verlag.

(1982). The robustness of LISREL against small sample sizes in factor analysis models. In *Systems under Indirect Observation: Causality, Structure, Prediction*, K. G. Jöreskog & H. Wold (Eds.), Part 1, pp. 149–73. Amsterdam: North Holland.

(1983). *On the Robustness of LISREL (Maximum Likelihood Estimation) against Small Sample Size and Non-Normality*. Doctoral dissertation, University of Groningen.

(1985). Non-convergence, improper solutions, and starting values in LISREL maximum likelihood estimation. *Psychometrika, 50*, 229–42.

Bradley, J. V. (1977). A common situation conducive to bizarre distribution shapes. *American Statistician, 31*, 147–50.

Browne, M. W. (1982). Covariance structures. In *Topics in Applied Multivariate Analysis*, D. M. Hawkins (Ed.), pp. 72–141. Cambridge University Press.

(1984). Asymptotically distribution-free methods for the analysis of covariance structures. *British Journal of Mathematical and Statistical Psychology, 37*, 62–83.

Duncan, G. T., Haller, A. O., & Portes, A. (1968). Peer influences on aspirations: A reinterpretation. *American Journal of Sociology, 74*, 119–37.

Gnanadesikan, R. (1977). *Methods for Statistical Data Analysis of Multivariate Observations*, New York: Wiley.

International Mathematical and Statistical Libraries. (1982). *IMSL Library: Reference Manual*, Vol. 2, Edition 9. Houston, TX.

Jöreskog, K. G. (1970). A general method for analysis of covariance structures. *Biometrika, 57*, 239–51.

(1973) A general method for estimating a linear structural equation system. In *Structural Equation Models in the Social Sciences*, A. S. Goldberger & O. D. Duncan (Eds.), pp. 85–112. New York: Seminar Press.

(1978) Structural analysis of covariance and correlation matrices. *Psychometrika, 43*, 443–77.

(1982a). Analysis of covariance structures. (with discussion) *Scandinavian Journal of Statistics, 8*, 65–92.

(1982b). The LISREL approach to causal model-builduing in the social sciences. In *Systems under Indirect Observation: Causality, Structure, Prediction*, K. G. Jöreskog & H. Wold (Eds.), Part 1, pp. 81–99. Amsterdam: North Holland.

Jöreskog, K. G., & Sörbom, D. (1984). *LISREL VI: Analysis of Linear Structural Relationships by Maximum Likelihood, Instrumental Variables, and Least Squares Methods. User's Guide.* University of Uppsala, Department of Statistics.

Krane, W. R., & McDonald, R. P. (1978). Scale invariance and the factor analysis of correlation matrices. *British Journal of Mathematical and Statistical Psychology, 31*, 218–28.

Lawley, D. N., & Maxwell, A. E. (1971). *Factor Analysis as a Statistical Method*, 2nd ed. London: Butterworth.

Lee, S. Y. (1980). Estimation of covariance structure models with parameters subject to functional restraints. *Psychometrika, 45,* 309–24.

Muthén, B. (1983). Latent variable structural equation modeling with categorical data. *Journal of Econometrics, 22,* 43–65.

(1984) A general structural equation model with dichotomous, ordered categorical, and continuous latent variable indicators. *Psychometrika, 49,* 115–32.

Olsson, U. (1979a). On the robustness of factor analysis against crude classification of observations. *Multivariate Behavioral Research, 14,* 485–500.

(1979b). Maximum likelihood estimation of the polychoric correlation coefficient. *Psychometrika, 44,* 443–60.

Olsson, U., Drasgow, F., & Dorans, N. J. (1982). The polyserial correlation coefficient. *Psychometrika, 47,* 337–51.

Rindskopf, D. (1983). Parameterizing inequality constraints on unique variances in linear structural models. *Psychometrika, 48,* 73–83.

(1984) Using phantom and imaginary latent variables to parameterize constraints in linear structural models. *Psychometrika, 49,* 37–47.

Shapiro, S. S, & Francia, R. S. (1972). An approximate analysis of variance test for normality. *Journal of the American Statistical Association, 67,* 215–16.

Wheaton, B., Muthén, B., Alwin, D. F., & Summers, G. F. (1977). Assessing reliability and stability in panel models. In *Sociological Methodology 1977,* D. R. Heise (Ed.), pp. 84–136. San Francisco: Jossey-Bass.

10

An inquiry into the effects of outliers on estimates of a structural equation model of basic skills assessment

JOAN K. GALLINI AND JIM F. CASTEEL

Little is known about the behavior of LISREL estimates when distributions are contaminated by outlying observations. Monte Carlo approaches have typically been used to investigate the robustness of maximum likelihood techniques in factor analysis models (Fuller & Hemmerle 1966; Olsson 1979; Gallini & Mandeville 1984; Boomsma, Chapter 9 in this volume) or to examine departures from normality (Andrews, Gnanadesikan, & Warner 1973; Gnanadesikan 1977). Such studies have yielded important results concerning the robustness of maximum likelihood estimates under various conditions. However, the Monte Carlo approach is atypical of the situation faced by the practicing researcher dealing with a data set in which the "true" structure in the population is unknown.

In this chapter the influence of outliers on parameter estimates is addressed in a real data set. The LISREL model is examined using real data in which the relationships may be atypical owing to the influence of outliers. A robust estimation technique (Tukey 1960) is employed to identify outlying observations. The consequences for model fit in samples of variable sizes are examined when these outliers are removed from the sample. The major aim of the chapter is to provide the researcher with a practical strategy for the detection of outliers in the context of structural modeling and an indication of their effects on parameter estimates.

The model

In 1978 the South Carolina legislature established the Basic Skills Assessment Program (BSAP). The BSAP tests of reading and mathematics were field-tested in 1980 and administered statewide in the spring of 1981 (South Carolina Department of Education 1981). This study uses the first grade BSAP test data from 1981 matched with the students' 1980 "readiness" test scores on the Cognitive Skills Assessment Battery (CSAB; Boehm and Slater 1977) collected by the South Carolina Department of

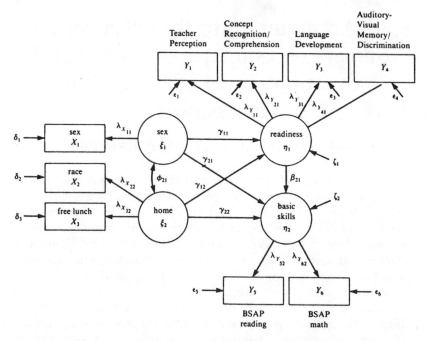

Figure 10.1. Structural equation model for the BSAP.

Education. Information on sex, race, and free-lunch status was also collected for all students.

A recursive structural equation model was formulated for the BSAP (Figure 10.1). The causal ordering of variables in the model was determined by their time ordering. Demographic variables were specified to be causally prior to achievement variables; variables measured in 1980 were specified to be causally prior to those measured in 1981.

The model consists of two exogenous latent constructs, "home" and "sex." The home construct has two indicators, "race" and "free-lunch status" (free-lunch status is interpreted as an indicator of socioeconomic status derived from eligibility for free, reduced, or full-cost school lunches). The two endogenous constructs are "readiness for first grade" and "basic skills acquired by the end of first grade." Readiness for first grade was measured by the CSAB. A previous factor analysis of the CSAB identified the four indicators shown in the model: "teacher perception" (ATSO), "concept recognition/comprehension" (CRC), "language development" (LD), and "auditory–visual memory/discrimination" (AVM) (Gallini and Mappus 1981). Basic skills were measured by the test of the South Carolina BSAP and had two indicators: "reading" and "math."

Table 10.1. *LISREL model specifications*

MO	NY = 6	NX = 3	NE = 2	NK = 2	
LX = FU, FI	LY = FU, FI	TD = DI, FR	TE = DI, FR		
PH = SY, FR	GA = FU, FR	BE = FU, FI	PS = DI, FR		
Free	LX (2, 2)	LY (2, 1)	LY (3, 1)	LY (4, 1)	LY (6, 2)	BE (2, 1)
Fixed	PH (1, 1)	TD (1, 1)			
VA 1.0	LX (3, 2)	LX (1, 1)	LY (1, 1)	LY (5, 2)	
VA .0	LX (2, 1)	LX (3, 1)	LX (1, 2)	LY (5, 1)	
VA .0	LY (6, 1)	LY (1, 2)	LY (2, 2)	LY (3, 2)	
VA .0	LY (4, 2)	BE (1, 1)	BE (2, 2)	BE (1, 2)	
VA .4	PH (1, 1)				
VA .05	TD (1, 1)				
ST .4	TD (2, 2)	TD (3, 3)			

Model specifications for the free and fixed elements are shown in Table 10.1 in LISREL notation (Jöreskog & Sörbom 1981).

Method

A random sample of 4,976 first graders in South Carolina comprised the total data set. Random samples of 100, 500, and 1,500 were selected for the structural equation analysis to examine the effects of different sample sizes. The smaller samples were nested within the total 4,976 but were selected so as to be independent of one another.

The data were then systematically trimmed by a method commonly used to "robustify" regression parameters so as to reduce the effects of outlying observations. Huynh (1982) compared four such techniques and found little practical differences among them; all four produced regression coefficients that were significantly different from the ordinary least squares solution but were not significantly different from one another. In addition, after the removal of observations identified by the robust techniques as outliers, the ordinary least squares regression on the remaining observations produced regression coefficients virtually identical to the robust estimates. This study used biweight estimates, a technique proposed by Tukey (1960; see Hogg 1979 for a list of references). The method divides regression residuals by a scale "d" (similar to σ in the normal error model), and the resulting x is multiplied by the function ψ, which is defined as

$$\psi(x) = x\{1 - (x/k)^2\}^2, \quad |x| \leqslant k$$
$$= 0, \quad |x| > k$$

where k is a tuning constant typically set at 5.0. An iterative weighted least

Table 10.2. *Comparison of regression estimates for math*

Estimate	Ols	Tukey
R^2	.362	.407
Intercept	12.357	13.210
1 (sex)	0.104	0.139
2 (race)	0.620	0.465
3 (free lunch)	0.190	0.184
4 (teacher)	0.031	0.058
5 (concept)	0.242	0.256
6 (language)	0.026	0.008
7 (memory)	0.191	0.147

Table 10.3. *Comparison of regression estimates for reading*

Estimate	Ols	Tukey
R^2	.439	.524
Intercept	.147	−2.334
1 (sex)	1.877	2.163
2 (race)	0.364	0.386
3 (free lunch)	0.971	0.840
4 (teacher)	0.043	0.031
5 (concept)	0.580	0.642
6 (language)	0.137	0.128
7 (memory)	0.233	0.260

squares process must be employed, and a program in Statistical Analysis Systems (1979; Casteel & Huynh 1982) was used. This process, based on the magnitude of the residuals from the robust regression line, results in weights in the range from 0 to 1, where 0 indicates an extreme outlier.

Regressions were run on the data set to compare ordinary least squares (Ols) and robust estimates. Two regression models were examined: (1) the regression of math on sex, race, free lunch, and the four factors of the CSAB; and (2) the regression of reading on the same set of variables. Tables 10.2 and 10.3 show the results of the regression comparing Ols and the robust estimates. For both math and reading the robust method produces an increase in the multiple correlation for the model.

Although any of a number of approaches might be used to reduce the effect of outlying observations in the robust regressions, simply removing the outliers has been shown to be essentially equivalent to other robustifying techniques (Huynh 1982). In order to heavily trim outliers from the comparison data for the purpose of this study (∼20% of the observations were removed) a .75 criterion weight was selected. Observations with weights less than .75 were assumed to be outliers and were removed from each sample. This process was completed independently for math and reading within the total sample and each of the subsamples, allowing each subsample to approximate its own robust regression parameters. Consequently, observations distant from either regression line, math or reading, were removed. For the total sample, this procedure removed 224 observations ($\sim 4.5\%$) due to reading alone, 425 observations ($\sim 8.5\%$) due to math alone, and another 290 observations ($\sim 5.8\%$) identified by both math and reading. This resulted in a new total sample size of 4,037 (19% trimmed), whereas the subsamples were independently reduced to sizes of 75 (25% trimmed), 405 (19% trimmed), and 1,189 (21% trimmed), respectively.

Figures 10.2 and 10.3 show the residuals plotted against the predicted values for both reading and math using the entire sample ($N = 4,976$). The vertical lines represent the approximate boundaries beyond which outliers were removed. This approach removes observations that may be improperly measured or perhaps come from another population but that are known to depart from a normal distribution around a multiple linear regression. Thus, only the magnitude of the residuals from the multiple regressions indicates outliers. It follows that observations that depart from the regression line are not necessarily the most extreme points in the distribution of the dependent variables, which, though large in absolute value, may be quite close to the regression line. The purpose of this chapter is to examine the robustness of parameter estimates in structural equation models when the data contain outliers.

Results

.The LISREL VI computer program was employed to estimate the structural equation model for each original data set and each "robustified" data set (with the outliers removed). Table 10.4 presents the chi-square tests for overall model fit. Whereas all the chi-squares are relatively large, the robustifying technique resulted in significantly reduced chi-squares in three of four cases. The chi-square fit statistic, however, is dependent on sample size. The goodness-of-fit index (GFI) and adjusted goodness-of-fit statistics (AGFI) (adjusted for degrees of freedom) are independent of sample size. These are shown in Table 10.5. The goodness-of-fit index is relatively high for both original and robust data sets of each size considered (ranging from .859 to .979). They suggest that the outliers did not have a major impact on the overall model fit; the differences between the goodness-of-fit for the original and robustified data sets ranged from .002 to .028. Table 10.5 also reports mean square residuals, another measure of overall model fit. This index takes its metric from

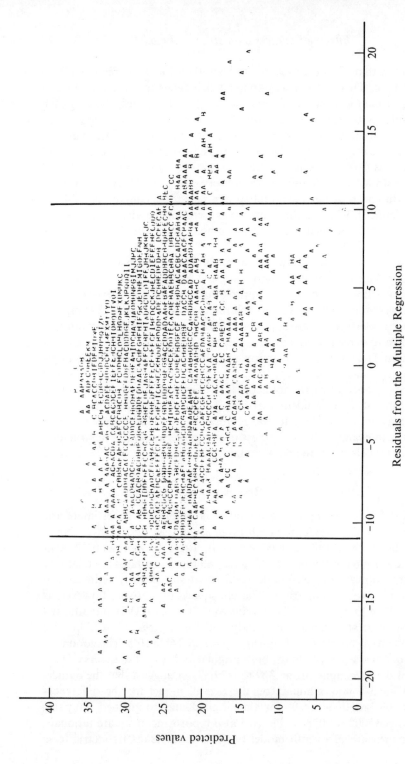

Figure 10.2. Residuals plotted against predicted values for reading regression with the entire sample ($N = 4,976$). The residual scatter plot for the robust regressions is represented between the parallel lines. A denotes one observation; B, two observations; etc. Note: 168 observations had missing values; 4 were hidden.

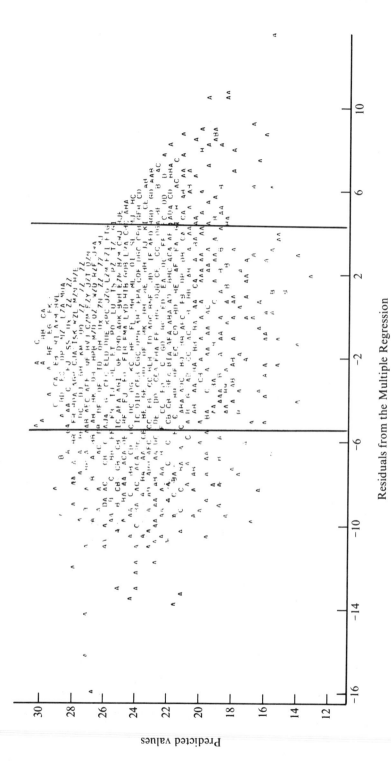

Figure 10.3. Residuals plotted against predicted values for math regression with the entire sample ($N = 4,976$). The residual scatter plot for the robust regressions is represented between the parallel lines. A denotes one observation; B, two observations; etc. Note: 166 observations had missing values; 214 were hidden.

Table 10.4. *Chi-square fit statistics for models*

Data set	Sample size	χ^2	d.f.	Difference
Original	100	77.25	22	−28.50
Robustified	75	48.75	22	
Original	500	64.10	22	−8.71
Robustified	405	55.39	22	
Original	1,500	140.04	22	−42.80
Robustified	1,189	97.24	21	
Original	4,976	550.63	22	−65.07
Robustified	4,037	485.56	22	

Table 10.5. *Goodness-of-fit and root mean square residuals for models*

Data sets	Sample size	d.f.	GFI	AGFI	Mean square residuals
Original	100	22	.859	.711	1.158
	500	22	.973	.945	0.471
	1,500	22	.979	.957	0.342
	4,976	22	.978	.955	0.429
Robustified	75	22	.887	.768	0.526
	405	22	.971	.940	0.377
	1,189	22	.974	.947	0.277
	4,037	22	.970	.938	0.375

comparing the observed variances and covariances; hence, it is not so useful for models comparing different data sets. All of the fit statistics could probably be improved by allowing for correlated errors in the model. However, the primary focus of this study is the bias in parameter estimates for a given model when estimated for data containing outliers. The correlated errors were omitted in order to keep the model relatively simple.

Further analysis involved an evaluation and comparison of the individual parameter estimates for the original versus the robust data sets. The LISREL estimates for the model are given in Table 10.6 and their respective standard errors in Table 10.7. A large decrease occurs from the original to the robustified data sets for the estimates of the equation residual variance (ψ_{22}) for the LISREL regressions of math achievement (η_2) on the other variables in the model. This reduction is expected as a direct result of removing error variance ($1 - \psi_{22}$) in the robustifying process.

Table 10.6. *LISREL parameter estimates for original and robust data sets*[a]

Parameter	N = 100 original	N = 75 robust	N = 500 original	N = 405 robust	N = 1,500 original	N = 1,189 robust	N = 4,976 original	N = 4,037 robust
λ^Y_{21}	3.424	3.109	2.663	2.316	2.401	2.386	2.316	2.426
λ^Y_{31}	2.210	1.343	1.454	1.296	1.412	1.401	1.388	1.370
λ^Y_{41}	3.679	2.453	2.773	2.576	2.399	2.306	2.326	2.326
λ^Y_{62}	0.480	0.378	0.538	0.455	0.482	0.431	0.490	0.436
λ^X_{11}	0.418	0.387	0.652	0.707	0.707	0.707	0.707	0.707
λ^X_{22}	0.453	0.540	0.461	0.493	0.413	0.405	0.412	0.394
β_{21}	4.194	3.000	3.001	2.894	2.943	3.140	2.676	3.155
γ_{11}	0.166	0.240	0.959	1.069	0.398	0.369	0.434	0.382
γ_{21}	1.340	3.085	1.072	0.936	0.213*	0.292*	0.747	0.565
γ_{12}	0.792	1.116	1.122	1.303	1.090	1.115	1.095	1.024
γ_{22}	0.230	1.442*	1.056	1.163	0.800	0.599	1.066	0.676
ϕ_{21}	0.040*	0.013*	0.998*	-0.017*	0.006*	0.005*	0.006*	0.007*
ϕ_{22}	0.729	0.630	0.564	0.548	0.702	0.716	0.679	0.710
ψ_{11}	0.828*	1.156	1.979	2.185	2.242	2.205	2.661	2.301
ψ_{22}	15.612	0.086*	12.011	2.736	12.294	1.736	14.926	3.400
θ^ε_{11}	7.694	5.618	5.982	6.085	5.946	5.756	5.984	5.890
θ^ε_{22}	8.218	6.002	12.157	11.473	9.689	8.873	10.542	8.553
θ^ε_{33}	7.342	7.585	9.556	8.920	9.311	9.906	9.361	9.735
θ^ε_{44}	9.893	9.640	11.160	9.754	11.378	10.634	11.803	11.661
θ^ε_{55}	15.587	10.261	17.627	17.361	13.512	11.291	13.510	12.647
θ^ε_{66}	4.221	2.961	5.702	3.086	5.207	2.832	5.918	3.258
θ^δ_{22}	0.101	0.066	0.130	0.117	0.130	0.133	0.135	0.140
θ^δ_{33}	0.171*	0.260	0.336	0.352	0.198	0.184	0.221	0.190

[a] Asterisk denotes parameters that are less than twice their standard error.

Table 10.7. Standard errors for the original and robust data set estimates

Parameter	$N = 100$ original	$N = 75$ robust	$N = 500$ original	$N = 405$ robust	$N = 1,500$ original	$N = 1,189$ robust	$N = 4,976$ original	$N = 4,037$ robust
λ^y_{21}	0.952	0.694	0.206	0.189	0.107	0.113	0.055	0.063
λ^y_{31}	0.641	0.372	0.130	0.124	0.074	0.080	0.038	0.044
λ^y_{41}	1.024	0.584	0.211	0.202	0.109	0.112	0.056	0.063
λ^y_{62}	0.060	0.048	0.027	0.023	0.014	0.012	0.008	0.007
λ^x_{11}	0.051	0.058	0.027	0.030	0.016	0.018	0.009	0.010
λ^x_{22}	0.078	0.084	0.053	0.054	0.025	0.026	0.015	0.015
β_{21}	1.335	0.799	0.291	0.271	0.156	0.160	0.077	0.090
γ_{11}	0.232	0.328	0.153	0.179	0.082	0.091	0.049	0.050
γ_{21}	1.142	0.895	0.480	0.429	0.241	0.201	0.139	0.118
γ_{12}	0.265	0.323	0.164	0.189	0.086	0.094	0.051	0.052
γ_{22}	0.954	0.887	0.472	0.436	0.227	0.191	0.131	0.109
ϕ_{21}	0.077	0.086	0.028	0.031	0.017	0.019	0.009	0.010
ϕ_{22}	0.166	0.160	0.080	0.080	0.049	0.054	0.028	0.032
ψ_{11}	0.463	0.546	0.316	0.372	0.201	0.216	0.125	0.124
ψ_{22}	4.821	2.716	1.932	1.345	1.128	0.698	0.689	0.441
θ^ε_{11}	1.125	0.966	0.406	0.460	0.237	0.252	0.133	0.141
θ^ε_{22}	1.722	1.744	1.061	1.012	0.515	0.487	0.305	0.270
θ^ε_{33}	1.222	1.325	0.673	0.681	0.400	0.438	0.214	0.235
θ^ε_{44}	2.034	1.776	1.046	0.983	0.565	0.539	0.328	0.321
θ^ε_{55}	4.539	2.867	1.976	1.704	1.058	0.744	0.632	0.466
θ^ε_{66}	1.094	0.589	0.954	0.328	0.289	0.159	0.181	0.101
θ^δ_{22}	0.026	0.025	0.015	0.016	0.008	0.008	0.005	0.005
θ^δ_{33}	0.111	0.089	0.064	0.060	0.038	0.040	0.022	0.025

No particular directional changes in the parameter estimates can be expected from a technique that simply reduces bias. However, for this set of data some patterns were detected when bias was reduced in the original data sets. As shown in Table 10.6, there are consistent but small decreases in the factor loadings of the indicators on the latent constructs (λ parameters) from the original to the robust data sets at each sample size. A similar pattern appears among the measurement error variances associated with those loadings (θ^ε and θ^δ parameters).

Further interpretation of the impact on LISREL estimates of removing outliers necessitates examination of the standard errors in Table 10.7. As would be expected from large-sample theory, the standard errors decrease as the sample size increases. The trend is consistent across the four original data sets as well as across the four robustified data sets. Although this observation is useful, it is not within the constraints of this study to examine further the effect of sample size. Rather, emphasis is given to the effect of the removal of outliers on improved estimates, that is, decreases in standard errors from the original to the robustified data sets.

If observations were randomly removed from a data set, the standard errors of the LISREL estimates would be expected to increase owing to the reduction in sample size. However, if the process of removing selected observations were not random but instead based on a procedure logically related to the specification of the model and intended to improve estimates, the standard errors would remain the same or decrease. Although the parameter estimates might change, robustification would be of little practical use if the standard errors remained the same, since this would indicate no improvement in the precision of estimated values. The standard errors reported in Table 10.7 show several trends. Of the 92 standard errors, 4 show no change, 45 decrease, and 43 increase when outlying observations are removed. Although the increases and decreases are almost evenly split, it must be noted that the average decrease is 0.216 whereas the average increase is only 0.017. In fact, overall there is an average decrease in the standard errors of the LISREL estimates of 0.098 when the sample is trimmed by removing outliers. Examining only changes greater than 0.01 in absolute value reveals 35 decreased standard errors and only 14 increased standard errors as the data sets are robustified; using a criterion of 10 percent change indicates 28 decreases and 21 increases in standard errors.

Another trend in the standard errors may be observed in the interaction between the sample size and the robustifying process. In small samples, which naturally have larger standard errors, the robustifying process has the greatest effect; the efficacy of removing outliers decreases as the sample size increases. In fact, the average decreases in the standard errors of the

LISREL estimates when the samples of 100, 500, 1,500, and 4,976 were robustified were 0.264, 0.068, 0.020, and 0.039, respectively.

Conclusions

This chapter demonstrates the effects of outliers on parameter estimates in a structural equation model using an empirical data set. The approach described here involved a series of multiple regressions and robust multiple regressions and the removal of outlying observations beyond a criterion point based on the robust regressions.

The results suggest that careful consideration should be given to robustifying elements in a sample matrix when the sample size is small, before estimating structural equation models. If outliers are suspected, whether due to improperly identified samples, incorrect measurement, data contamination, or other factors, some approach to reducing the effect of the outliers should be considered (Huber 1964, 1973).

The smaller effects found with the large data sets would presumably be even smaller if different techniques were used for robustifying the data. The method employed in this study removed a similar proportion of the data in all samples. The use of a method based strictly on the definition of outliers as influential observations would result in the removal of a smaller percentage of observations from large data sets and would thus reduce the effect.

As demonstrated by this study, an increase in R^2 due to robust regression provides initial evidence of outliers and may indicate whether data should be robustified before LISREL analysis. The determination of what constitutes a substantial change must be viewed in terms of the specific situation. For example, in the present study, the changes in R^2 may appear to be small in absolute value (from .362 to .407 and from .439 to .524); however, given the large sample size ($N = 4,976$) on which the robust techniques were based, these increases seem sufficiently substantial to warrant investigation. Such an increase in R^2 may indicate the need to robustify the data before the LISREL analysis. Consistent decreases in the standard errors of the estimates as shown in the LISREL results of this chapter provide further support for the utility of robustification of a given data set containing outliers. If there is a lack of initial evidence of outliers, the researcher should employ the original data set in the LISREL analysis.

As shown in this chapter, it is of greatest advantage to apply robust methods to small samples; in all instances the parameter estimates and their standard errors showed relatively larger decreases in the small data sets when outliers were removed. Indeed, with sample sizes larger than 500, robust methods probably produce only minimal changes and may be unnecessary; smaller samples, however, should be carefully examined for outliers. Such findings are of particular practical significance, because social science research typically employs small samples.

References

Andrews, D. F., Gnanadesikan, R., & Warner, J. L. (1973). Methods for assessing multivariate normality. In P. R. Krishnaiah (Ed.), *Multivariate analysis–III.* New York: Academic Press, 95–116.

Boehm, A. E., & Slater, B. R. (1977) *Cognitive Skills Assessment Battery teacher's manual.* New York: Columbia Teacher's College.

Casteel, J. F., & Huynh, H. (1982, March). *Robust regression using SAS.* Paper presented at the annual meeting of the American Educational Research Association, New York.

Fuller, E. L., Hemmerle, W. J. (1966). Robustness of the maximum-likelihood estimation procedure in factor analysis. *Psychometrika, 31,* 255–66.

Gallini, J., & Mandeville, G. (1984). Misspecification error in structural equation models: A Monte Carlo approach. *Journal of Experimental Education, 53*(1), 9–19.

Gallini, J., & Mappus, L. (1981). *A correlation study of teachers' observations of first graders' behavior during testing and readiness/basic skills performance: Preliminary results.* Paper presented at the Third Annual USC Conference on Educational Issues and Research, Columbia, South Carolina.

Gnanadesikan, R. (1977). *Methods of statistical data analysis of multivariate observations.* New York: Wiley.

Hogg, R. V. (1979). Statistical robustness: One view of its use in application today. *American Statistician, 33,* 108–15.

Huber, P. J. (1964). Robust estimation of a location parameter. *Annals of Mathematical Statistics, 35,* 73–101.

(1973). Robust regression: Asymptotics, conjecture, and Monte Carlo. *Annals of Statistics, 1,* 799–821.

Huynh, H. (1982). A comparison of four approaches to robust regression. *Psychological Bulletin, 92,* 505–12.

Jöreskog, K. G., & Sörbom, D. (1981). *LISREL VI: A general computer program for estimating a linear structural equation system.* Chicago: International Educational Resources.

Olsson, U. (1979). On the robustness of factor analysis against crude classification of the observations. *Multivariate Behavioral Research, 14,* 485–500.

Statistical Analysis Systems Institute. (1979). *SAS user's guide.* Raleigh, NC.

South Carolina Department of Education. (1981). *Basic skills assessment program: Reading and math tests.* Columbia, SC.

Tukey, J. W. (1960). A survey of sampling from contaminated distributions. In I. Olkin (Ed.), *Contributions to probability and statistics.* Stanford, CA: Stanford University Press, 299–308.

11

Testing structural equation models

W. E. SARIS, J. DEN RONDEN, AND A. SATORRA

Introduction

An important use of structural modeling is the testing of theories. The plausibility of hypotheses concerning causal mechanisms depends on the empirical support they receive from data. Thus, any technique that analyzes causal structures should include a means of assessing the disagreement between the model and the data. However, even when a test of the agreement between the data and the theoretical model is available, we also require a means of assessing the probability that the results are due to characteristics of the research design itself. There must be a reasonable chance of rejecting incorrect theories independently of the research design. The probability of rejecting an incorrect model is referred to as the "power of the test." Structural modeling provides estimates of the model parameters and a formal test for deciding whether a theory should be rejected, given the data. However, the standard use of the likelihood ratio test statistic is not without problems. In the case of a large sample, the test very often leads to rejection, whereas in the case of a small sample the test rarely leads to the rejection of the model. Other indices of model fit have been suggested (Wheaton et al. 1977; Bentler & Bonnet 1980; Fornell & Larcker 1981; Hoelter 1983) that take into account the impact of the sample size on the test; however, the efficacy of all of these indices depends on the power of the test. Satorra and Saris (1982a,b) have developed a procedure to determine the power of the likelihood ratio test in structural models. Given the knowledge of its power for a particular model, a criterion for the evaluation of structural equation models that takes Type I and Type II errors into account can be formulated.

This chapter discusses the following:

1. problems that arise when the fit of structural equation models is not formally assessed,
2. problems associated with the likelihood ratio test statistic when a specific significance level (conventionally .05) is used,
3. problems of alternative testing procedures, and
4. a procedure for testing the fit of models that takes account of the power of the test.

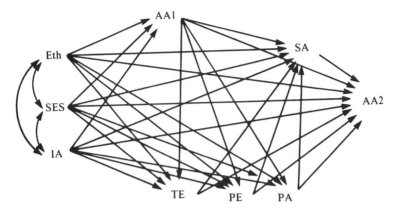

Figure 11.1. Clifton's model. Eth, Ethnicity (grade 9); SES, Socioeconomic Status (gr. 9); IA, Intellectual Ability; AA1, Academic Achievement (gr. 9); TE Teachers' Expectations (gr. 10); PE, Parenting Expectations (gr. 10); PA, Peer Aspirations (gr. 10); SA, Student Aspirations (gr. 10); AA2, Academic Achievement (gr. 11).

These issues are illustrated by a secondary analysis of data from articles published during the period 1979–82. Fifteen articles that report the use of path analysis and 24 that report LISREL analysis were selected for study. For the 15 studies that apply path analysis we illustrate the problems of the path analytic approach by focusing on the way the data were analyzed. For the 24 LISREL applications, we report and examine the means by which the researcher tried to overcome the problems associated with the likelihood ratio test statistic. Finally, we illustrate an alternative testing procedure.

Implications of failing to test the fit of a model

The standard practice of applying structural modeling methods is illustrated by the example in Figure 11.1, taken from Clifton (1981). The coefficients of the model were estimated by ordinary least squares regression. This analysis is not a sufficient means of evaluating the nonsaturated model postulated, because there are no criteria by which to decide whether the model actually does or does not fit the data. In this model some of the effects among intervening variables are hypothesized to be zero, but no tests of these hypotheses were undertaken in the original path analysis. This is a serious methodological omission, because it means that there is no evaluation of the fit of the model to the data. The relaxing of parameters formally constrained to zero may result in changes in the values of the other parameters if the hypothesized model is misspecified. For instance, it seems plausible to argue not only that Parental Expectations (PE) are determined by background variables but that they are partly dependent on Teachers' Expectations (TE). When this relationship is included in the model, not only is the direct effect of Teachers' Expectations on Parental Expectations statistically significant, but the change is accompanied by a substantial reduction in the direct effect of Academic Achievement (AAI) on Parental Expectations and of Socio-economic Status (SES) on Parental Expectations. Thus, the interpretation of the results in models that do not formally test the fit of the model against the data is suspect.

Problems with the .05 significance level

The general LISREL procedure provides a likelihood ratio test statistic for assessing the agreement between the hypothesized causal structure and the data, and this can be routinely used to test the fit of models. This test statistic is based on a comparison of the value of the likelihood function for the estimated model with that of a fully saturated model. The fully saturated model (zero degrees of freedom) has a perfect fit and therefore represents the minimum value possible for the likelihood function. If the ratio of these values is represented by R, the test statistic $(T = -2 \log R)$ has a chi-square distribution. However, this is true only if the model is correct, the observed variables are normally distributed, and the sample is large.[1] The following decision rule is used for a test at the α level of significance. If $t^{d.f.} < C(\alpha)$ the model is rejected, where t denotes the observed value of the test statistic T, d.f. the number of degrees of freedom, which is equal to the number of overidentifying restrictions, and $C(\alpha)$ the value for which $P(t > C) = \alpha$. This value $C(\alpha)$ is obtained from a table for the chi-square distribution. We applied this test to the path analysis models that we examined to evaluate their fit to the data.

Table 11.1 shows that, in general, the models tested on a small data set were accepted, whereas those tested on a large data set were rejected. In total, 17 of the 29 models analyzed were rejected as having an unacceptable fit at $\alpha \leqslant .05$. Immediately we see one of the problems associated with the use of the LISREL test statistic for assessing the fit of the model: It is difficult to know whether the fit is due to the hypothesized structure or to the sample size in small samples.

Alternative testing procedures used in practice

An awareness of this problem has led users of the LISREL program to employ alternative procedures for deciding whether a model is tenable.

Table 11.1. *"Fit" of path models published in journals, 1979–82*

Author	N	t	d.f.	Decision[a]
Rosa & Maswe (1980)	15	0.7	1	A
	15	2.6	3	A
	18	1.6	6	A
	18	1.8	6	A
Morgan & Fitzgerald (1980)	17	1.1	2	A
	17	19.3	6	R
	20	1.5	2	A
	20	2.9	4	A
Messner (1983)	50	5.1	3	A
Ammerman (1980)	72	4.6	6	A
Rosenstein (1981)	125	6.5	5	A
	209	4.5	5	A
Perkins & Fawlkes (1980)	286	35.1	8	R
	286	32.1	8	R
Clifton (1981)	315	316.1	3	R
	579	345.3	3	R
Shover, Norland, & Thornton (1979)	394	53.8	8	R
	394	45.0	7	R
	492	91.5	7	R
	492	90.5	7	R
Spitze & Spaeth (1979)	411	138.5	17	R
Ross & Duff (1983)	422	64.7	18	R
Baldassare & Protask (1982)	604	218.2	21	R
Speare Korbrin, & Kingskade (1983)	808	12.8	10	A
Robinson & Kelley (1979)	1,120	21.9	7	R
Strickland (1982)	2,414	545.2	16	R
Hanks (1982)	10,245	1,155.0	7	R
	10,245	1,155.1	7	R
	10,245	153.7	6	R

[a] A, accept; R, reject.

When we examined the 24 LISREL applications selected from the literature, we found that the most frequently used procedure for assessing the fit of a model was the ratio of the value of the test statistic to the degrees of freedom in the model. This index was used in half of the studies examined, sometimes in combination with other decision criteria.[2] A second procedure for assessing the fit of a model is to compare nested models[3] using the test statistic D, which is the difference between t_1 and t_2, where t_1 refers to a more restricted model than t_2. Four of the studies used this procedure.

In our view, these procedures are not very helpful. The first procedure was suggested by Wheaton et al. (1977) to deal with the effect of large sample size on the test statistic, and on the basis of their experience from inspecting the sizes of the residuals that accompany variable chi-square values, they suggested that a ratio of around 5 was reasonable when the sample size is about 1,000. The main effect of this rule of thumb is to increase the probability of accepting a model because the critical (cut off) point in the chi-square distribution then corresponds not to the .05 significance level, but to some lower significance level. For example, with d.f. = 10 and a ratio of the chi-square statistic T to the degrees of freedom equal to 5, the significance level is .027 $\times$ 10^{-5}, which is considerably smaller than .05. The $R = 5$ criterion thus corresponds to a probability for the chi-square statistic somewhat below $\alpha = .05$. The power of the test will be reduced by this shift in the significance level; although it may still be acceptable, there is no guarantee of this. Furthermore, $R = 5$ is a rather arbitrary criterion, as can be seen from the various statements about the criterion for rejection. Miller and Conaty (1982) state, "[F]or a sample of given size, the lower the chi-square per degree of freedom the better the model fits the data" without reference to a specific quantity, but Dalton (1981) suggests that "... a 10:1 ratio of chi-square to degrees of freedom is often considered as a good fit." Matsueda (1982) stated that "... the chi-square is over 4 times the degrees of freedom indicating a poor fit" (sample size = 1,140).

The utility of the procedure for comparing the fit of nested models is also limited, because the impact of sample size is again not neutralized. When the sample size is small, a restriction of any parameter in an unrestricted model will in general be tenable. This can occur even when a large effect is set equal to zero. On the other hand, when the sample size is large, restricting a parameter, even one that has a small value, is quite likely to yield a significant increase in the test statistic. Obviously, the main weakness of these procedures is that the issue of the power of the test is not adequately considered. Satorra and Saris (1982a,b) have developed a procedure to evaluate the power of such tests in the context of LISREL modeling. The main idea behind this procedure is explained in the next section and applied in a subsequent section.

The power of a test of the model

Figures 11.2a and 11.2b present two different situations. In both figures the curve on the left is the distribution of the test statistic when the model is correct, with nine degrees of freedom. The curve to the right is the distribution of the test statistic when the model is incorrect. In Figure 11.2 this distribution deviates considerably from the distribution for the correct model, whereas in Figure 11.3 the distributions are approximately the same.

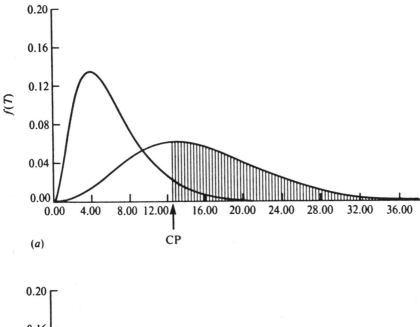

(a)

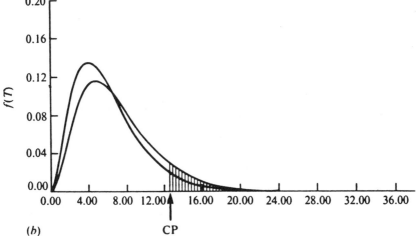

(b)

Figure 11.2. (a) Distribution of the test statistic for a correct model (left curve) and an incorrect model (right curve), which differ considerably.
(b) Distribution of the test statistic for a correct model (left curve) and an incorrect model (right curve), with differ little. In both graphs, T is the test statistic; CP, the criterion point. Shaded area is the probability of the modeling rejected if the model is incorrect.

If Figure 11.2a is the correct description of the situation and we test at the .05 significance level, the test will lead to rejection in nearly all samples, because the test statistic will almost always be larger than the critical value at the .05 level (16.9 for d.f. = 9). If the shift in distribution presented in Figure 11.2 is due to a substantial misspecification in the model, the test would be very useful. However, if the misspecification is minor – for example, if a standardized coefficient is not zero, as assumed but .01 – this test would be very unattractive. In the case of a minor misspecification we do not necessarily want to reject the model. However, if Figure 11.2b presents the correct situation, the opposite problem arises. When the specification error is very small the test used is acceptable, but when the error is large the test is not acceptable, because it does not detect serious misspecification. It would reject clearly incorrect models almost as often as the correct model.

Both cases illustrate the importance of knowledge about the probability that an incorrect model will be rejected, in other words the power of the test. Satorra and Saris (1982a,b) have developed a procedure to determine the power of the test based on the result that the distribution of the test statistic in the case of an incorrect model approaches the noncentral chi-square distribution with a noncentrality parameter λ. This noncentrality parameter specifies how far the distribution shifts to the right and can be computed routinely using the LISREL program.[4] As an illustration, it is instructive to examine the computation of the power of the test for some of the path models discussed earlier. Table 11.2 shows the probability of rejecting the model at the .05 significance level when it is compared with the alternative model in which one of the relationships originally specified to be zero is .1, .2, .3, .4, .5, respectively, in the population.

This table clearly gives an explanation for the results reported in Table 11.1. When the sample size is small, the probability of rejecting the model is small, even if there is a moderately large specification error. When the sample size is large, however, the test statistic is particularly sensitive to small specification errors, and the model is rejected most of the time. But the sample size is not the only determinant of the power of the test. The values of the other parameters of the model are also important. Therefore, it is not enough to correct the .05 level test for the effect of sample size alone (Bentler & Bonett 1980; Hoelter 1983). It is more appropriate to take account of the power of the test directly, as discussed below. Speaking of the power of the test is in fact a simplification, because the power of the test differs according to the size of the specification error, the value of the model parameters, and the sample size. Nevertheless, we use the expression "the power of the test" to indicate the sensitivity of the test in a particular situation for specification errors of specified size.

Table 11.2. *Power of path models at the .05 significance level*

Author	N	Power[a]				
		(0.1)	(0.2)	(0.3)	(0.4)	(0.5)
Rosa & Masure (1980)	15	.07	.15	.30	.55	.75
Morgan & Fitzgerald (1980)	17	.06	.12	.64	—[b]	—[b]
Messner (1983)	50	.08	.22	.48	.78	.96
Ammerman (1980)	72	.07	.16	.36	.67	.92
Rosenstein (1981)	209	.12	.48	.94	1.0	1.0
Perkins & Fawlkes (1980)	286	.35	.95	.99	1.0	1.0
Shover et al. (1979)	394	.35	.94	1.0	1.0	1.0
Spitze & Spaeth (1979)	411	.20	.80	1.0	1.0	1.0
Ross & Duff (1983)	422	.24	.91	1.0	1.0	1.0
Clifton (1981)	579	.28	.87	1.0	1.0	1.0
Baldassare & Protask (1982)	604	.60	.10	.19	.39	.71
Speare et al. (1983)	808	.34	.97	1.0	1.0	1.0
Robinson & Kellery (1979)	1,120	.81	1.0	1.0	1.0	1.0
Strickland (1982)	2,414	.97	1.0	1.0	1.0	1.0
Hanks (1982)	10,245	1.0	1.0	1.0	1.0	1.0

[a] Numbers in parentheses represent value of parameter in alternative specification of the model.
[b] The matrix is not positive definite.

The proposed testing strategy

Four different decision situations should be distinguished in the testing of models. These distinctions are made on the basis of the value of the test statistic and the power of the test. Table 11.3 presents the four decision situations.

Case I. The first case is characterized by a test statistic that is larger than the critical value at the .05 level, and the power of the test is not too high; hence, small misspecifications do not lead to a rejection of the model.[5] In such situations a test statistic that is larger than the critical value is likely to be due to large misspecification in the model. Therefore, the model should be rejected.

Case II. The test statistic is again larger than the critical value, but in this case the power is also high. Therefore, it is not clear whether the model contains large or small specification errors, because even small specification errors lead to high values of the test statistic in this case. Given this unclear situation, it is necessary to adjust the test in order to make it more decisive. These adjustments are discussed later.

Table 11.3. *Four decision situations*

	Power low	Power high
$t > C(.05)$	I (reject null hypothesis)	II (adjust test)
$t < C(.05)$	III (adjust test)	IV (accept null hypothesis)

Case III. The value of the test statistic is now smaller than the critical value, but the power is again low. This means that even large specification errors have a low probability of being detected. The situation is again unclear and it is necessary to adjust the test by increasing the sample size.

Case IV. Here the decision is clear. The test statistic is lower than the critical value at the .05 level, and the power is high. In this situation we know that substantial specification errors would be detected. Therefore, a test statistic that is smaller than the critical value suggests that the model does not deviate substantially from the correct model.

There are two possibilities for adjusting the test in cases II and III. The first involves an adjustment of the significance level. In Figure 11.2a we presented the distribution of the test statistic for a correctly specified and an incorrectly specified model. From this figure it can be seen that by changing the significance level of the test it is possible to change the critical value and also the power of the test. For instance, if the power is too low (case III), we can increase it by increasing the significance level at which the test is evaluated. In this way the critical value of the test moves to the left with a consequent increase in power. If however, the power is too high (case II), owing to a large sample, it can be reduced by a decrease in the significance level at which the test is evaluated.

If the decision situation is like that presented in Figure 11.2b, there is no way of adjusting the test by a shift in the level at which it is evaluated. In such a case, an adjustment of the sample size is necessary. Since the value of the noncentrality parameter λ is a linear function ot the sample size, it follows that the necessary sample size for a test with a fixed amount of power can be determined in the following way:

$$\frac{\text{required value of } \lambda \times \text{ the sample size used}}{\text{value of } \lambda \text{ for the estimated model}} = \text{required sample size}$$

Finally, this testing strategy can be applied to comparisons of nested models. There the test statistic D is used, which is equal to the difference between the value t_1 of the test statistic T_1 for the more restrictive model and the value t_2 of the test statistic T_2 for the alternative, less restricted model. The degrees of freedom for this test are equal to the difference in the degrees of freedom between the models. Again, the test statistic D is distributed asymptotically as a chi-square variable if the restrictions are correct and as a noncentral chi-square variable if the restrictions are incorrect.[6] Again, we have to take account of the power of the test, because the four cases detailed above may occur here as well. An example of the application of these tests is now presented.

Applications

Taking Table 11.3 as a guide, we present one example for each decision situation. Simultaneously, we illustrate briefly how the procedure can serve as an alternative to the normal testing procedures.[7]

Case I: Rejection of a model on the basis of the standard chi-square test when the power of the test is low.

Wheaton et al. (1977) present a model of the stability over time of alienation and its relation to background variables such as education and occupation. The analysis employs data measured at two points in time and is also discussed in Jöreskog and Sörbom (1981) and Bentler and Bonett (1980). The model is shown in Figure 11.3.

From the chi-square statistic for the fit of the basic model ($\chi^2_6 = 71.5$) one would conclude that the model is not compatible with the data at the .05 level of significance. Following Wheaton et al. we inquire whether the assumption of uncorrelated errors between the same measures at different points in time ($\varepsilon_1, \varepsilon_3$ and $\varepsilon_2, \varepsilon_4$) accounts for the lack of fit. If we assume that both of these correlations are equal to .1, the probability of rejecting the model at the .05 significance level equals .09.[8] Only if the correlated errors are high will the test of the model fit have high power (e.g., when the correlation is assumed to be .4, the power of the test is .98).

This corresponds to the first decision situation in Table 11.3, where the lack of fit is not due merely to small errors of specification in the model. To obtain an acceptable fit the model thus requires significant alteration. Note that, in this case, the test statistic does produce a reliable indication of the lack of fit, because rejection points to large misspecifications in the model. Hence, assessing the fit by other criteria, as was done by Wheaton et al. (1977) and by Bentler and Bonett (1980), is unnecessary.

Case II: Rejection of a model on the basis of the standard chi-square test when the power of the test is high.

In order to illustrate the second possibility we discuss a study concerned with the determinants of the choice of secondary school (Saris & Stronkhorst 1984). The model, shown in Figure 11.4, does not have an acceptable fit at the .05 significance level.

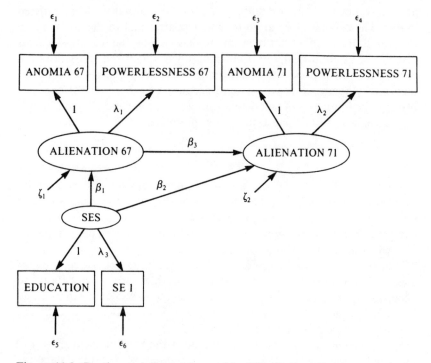

Figure 11.3. Bentler and Bonnett's model. SES, Socioeconomic status; SEI, Socio-Economic Index.

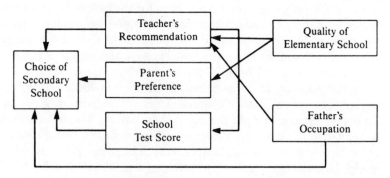

Figure 11.4. Saris's model.

Proceeding in an exploratory way, we relax additional restrictions in order to obtain a better-fitting model. The question is whether the changes are really necessary or whether they merely capitalize on chance by fitting the model to this particular data set. For this we require a test of the importance of the difference between the null model and the final model derived through the exploratory fitting process. Obviously, such a test has to be done on new data and not on the old data from which the modifications derive. We reestimate the model from a second data set with the same variables but for a different point in time, consisting of 1,738 cases. The formulation of the problem implies that we have to test the fit of the null model against that of the modified model by examining the test statistic D for the new data set. First, we evaluate the power of the standard .05-level test of model fit. We test the hypothesis that $\gamma_{31} = \gamma_{22} = \gamma_{41} = \beta_{32} = 0$ against the alternative, that these parameters are all equal to 0.1, that is, that the modifications are all minor. The power of this test indicates that the probability of rejecting the null model, when the additional parameters are all equal to 0.1, is 1.0 ($\lambda = 138.12$). However, we think that this test is too critical for the substantive nature of the hypothesis; for example, if these parameters were as small as 0.04, the probability of rejecting the model would still equal .95. Thus, the power of the test of this hypothesis is high even when the original model contains only minor misspecifications. Obviously, we may not wish to reject the model in such a case and would prefer a test with somewhat less power. We can obtain this by reducing the significance level of the test. However, shifting the significance level will not always provide the user with a reasonable test. For instance, in the present case, when the significance level is set to .001, the power of the test is still equal to 1.0. Reducing the significance level even further raises problems because the standard statistical tables do not provide information for very low significance levels. Therefore, we suggest an alternative way of assessing the appropriateness of the model. If we want to test the hypothesis, that $\gamma_{31} = \gamma_{32} = \gamma_{41} = \beta_{32} = 0$ against the alternative, that these parameters all equal 0.1, we first choose the amount of power we want to have, say .8. Next we obtain the critical point C, such that the noncentral chi-square distributed test statistic $T(\lambda)$ exceeds the value C with probability .8. Since this information is not readily available from published tables, we use the result that the noncentral chi-square distribution can be approximated by the standard normal distribution. In this way it is possible to determine C' (an approximation to C) by the formula

$$C' = (\text{d.f.} + \lambda) - Z_p \times \sqrt{2(\text{d.f.} + 2\lambda)}$$

where Z_p denotes the z value (from the table of the standard normal), such that $p(z < Z_p) = \text{power}$.

In our example, choosing the power to be .8, we calculate the critical point

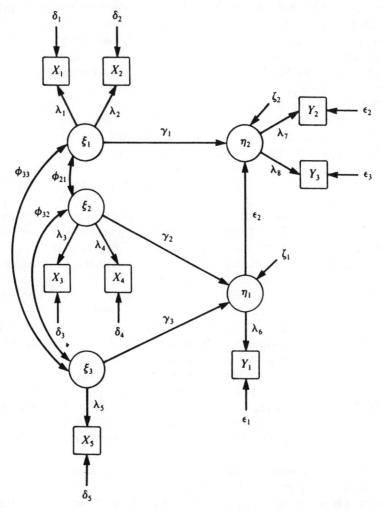

Figure 11.5. Bagozzi's model. ξ_1, Achievement Motivation; ξ_2, Task-Specific Self-esteem; ξ_3, Verbal Intelligence; η_1, Performance; η_2, Job Satisfaction.

$$C' = (4 + 138.12) - .84 \sqrt{2(4 + 2 \times 138.12)} = 122.23$$

Now, from the null model and the alternative model, we obtain

$$d = t_1 - t_2 = 71.26 - 0.16 = 71.10$$

This value is smaller than C'; thus, the null hypothesis should not be rejected. Therefore, for this data set we do not have to relax the four restrictions found to increase the fit of the model in the earlier exploratory analysis.

Note that this conclusion would not have been reached by a comparison of the nested models without taking into account the power of the test. The use of the .05 level test of D would have led to rejection of the null hypothesis.

Case III: Acceptance of a model on basis of the standard chi-square test when the power of the test is low.

The third example involves a model presented by Bagozzi (1980) and is depicted in Figure 11.5. The model is not rejected at the standard .05 significance level. As can be seen in the figure one of the restrictions is that Achievement Motivation does not have a direct effect on Performance. Assuming that we wish to test this hypothesis, we estimate the power and find that the test is not very conclusive. For instance, if this direct effect was 0.1, the probability of rejecting the model equals .07. If the effect was 0.3 the power of the model would be .38, and if it was 0.5 the power would be .79. Hence, we see that in this case the model test is sensitive only to large misspecifications.

No conclusion can be drawn from the .05 significance level test alone in this model because the power is too low. Adjusting the significance level criterion does not help very much.[9] The only solution in this case, therefore, is to do the research again, this time with a larger sample size. The sample size needed to obtain a test with a power of .8 for a misspecification error of 0.1 is $(19/0.7914) \times 122 = 2,929$, rather than the much smaller sample employed in the original study.

Tests in small samples can therefore be particularly misleading because of the tendency to accept a model with little chance of being rejected by the test. The evaluation of the power of the test can make us aware of this problem.

Case IV: Acceptance of a model on the basis of the standard chi-square test when the power of the test is high.

The final example is drawn from Bollen's (1980) model of the measurement of political democracy (Figure 11.6). The main concern here is to examine whether two theoretically distinct constructs of Political Democracy are empirically separable in this small sample ($N = 113$). From a comparison of nested models Bollen concludes that they are not separable. However, as we have seen, one should be careful when drawing conclusions from small samples. We evaluate whether the model would have a reasonable chance of being rejected if the correlation between the two constructs differed from 1.0 in the population. A strong test of this would be to assess whether a deviation of .1 would be detected in the model-testing procedure. Hence, the issue is whether the power would be

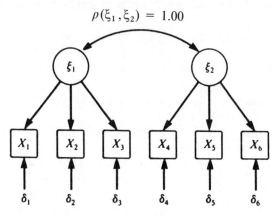

$$\rho(\xi_1,\xi_2) = 1.00$$

Figure 11.6. Bollen's model. ξ_1, Political Liberty; ξ_2, Popular Sovereignty.

high if the true relationship were .9 instead of 1.0. Although the sample size is not very large, the power of the test is actually quite high (.85), and the power would be .93 if the relationship were .89 rather than 1.0.[10] Bollen's test statistic indeed has a smaller value than the critical value of the .05-level test. Therefore, on the basis of this additional evidence we agree with the conclusion that the structures are not empirically separable, although Bollen did not have sufficient evidence to draw this conclusion on the basis of the chi-square test alone.

Conclusion

In our view the procedures for testing structural equation models have not been sufficiently rigorous. The lack of a formalized criterion for testing a model in path analysis affects the validity of the conclusions drawn. In the LISREL context we find that the frequently used test procedures may be inappropriate in some situations, for none of these procedures provides any control over the power of the test. Furthermore, these procedures give the researcher too much freedom to accept or to reject a model since they are to a large extent arbitrary.[11] We suggested an enhanced testing strategy that takes into account the power of the test. This procedure requires the researcher to specify an alternative model and to choose specific values of parameters for which the power of the test is to be evaluated. The researcher also has to determine how powerful the test should be. We consider that a proper procedure for testing causal models is essential for progress in the nonexperimental sciences, and this means that researchers should evaluate the power of the test they use.

Several of the decisions required in this enhanced testing procedure seem to be rather arbitrary and dependent on the state of development in a given field of research. For example, there is as yet no working rule of thumb to indicate what is a generally acceptable level of power for an appropriate test of model fit. However, this problem is analogous to the choice of a probability level in significance testing, where the .05 level has gained currency as an accepted working rule of thumb. We have illustrated that even a somewhat arbitrary choice for the power of the test is better than the usual approach, in which the power of the test is completely ignored. The purpose of the examples was also to show that the sample size is not the only important determining factor for the power of the test. Even in small data sets tests can be very powerful. The true magnitude of the parameters in a model is at least as important as sample size. For a more detailed discussion we refer the reader to Saris and Stronkhorst (1984).

Appendix

The value of the noncentrality parameter λ can be computed by the following procedure:

1. Choose an alternative model and the parameter values against which to test the estimated model. The alternative parameter values chosen should provide a substantively meaningful test of the model.
2. Compute the population variance–covariance matrix implied by the alternative parameter values. This can be done with LISREL by specifying fixed values for the parameters of the model or by hand, using the equations for the relationships in the model.
3. Compute the parameter values for the original model using this derived variance–covariance matrix as input to the analysis. The sample size is specified to be the same as that in the original sample.
4. The test statistic for the fit of the model in this analysis provides an approximation for the noncentrality parameter λ. From the value of λ, the degrees of freedom, and the significance level of the test chosen, the power of the test can be obtained from tables for the noncentral chi-square distribution (Harter et al. 1970).

See Saris and Stronkhorst (1984) for a more detailed discussion of the procedure, and for examples.

Notes

1. See Chapters 9 and 13 for a discussion of empirical findings relating to the robustness of this measure.

2. Some authors use this index in combination with other criteria, such as the size of the first-order derivatives (Matsueda 1982), the absolute magnitude of the residuals (Knoke 1979; Sullivan et al. 1979), or probability level (Portes, Parker, & Cobas 1980).

3. One model is said to be nested within a second if the latter can be obtained by adding parameters to the former. In this case, the difference between the values of the test statistic, denoted D, is distributed as a chi-square variable, with degrees of freedom equal to the difference between the degrees of freedom of the two models. If D is statistically significant, the more relaxed (less restricted) model provides a better fit to the data than the more restricted model.

4. For details of the computation see the Appendix of this chapter. Provision for implementing this procedure is made in LISREL VII and later versions.

5. By "too high power" we mean that substantively uninteresting deviations from the model would lead to the rejection of the model. In general we think that a deviation of 0.1 should be detected with rather high (say, 0.8) power, but the model should not be rejected in case of smaller deviations.

6. This result holds under the condition that the less restricted model has an acceptable fit. Otherwise, the test statistic D may not be distributed as a chi-square variable, even if the hypothesis that the restricted parameters are zero is correct. If the initial model, in this case the less restrictive model, does not have an acceptable fit, the test of a difference between the two models would be rejected too frequently (Satorra & Saris 1982a,b).

7. For a more detailed illustration of the application of these procedures see Saris and Stronkhorst (1984, pp. 201–14).

8. The reported power values are computed at the .05 significance level, unless specified otherwise.

9. For instance, when the significance level is set to .2, the probability of detecting an effect of 0.1 is only .25; the effect has to equal 0.4 before there is a reasonable chance of rejecting the model (power = .8710).

10. Following Bollen (1980) we computed the power for the test statistic D with the degrees of freedom specified to be 1.

11. Hoelter (1983) proposed another goodness-of-fit index to overcome the problems associated with the power of the test, which focuses on the sample size. In our view this index is not appropriate, because (1) the sample size is not the only determinant of the power, and (2) most likely there will be no consensus among researchers about the acceptance region.

References

Ammerman, N. T. (1980). The civil rights movement and the clergy in a southern community. *Sociological Analysis, 41*, 339–50.

Bagozzi, R. P. (1980). Performance and satisfaction in an industrial sales force: An examination of their antecedents and simultaneity. *Journal of Marketing, 44*, 65–77.

Baldassare, M., & Protask, W. (1982). Growth controls, population growth, and community satisfaction. *American Sociological Review, 47*, 339–46.

Bentler, P., & Bonett, D. G. (1980). Significance tests and goodness of fit in the analysis of covariance structures. *Psychological Bulletin, 88*, No. 3, 588–606.

Bollen K. A. (1980). Issues in the comparative measurement of political democracy. *American Sociological Review, 45*, 370–91.

Clifton, R. A. (1981). Ethnic differences in the academic achievement process in Canada. *Social Science Research, 10*, 67–87.

Dalton, D. A. (1981). Reassessing parental socialization: Indicator unreliability versus generational transfer. *American Political Science Review, 74*, 421–31.

Fornell, C., & Larcker, D. F. (1981). Evaluating structural equation models with unobservable variables and measurement error. *Journal of Marketing Research, 18*, 39–50.

Hanks, M. (1982). Youth, voluntary associations and political socialization, *Social Forces, 60*(82), 211–23.

Harter, H. L., & Owen, O. B. (1970). *Selected Tables in Mathematical Statistics*. Chicago: Markham.

Hoelter, J. (1983). The analysis of covariance structures: Goodness of fit indices. *Sociological Methods and Research, 11*, 325–44.

Jöreskog, K. G., & Sörbom, D. (1981). *LISREL V: Analysis of linear structural relationships by the method of maximum likelihood*. Chicago: National Educational Resources.

Knoke, D. (1979). Stratification and the dimensions of American political orientations. *American Journal of Political Science, 23*, 772–91.

Matsueda, R. L. (1982). Testing control theory and differential association: A causal modeling approach. *American Sociological Review, 47*, 489–504.

Messner, S. F. (1983). Societal development, social equality and homicide: A cross-national test of a Durkheimian model. *Social Forces, 61*(83), 456–74.

Miller, G. A., & Conaty, J. (1982). Comparative organization analysis: Sampling and measurement. *Social Science Research, 11*, 141–52.

Morgan, D. R., & Fitzgerald, M. (1980). A causal perspective on school segregation among American states: A research note. *Social Forces, 58*, 329–335.

Perkins, J., & Fawlkes, R. V. (1980). Opinion representation versus social representation; or, why women can not run as women and win. *American Political Science Review, 74*, 92–103.

Portes, A., Parker, N., & Cobas, J. (1981). Assimilation or consciousness: Perception of U.S. society among recent Latin American immigrants to the United States. *Social Forces, 59*, 200–24.

Robinson, R. V., & Kelley, J. (1979). Class as conceived by Marx and Dahrendorf: Effects on income inequality and politics in the United States and Great Britain. *American Sociological Review, 44*, 38–58.

Rosa E., & Mazur, A. (1980). Incipient status in small groups. *Social Forces, 58*, 18–37.

Rosenstein, C. (1981). The liability of ethnicity in Israel. *Social Forces, 59*, 667–86.

Ross, C. E., & Duff, R. S. (1983). Medical care, living conditions, and children's well-being. *Social Forces, 61,* 225–40.

Saris, W. E., & Stronkhorst, L. H. (1984). *Introduction to Causal Modeling in Non-Experimental Research.* Amsterdam: Sociometric Research foundation.

Satorra, A., & Saris, W. E. (1982a). Power of the likelihood test for structural equation models. Free University Amsterdam, Department of Methods and Techniques.

   (1982b). The accuracy of a procedure for calculating the power of the likelihood ratio test as used within the Lisrel framework. Amsterdam: Sociometric Research.

Shover, N., Norland, J., & Thornton, W. (1979). Gender roles and delinquency. *Social Forces, 58,* 162–75.

Speare, A., Kobrin, F., & Kingskade, W. (1983). The influence of socioeconomic bonds and satisfaction on interstate migration. *Social Forces, 61,* 551–74.

Spitze, G. D., & Spaeth, J. L. (1979). Employment among married female college graduates. *Social Science Research, 8,* 184–99.

Strickland, D. E. (1982). Social learning and deviant behavior: A specific test of a general theory – a Comment and Critique. *American Sociological Review, 47,* 162–66.

Sullivan, J. L., Piereson, J. L., Marcus, G. E., & Feldman, S. (1979). The more things change, the more they stay the same: The stability of mass belief systems. *American Journal of Political Science, 23,* 176–92.

Wheaton, B., Muthén, B., Alwin, D. F., & Summers, F. (1977). Assessing the reliability and stability in panel models. In D. R. Heise (ed.), *Sociological Methodology* (pp. 84–136). San Francisco: Jossey-Bass.

12

LISREL models for inequality constraints in factor and regression analysis

HENK KELDERMAN

Introduction

In the analysis of covariance structures using LISREL, models are specified by restricting the parameters in the LISREL matrices to be equal to a predetermined value (fixed parameters) or to be equal to one another (Jöreskog 1970, 1974, 1978; Jöreskog & Sörbom 1978). In many applications, these restrictions lead to models that are either more restrictive or more relaxed than what we have in mind. Often the analyst would like to specify certain parameters to be larger than a predetermined value (usually zero) or larger than another parameter.

Lee (1980) and McDonald (1980) have described methods for estimating parameters of covariance structure models subject to inequality constraints: Lee uses a penalty function and McDonald a reparametrization method. Both methods are very general but require special algorithms or some ad hoc programming. In this chapter, it is shown that McDonald's reparametrization method can be formulated as a standard LISREL model. The model can be used to put lower bounds on factor loadings, regression weights, and error variances, as well as inequalities between regression coefficients or factor loadings. Moreover, regression coefficients or factor loadings can be specified to exceed one another by a predetermined amount. Before developing a general LISREL model to handle these constraints, I start with an example from multiple regression analysis.

In Figure 12.1 a model is depicted for the regression of achieved educational level y on intelligence x_1 and SES (socioeconomic status) x_2, where β_1 and β_2 are the regression coefficients corresponding to x_1 and x_2. In LISREL, the model can be specified by

$$\Gamma = [\gamma_1 \quad \gamma_2]$$

and $\Lambda_y = I$ and $\theta^\varepsilon = 0$, where $\beta_1 = \gamma_1$ and $\beta_2 = \gamma_2$ are the parameters to be estimated. The structural equation system then becomes

222   HENK KELDERMAN

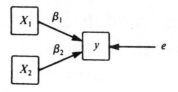

Figure 12.1. Model for the regression of achieved educational level y on intelligence x_1 and SES x_2.

$$y = \mathbf{\Gamma x} + e = [\beta_1 \quad \beta_2]\begin{bmatrix} x_1 \\ x_2 \end{bmatrix} + e = \beta_1 x_1 + \beta_2 x_2 = e$$

In this model the β-weights are unrestricted; they may be either positive or negative. Since negative coefficients for the regression of achieved educational level on intelligence and SES are highly implausible from a substantive point of view, the analyst might want to estimate a model in which the values of β_1 and β_2 are restricted a priori to be nonnegative.

In LISREL such a model can be specified by

$$\mathbf{\Lambda}_y = [\lambda_1 \quad \lambda_2] \quad \text{and} \quad \mathbf{\Gamma} = \begin{bmatrix} \gamma_{11} & 0 \\ 0 & \gamma_{22} \end{bmatrix}$$

with $\lambda_1 = \gamma_{11} = \alpha_1$ and $\lambda_2 = \gamma_{22} = \alpha_2$ and setting fixed x, $\mathbf{B} = \mathbf{0}$ and $\mathbf{\Psi} = \mathbf{0}$. The LISREL system then becomes

$$\mathbf{\eta} = \mathbf{\Gamma\xi}, \quad \mathbf{y} = \mathbf{\Lambda}_y\mathbf{\eta} + \mathbf{\varepsilon}, \quad \mathbf{x} = \mathbf{\xi}$$

Substituting for ξ and η and writing $e = \varepsilon$ yields

$$\begin{aligned} y &= \mathbf{\Lambda}_y\mathbf{\Gamma x} + e \\ &= [\alpha_1 \quad \alpha_2]\begin{bmatrix} \alpha_1 & 0 \\ 0 & \alpha_2 \end{bmatrix}\begin{bmatrix} x_1 \\ x_2 \end{bmatrix} + e \\ &= [\alpha_1^2 \quad \alpha_2^2]\begin{bmatrix} x_1 \\ x_2 \end{bmatrix} + e \\ &= \alpha_1^2 x_1 + \alpha_2^2 x_2 + e \end{aligned}$$

That is, the regression weights β_1 and β_2 are now estimated as the squares α_1^2 and α_2^2, which are always nonnegative. Thus, a model with inequality constraints can be formulated by using the additional $\mathbf{\Lambda}_y$ matrix. This matrix was set equal to the identity matrix in the unrestricted case.

Furthermore, the analyst might hypothesize that a change of one unit on x_1 might give a larger effect on y than a change of one unit on x_2, that is, that β_1 is larger than β_2. This restriction can be imposed by setting γ_{21} = α_2 in addition to the restriction above; that is,

$$\Gamma = \begin{bmatrix} \alpha_1 & \\ \alpha_2 & \alpha_2 \end{bmatrix}$$

so that

$$y = \Lambda_y\Gamma\mathbf{x} = e$$

$$= [\alpha_1 \quad \alpha_2]\begin{bmatrix} \alpha_1 & 0 \\ \alpha_2 & \alpha_2 \end{bmatrix}\begin{bmatrix} x_1 \\ x_2 \end{bmatrix} + e$$

$$= [\alpha_1^2 + \alpha_2^2 \quad \alpha_2^2]\begin{bmatrix} x_1 \\ x_2 \end{bmatrix} + e$$

$$= (\alpha_1^2 + \alpha_2^2)x_1 + \alpha_2^2 x_2 + e$$

so that the regression coefficient $\beta_1 = \alpha_1^2 + \alpha_2^2$ is specified to exceed the regression coefficient $\beta_2 = \alpha_2^2$ by the positive amount α_1^2.

This method (i.e., the use of the matrix product $\Lambda_y\Gamma$ to set inequality constraints) can also be used to set inequality constraints on factor loadings. If an observed variable is an indicator of an unmeasured construct or factor, we almost always expect its loading to be nonnegative. Usually, the loading is also expected to be larger than a certain value, say 0.30, to justify the claim that the observed variable is an indicator of the factor. Specifying the loading as entirely free or fixed does not adequately represent our hypothesis.

Another example is the analysis of measures constructed in a multitrait–multimethod matrix (Campbell & Fiske 1959). Campbell and Fiske state as a validity criterion that a variable must correlate higher with a variable measuring the same trait by a different method than with a variable measuring another trait by the same method. If the correlations between the variables are explained by a confirmatory factor analysis model with trait and method factors, this criterion essentially requires that a variable's trait-factor loading is larger than its method-factor loading.

In factor analysis another problem that requires inequality constraints is the occurrence of Heywood cases (i.e., nonpositive residual variances). Heywood cases can be prevented by specifying the error term of each variable as a factor and then specifying the factor loadings to be positive by the method shown before. This chapter, however, describes a somewhat simpler method that avoids the use of the Γ matrix.

The next section describes the type of models with inequality constraints that can be formulated within the LISREL framework. Then different cases of inequality constraints are discussed: lower bounds on residual variances and inequality constraints on regression coefficients or factor loadings, both for one variable and for several independent variables or factors. Two empirical examples are given: a confirmatory factor analysis from the measurement of intelligence and an example from educational sociology. The latter example shows that inequality constraints can also be used to specify regression analysis models with predictors that have only ordinal-scale properties.

Scope of the model

In this chapter we consider the model

$$\mathbf{y} = \mathbf{D}\mathbf{z} + \mathbf{e} \tag{12.1}$$

where $\mathbf{y}' = (y_1, y_2, \ldots, y_p)$ is a vector of observed dependent variables, $\mathbf{z}' = (z_1, z_2, \ldots, z_r)$ is a vector of observed or unobserved independent variables, $\mathbf{e}' = (e_1, e_2, \ldots, e_p)$ is a vector of residuals, and $\mathbf{D}(p \times r)$ is a matrix of coefficients (regression coefficients, factor loadings). If the variables in $\mathbf{z}$ are all unobserved, the model in (12.1) is the factor analysis model and if $\mathbf{z}$ is observed, the model in (12.1) is the simultaneous equations regression model. In general, $\mathbf{z}$ may contain both observed variables and unobserved variables.

In the model represented by (12.1) it is assumed, without loss of generality, that the population means of the variables $\mathbf{y}$, $\mathbf{z}$, and $\mathbf{e}$ are zero. Denote the q observed independent variables by $\mathbf{x}' = (x_1, x_2, \ldots, x_q)$ and the remaining $r - q$ unobserved independent variables by $\omega' = (\omega_1, \leqq_2, \ldots, \omega_{r-q})$ and let $\mathbf{z}' = (\mathbf{x}', \omega')$ and define a partitioned matrix $\mathbf{S}(q \times r) = [\mathbf{I} \ \mathbf{0}]$ that picks the observed variables from $\mathbf{z}$ and ignores the unobserved variables; that is,

$$\mathbf{x} = \mathbf{S}\mathbf{z} \tag{12.2}$$

Assuming that the population covariances between the residuals and the independent variables are zero, it follows from (12.1) and (12.2) that the covariance matrix of the observed variables $\boldsymbol{\Sigma}$ has the structure

$$\boldsymbol{\Sigma} = \left[\begin{array}{c|c} \boldsymbol{\Sigma}_{yy} & \boldsymbol{\Sigma}_{yx} \\ \hline \boldsymbol{\Sigma}_{xy} & \boldsymbol{\Sigma}_{xx} \end{array} \right] = \left[\begin{array}{c|c} \mathbf{D}\mathbf{C}\mathbf{D}' + \mathbf{E}^2 & \mathbf{D}\mathbf{C}\mathbf{S}' \\ \hline \mathbf{S}\mathbf{C}\mathbf{D}' & \mathbf{S}\mathbf{C}\mathbf{S}' \end{array} \right] \tag{12.3}$$

where $\boldsymbol{\Sigma}_{yy}$, $\boldsymbol{\Sigma}_{yx}$, and $\boldsymbol{\Sigma}_{xx}$ are the matrices of population covariances between the y variables, between y and x variables, and between the x variables and $\boldsymbol{\Sigma}_{xy} = \boldsymbol{\Sigma}'_{yx}$.

On the right side of (12.3) $\mathbf{C}$ is the population covariance matrix of the independent variables $\mathbf{z}$, and $\mathbf{E}^2$ is the covariance matrix of residuals $\mathbf{e}$. Throughout this chapter we assume that $\mathbf{E}^2$ is a diagonal matrix with

residual variances on the diagonal, If there are no unobserved indepen-
dent variables, the matrix $\mathbf{S}$ is an identity matrix and $\mathbf{C} = \boldsymbol{\Sigma}_{xx}$. If there are
no observed independent variables, there are no $\boldsymbol{\Sigma}_{yx}$, $\boldsymbol{\Sigma}_{xy}$, and $\boldsymbol{\Sigma}_{xx}$ and we
have the factor analysis model.

The covariance matrix in (12.3) is a special case of the general LISREL
model, where $\boldsymbol{\Lambda}_y$, $\boldsymbol{\Lambda}_x$, $\boldsymbol{\Phi}$, and $\boldsymbol{\theta}_\varepsilon$ are set equal to $\mathbf{D}$, $\mathbf{S}$, $\mathbf{C}$, and $\mathbf{E}^2$,
respectively.

Special cases of (12.3) are obtained by setting parameters equal to a
predetermined (usually zero) value or equal to one another; that is, if ρ_1
and ρ_2 are parameters, one can write

$$\rho_1 = c_1 \qquad \text{or} \qquad \rho_1 = \rho_2$$

McDonald (1980), however, also considers restrictions of the form

$$\rho_1 = c_1 + \alpha_1^2 \qquad \text{or} \qquad \rho_2 = \rho_1 + c_2 + \alpha_2^2 \qquad (12.4)$$

where c_1 and c_2 are constants and α_1 and α_2 are parameters to be
estimated: the derived parameters. If the derived parameters α_1 and α_2 are
estimated instead of the original parameters ρ_1 and ρ_2, the latter satisfy
the inequality constraints

$$\rho_1 \geqq c_1 \qquad \text{and} \qquad \rho_2 \geqq \rho_1 + c_2$$

respectively. This is true because the squares α_1^2 and α_2^2 are nonnegative. In
this chapter, restrictions of type (12.4) are imposed on the matrix $\mathbf{E}^2$ of
residual variances and the coefficient matrix $\mathbf{D}$ of the model in (12.3) by
rewriting the matrices as

$$\mathbf{E}^2 = \mathbf{N} \cdot \mathbf{N} + \mathbf{Q} \qquad (12.5)$$

and

$$\mathbf{D} = \mathbf{K} \cdot \mathbf{L} + \mathbf{M} \qquad (12.6)$$

where $\mathbf{Q}$ and $\mathbf{M}$ contain fixed constants and $\mathbf{N}$, $\mathbf{K}$, and $\mathbf{L}$ contain the
derived parameters to be estimated. To show how (12.5) and (12.6) can be
used to specify inequality constraints, and how (12.3) using (12.5) and
(12.6) can be specified as a LISREL model, I consider some special cases.
A simple case is (12.3) with lower bounds on the residual variances.

Lower bounds on residual variances

Lower bounds on the estimates of residual variances may be useful to
prevent nonpositive estimates (Heywood cases) (Jöreskog 1967) or to
incorporate prior knowledge of the amount of measurement error in
the model. To impose lower bounds on residual variance estimates let

$\mathbf{Q} = \mathrm{diag}\{q_1, q_2, \ldots, q_p\}$ be a diagonal matrix of lower bounds and $\mathbf{N} = \mathrm{diag}\{v_1, v_2, \ldots, v_p\}$ a diagonal matrix of derived parameters to be estimated. Using (12.5) we then have (for $p = 3$)

$$
\begin{aligned}
&\overset{\displaystyle \mathbf{E}}{\begin{bmatrix} \sigma_{e_1}^2 & & \\ & \sigma_{e_2}^2 & \\ & & \sigma_{e_3}^2 \end{bmatrix}} \\[2mm]
&= \overset{\displaystyle \mathbf{N}}{\begin{bmatrix} v_1 & & \\ & v_2 & \\ & & v_3 \end{bmatrix}} \overset{\displaystyle \mathbf{N}}{\begin{bmatrix} v_1 & & \\ & v_2 & \\ & & v_3 \end{bmatrix}} + \overset{\displaystyle \mathbf{Q}}{\begin{bmatrix} q_1 & & \\ & q_2 & \\ & & q_3 \end{bmatrix}} \\[2mm]
&= \begin{bmatrix} v_1^2 + q_1 & & \\ & v_2^2 + q_2 & \\ & & v_3^2 + q_3 \end{bmatrix}
\end{aligned}
$$

and the residual variance estimates satisfy the inequality constraints

$$\sigma_{e_i}^2 \geqq q_i$$

for all i.

LISREL specification

To specify the model in (12.3) with restrictions (12.5) as a LISREL model, let

$$\Lambda_y = [\mathbf{D}_{p \times r} \quad \mathbf{N}_{p \times p}], \qquad \Lambda_x = [\mathbf{S}_{q \times r} \quad \mathbf{O}_{q \times p}]$$

$$\Phi = \begin{bmatrix} \mathbf{C}_{r \times r} & \mathbf{O}_{r \times p} \\ \mathbf{O}_{r \times p} & \mathbf{I}_{p \times p} \end{bmatrix} \quad \text{and} \quad \theta_\varepsilon = \mathbf{Q}_{p \times p}$$

where Λ_y, Λ_x, and Φ are partitioned matrices. It is readily verified that this yields

$$\Sigma = \begin{bmatrix} \Lambda_y \Phi \Lambda_z' + \theta_\varepsilon & \Lambda_y \Phi \Lambda_x' \\ \Lambda_x \Phi \Lambda_y' & \Lambda_x \Phi \Lambda_x' \end{bmatrix} = \begin{bmatrix} \mathbf{DCD}' + \mathbf{NN}' + \mathbf{Q} & \mathbf{DCS}' \\ \mathbf{SCD}' & \mathbf{SCS}' \end{bmatrix}$$

which is equal to (12.3) with restrictions (12.5).

For example, Figure 12.2 shows a factor analysis model with one factor ω and three observed variables y_1, y_2, and y_3. Suppose y_1, y_2, and y_3 have variance equal to 1 and reliabilities 0.80, 0.78, and 0.85, respectively, so

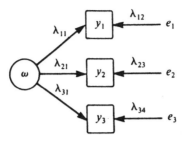

Figure 12.2. Factor analysis model.

that we do not expect the residual variances $\sigma_{e_1}^2$, $\sigma_{e_2}^2$, and $\sigma_{e_3}^2$ to be lower than 0.20, 0.22, and 0.15, respectively. To specify those lower bounds in LISREL we write

$$\boldsymbol{\theta}_\varepsilon(=\mathbf{Q}) = \begin{bmatrix} 0.20 & & \\ & 0.22 & \\ & & 0.15 \end{bmatrix}$$

$$\boldsymbol{\Lambda}_y = \begin{bmatrix} \lambda_{11} & \lambda_{12} & \\ \lambda_{21} & & \lambda_{23} \\ \lambda_{31} & & \lambda_{34} \end{bmatrix}$$

and

$$\boldsymbol{\phi} = \begin{bmatrix} 1 & & & \\ & 1 & & \\ & & 1 & \\ & & & 1 \end{bmatrix}$$

so that the covariance matrix becomes

$$\Sigma = \begin{array}{ccc} \lambda_{11}^2 + \lambda_{12}^2 + 0.20 & \lambda_{11}\lambda_{21} & \lambda_{11}\lambda_{31} \\ \lambda_{21}\lambda_{11} & \lambda_{21}^2 + \lambda_{23}^2 + 0.22 & \lambda_{21}\lambda_{31} \\ \lambda_{31}\lambda_{11} & \lambda_{31}\lambda_{21} & \lambda_{31}^2 + \lambda_{34}^2 + 0.15 \end{array}$$

with $\sigma_{e_1}^2 = \lambda_{12}^2 + 0.20$, which is larger than 0.20.

Inequality constraints on D: one independent variable

We now consider inequality constraints on the elements of the coefficient matrix **D** in (12.1). The elements of **D** may be regression weights or factor loadings, depending on whether the independent variables are observed or unobserved. The method for imposing inequality constraints is the same in both cases. Therefore, in the following treatment no distinction is made between them. In the following the word "coefficient" may refer to regression coefficient or factor loading. If there is only one independent variable ($r = 1$), the coefficient matrix $\mathbf{D}(p \times r)$ is a column vector. To ensure that the coefficients $\mathbf{D}' = (\delta_1, \delta_2, \ldots, \delta_p)$ are larger than $\mathbf{M}' = (m_1, m_2, \ldots, m_p)$, equation (12.6) must have the form

$$
\begin{matrix} \mathbf{D} \\ \begin{bmatrix} \delta_1 \\ \delta_2 \\ \delta_3 \end{bmatrix} \end{matrix}
=
\begin{matrix} \mathbf{K} \\ \begin{bmatrix} \alpha_1 & & \\ & \alpha_2 & \\ & & \alpha_3 \end{bmatrix} \end{matrix}
\begin{matrix} \mathbf{L} \\ \begin{bmatrix} \alpha_1 \\ \alpha_2 \\ \alpha_3 \end{bmatrix} \end{matrix}
+
\begin{matrix} \mathbf{M} \\ \begin{bmatrix} m_1 \\ m_2 \\ m_3 \end{bmatrix} \end{matrix}
\tag{12.7}
$$

where $p = 3$, $k_{ij} = 0$ ($i \neq j$), $k_{ii} = \alpha_i$, and $l_i = \alpha_i$. It is easily verified that this yields

$$\delta_i = \alpha_i^2 + m_i$$

that is, $\delta_1 \geq m_i$ for all i. The off-diagonal elements of $\mathbf{K}$ can be used to set inequality constraints *between* coefficients. To specify δ_i to be bounded below by another coefficient δ_j, the element k_{ij} of $\mathbf{K}$ must be set equal to α_j. For example, if $p = 3$,

$$
\begin{matrix} \mathbf{D} \\ \begin{bmatrix} \delta_1 \\ \delta_2 \\ \delta_3 \end{bmatrix} \end{matrix}
=
\begin{matrix} \mathbf{K} \\ \begin{bmatrix} \alpha_1 & \alpha_2 & \\ & \alpha_2 & \\ & & \alpha_3 \end{bmatrix} \end{matrix}
\begin{matrix} \mathbf{L} \\ \begin{bmatrix} \alpha_1 \\ \alpha_2 \\ \alpha_3 \end{bmatrix} \end{matrix}
+
\begin{matrix} \mathbf{M} \\ \begin{bmatrix} m_1 \\ m_2 \\ m_3 \end{bmatrix} \end{matrix}
$$

$$
=
\begin{bmatrix} \alpha_1^2 + \alpha_2^2 + m_1 \\ \alpha_2^2 \phantom{{}+\alpha_2^2} + m_2 \\ \alpha_3^2 \phantom{{}+\alpha_2^2} + m_3 \end{bmatrix}
=
\begin{bmatrix} \delta_2 + \alpha_1^2 + m_1 - m_2 \\ \alpha_2^2 + m_2 \\ \alpha_3^2 + m_3 \end{bmatrix}
$$

restricts δ_1 to exceed δ_2 by at least the value $m_1 - m_2$ and puts lower bounds m_2 and m_3 on δ_2 and δ_3, respectively. In similar fashion, inequalities can be set between several coefficients. For example, consider

$$
\begin{matrix} \mathbf{D} \\ \begin{bmatrix} \delta_1 \\ \delta_2 \\ \delta_3 \end{bmatrix} \end{matrix}
=
\begin{matrix} \mathbf{K} \\ \begin{bmatrix} \alpha_1 & \alpha_2 & \\ & \alpha_2 & \\ \alpha_1 & \alpha_2 & \alpha_3 \end{bmatrix} \end{matrix}
\begin{matrix} \mathbf{L} \\ \begin{bmatrix} \alpha_1 \\ \alpha_2 \\ \alpha_3 \end{bmatrix} \end{matrix}
+
\begin{matrix} \mathbf{M} \\ \begin{bmatrix} m_1 \\ m_2 \\ m_3 \end{bmatrix} \end{matrix}
$$

$$
=
\begin{bmatrix} \alpha_1^2 + \alpha_2^2 + m_1 \\ \alpha_2^2 + m_2 \\ \alpha_1^2 + \alpha_2^2 + \alpha_3^2 + m_3 \end{bmatrix}
=
\begin{bmatrix} \delta_2 + \alpha_1^2 + m_1 - m_2 \\ \alpha_2^2 + m_2 \\ \delta_1 + \alpha_3^2 + m_3 - m_1 \end{bmatrix}
\tag{12.8}
$$

which specifies δ_1 to exceed δ_2 by $m_1 - m_2$, δ_3 to exceed δ_1 by $m_3 - m_1$, and δ_2 to be larger than or equal to m_2.

In the specification of inequality constraints using (12.6), two rules must be followed. First, all inequalities implied by the intended inequality constraints should be specified. For example, if $\delta_1 > \delta_2$ (i.e., $k_{12} = \alpha_2$) and $\delta_3 > \delta_1$ (i.e., $k_{31} = \alpha_1$) [as in example (12.8)], the implied inequality $\delta_3 > \delta_2$ should be specified by $k_{32} = \alpha_2$. Second, a coefficient should not be specified to be larger than or equal to two other coefficients at the same time. For example, $k_{12} = \alpha_2$ and $k_{13} = \alpha_3$ does not result in $\delta_1 > \delta_2$ and $\delta_1 > \delta_3$, but in $\delta_1 > \delta_2 + \delta_3$, which is obviously not intended.

In (12.7) and (12.8) all coefficients δ_i are bounded below. If necessary, these lower bounds can be removed by setting the corresponding element δ_i of L equal to 1 instead of α_i. Furthermore, coefficients δ_i can be set equal to a predetermined value m_i by setting the corresponding elements k_{ij} and l_i equal to zero. Finally, if there is no inequality constraint between two or more parameters, they can be set equal to one another by setting their corresponding elements in K, L, and M equal to one another. For example, in the model

$$
\begin{array}{cccc}
\mathbf{D} & \mathbf{K} & \mathbf{L} & \mathbf{M} \\
\begin{bmatrix} \delta_1 \\ \delta_2 \\ \delta_3 \\ \delta_4 \end{bmatrix} = & \begin{bmatrix} \alpha_1 & \alpha_2 & & \\ & \alpha_2 & & \\ & & \alpha_2 & \\ & & & 0 \end{bmatrix} & \begin{bmatrix} \alpha_1 \\ 1 \\ 1 \\ 0 \end{bmatrix} & + \begin{bmatrix} m_1 \\ m_2 \\ m_2 \\ m_4 \end{bmatrix}
\end{array}
$$

$$
= \begin{bmatrix} \alpha_1^2 + \alpha_2 + m_1 \\ \alpha_2 + m_2 \\ \alpha_2 + m_2 \\ m_4 \end{bmatrix} = \begin{bmatrix} \delta_2 + \alpha_1^2 + m_1 - m_2 \\ \delta_2 \\ \delta_2 \\ m_4 \end{bmatrix}
$$

the coefficient δ_4 is set equal to the fixed value m_4, δ_2 and δ_3 are set equal to each other, and δ_1 exceeds δ_2 by at least $m_1 - m_2$.

It is important to note that in this example the fourth column of K and the fourth row of L can be left out since they consist of zeros only. Consequently, the number of columns of K and rows of L need not be larger than the number of free and constrained parameters in D. This is of great practical value, since it considerably reduces the memory storage needed to run the program. Let us now generalize these results to the case of several independent variables.

Inequality constraints on D: several independent variables

If there are r (≥ 2) independent variables, the coefficient matrix D has r columns, say $\mathbf{D}_i$ ($i = 1, \ldots, r$). To restrict each column to be equal to

$$\mathbf{D}_i = \mathbf{K}_i \cdot \mathbf{L}_i + \mathbf{M}_i$$

where $\mathbf{K}_i$, $\mathbf{L}_i$, and $\mathbf{M}_i$ have fixed, free, and constrained parameters in the appropriate places, we must write the full coefficient matrix D as

$$\text{D} \qquad\qquad \text{K} \qquad\qquad \text{L} \qquad\qquad \text{M}$$

$$[\text{D}_1 \ \text{D}_2 \ldots \text{D}_r] = [\text{K}_1 \ \text{K}_2 \ldots \text{K}_r] \begin{bmatrix} \text{L}_1 & & \\ & \text{L}_2 & \\ & & \ddots \\ & & & \text{L}_r \end{bmatrix} + [\text{M}_1 \ \text{M}_2 \ldots \text{M}_r]$$

$$= [\text{K}_1 \cdot \text{L}_1 + \text{M}_1 \ \ \text{K}_2 \cdot \text{L}_2 + \text{M}_2 \ \ldots \ \text{K}_r \cdot \text{L}_r + \text{M}_r]$$

For example, if there are $p = 3$ dependent variables and $r = 2$ independent variables we have

$$\text{D} \qquad\qquad\qquad \text{K} \qquad\qquad\qquad \text{L} \qquad\qquad \text{M}$$

$$\begin{bmatrix} \delta_{11} & \delta_{12} \\ \delta_{21} & \delta_{22} \\ \delta_{31} & \delta_{32} \end{bmatrix} = \begin{bmatrix} \alpha_{11} & & & \alpha_{12} & & \\ & \alpha_{21} & & & \alpha_{22} & \\ & & \alpha_{31} & & & \alpha_{32} \end{bmatrix} \begin{bmatrix} \alpha_{11} \\ \alpha_{21} \\ \alpha_{31} \\ \alpha_{12} \\ \alpha_{22} \\ \alpha_{32} \end{bmatrix} = \begin{bmatrix} m_{11} & m_{12} \\ m_{21} & m_{22} \\ m_{31} & m_{32} \end{bmatrix}$$

$$= \begin{bmatrix} \alpha_{11}^2 + m_{11} & \alpha_{12}^2 + m_{11} \\ \alpha_{21}^2 + m_{21} & \alpha_{22}^2 + m_{22} \\ \alpha_{31}^2 + m_{31} & \alpha_{32}^2 + m_{32} \end{bmatrix} \qquad\qquad (12.9)$$

where $k_{i,i+(j-1)p} = \alpha_{ij}$ and $l_{i+(j-1)p,j} = \alpha_{ij}$ ($i = 1,2,3; j = 1,2$), and zero otherwise, restricts each coefficient δ_{ij} to be larger than or equal to the constant m_{ij}.

As before, the zero elements of K can be used to set inequality constraints between coefficients of the same column of D. Moreover, the zero elements in L can be used to set inequality constraints between coefficients of the same *row* of D.

To set columnwise inequalities

$$\delta_{i'j} \geq \delta_{ij} + m_{i'j} - m_{ij}, \qquad i' \neq i$$

we must specify

$$k'_{i,i+(j-1)p} = \alpha_{ij}$$

And to set rowwise inequalities

$$\delta_{i'j} \geq \delta_{ij} + m_{ij'} - m_{ij}, \qquad j' \neq j$$

we must specify

$$l_{i+(j-1)p,j'} = \alpha_{ij}$$

As an example of rowwise inequality constraints consider

$$\begin{bmatrix} \delta_{11} & \delta_{12} \\ \delta_{21} & \delta_{22} \\ \delta_{31} & \delta_{32} \end{bmatrix} = \begin{bmatrix} \alpha_{11} & & \alpha_{12} & \\ & \alpha_{21} & & \alpha_{22} \\ & & \alpha_{31} & & \alpha_{32} \end{bmatrix} \begin{bmatrix} \alpha_{11} \\ \alpha_{21} \\ \alpha_{31} \\ \alpha_{12} & \alpha_{12} \\ \alpha_{22} & \alpha_{22} \\ \alpha_{32} & \alpha_{32} \end{bmatrix} + \begin{bmatrix} m_{11} & m_{12} \\ m_{21} & m_{22} \\ m_{31} & m_{32} \end{bmatrix}$$

$$\begin{bmatrix} \alpha_{11}^2 + \alpha_{12}^2 + m_{11} & \alpha_{12}^2 + m_{12} \\ \alpha_{21}^2 + \alpha_{22}^2 + m_{21} & \alpha_{22}^2 + m_{22} \\ \alpha_{31}^2 + \alpha_{32}^2 + m_{31} & \alpha_{32}^2 + m_{32} \end{bmatrix}$$

$$= \begin{bmatrix} \delta_{12} + \alpha_{11}^2 + m_{11} - m_{12} & \alpha_{12}^2 \, \text{r} \, m_{12} \\ \delta_{22} + \alpha_{21}^2 + m_{21} - m_{22} & \alpha_{22}^2 \, \text{r} \, m_{22} \\ \delta_{32} + \alpha_{31} + m_{31} - m_{32} & \alpha_{32} + m_{32} \end{bmatrix}$$

which specifies that the coefficients δ_{i1} on the first independent variable (e.g., a trait factor) exceed the coefficients δ_{i2} on the second independent variable (e.g., a method factor) by the amount $m_{i1} - m_{i2}$. In addition, the coefficients of the second independent variable are specified to be larger than m_{i2}.

Columnwise and rowwise inequalities may be specified in the same model, but no coefficient should be subjected to both columnwise and rowwise inequality constraints at the same time. This will not give the desired results. Also, as with one independent variable, implied inequalities must also be specified. For example, if $\delta_{11} \geqslant \delta_{12}$ and $\delta_{12} \geqslant \delta_{13}$ is specified, $\delta_{11} \geqslant \delta_{13}$ must also be specified. Furthermore, if a coefficient is specified to exceed two parameters at the same time, an inequality should be specified between these two parameters; that is, $\delta_{11} \geqslant \delta_{12}$ and $\delta_{11} \geqslant \delta_{13}$ should not be specified unless either $\delta_{12} \geqslant \delta_{13}$ or $\delta_{13} \geqslant \delta_{12}$ is also specified.

As before, lower bounds can be removed by setting elements of **L** equal to 1; coefficients can be set equal to a predetermined value m by setting the corresponding elements in **K** and **L** equal to zero; and coefficients can be set equal to one another by setting the corresponding elements of **K**, **L**, and **M** equal to one another. However, care should be taken to ensure that the inequality and equality constraints are not specified for the same pairs of coefficients. Let us now look at the LISREL specification of inequality constraints on coefficients.

LISREL specification

To specify the model in (12.3) with restrictions (12.6), we distinguish between two cases: a zero and a nonzero constant matrix **M**. If **M** is zero, the LISREL specification is simply

$$\mathbf{\Lambda}_y = \mathbf{K}_{p \times (p \cdot r)}, \quad \mathbf{\Gamma} = \mathbf{L}_{(p \cdot r) \times r}$$

$$\mathbf{\Phi} = \mathbf{C}_{r \times r}, \quad \mathbf{\Lambda}_x = \mathbf{S}_{q \times r}, \quad \mathbf{\theta}_\varepsilon = \mathbf{E}^2_{p \times p}$$

where $\mathbf{K}$, $\mathbf{L}$, $\mathbf{C}$, $\mathbf{S}$, and $\mathbf{E}^2$ contain fixed, free, and constrained parameters in the appropriate places. This LISREL specification gives the population covariance matrix

$$\mathbf{\Sigma} = \begin{bmatrix} \mathbf{\Sigma}_{yy} & \mathbf{\Sigma}_{yx} \\ \mathbf{\Sigma}_{xy} & \mathbf{\Sigma}_{xx} \end{bmatrix} = \begin{bmatrix} \mathbf{\Lambda}_y \mathbf{\Gamma} \mathbf{\Phi} \mathbf{\Gamma}' \mathbf{\Lambda}'_y + \mathbf{\theta}_\varepsilon & \mathbf{\Lambda}_y \mathbf{\Gamma} \mathbf{\Phi} \mathbf{\Lambda}'_x \\ \mathbf{\Lambda}_x \mathbf{\Phi} \mathbf{\Gamma}' \mathbf{\Lambda}'_y & \mathbf{\Lambda}_x \mathbf{\Phi} \mathbf{\Lambda}'_x \end{bmatrix}$$

$$= \begin{bmatrix} \mathbf{KLCL'K'} + \mathbf{E}^2 & \mathbf{KLCS'} \\ \mathbf{SCL'K'} & \mathbf{SCS'} \end{bmatrix} \qquad (12.10)$$

which is equal to (12.3) with $\mathbf{D} = \mathbf{K} \cdot \mathbf{L}$.

If $\mathbf{M}$ is nonzero, however, the LISREL specification becomes more complex. We must then specify

$$\mathbf{\Lambda}_y = [\mathbf{K}_{p \times (p \cdot r)} \quad \mathbf{M}_{p \times r}], \quad \mathbf{\Gamma} = \begin{bmatrix} \mathbf{L}_{(p \cdot r) \times r} \\ \mathbf{I}_{r \times r} \end{bmatrix}$$

$$\mathbf{\Phi} = \mathbf{C}_{r \times r}, \quad \mathbf{\Lambda}_x = \mathbf{S}_{q \times r}, \quad \mathbf{\theta}_\varepsilon = \mathbf{E}^2_{p \times p} \qquad (12.11)$$

where the LISREL matrices $\mathbf{\Lambda}_y$ and $\mathbf{\Gamma}$ are partitioned matrices and $\mathbf{K}$, $\mathbf{L}$, $\mathbf{M}$, $\mathbf{C}$, $\mathbf{S}$, and $\mathbf{E}^2$ contain fixed, free, and constrained parameters in the appropriate places. It can be shown that (12.10) with LISREL matrices (12.11) yields

$$\mathbf{\Sigma} = \begin{bmatrix} \mathbf{\Sigma}_{yy} & \mathbf{\Sigma}_{yx} \\ \mathbf{\Sigma}_{xy} & \mathbf{\Sigma}_{xx} \end{bmatrix} = \begin{bmatrix} (\mathbf{K} \cdot \mathbf{L} + \mathbf{M})\mathbf{C}(\mathbf{K} \cdot \mathbf{L} + \mathbf{M})'^2 + \mathbf{E} & (\mathbf{K} \cdot \mathbf{L} + \mathbf{M})\mathbf{CS'} \\ \mathbf{SC}(\mathbf{K} \cdot \mathbf{L} + \mathbf{M})' & \mathbf{SCS'} \end{bmatrix}$$

which is equal to (12.3) with restrictions (12.6). A remark must be made about the factor analysis case. If all independent variables are unobserved variables, there are no x variables and no $\mathbf{\Sigma}_{xy}$, $\mathbf{\Sigma}_{yx}$, $\mathbf{\Sigma}_{xx}$, and $\mathbf{\Lambda}_x$. A technical problem then is that LISREL does not permit the use of the matrix $\mathbf{\Gamma}$. To overcome this, specify one dummy x variable with variance one and zero correlations with the y variables; that is, extend the observed covariance matrix with

$$\mathbf{S}_{xx} = 1 \quad \text{and} \quad \mathbf{S}_{xy} = \mathbf{O}_{1 \times p}$$

Now make the corresponding submatrices of $\mathbf{\Sigma}_{xx}$ and $\mathbf{\Sigma}_{xy}$ equal to this by writing [see (12.10)]

$$\mathbf{\Lambda}_x = \mathbf{O}_{1 \times r} \quad \text{and} \quad \mathbf{\theta}_\delta = 1$$

Since the observed and the expected covariance matrices are extended with the same elements, the fit of the model stays the same. We have only to adjust the number of degrees of freedom. The number of degrees of freedom is the number of possibly different (co)variances in S minus the number of parameters to be estimated. By this trick we add $p + 1$ (co)variances to S. Since Λ_x and θ_δ are fixed, we add no parameters to be estimated. Therefore, to obtain the correct degrees of freedom we have to subtract $p + 1$ from the degrees of freedom in the LISREL output. In the LISREL models above, the matrices Λ_y and Γ are large. As remarked earlier, if both the ith column of Λ_y and the ith row of Γ consist of zeros, they can be deleted. This may considerably reduce the memory storage requirements of the LISREL program.

Empirical example 1

Guilford's (1971) structure-of-intellect model is a taxonomy of basic human abilities. In this model each ability is classified by three facets: operation, content, and product. The *operation* facet refers to the subjects' intellectual processing of information. Five types of operation are distinguished: cognition (C), memory (M), divergent production (D), convergent production (P), and evaluation (E). The *content* facet refers to the content of the information and has four categories: figural (F), symbolic (S), semantic (M), and behavioral (B). Finally, the *product* facet pertains to the form of the information and has six categories: units (U), classes (C), relations (R), systems (S), transformations (T), and implications (I).

In the Aptitude Research Project (Guilford 1971) tests were constructed for specific combinations of operation, content, and product facets. Guilford's hypothesis was that the performance of subjects on these tests depends on latent ability factors defined by a specific combination of operation, content, and product facets. An alternative hypothesis is that the test performance depends on separate operation, content, and product ability factors (Guttman 1965; Cronbach 1971). Both hypotheses can be formulated as models for tests constructed in a facet design (Mulaik 1975; Mellenbergh et al. 1979). To compare the fit of both models Kelderman, Mellenbergh, and Elshout (1981) reanalyzed seven data sets from the Aptitude Research Project by covariance structure analysis. Unfortunately, for the alternative model the solution did not converge for six of the seven analyses. Moreover, the intermediate estimates contained many negative loadings and residual variances. Since there was no convergent solution, it was not possible to compose parameter estimates and model fit for the two competing hypotheses.

In Table 12.1 the results for a respecified model (Tenopyr, Guilford, &

Table 12.1. *Parameter estimates of alternative model specifications for Guilford data*

Test	Problem type	Operation		Content		Product			Residual variance
		Cognition	Memory	Symbolic	Behavioral	Classes	Relation	Systems	
1	CSC	0.13(0.14)		0.61(0.62)		0.15(0.05)			0.52(0.54)
2	CSC	0.00(−0.09)		0.68(0.73)		0.73(2.10)			0.00(−3.88)
3	CSR	0.23(0.20)		0.55(0.57)			0.03(0.01)		0.56(0.57)
4	CSR	0.37(0.46)		0.48(0.46)			0.13(0.04)		0.50(0.45)
5	CSS	0.35(0.38)		0.26(0.26)				0.00(0.03)	0.75(0.73)
6	CSS	0.19(0.22)		0.57(0.55)				0.00(0.17)	0.57(0.54)
7	CBC	0.61(0.50)			0.06(0.29)	0.06(0.06)			0.62(0.66)
8	CBC	0.40(0.30)			0.25(0.39)	0.00(0.01)			0.78(0.76)
9	CBR	0.40(0.29)			0.34(0.43)		0.00(−0.01)		0.73(0.73)
10	CBR	0.53(0.46)			0.06(0.26)		0.09(0.02)		0.70(0.72)
11	CBS	0.53(0.41)			0.35(0.49)			0.00(0.29)	0.60(0.52)
12	CBS	0.37(0.31)			0.45(0.43)			0.00(0.04)	0.66(0.72)
13	MSC		0.78(0.79)	0.52(0.53)		0.00(0.00)			0.12(0.09)
14	MSC		0.59(0.56)	0.50(0.52)		0.00(−0.01)			0.40(0.42)
15	MSR		0.12(0.10)	0.72(0.73)			0.12(0.04)		0.45(0.46)
16	MSR		0.10(0.11)	0.39(0.38)			0.00(3.19)		0.00(−9.34)
17	MSS		0.41(0.39)	0.42(0.44)				0.00(−0.17)	0.65(0.63)
18	MSS		0.29(0.25)	0.47(0.52)				0.00(−0.35)	0.70(0.56)

Note: Omitted loadings were fixed at zero. Main coefficients pertain to the restricted model and coefficients in parentheses pertain to the unconstrained model.

Hoepfner 1966) are given. The model is an alternative specification with uncorrelated factors in which all loadings and residual variances are restricted to be nonnegative. The intermediate parameter values for the unrestricted model after 184 iterations are indicated in parentheses. The nonconvergent resolution for the unrestricted model is clearly unacceptable; there are two negative residual variances, two loadings larger than 1, and some negative loadings. The restricted model converged after 51 iterations and yielded a chi-square statistic of 244 with 99 degrees of freedom; the model must clearly be rejected. The parameter estimates show that variables 2 and 16 have zero residual variance and that the product factors are not present (i.e., all their factor loadings are approximately zero). The latter is consistent with earlier results of Cronbach (1971) and Merrifield (Cronbach & Snow 1977, p. 157), who found support for an alternative hypothesis with only two facets: operations and content. But even if the degrees of freedom of the product loadings are not counted, the model in Table 12.1 must still be rejected (χ^2 = 244 with DF = 99 + 18 = 117, $p < 0.001$).

Empirical example 2

In the Netherlands every year, all 18-year-old boys are tested for national service. Van Meerum and van Peet (1976) took a sample of the 1972 draft to analyze the effect of environment and intelligence on achieved educational level. They converted completed grades and school types to a scale from 0 to 100 describing the level of education achieved. Furthermore, they registered, among other things, the number of children in the family (1–8 or more) from which the draftee came and his score (0–04) on Raven's Progressive Matrices Test – a nonverbal measure of general intelligence (Raven 1938).

To illustrate the use of inequality constraints in (dummy) regression analysis we start with Model 12.1:

$$y = \mu + \beta_1 z_1 + \beta_2 z_2 + \ldots + \beta_7 z_7 + \beta_8 z_8 + \gamma x + e$$

where y is the education score, x is the intelligence score, and $z_1, \ldots, z_8$ are dummy variables with the following values:

z_1 = 1 if there is one child in the family; 0 otherwise
$\vdots$
z_7 = 1 if there are seven children in the family; 0 otherwise
z_8 = 1 if there are eight or more children in the family; 0 otherwise

The dummy variables $z_1, \ldots, z_8$ and x are considered to be fixed.
There is an indeterminacy in this model; adding a constant c to μ and

Table 12.2. *Parameter estimates, coefficients of determination, and F-statistics of models for army data* ($N = 6,889$)

| Model | Parameter | | | | | | | | γ | R^2 | F | d.f. |
	μ	β_1	β_2	β_3	β_4	β_5	β_6	β_7	β_8				
12.1	−9.42	5.27	5.20	4.89	3.06	0.88	1.71	−0.21	0.00[a]	1.61	0.77	2,848.24	(8,6891)
12.2	−9.48	5.32	5.31	4.99	3.17	1.31	1.31	0.05	0.00[a]	1.61	0.77	2,848.24	(8,6891)
12.3	−10.00	6.76	5.80	4.83	3.87	2.90	1.93	0.97	0.00[a]	1.61	0.77	11,383.78	(2,6897)

[a]Fixed at zero.

subtracting c from each β_i does not change the model – a standard situation when dummy variables are used. To remove this indeterminacy we set β_8 equal to zero or, equivalently, remove z_8 from the model.

Table 12.2 gives the LISREL estimates for Model 12.1. The estimates were obtained by analyzing the matrix of moments about zero of the variables y, $z_1, \ldots, z_7$, x, and a constant variable consisting of ones, to estimate μ. From Table 12.2 it is seen that, for families of up to five children, the β parameters tend to get smaller as the family becomes larger.

In Model 12.2 we specify that draftees from larger families have a lower level of education; that is, we set $\beta_i \geqslant \beta_{i+1}$ or, equivalently,

$$\begin{aligned} \beta_i &= \beta_{i+1} + \alpha_i^2, \qquad i = 1, \ldots, 7 \\ &= \alpha_i^2 + \ldots + \alpha_1^2 \end{aligned}$$

where the parameters α are estimated. This model allows us to specify that the effect of increasing family size is ordinal. If we let the LISREL variables $\mathbf{y}$, $\mathbf{x}$, and $\boldsymbol{\varepsilon}$ be $\mathbf{y} = y$, $\mathbf{x}' = (1, z_1, \ldots, z_7, x)$, and $\boldsymbol{\varepsilon} = e$, Model 12.1 with the restrictions of Model 12.2 becomes in LISREL notation

$$\mathbf{y} = \mathbf{\Lambda}_y \mathbf{\Gamma} \mathbf{x} + \boldsymbol{\varepsilon} \tag{12.12}$$

with

$$\mathbf{\Lambda}_y' = (\mu, \alpha_1, \alpha_2, \alpha_3, \alpha_4, \alpha_5, \alpha_6, \alpha_7, \gamma) \tag{12.13}$$

and

$$\mathbf{\Gamma} = \begin{bmatrix} 1 & 0 & 0 & 0 & 0 & 0 & 0 & 0 & 0 \\ 0 & \alpha_1 & 0 & 0 & 0 & 0 & 0 & 0 & 0 \\ 0 & \alpha_2 & \alpha_2 & 0 & 0 & 0 & 0 & 0 & 0 \\ 0 & \alpha_3 & \alpha_3 & \alpha_3 & 0 & 0 & 0 & 0 & 0 \\ 0 & \alpha_4 & \alpha_4 & \alpha_4 & \alpha_4 & 0 & 0 & 0 & 0 \\ 0 & \alpha_5 & \alpha_5 & \alpha_5 & \alpha_5 & \alpha_5 & 0 & 0 & 0 \\ 0 & \alpha_6 & \alpha_6 & \alpha_6 & \alpha_6 & \alpha_6 & \alpha_6 & 0 & 0 \\ 0 & \alpha_7 & \alpha_7 & \alpha_7 & \alpha_7 & \alpha_7 & \alpha_7 & \alpha_7 & 0 \\ 0 & 0 & 0 & 0 & 0 & 0 & 0 & 0 & 1 \end{bmatrix} \tag{12.14}$$

so that

$$\mathbf{y} = (\mu, \alpha_1^2 + \ldots + \alpha_7^2, \alpha_2^2 + \ldots + \alpha_7^2, \ldots, \alpha_6^2 + \alpha_7^2, \alpha_7^2, \gamma)\mathbf{x} + \boldsymbol{\varepsilon}$$

and from Model 12.2

$$\begin{aligned} \mathbf{y} &= (\mu, \beta_1, \beta_2, \ldots, \beta_7, \gamma)\mathbf{x} + \boldsymbol{\varepsilon} \\ y &= \mu + \beta_1 z_1 + \ldots + \beta_7 z_7 + \gamma x + e \end{aligned}$$

In the LISREL input, the elements of $\mathbf{\Lambda}_y$ in the position of the letters μ, $\alpha_1, \ldots, \alpha_7, \gamma$ are specified as free parameters, whereas elements of $\mathbf{\Gamma}$ in the position of the letters $\alpha_1, \ldots, \alpha_7$ are set equal to the elements of Λ_y in the position of the same letter $\alpha_1, \ldots, \alpha_7$. Furthermore, the matrix $\Phi(q \times q)$ is specified as a free symmetric matrix that neutralizes $\Lambda_x = \mathbf{I}$, $\mathbf{B} = \mathbf{0}$, $\Psi = \mathbf{0}$, $\theta_\delta = \mathbf{0}$. In Model 12.3 we additionally specify that the α_i's ($i = 1, \ldots, 7$) are equal to one another:

$$\beta_i = \beta_{i+1} + \alpha^2, \qquad i = 1, \ldots, 7$$

This allows us to specify the additional constraint that the effect of an increase in family size of one unit has the same influence on educational achievement for all family sizes; that is, i specifies that the relation between educational achievement and the number of children in the family is linear. Model 12.3 has the same LISREL specification as Model 12.2 except that all λ and γ parameters corresponding to α in Λ_y and Γ are restricted to be equal. From Table 12.2 it is seen that, although the estimates of the β parameters are different, Model 12.2 and Model 12.3 predict educational achievement as well as Model 12.1 does.

Concluding remarks

In this chapter it is shown that inequality constraints on factor loadings and regression coefficients can be handled within the general LISREL model. There are, however, some limitations on the imposition of inequality constraints in LISREL.

First, parameters can be specified to be larger but not to be smaller than a certain constant. Second, parameters can be specified to exceed another parameter only if both parameters are in the same row or the same column of the coefficient matrix. Third, parameters cannot be specified to exceed two other parameters at the same time, unless there is an inequality constraint between these parameters. The first two limitations do not exist in McDonald's (1980) COSAN model for the analysis of covariance structures. In COSAN, functional restraints between parameters can be imposed by "scalar specification."

Another problem concerns the comparison of model fit. If Model A is obtained by imposing inequality constraints on the parameters of Model B, the set of covariance matrices consistent with Model A is a proper subset of the set of covariance matrices consistent with Model B. Consequently, Model A is a submodel of Model B. Their difference in fit, however, cannot be compared by using their difference in chi-square statistics, since their difference in degrees of freedom is zero. This is because both Model A and Model B have the same number of parameters to be estimated and thus the same number of degrees of freedom. The models should therefore be compared by comparing the right-tail probabilities of their chi-square statistics or some other measure of fit.

In the examples we have not reported standard errors, since it is unclear how the standard errors of the parameters of interest (e.g., factor loadings) can be calculated from the standard errors of the derived parameters α. Furthermore, it was observed that the calculated standard errors of derived parameters were very large if the parameter was equal to zero, that is, if the corresponding model parameter was equal to its lower bound. This can be explained by the fact that the likelihood is not continuous at that point. The standard errors are then undefined, since they are calculated from the second derivatives of the likelihood function.

References

Campbell, D. T., & Fiske, D. W., (1959). Convergent and discriminant validation by the multitrait–multimethod matrix. In W. A. Mehrens & R. L. Ebel (eds.), *Principles of educational and psychological measurement*. Chicago: Rand McNally.

Cronbach, L. J. (1971). Test validation. In R. L. Thorndike (Ed.), *Educational measurement* (2nd ed., pp. 443–507). Washington, D.C.: American Council on Education.

Cronbach, L. J., & Snow, R. E. (1977). *Aptitudes and instructional methods*. New York: Irvington.

Guilford, J. P. (1971). *The nature of human intelligence*. New York: McGraw-Hill.

Guttman, L. (1965). A faceted definition of intelligence. In R. Eifermann (Ed.), *Scripta Hieroslmitana* (pp. 161–81). Jerusalem: Magnes Press.

Jöreskog, K. G. (1967). Some contributions to maximum likelihood factor analysis. *Psychometrika, 32*, 443–82.

   (1970). A general model for analysis of covariance structures. *Biometrika, 57*, 239–51.

   (1974). Analyzing psychological data by structural analysis of covariance matrices. In D. H. Krantz, R. C. Atkinson, R. D. Luce, & P. Suppes (Eds.), *Contemporary developments in mathematical psychology, Vol. 2: Measurement, psychophysics, and neural information processing*. San Francisco: Freeman.

   (1978). Structural analysis of covariance and correlation matrices. *Psychometrika, 43*, 443–77.

Jöreskog, K. G., & Sörbom, D. (1978). *LISREL IV: A general computer program for estimation of linear structural equation systems by maximum likelihood methods*. University of Uppsala, Department of Statistics.

Kelderman, H., Mellenbergh, G. J., & Elshout, J. (1981). Guilford's facet theory of intelligence: An empirical comparison of models. *Multivariate Behavioral Research, 16*, 37–62.

Lee, S. Y. (1980). Estimation of covariance structure models with parameters subject to functional restraints. *Psychometrika*, *45*, 309–24.

McDonald, R. P. (1980). A simple comprehensive model for the analysis of covariance structures: Some remarks on applications. *British Journal of Mathematical and Statistical Psychology*, *33*, 161–83.

Mellenbergh, G. J., Kelderman, H., Stijlen, J. G., & Zondag, E. (1979). Linear models for the analysis and construction of instruments in a facet design. *Psychological Bulletin*, *86*, 766–76.

Mulaik, S. A. (1975). Confirmatory factor analysis. In D. J. Amick & H. J. Walberg (Eds.), *Introductory multivariate analysis*. Berkeley, CA: McCutchan, 1975

Raven, J. C. (1938). *Progressive matrices*. London: Lewis.

Tenopyr, M. L., Guilford, J. P., & Hoepfner, R. A. (1966). *A factor analysis of symbolic memory abilities*. Reports of the Psychology Laboratory, No. 38. Los Angeles: University of Southern California.

van Meerem, L. M., & van Peet, A. A. J. (1976). Intellectuele reserve als indicatie voor gelijkheid van kansen. *Tijdschrift voor Onderwijs Research*, *1*, 241–55.

13

Issues and problems in the application of structural equation models

PETER CUTTANCE

Introduction

Although structural equation and covariance structure modeling has become more widely used during the past few years, there have been numerous suggestions that it may not be suitable for many of the models and data found in the social and behavioral sciences. Several studies of the behavior of structural modeling methods in conditions that approximate those found in practice have now been completed. They provide a fairly clear idea of when these methods are appropriate given particular model and data conditions.

Chapter 2 in this volume sets out the statistical model in matrix notation and specifies the assumptions required in order to estimate and test its fit to data. In this chapter we discuss methodological and statistical issues encountered in the application of structural modeling. Particular attention is paid to the evaluation of the robustness of the method to violation of the assumptions made in estimating the parameters of the model and testing its fit to the data.

General methodological and statistical issues

In this section we discuss several methodological issues encountered in the application of structural equation modeling. These include the specification of alternative models, the choice of a statistic to represent the relationship between noninterval measurement scales, the treatment of interactions, the relationship between exploratory and confirmatory modeling, and issues arising from the unit of analysis and sampling method employed in the collection of nonexperimental data.

Exploratory and confirmatory methods

The basic difference between exploratory and confirmatory modeling is related to the way that theory and data interact in the analysis. In an exploratory analysis the data are analyzed primarily on the basis of statistical models (ranging from those based on simple descriptive statistics to the complex statistical models underlying such techniques as factor analysis) and substantive theory is introduced post hoc at the point where the researcher is trying to interpret the results of such analyses. In contrast, a confirmatory analysis requires the researcher to put forward a formal model based on substantive considerations at the outset. A statistical model that parallels this substantive model is then constructed and tested against the data. Put another way, exploratory analyses attempt to glean statistical evidence from the data, which is then interpreted in an extra statistical framework, whereas confirmatory modeling constructs its models in an extra statistical framework and then tests their efficacy in a statistical framework (Cuttance 1985a,b).

The analyses typically conducted with structural modeling methods contain both exploratory and confirmatory elements. However, it is important to recognize that, when the data are treated as a single sample for analysis purposes, the confirmatory phase should precede the exploratory phase, a reversal of much social science practice. A researcher using structural modeling techniques must first have a substantive model from which to construct a mathematical representation of the social or behavioral process of interest. The object of constructing the mathematical representation of the process is to provide a means of testing whether the model accounts for the underlying grid of relationships in the data. This amounts to an attempt to prove or "confirm" the null hypothesis represented in the specification of the model, something that runs counter to established scientific practice. The information gained from the attempt, however, is employed as evidence that indicates whether the model posited could explain the relationships in the data, within the bounds of sampling error, in which case we say that the model *fits* the data.

The discovery that a particular model fits the data does not, however, imply that it is necessarily a true representation of the real-world processes that actually generated the data. Alternative models may fit the data equally well (Toulmin 1953, pp. 113–15), and until all such models were tested and tests designed to differentiate among the efficacy of each, we could not say with certitude which model was the true model. Of course, we can never know all such models; hence, progress rests on the idea of accumulating evidence about competing models and making extrastatistical assessments of the evidence in support of each.

Often the model posited does not fit the data satisfactorily. In this case we can either reject the model and construct alternative models and test them against the data, or move into an exploratory phase in the context of the original model. Any subsequent changes made in the model then represent ad hoc adjustments of the substantive model originally posited. In general, we are interested in whether relatively minor adjustments of the model will accommodate the discrepancy between it and the data. If major changes in the original model are required, it is clear that this model is not capable of explaining the data; hence, the substantive model underlying it does not describe the processes that generated the data. The interpretation of a model that has undergone major change through a series of adjustments of the data is clearly of an exploratory nature. As in any interpretation of the findings from an exploratory analysis, caution must be exercised because many alternative models, hence many different substantive interpretations, could explain any given data structure. MacCallum (1985) investigated the process of the exploratory fitting of models in simulated data, that is, data for which the true model was known. He found that only about half of the exploratory searches located the true model, even when starting from a model that was misspecified by only one or two parameters. He obtained this limited rate of success for such models in samples of 300 observations, which were assumed to be population data, and his success rate in smaller samples ($N = 100$) was zero. However, we are usually working with sample rather than population data, and the data structure analyzed represents the population data structure with some degree of uncertainty. Hence, the probability of locating the correct model by exploratory methods when sample data are used is even less than the limited success rate obtained by MacCallum, particularly so when it is further recognized that his models of the true population structures are gross simplifications of the structure that we investigate in social and behavioral research. An exploratory analysis of data thus entails the risk of inducing an interpretation founded on the idiosyncracies of individual samples. This explains why many highly parametrized models that are developed by exploratory fitting procedures in one sample often fail to fit the data from another sample. Any parameters that fit the model to the specific sampling fluctuations contained in the first sample cannot be expected to fit the particular sampling fluctuations contained in the second sample.

Another point of relevance to estimates of parameters based on exploratory analyses is related to the use of significance testing. The degree of probability associated with a confirmatory test of the fit of a model that has been constructed from an exploratory analysis of the same data tells us nothing about the true parameter values in the population. The exploratory analysis will have been based on an iterative process that could, if taken to its logical conclusion, eventually describe all the variation in the sample. Then the model would fit the data perfectly in an analytic or descriptive sense, rather than in a probabilistic sense (Cliff

1983; MacCallum 1985). Any model derived from an exploratory procedure can be tested with respect to its capacity to describe the true
structures in the population only if tested against samples other than that
on which it was developed.

In contrast, a confirmatory analysis aims to test whether a given model
could have generated the structure of relationships in the data (as
represented by the means of and covariances among variables) within the
bounds of sampling error; hence, it tests whether the model could
represent the true model for the population. Cudeck and Browne (1983)
have argued that such a strategy is not strictly appropriate given the
under-developed state of most social and behavioral science theories.
They suggest that a more realistic objective would be to employ a cross-
validation strategy to develop models that will perform optimally in future
samples. Their cross-validation strategy for the development of models is
based on an exploratory analysis of a subsample of the data and its
subsequent replication in a second subsample of the data. They found that
a double cross validation, that is, exploratory fitting of models in each half
of the data with replication to the other half of the data, provided models
that, although often rejected by the chi-square test statistic in the
replication sample, did not differ very much substantively. Highly parametrized exploratory models, which thus fit the data well in the initial
subsample, did not necessarily replicate better than models with fewer
parameters. This reflects the nature of the exploratory fitting of models to
data: Many parameters in the model may be doing little more than fitting
the model to the sampling fluctuations in the (sample of) data analyzed.
These parameters are irrelevant to the true population model; hence, they
are of no substantive value when the model is cross-validated against
other samples drawn from the same population.

The problems of superfluous parameters associated with the idiosyncracies of particular samples highlights the desirability of formally
specifying alternative models that could have generated the data.
Although the idea of specifying alternative models is often argued to be
impractical, it should be one of the explicit functions of a literature review.
Indeed, the methodology of confirmatory modeling can be viewed as one
in which the strategy of cross validation is *writ large*. Individual studies do
not exist in vacuo, but rather in the context of antecedent cognate research
and practical knowledge. One of the essential functions of research is to
formalize such knowledge by constructing conceptual models of the
process under investigation. When contradictory or incompatible formulations of the evidence embodied in this extant knowledge are revealed,
they provide a basis for competing explanatory models. Confirmatory
modeling aimed at evaluating which of the alternative models formulated

may best account for the relationships in the data can then be viewed as a cross validation, or replication, of models derived from previous empirical and theoretical work. If the data are made available to other researchers, this process need not even require that a given study consider more than a single model; that is, there is no necessity for competing models to be evaluated within the confines of an individual research program. However, when a research program aims to make prescriptive recommendations to inform policy or practice, it is highly desirable that competing models be entertained as a means of assessing the validity of any conclusions reached on the basis of particular models.

There is a sense in which the form of cross validation embodied in a confirmatory method as outlined above is more robust than cross validation among subsamples within a study. When the cross validation is based on models evaluated in separate studies employing different data, the samples of data are truly independent, whereas subsamples within a study share biases and other characteristics derived from their common sampling frame and data collection procedures. Needless to say, this assumes that the different studies draw their samples from the same relevant universe of observations.

Measurement issues

Measurement issues in structural modeling include the following: (1) the nature of measurement in the social and behavioral sciences, (2) the selection of appropriate measurement scales to fit the framework and statistical assumptions, and (3) the standardization problems arising out of the need to interpret parameter estimates across samples, and subgroups, and to compare parameters within a model.

Epistemological problems arise in the process of measurement and its relation to the substantive theoretical framework through which the phenomena of interest are observed. In order to measure a social event it is necessary first to formulate a theory of what that event is and how it fits into the structure of the phenomena with which it is associated. The divisions in the *scale* of a measurement instrument are used to locate an observation of the event into a category that is meaningful in terms of the substantive concepts of the theory employed to describe and explain the phenomena under investigation.

The relevance of these issues lies in their salience in understanding the relation of *measurement models* to *structural models* in structural modeling. Essentially, measurement models have meaning only in the context of the theory that underlies the substantive relationships embodied in the structural model. Thus, it makes sense to estimate the parameters for the structural and measurement models simultaneously. Those who argue for a two-step procedure in which the measurement model parameters are estimated in the first step independently of the structural model, and are then held constant in the second stage while the parameters of the structural model are estimated, implicitly deny the theory-laden nature of measurement. Burt (1976), however, found that the parameter estimates for models varied little regardless of whether they were estimated by such a two-stage procedure or simultaneously. He did note, however, an exception when the signs implied by variable loading across constructs and the estimated correlations among constructs conflicted with the signs for the observed correlations among variables. Burt's discussion does not recognize the *necessary* logical relationship between measurement and theory, and he discusses the relationship between measurement and structural parameters as if they were epistemologically independent.

The choice of a measurement scale for a variable also involves a decision about its interval or categorical nature. These issues were discussed briefly in Chapter 1 dealing with framework assumptions for structural modeling. However, measures of the degree to which variables covary were not discussed.

An elementary expression of the degree to which two continuous variables covary is the average of the cross products between them,

$$\text{mean cross product} = \frac{1}{N}\sum X_i Y_i$$

where X_i and Y_i are any two variables and i refers to the $i = 1, \ldots, N$ observations in the sample.

This measure is known as the moment about the origin, and it contains information on the location of the means of the variables with respect to the origin in addition to the covariation among the variables. The mean cross-product matrix for all variables in a model is called the *moment matrix*, and this matrix should be analyzed if the model contains parameters estimating measures of location such as equation intercepts or factor means.

If each variable is centered so about its mean is zero, information on the native origin for the measuring scale is lost. The covariation among continuous interval variables is known as their *covariance*. The covariance is expressed as the mean cross product between the centered scores for the variables:

$$\text{cov}(X_i Y_i) = \frac{1}{N}\sum (X_i - X)(Y_i - Y)$$

If the variables are standardized to have standard deviations of unity, in addition to being centered about their means, the measure of covariation between them is known as the Pearson product–moment correlation coefficient. The standardized variables are the original scores subtracted from the mean and divided by their standard deviation:

$$\text{standardized variable} = \frac{X_i - \bar{X}}{\sqrt{\sum(X_i - \bar{X})^2/N}}$$

The correlation coefficient is then expressed as

$$\text{correlation } r = \frac{1}{N}\sum\left[\frac{X_i - \bar{X}}{\sqrt{\sum(X_i - \bar{X})^2/N}}\right]\left[\frac{Y_i - \bar{Y}}{\sqrt{\sum(Y_i - \bar{Y})^2/N}}\right]$$

Now, the numerator times $1/N$ is the same as the formula for the covariance between X and Y, and the denominator reduces to the product of the variances; thus,

$$\text{correlation } r = \frac{\text{cov}(X, Y)}{\text{var}(X)\,\text{var}(Y)}$$

Although the above measures of covariation are presented in many basic statistics books, their direct implications as measures of covariation in the types of data usually encountered in the social and behavioral sciences are not always understood. The principal assumption invoked when these measures are employed as measures of covariation is that the measurement scales are interval in nature and that the relationships among variables are linear.

When a weaker assumption of ordered polytomous measurement scales is employed, the above measures capture only the linear component of any covariation and fail to capture any nonlinear component; hence, the estimates of total covariation among such variables may be attenuated. This means that the estimates of covariation for data commonly encountered in social and behavioral research typically underestimate the strength of the true relationship among variables. In the context of regression analysis we can test for well-behaved nonlinear components of the relationship between the dependent and independent variables by specifying a polynomial function for the independent variables. However, simple polynomial functions may not capture the all-nonlinearity in the bivariate relationships.

The measures of covariation described above are also affected by nonnormal skewness and kurtosis when employed as summary measures of covariation in the data. Thus, there is a prima facie case for investigating the robustness of linear measures of covariation to departures from linearity, skewness, and deviations from the kurtosis of the normal distribution.[1]

It is clear that the above measures of covariation depend on the scaling of variables. If the scaling is interval in character, the interpretation of the measures is invariant to a shift in location of the origin. This is due to the fact that a fixed distance on an interval scale has the same interpretation regardless of where on the scale it is located. However, if we relax this assumption of an interval scale and assume only that the measurement scale is an ordered polytomous scale, the interpretation of covariation in terms of the measures outlined above will not be invariant to changes in the value at which each category is located. For example, a scale with assigned values of 1, 2, 3, 4, 5 for its categories may provide quite different estimates of covariation with other variables from those obtained by an alternative assignment of the values of 1, 4, 5, 11, 37, respectively. In social science research, measurement scales are often of an ordered polytomous character. Hence, the robustness of measures of covariation to alternative scalings (metric) of the measures is of considerable interest. Departures from the assumption of interval-level scaling will generally attenuate the estimate of covariation among variables.

One solution to the problem of calculating covariances for variables with an ordered noninterval (ordinal) metric is to assume that each of the variables has an underlying normal distribution in the population and to rescale each to an interval-level variable on the basis of this underlying distribution. New thresholds are calculated for the values at which categories of the variables are defined on the scale on the basis of the frequency of observations in each category for each variable. We refer to this as normal scoring. Since the choice of a normal distribution is arbitrary, the units of the scale are also calculated on this basis. The product–moment correlation among these normally scored variables can then be employed as a measure of covariation among them. Since the normalized scores have an arbitrary metric, the measure of location (mean) for the variable is also arbitrary and is usually set at zero. The distribution of the variable is usually also arbitrarily defined to have unit variance, in which case the resulting unit of measurement for the variable is commonly referred to as a z-score.

Treating each variable distribution independently, however, may not be the most effective way of summarizing the covariation between pairs of variables. An alternative is to estimate the covariation between each pair of variables from their joint distribution. Two approaches are available in this case. The first is to calculate the canonical correlation between each pair of variables (Kendall & Stuart 1961, pp. 568–73). The canonical correlation calculates optimal score values for the two variables that maximize their product–moment correlation, subject to the assumption that each has mean zero and unit variance.

The second approach is to assume that each variable corresponds to a latent variable with a continuous distribution. New threshold values for each category value are then calculated on the assumption that the joint distribution between the pair of latent variables is normal (Jöreskog & Sörbom 1985). The polychoric correlation is estimated by maximum likelihood methods as the correlation between pairs of these latent variables.

One consequence of these approaches is that truncated or censored distributions are simply a special case of the general distribution for an ordinal variable. Censored distributions are relatively common in social and behavioral science measurement (Maddala 1984). Examples are floor and ceiling effects in cognitive tests, educational qualifications measured in years of schooling, and employment status.

Although these measures provide a means by which alternative measures of covariation can be calculated, they presuppose that the respective bivariate distributions are normal. If it is only our poor measurement instruments that make it appear otherwise in many cases, these alternative measures of covariation are to be preferred to any that are based on the raw scores for observed variables. A measure of covariation based directly on the raw score product–moment correlation coefficient is often severely attenuated, and this may be one of the reasons that such estimates are predominantly in the range .0–.5 for variables thought to be associated from a theoretical perspective. Many conceptual variables could be viewed as normally distributed in the general population, and even when this is not the case it may be reasonable to approximate them as being normally distributed, particularly if the metric in which they are measured in most research is somewhat arbitrary. Alternative categories that reflected a more normal distribution could be devised in many cases. The conceptual variable of educational attainment is sometimes measured as "years of schooling." This results in a distribution with an upper tail that is thicker than that of a normal distribution and a lower tail that is truncated. The conceptual variable, however, is continuous and extends beyond the range captured in the observed variable. A more appropriate measuring scale would extend the tails of the observed distribution and match the distribution of the theoretical variable better. Such adjustments would result in many variables with an observed distribution that is more like the normal distribution. Conceptually, the normal scoring, canonical correlation, and polychoric correlation coefficients all appeal to these ideas for their validity as measures of covariation among observed variables.

All the measures of covariation discussed above, with the exception of the moments about the origin and the covariance between two variables, are standardized measures. That is, they have arbitrarily defined location and variance parameters. Kim and Ferree (1981) provide a lucid discussion of standardization in social and behavioral science research. One objective of standardization is to allow for comparison, either across samples or across variables and constructs within a model. The methods commonly employed to estimate structural models, however, are not all suitable when standardized measures of covariation are employed as the basic input to the analysis. This is because these estimators have been developed for the normal theory properties of the covariance matrix. We return to this issue later in the discussion of the various estimators available.

Sampling issues

Since the mid-1970s, there has been a considerable volume of research on the consequences of analyzing nonexperimental data based on sampling schemes that are not of a simple random nature (e.g., cluster sampling) when the model assumes that the data are drawn from a simple random sample from the population (Holt, Smith, & Winter 1980, Scott & Holt 1982). The problem is closely related to the estimation problems associated with the "unit of analysis" issue discussed in educational and sociological research. The unit of analysis issue concerns the appropriate level of observation for modeling hierarchical phenomena. It has been widely discussed under the rubric of "contextual analysis" and "ecological analysis" (Boyd & Iversen 1979; Burstein 1980) and has recently been reformulated as the multilevel statistical model (Mason, Wong, & Entwistle 1985, Aitkin & Longford 1986; Goldstein 1986; Raudenbush & Bryk 1986a,b).

Cluster sampling methods and observations on intact units with a multilevel structure (e.g., pupils within schools) give rise to observations that do not satisfy the independence assumption of linear models. That is, the observations (on pupils) within clusters or observational units (schools) are not independent of one another, but rather have some degree of variation in common for all pupils within each school. Thus, pupils sampled within schools show more similarity (less variation) than pupils in a sample drawn randomly across schools. Hence, observations on pupils within schools are correlated (nonindependence). This lack of independence among observations is due to the fact that higher-level (school-level) factors influence the score for all observations (pupils) within each higher-level unit. The statistical implications of these issues are discussed in a later section.

Estimation

In this section we consider the role of assumptions outlined in earlier sections for the estimation of model parameters. A range of estimators and the assumptions on which they are based are discussed in order to ascertain those features of estimators that might raise questions about their application in certain situations. The estimation of parameters is closely related to the problems of identification and testing.

Identification

A good general introductory exposition of the formal aspects of the identification problem is available in Saris and Stronkhorst (1984); more formal and advanced discussions are available in standard econometric texts (e.g., Wonnacott & Wonnacott 1985; Pindyke & Rubinfeld 1981). A model is said to be identified if its parameters are uniquely determined by the variances and covariances among the observed variables in the model. The statistical assumptions S1–S4 outlined in Chapter 2 go a long way toward identifying the parameters of the model. They provide a mathematical framework for expressing the variances and covariances among the observed variables as combinations of parameters in the model. This, however, takes the form of a mathematical relationship between the hypothesized population variances and covariances and the model parameters, and no considerations related to sampling from the population formally enter into the problem. In consequence, the evaluation of the identification status of a model cannot be assessed fully on the basis of an empirical test of the model against sample data. Such data-based evaluations of identification can be misleading (Krane & McDonald 1979). A model may appear to be empirically identified in a sample when it is actually underidentified in the population. Likewise, a model could be judged to be underidentified in a sample even if it is identified in the population. The reason for these perverse conclusions are to be found in the random fluctuations that occur in data sampled from a population. Large sample sizes are some insurance against the occurrence of such phenomena, but they do not obviate the need to evaluate the identifiability of model parameters more formally. The LISREL program performs an empirical test of identifiability, but because it is based on the sample data it may occasionally give a misleading diagnostic on the identifiability of a model. Although Jöreskog and Sörbom (1981) suggest that the empirical test will "almost certainly" be correct, one is advised to be careful when samples are small.

Alternative estimators

Structural modeling methods employed in social and behavioral sciences can be thought of as a merger of models developed in econometrics and psychometrics (Goldberger 1971), the structural model relating to the former and the measurement models relating to the latter. The factor analysis model developed in psychometrics can be estimated by least squares methods once sufficient restrictions have been placed on it for identification purposes. However, it was clear early in the development of simultaneous equation modeling methods in econometrics that independence between disturbances and the "independent" variables in equations would be unrealistic, especially since lagged time-dependent variables were likely to appear in equations as both dependent variables and independent variables. Most introductory econometrics textbooks (Johnston 1972; Pindyke & Rubinfeld 1981) demonstrate that the method of ordinary least squares (OLS) produces biased and inconsistent estimates of the model parameters under such conditions.

The method of two-stage least squares (2SLS) was developed to deal with problems caused by a lack of independence between the equation disturbances and independent variables. More complex models consisting of several equations require even more elaborate methods that simultaneously estimate all parameters in the model.[2] Maximum likelihood (ML) and generalized least squares (GLS) estimators have been developed for estimating the parameters in complex multiequation models. LISREL (VI and earlier versions) allows the user the option of selecting from four different estimators: OLS, GLS, ML, and an instrumental variables estimator (IV), which is similar to 2SLS. The program uses the OLS and IV estimators as methods of obtaining initial estimates of the parameters. These estimates are then employed as initial values for the iterative ML and GLS estimators. In some models the OLS and IV estimators are efficient unbiased estimators of the parameters – for example, for a single regression equation with no lagged independent variables. For multiequation and more complex models, however, they are generally less efficient than the GLS or ML estimates. For many models – for example, those with lagged independent variables or reciprocal influences among dependent variables, the OLS and IV estimators also produce biased estimates of the parameters.

The basic principle of the OLS, IV, and GLS methods is to minimize the discrepancy between the estimates of variances and covariances implied by the parameter estimates Σ and the estimated population variances and covariances derived from the data in the sample S; that is, the estimator minimizes a function of $|S - \Sigma|$. However, the estimates of the population variances and covariances are themselves not known exactly but subject to sampling error. Estimates of parameters in a model will also be affected by this characteristic of the basic input to the analysis. Information on this sampling variation can be employed to derive more efficient estimates of the model parameters. This is done by weighting the discrepancy function to be minimized by the variances and covariances of the covariance matrix fed into the model. Hence, a more advanced estimation method would minimize a function of $|\mathbf{W}(\mathbf{S} - \Sigma)|$, where $\mathbf{W}$ is a weight matrix based on the variances and covariances of the estimated covariance matrix for the data. The OLS method ignores this refinement by setting $\mathbf{W} = \mathbf{I}$; that is, all elements of the covariance matrix estimated from the data are assumed to be estimated with equal precision. For this reason the OLS method is commonly referred to as unweighted least squares (ULS). The GLS method estimates $\mathbf{W}$ under the assumption that the data have a multivariate normal distribution.

The ML method of estimation is based on an approach that is quite different from that of the least squares estimators. It finds the combination of parameter values that maximizes the likelihood of the sample covariances. In order to do this it must assume that the probability density function for the variables is known. This probability density function is referred to as the *prior* distribution assumed for the variables in the population. The prior must be specified a priori, if for no other reason than that the data are assumed to be only a sample from the population and hence the exact population distribution is not known. Various prior distributions can be assumed in applications of the ML method, but the one most commonly specified in ML estimators for structural models is the multivariate normal distribution. Given the sample size, the observed (sample) covariances, the prior distribution to be assumed for the population, and the model specification, the method then employs a numerical procedure to find the parameter values that maximize the likelihood for the estimated covariances.

Three other estimators have also been developed for structural equation models. The first of these is a modified GLS estimator that allows for the relaxation of the strict assumption of multivariate normality by allowing for skewness in the multivariate distribution (Browne 1982; Bentler 1983a,b). Browne showed that deviation from normal kurtosis rather than skewness was likely to distort estimates for methods that assumed a multivariate normal distribution. This estimator still requires that the multivariate distribution of the variables have the same kurtotic characteristics as the multivariate normal distribution. But skewness and kurtosis are nearly always found to vary together; hence, it is unlikely in practice that this assumption about the multivariate distribution for the variables will be satisfied in many cases where the assumption of multivariate normality is not satisfied.

Browne (1984), however, has developed another more general estimator that relaxes both the assumptions of normal skewness and normal kurtosis, so that the assumption of multivariate normality can be dispensed with. This is referred to as the asymptotically distribution-free (ADF) best generalized least squares estimator. Both the modified GLS estimator and the ADF estimator estimate the weight matrix **W** as a complex function of the variances and covariances of the estimates of the population covariances. The normal-theory (unmodified) GLS estimator is implemented in LISREL VI (and the ML estimator can be shown to be equivalent to it), and the ADF estimator is implemented in LISREL VII, where it is called the WLS estimator.

Muthén (1978, 1984) developed another estimator that explicitly deals with the categorical nature of variables. It is referred to as the categorical variable methodology (CVM) estimator, and it avoids the use of Pearson product–moment correlations and metric covariances among variables by fitting the model directly to the estimated latent correlations underlying the observed categorical variables. In essence, it assumes a multivariate normal distribution for the latent continuous variables underlying the observed categorical variables. This estimator can also be represented by the discrepancy function for the GLS estimator with a specific form for the weight matrix **W**. This estimator is not available in LISREL VI and earlier versions, because the estimates that use the polychoric correlations do not take into account the appropriate weight matrix and hence are not asymptotically efficient. LISREL VII does, however, provide an estimator similar to Muthén's CVM estimator. It requires that the WLS estimator be employed with an input matrix of polychoric correlations.

The ULS estimator is not scale-free, which means that a set of estimates derived from the covariance matrix are not a simple linear transformation of those based on the (standardized) correlation matrix or any other rescaling of the variables. The other estimators and the CVM estimator are scale-free; thus, the researcher does not have to be particularly concerned about the scaling of variables in the sense that estimators for different scalings relate to one another through a direct transformation function. This is important because many variables in social and behavioral science research are expressed on what is essentially an arbitrary scale – for example, 18–83 for a scale of occupational prestige in one study (Goldthorpe & Hope 1974) and a scale of 1 to 21 (Stewart, Prandy, & Blackburn 1980) in another. Differences in scaling are also inherent in scores for variables derived as a weighted sum of a set of items, such as test scores or scores for a measure of neuroticism or disability measured by instruments that may contain different numbers of items in different studies. Furthermore, as discussed earlier, the measures of covariation available for ordinal variables usually entail an arbitrary standardization of variable measurement scales.

The GLS and ML estimators are asymptotically unbiased and asymptotically efficient under the assumption of multivariate normality. This means that in large samples they provide unbiased estimates with minimum sampling variation. The concept of a "large sample" derives from the calculus of probability density functions for the variables and corresponds to the statement that under integration these properties will hold in the limit as the sample size tends toward infinity. Thus, we cannot say a priori how many observations constitute a large sample, since it depends on the probability density function for the particular population from which the sample is drawn. Samples in the social and behavioral sciences typically range in size from 50–100 in studies using intensive interviews, through 100–1,000 in many social psychological studies, and 3,000–5,000 or more in large-scale sociological, educational, and medical surveys. Although experience suggests that it is relatively safe to assume asymptotic behavior for these estimators in samples of 1,000 or more observations, it is not clear whether similar assumptions can be made in samples as small as 100 observations. Evidence from simulation studies of the types of structural models used in econometrics suggests that limited-information estimators for parameters in one equation at a time (OLS, IV) perform fairly well even in small samples of 30 to 50 observations (Mösbaek & Wold 1970). So-called full-information estimators (those that estimate the parameters in all equations simultaneously, such as ML, GLS, ADF, and CVM) are generally found to be less stable in such small samples. Since limited-information estimators are theoretically less efficient than full-information estimates in many structural modeling situations, there is a potential trade-off between sample size and the performance of estimators. Whether this holds for structural models of the type typically used in the social and behavioral sciences has been the subject of various simulation studies, the most extensive of which is reported in Chapter 9. In the section below on robustness, other research in this area is discussed.

Assessment of fit and the evaluation of models

The assessment of model fit has probably received more attention in the literature than any other aspect of structural modeling. Most discussion has focused on the likelihood ratio test statistic for such models. This provides a test of model fit with desirable theoretical properties (it has an asymptotic chi-square distribution) under certain conditions. Since it is realized that the conditions required for this test of fit will be only approximately satisfied, other measures of the fit of a model are also important.

At the most general level, the validity of a model should be evaluated on methodological criteria for the reasonableness of the parameter estimates. For example, models that have estimates of correlations greater than unity in absolute value or that have negative variances (Heywood cases) do not satisfy basic methodological criteria. Various measures of the amount of variance accounted for by a model and of the difference between the observed covariances and those implied by the model have been developed.

We use the phrase "test of the fit" of a model to refer to parametric statistical tests, that is, those based on a particular statistical distribution, and the phrase "evaluation of the model" to refer to measures of the methodological validity of a model. These measures include various indices of the fit of a model, but their distributional properties are unknown: hence, they are not *test statistics* in the usual sense, but heuristic indicators of how well a model performs.

Evaluation of the model

Methods for assessing the methodological validity of a model have been somewhat neglected in the literature. It is assumed that every researcher knows about them and employs them routinely in structural modeling. However, we believe that their use deserves more prominence. First we discuss general requirements for the estimates of model parameters to be methodologically valid, and second we discuss various indices of model fit.

At the most fundamental level of evaluation of a model, one must ask, "Are the parameter estimates plausible?" This entails an inspection of the estimates to ascertain whether all estimated and implied correlations are in the range |0–1| and whether all the estimated variances of latent constructs, error, and residual terms are positive. Furthermore, all estimates of squared multiple correlations for the observed variables and coefficients of determination for the structural equations should be positive. Other indicators that something might be amiss are large standard errors and highly correlated parameter estimates. A message indicating that a correlation or covariance matrix is not positive definite is also indicative of weaknesses in the model, unless the constraints placed on parameters (e.g., an error variance constrained to be zero) are the reason for the matrix being nonpositive definite. If any of these criteria are not met, they indicate that the model estimates are not logically plausible.

The next level of evaluation involves an assessment of whether the estimates of construct loadings are sufficiently high to justify the interpretation of the constructs as measuring an underlying theoretical construct. If, using a common rule of thumb, all standardized loadings for a particular construct were less than 0.3, it would seem inappropriate to interpret the construct as a measure of an underlying variable of substantive importance in relation to its indicators. In essence, this situation would suggest that the indicators had little validity vis-à-vis the construct concerned. Indicators of greater validity will result in high standardized construct loadings in the model. A model with weak relationships between constructs and their indicators makes little substantive or methodological sense. Fornell and Larcker (1981) have argued that this is a weakness in structural modeling, but in reality it merely reflects the fact that poor measurement cannot yield a substantively valid model. The use of high-powered statistical tests cannot compensate for a lack of theoretical substance in a model. Hence, the argument of Fornell and Larcker that models with low correlations among observed variables lead to estimates of strong relationships among constructs is somewhat specious. It fails to take account of the fact that such a model would be substantively invalid because the constructs themselves would fail to capture a substantively meaningful portion of the variance shared by their indicators. Statistically, low correlations among indicators of a construct imply that there is little variance among them.

The squared multiple correlation for an observed variable indicates the proportion of its variance that is accounted for by the latent construct. Large multiple correlations indicate that a high proportion of the variance in the observed variable is accounted for by the latent construct, hence that it is a valid indicator of that construct. A low squared multiple correlation indicates that the indicator is a weak or invalid measure of the construct concerned.

The third level of evaluation concerns the amount of variance accounted for in each structural equation of the model. The squared multiple correlation for each equation is the structural modeling analogue of the squared multiple correlation R^2 in regression analysis. High values indicate that a large proportion of the variance in the "dependent" latent construct in the equation is accounted for by the "independent" latent constructs in the equation. Hence, the difference between the statistic for regression models and for an equation in a structural model is related to the fact that regression models are based on relationships among *observed variables*, whereas structural models are based on relationships among *latent constructs*. A summary measure of the multiple correlation across all structural equations is provided by the coefficient of determination for the model. In addition, the LISREL program provides a coefficient of determination for all *observed* variables jointly. This coefficient for the observed variables is analogous to the squared multiple correlation for the regression of the dependent observed variables on all other observed variables in the model. Although it is rarely the objective of a model to explain the variation in all the endogenous constructs, a model with low squared multiple correlations for intervening endogenous constructs may be considered to be an inadequate representation of the processes that generated the data. Thus, a given model may be evaluated as being more adequate for some relationships (equations in the model) than for others. We will almost always wish to apply a test of adequacy to the model for its capacity to explain the variation in the main dependent construct. This is usually the final endogenous construct in a recursive model. In a reciprocal effects model the focus is on more than a single construct, and in a covariance structure model (e.g., a multimethod-multitrait or factor analysis model) the focus is on several latent constructs jointly.

The fourth level of the evaluation of a model concerns its capacity to reproduce the covariance structure among the observed variables. This is known as assessing the fit of the model. We shall discuss measures of fit that are not based on distributional assumptions initially and then move on to measures based on test statistics for which statistical tests are available.

Several measures of fit are employed in research published in the literature, and we shall discuss each of these in turn. The object of evaluating the fit of a model is to assess how well the structure of relationships specified in the given model accounts for the variances and covariances among the observed variables in the model. A completely saturated model, that is, a model that is equivalent to a regression model between the observed dependent and all observed independent variables, exactly describes all of the covariation among the observed variables in terms of the model parameters. Such a model has zero degrees of freedom. Structural equation models, however, aim to describe the covariation among the observed variables in terms of the model's parameters by positing a simpler structure relating not the observed but the unobserved variables (latent constructs) of the substantive model to one another. Such a model usually specifies that certain paths are zero; that is, a latent construct may be specified to influence a second latent construct but not to influence a third latent construct. In terms of a path diagram, some paths are thus omitted. This means that not all specifications of a model may account for the covariation among the observed variables equally well. In mathematical terms we calculate the fit of a model as a function of $|S - \Sigma|$

representing the differences between the observed covariances and the covariances implied by the model estimates for the particular model specified.[3]

A first guide to the fit of a model can thus be gained from an inspection of the residuals arising from the difference between the covariances and variances for the observed data and those implied by the model estimates. These are printed in the LISREL output as the "residuals," and their average is represented by the root mean square residual. A problem in interpreting these residuals is that their magnitude is dependent on the magnitude of the variances and covariances in the model. Also, since the covariances calculated from parameter estimates are subject to sampling variation reflected in the standard errors of the parameter estimates, it makes sense for comparative purposes to normalize these calculated residuals by dividing them by their standard error. If we then make an assumption that the normalized residuals have a normal distribution, we can present them as a quantile–quantile (Q–Q) plot.[4] The straight line from the bottom left to the top right of a Q–Q plot represents the trace line for the quantiles from a cumulative normal distribution. Hence, if the normalized residuals represent purely random variation in the difference between the observed and the fitted covariances, they will all fall along this diagonal line. If the residuals in the Q–Q plot fall roughly along a line that is steeper than the diagonal, they indicate that the model is overfitting the data. In this case the spread of the residuals is less than that which would be expected; that is, they are more closely bunched about zero (too few points in the "tails," and too many in the center, of the distribution) than they would be if they represented a random variable from a standard normal distribution. The reverse case of a flatter slope than the diagonal indicates residuals with a greater spread than that expected for a random normal deviate. Any model for which the residuals follow roughly a straight line can be considered adequate. Those with a flatter slope have a poor fit, as do those with residuals that do not approximate a straight line on the Q–Q plot. Models with a straight line that is considerably steeper than the diagonal must be interpreted cautiously, since some of their parameters may be modeling mere sampling fluctuations in the data rather than real relationships that could be replicated in other data. Parameters that mainly reflect sampling variation do not represent any feature of the underlying population; hence, they have no substantive interpretation in terms that generalize to the population of interest. Thus, Q–Q plots with a steep slope indicate that the model is *overfitting* the real (substantive) relationships in the data.

Those Q–Q plots that exhibit nonlinearities indicate that the model fits some variances and covariances considerably better, or worse, than others and that the normalized residuals do not have a normal distribution. This usually indicates that the model is poorly specified. An inspection of the normalized residuals will usually indicate that some of the variances and covariances are poorly fitted.

The LISREL program provides two summary measures of the fit of the overall model in addition to the likelihood ratio test statistic. The two summary measures are the goodness-of-fit index (GFI) and the adjusted goodness-of-fit index (AGFI). Both of these indices generally have a range of 0 to 1, although under some circumstances they can be negative. Values close to 1 indicate that the model accounts for most of the joint variances and covariances among observed variables in the model. The AGFI index adjusts this value for the degrees of freedom in the model. The sampling distributions for these measures are not known; thus, they cannot be employed as test statistics to indicate whether the proportion of the covariances and variances not accounted for are higher than would be expected by chance alone. Their use is as a heuristic guide to the overall adequacy of the model. Although no working rules of thumb have yet been established, it would seem reasonable on the basis of experience gained thus far to say that models with an AGFI of less than .8 are inadequate and that most acceptable models would appear to have an AGFI index of greater than .9.[5] Bentler and Bonnet (1980) and Saris and Stronkhorst (1984) have suggested alternative indices based on the proportion of the variances and covariances among the observed variables accounted for by a model. They differ somewhat from that produced by the LISREL program and require the researcher to specify an alternative null model to the fully saturated null model employed in calculating the fit statistics in LISREL. Like the AGFI and GFI they cannot be interpreted in the same way as squared multiple correlations since they are not measures of proportional reduction in error. Although they provide useful information about the fit of models in comparison with some prespecified null model, the interpretation of this information depends on the null model chosen as the base against which other models are compared. Tanaka (1982) provides examples of the use of these alternative fit indices.

Parametric tests of the fit of models

The main measure employed in tests of the fit of models is that based on the likelihood ratio test (LRT) statistic for the specified model against the alternative of the unconstrained (saturated) null model. Under the assumption of multivariate normality for the observed variables this test statistic has an asymptotic chi-square distribution. Thus, in large samples the fit of the model can be tested against that of the null model (which, since it is unconstrained, has perfect fit). If the specified model fits the observed sample variances and covariances as well as the null model, within the bounds of chance at some prespecified level (usually, $\alpha < .05$), the model is said to be a valid model for the population.

As is the case with most parametric statistical tests, the LRT statistic[6] is dependent on sample size. A practical consequence of this for the relatively simple models employed in the social and behavioral sciences is that fewer of them fit the data in large samples than in small samples. Thus, for practical purposes Jöreskog and Sörbom (1981) suggest that the LRT statistic should be treated as a heuristic index of the goodness-of-fit, along similar lines to the model evaluation measures already discussed, rather than as a test statistic. They suggest that the LRT statistic is sensitive to departures from the assumption of multivariate normality; thus, it is unwise to interpret it strictly as a test statistic in most situations, given the type of data available in the social and behavioral sciences. However, it is widely employed as a test statistic in the published literature. In the next section we assess findings of research on the robustness of the LRT statistic to violation of the assumptions of the model.

The LRT statistic is also used to test for differences in the fit of models that form a nested hierarchy. A set of models are said to be nested within a hierarchy if each can be formed from a subset of the parameters in the model immediately above in the hierarchy. Differences in the value of the LRT statistic among models that are related in a hierarchical structure have an asymptotic chi-square distribution. For example, the decrease in fit (increase in value of the LRT statistic) for a model formed by constraining one additional parameter in a baseline model can be tested as a chi-square statistic with one degree of freedom. As an approximate rule of thumb, a change in the test statistic of about the same magnitude as or larger than the difference in the degrees of freedom between the two models indicates a deterioration in fit for the more constrained model. That is, the deterioration in fit is greater than that expected by chance alone. The exact probability of the change in the value of the test statistic for a given difference in the degrees of freedom between two models can be ascertained from statistical tables for the chi-square distribution.

Two heuristic indices of fit based on the value of the LRT statistic for a model are (1) the test statistic divided by the degrees of freedom for the model and (2) critical N. The issues involved in using each of these ad hoc indices of model fit are discussed in Chapter 11. Dividing the test statistic by the degrees of freedom for the model is now considered an unreliable method of assessing the fit of a model. Critical N (Hoelter 1983; see also Chapter 5) calculates the sample size that would be required for the difference in the test statistic for two models to be statistically significant at some prespecified level (usually α = .05). If the sample size so calculated is considered sufficiently large, the model is assessed to be adequate. Sample sizes required for model estimates to be reliable are discussed below.

Robustness of estimation and testing procedures

The preceding sections and Chapter 2 outline the methodological and statistical assumptions made in structural modeling. Some of these are specific to the form of the statistical model on which LISREL is based, but most are applicable to a wide range of related models. The models developed and implemented in computer programs by Browne and Cudeck (1983; BENWEE), Bentler (1984; EQS), McDonald (1985; COSAN), and Muthén (personal communication; LISCOMP) are all close relatives.

When we speak of robustness in the context of statistical modeling we are referring to the degree to which the model will produce valid estimates and inferences when the methodological and statistical assumptions are not fully met. In general, we should expect that few of the assumptions will be fully met, and most violated to a greater or lesser degree. However, assumptions are not like an electronic switch, in which the current is either on or off. Rather, they are more like traffic laws, more or less observed, depending on the danger of violating them in particular circumstances. The task of this section is to delineate the circumstances and conditions under which structural modeling may lead us to the wrong answers. The features of social and behavioral science data that lead to the violation of the assumptions of structural modeling include distributional properties that lead to violation of the assumption of multivariate normality – skewness, leptokurtic (peaked) or platokurtic (flat) distributions, and multimodality; categorization of measurement scales; outliers; non-independent observations; and small samples. Studies of the robustness of structural modeling have investigated the influence of all these conditions, with one exception.

The exception is that of the nonindependence of observations discussed earlier under sampling issues. The most likely source of the noninde-pendence of observations is the multilevel and time-series nature of most social and behavioral science phenomena and the use of clustered sampling methods. It is probably true that a wide range of social and behavioral science data do not meet the assumption of independence among observations. Statistical methods for handling multilevel data are now being developed (Mason et al. 1985; Aitkin & Longford 1986;

Goldstein 1986; Raudenbush & Bryk 1986a,b), but there is no simple adjustment of the structural modeling framework that can be made in order to deal with nonindependent observations. We can, however, cope with the problem of the structural modeling framework by modeling each group (e.g., school) separately in a multigroup model, but this becomes intractable with more than a few groups, and such models typically lack power owing to the small number of observations in each higher-level unit. Furthermore, the results of the Monte Carlo study presented in Chapter 9 indicate that estimates of parameters and the test statistics are unstable in complex models when samples are small. The main substantive drawback of a strategy based on a multiple-group model, however, is that it does not allow for the modeling of substantive relationships across levels. Multilevel statistical models, however, cannot as yet deal with relationships among latent variables. One possibility that may be feasible is to use a multilevel statistical model to purge the covariance matrix of the effects of the nonindependence among observations and then employ this covariance matrix as input to structural modeling. The effect of ignoring any dependency among the observations in multilevel data, or that collected through clustered sampling methods, is an underestimation of the variances of the estimated population covariances for the observed variables.

Kish and Frankel (1974) have studied the consequences of clustering for estimating population location parameters (e.g., means), and Pfeffermann and Smith (1985), Scott and Holt (1982), and Holt et al. (1980), among others, have studied its effects on estimates of population regression parameters. Goldstein (1986), Aitkin and Longford (1986), Mason et al. (1985), and Raudenbush and Bryk (1986) have studied the effects of a lack of independence due to multilevel structures and have sought to deal with the problem by modeling the structure of errors at each level. We are not aware, however, of any attempts to consider the consequences of nonindependence due to sampling schemes or the multilevel character of data in the context of structural modeling.

Although there have not yet been any studies of the effect of varying degrees of dependence among observations on estimates and inferences in structural modeling, we can interpolate the findings from the effect in simple linear models, where it gives rise to unbiased but inefficient estimates. That is, the standard errors are underestimated – hence, the rule of thumb that it is advisable to double standard errors in regression models based on clustered samples. It would not be surprising if the consequences for standard errors in structural modeling were similar to those for regression models, but we should also expect that test statistics for the fit of structural models would also be affected.

The design of robustness studies

There have been two substantial investigations of the robustness of structural modeling (Boomsma, Chapter 9 in this volume, and 1983; Muthén & Kaplan 1985) and several smaller studies that have investigated particular aspects or robustness. There are essentially three modes of investigating the robustness of statistical models to particular estimation and testing procedures:

1. The most thorough, and expensive, method is to conduct a statistical study in which the features of models and data thought to influence the robustness of estimates and inferences are investigated in a Monte Carlo simulation. This design broadly follows that of a classical factorial experiment. In such a study artificial data of known properties are simulated a large number of times to provide estimates of the properties of estimators and test statistics under each specified set of model and data conditions. The theoretical asymptotic (large sample) estimates of the standard errors can also be derived from statistical theory for these models.

2. The performance of estimators and test statistics is investigated in a single sample of artificial data with known properties. A study of this kind can be thought of as a case study of one sample. Again the asymptotic standard errors can be derived theoretically for the models.

3. The estimates and inferences from alternative estimators are investigated for specific models in real data. In this case the "true structure" is not known, but the properties of the data and the specification of the models are known; thus, the estimates and test statistics for alternative estimators can be compared, given these.

The study by Boomsma and another by Jöreskog and Sörbom (1985) are the only ones to use a large-scale Monte Carlo design as outlined in design 1 above. Even then, Boomsma's design is restricted to the study of one estimator (ML) across a range of permutations of model and data characteristics. At the time of Boomsma's study, ML was the only estimator widely used. A similar study including ML, instrumental variables estimates, and GLS is underway (Hägglund 1985). Boomsma's study investigated a range of models under several distributional properties of the data and for various sample sizes. He conducted 300 replications of each experiment. The study by Muthén and Kaplan is a much smaller Monte Carlo investigation of the performance of ML, GLS, ADF, and CVM estimators in a single-factor model and is based on 25 replications of the experiment. The main feature of this study was its investigation of the effects of skewness and kurtosis on the estimators considered. Tanaka (1984) also used a Monte Carlo design of 20 replications to study the behavior of the ML and ADF estimators for variables with high positive kurtosis in a two-factor model. This investigation considered the effects for sample sizes of 100,500, and 1,500, whereas the Muthén and Kaplan study considered only the one sample size of 1,000. Although the Muthén–Kaplan and Tanaka studies are based on only a small number of replications of the experiments, they, in conjunction with Boomsma's study, provide more powerful evidence about the robustness of estimators and test statistics than studies conducted under designs 2 and 3 described above.

Jöreskog and Sörbom (1985) reported a Monte Carlo study that focused not on the parameters of the structural model, but rather on alternative estimates of the covariation among variables. The objective here was to ascertain the effects of nonnormal distributional properties of variables on different measures of covariation. Since all current estimators for structural models work from an estimate of the population covariation among variables, this approach breaks the problem of robustness into two components: the robustness of measures of covariation and the robustness of the estimators themselves. If unbiased measures of the covariation among variables could be found, these could be employed as the basic input to the analysis.

Studies that have employed artificial data for which the true structure is known but have considered only the one replication of the experiment include those of Bentler (1983b), Olsson (1979), and Fuller and Hemmerle (1966). Studies that have compared the performance of estimators and test statistics in real data those of include Browne (1982), Huba and Bentler (1983), Huba and Harlow (1983, 1985), Huba and Tanaka (1983), Huba, Wingard, and Bentler (1981), and Jöreskog and Goldberger (1972).

Together the studies to date tell us much about the performance of alternative estimators and their associated test statistics under varying model and data conditions. Below we review the findings for parameter estimates and for inferential test statistics: standard errors, confidence intervals, and the LRT statistic. The behavior of the model evaluation indices discussed earlier has not been studied in the context of varying model and data conditions. Since they represent empirical indices of model performance based on estimated parameters, it is possible that they also are not robust with respect to the true model that generated the data. If the assumptions of the particular estimators are met, the parameter estimates have the desirable theoretical properties of consistency and efficiency. Thus, they are unbiased and have the smallest possible standard errors in large samples. We discuss the findings from the robustness studies for estimators first and then consider the findings for the LRT statistic.

Robustness of parameter estimates and standard errors

Jöreskog and Sörbom's (1985) study of measures of covariation for ordinal variables considered six alternative measures:

1. the product–moment correlation using raw scores,
2. the product–moment correlation using normal scores,
3. the polychoric correlation,
4. the canonical correlation,
5. Spearman's rank order correlation, and
6. Kendall's τ_b coefficient.

The study simulated two sets of ordinal variables with assigned integer scores and a known population correlation coefficient of .60 300 times for samples of 100, 400, and 1,000 observations. In one simulation the pair of variables had three and four categories, and in the other they had five and seven categories. In the first simulation, the variables had relatively normal marginal distributions, and in the second, one had a U-shaped distribution and the other a skewed distribution. The findings of this study suggest that, although all estimators underestimated the true correlation, the polychoric correlation is least biased and the most consistent. Product–moment correlations based on normal scoring (bias < .06) and the canonical correlation (bias < .06) also performed relatively well. The bias for the polychoric correlation measure was less than .01 with variance < .01 for all sample sizes. The bias for the normal scoring and canonical correlation measures decreased as the number of categories in the variable increased. The bias for the product–moment correlation estimates based on raw scores was very large (> .50), representing an attenuation of the true correlation of more than 80 percent. The attenuation of the polychoric correlation, the canonical correlation, and the normal scoring product–moment correlation was of the order of 1, 9, and 9 percent, respectively. The attenuation factor for the Spearman and Kendall measures was of a similar order to that of the raw score product–moment correlation measure. Muthén and Kaplan (1985) reported that raw score product–moment correlations in the range .35–.45 were attenuated between 10 and 30 percent, depending on skewness and kurtosis. Browne (1982) has shown that kurtosis rather than skewness was the major theoretical threat to estimates of covariation based on raw scores. The Muthén and Kaplan study found that zero skewness and high kurtosis strongly attenuated estimates of correlations, but other cases with low kurtosis combined with moderate skewness also resulted in significant attenuation.

Jöreskog and Sörbom (1985) also reported a case study of measures of covariation for a mixture of interval and ordinal variables. The ordinal variables included one that was moderately skewed, with a U-shaped distribution, and another that was dichotomized. The polychoric/polyserial and canonical correlations were again the least biased and most consistent estimates of the true covariation among the variables in the data. For a two-factor model (Jöreskog 1978) and a sample $N = 200$, the model estimates based on these measures were also the least biased and most consistent. They performed better than those for the product–moment correlation calculated from either the raw scores or the normal scores for the variables. All estimates underestimated the factor loadings and overestimated the error variances in the model. None of the other studies that we consider below have reported their findings at this intermediate level at which the model summarizes the data as covariation between variable pairs. The Jöreskog and Sörbom (1985) study clearly suggests that at this level the polychoric/polyserial correlation and the canonical correlation measures are to be preferred to product–moment correlations based on either raw scores or normal scores or to the Spearman correlations or Kendall's τ_b measure as a summary measure of the covariation between pairs of ordinal variables or mixtures of ordinal and interval variables.

A general conclusion to be drawn from the studies of estimators of model parameters is that all estimators (ML, GLS, ADF, CVM) appear to produce relatively unbiased estimates when the distributional properties of the data do not represent extreme departures from normality. Muthén and Kaplan (1985) find no consistent bias in parameter estimates for any of the estimators when research designs for varying skewness and kurtosis are studied. They investigated a one-factor model with a skewness ranging from -0.3 to 2.9 in a sample of 1,000. This finding is in line with those of Boomsma (Chapter 9, this volume) for parameter estimates based on the ML estimator for a sample size of 400. He investigated models with variables ranging from a normal distribution to one with variables with skewness of up to 4.0 and a mean skewness of 2.5. The findings of Bentler (1983a), Huba and Bentler (1983), Huba and Harlow (1983, 1985), and Fuller and Hemmerle (1966) also suggest that ML and GLS parameter estimates are relatively unbiased in data with skewness and kurtosis in the range of most social and behavioral science data.[7] Browne (1982), however, found that the ML estimator consistently underestimated error variances for a one-factor model and highly nonnormal data (mean skewness = 4, mean kurtosis = 27). Further evidence that the ML estimator may produce biased estimates in strongly skewed or highly kurtotic data is provided by Olsson (1979) and Tanaka (1984). Olsson found that the degree of bias was greater for models in which the true factor loadings were highest.

It would appear that ML and GLS parameter estimates are relatively robust against skewness for a wide range of applications in the social and behavioral sciences. However, when severely skewed or highly kurtotic variables are present in a model, the ADF estimator should be used if possible.

Most of the studies noted above also found little evidence of bias in the estimated standard errors of parameters for the ML, GLS, and ADF estimators, even when data are moderately skewed. Muthén and Kaplan (1985) and Boomsma (Chapter 9), however, report that the standard deviations of the empirical distributions of the parameter estimates depart from expectation for ML and GLS when the data are skewed. They found that the standard deviation of the estimated parameters often exceeds the estimated standard deviation; hence, the estimated standard error is too conservative, even though Boomsma found that the value of the estimate itself over a large number of replications is unbiased. Thus, although both ML parameter estimates and standard errors appear to be unbiased in skewed data, we may sometimes be led into Type 1 errors (concluding that a parameter differs from zero when its true value does not), if we accept them at face value. Muthén and Kaplan obtained similar results for the ML and GLS estimators, but the ADF estimator appeared to behave appropriately even in the presence of quite strong skewness (all variables in model had skewness $= -2.08$) and kurtosis (all variables in model had kurtosis $= 4.113$).

Boomsma investigated the robustness of the ML estimates and standard errors to variation in sample size, to the degree of discreteness of the distributions of variables, and to estimation based on the correlation matrix. With small samples ($N \leqslant 100$) there was a much greater chance of improper solutions and of a failure to reach convergence, particularly when $N < 50$. For $N > 100$ there was no evidence of any systematic bias in parameter estimates or in estimated standard errors. Findings for models based on the analysis of correlation rather than covariance matrices mirrored these results when $N > 200$. However, these models overestimated the variation in standardized parameter estimates, thus leading to a conclusion that the parameter does not differ from zero more often than expected. Generally there appears to be little effect on parameter estimates and estimated standard errors related to variations in the number of categories in the measuring scales of discrete variables. Boomsma's investigation covered scales varying between two and five categories.

Since ML and GLS parameter estimates and standard errors are robust in the normal case, it would be convenient if the use of polychoric and tetrachoric correlations would provide a ready solution in the case of skewed variables. However, the ML and GLS estimators were developed for covariance structures, and polychoric and tetrachoric correlations, like product–moment correlations, do not conform to the statistical theory on which those estimators are based. The behavior of ML and GLS estimates for models based on polychoric correlations has not been widely studied. Jöreskog's (1985) case study of a two-factor model found that the parameter estimates using ML with polychoric/polyserial correlations as input were less biased with lower mean square error than those using product–moment correlations based on raw scores or normal scores or those based on canonical correlations. Huba and Harlow (1985) provide another indication of their likely behavior from a set of five case studies on real data. An analysis of the parameter estimates for the initial specification for each of their five models indicates that the correlation between the ADF estimates and ML–polychoric or ML–tetrachoric estimates is about .7–.9. The correlations between these estimates and the CVM estimates are of a similar order. The corresponding estimates of standard errors for ML–polychoric/tetrachoric and those for other estimators, however, show much lower agreement. The number of parameter estimates on which this comparison is based is not large (96), and the estimates are for only one data set per model; thus, caution is counseled in their interpretation. There appeared to be no clear pattern of over- or underestimation for the ML-polychoric/tetrachoric parameter estimates when compared with the ADF and CVM estimates. Huba and Harlow, however, concluded that the former estimators were the most deviant of those they studied. They found that improper solutions and outlier estimates were more likely to occur with the estimators based on polychoric and tetrachoric correlations than with the other estimators.

Muthén's (1984) CVM estimator fits the model to the estimated latent correlations among the observed discrete variables directly rather than fitting the model for the correlations among interval-level observed (raw score) variables. Muthén and Kaplan (1985) report findings for a moderately kurtotic (kurtosis = 2.9) and skewed (skewness = -2.0) model involving dichotomous variables. The CVM estimator produced unbiased parameter estimates but slightly overestimated the standard errors. The ML, GLS, and ADF estimators based on raw score product–moment correlations were generally found to be biased estimators of factor variance and errors but unbiased for factor loadings in this model. The degree of bias across the range of models studied increased with the extent of attenuation observed for the raw score product–moment correlation estimates of the true covariation in the data. In data with only moderate departures from normal kurtosis and skewness (both <1.3), however, the bias in the estimates was not large enough (<15%) to affect most substantive interpretations based directly on the magnitude of the parameter estimates. In the models where either skewness or kurtosis was >2, some parameter estimates for ML, GLS, and ADF were biased by up to 30 percent.

Overall, it seems safe to conclude that ML and GLS parameter estimates and estimated standard errors are robust against moderate departures from the skewness and kurtosis of the normal distribution for a range of factor analysis and structural equation models. This robustness is relatively solid for samples with $N > 200$, even if the model analyzes a correlation matrix rather than a covariance matrix. Robustness in smaller samples is somewhat more problematic, depending on the true population structure, model complexity, and so on but may be reasonable in samples as small as 100, and in some cases in even smaller samples. When the skewness and kurtosis of variables are more substantial, it is advisable to employ the ADF or the CVM estimator. A rule stipulating when to employ these estimators is difficult to specify, but a reasonable rule of thumb might be to use it in any situation when the skewness or kurtosis of variables in the model exceeds 2.0.

Now that the ADF estimator is more readily available, it is possible to check routinely whether the ML or GLS parameter estimates and estimated standard errors differ to any significant degree from it, although the ADF estimator may be too expensive to use as a frontline estimator. An alternative solution when the data are highly skewed is to collapse some categories in the measurement of the most skewed variables. Since the number of categories was found to have little influence on estimates, except that due to attenuation of covariances when the number of categories was severely reduced, a modest collapsing of categories in the tails of a distribution should have few deleterious effects. This, however, is of little help when the distribution is strongly censored or truncated, or for cases of perverse kurtosis. In such cases it would seem most appropriate to rely on the ADF estimator or to employ polychoric and polyserial correlations or canonical correlations as input to the analysis.

Robustness of the likelihood ratio test statistic

Most of the studies mentioned in the previous section have also investigated the robustness of the RT statistic. Again, however, most of the information we have is based on the study by Boomsma reported in Chapter 9, with other studies generally extending these findings to alternative estimators. We expect the LRT statistic to deviate from its expected chi-square distribution when the assumption of multivariate normality is violated.

Boomsma found that the robustness of the ML LRT statistic did not appear to be substantially affected by sample size. It tended to have a light tail with $N < 100$ and a somewhat heavy tail for larger samples, and outlier values were often observed. No other investigators have systematically studied the behavior of the statistic by varying sample sizes for other estimators. In several cases, however, the LRT statistic has been compared across estimators in the same sample.

The ML LRT statistic was found to behave reasonably well asymptotically when skewness was slight but tended to be overestimated when the skewness was moderate (mean skewness ≥ 0.56) or stronger (Boomsma, Chapter 9 in this volume). This results in rejection of the model too often when the value of the statistic is compared with the chi-square distribution. This finding is supported by those of Bentler (1983b), Huba and Bentler (1983), Browne (1982), Huba and Harlow (1983, 1985), Tanaka (1984), and Muthén and Kaplan (1985), who found that the ML LRT statistic is almost always larger, sometimes substantially so, than that for the ADF estimator. Huba and Harlow (1985) suggested that the ML statistic may overestimate in leptokurtic (peaked) distributions and underestimate in platokurtic (flat) distributions, but this is not borne out by the findings of Muthén and Kaplan (1985), that both ML and GLS consistently produce LRT statistics that are higher than that produced by ADF for the same models and data, exhibiting variation in these dimensions. Huba and Harlow (1983) had reported comparative results for two models that had widely varying skewness and kurtosis among their variable sets. Their skewness and kurtosis ranged from -0.47 to 3.08 and from -0.23 to 10.39 in the first model and -0.67 to 2.69 and -0.90 to 7.17, respectively, in the second model. They found that, compared with the ADF estimator, the ML estimator overestimated the LRT statistic in both models but that the GLS estimator underestimated it in the first model and overestimated it in the second model.

In the study by Muthén and Kaplan, which was based on a simple four-variable single-factor model in a sample of 1,000, the ML LRT statistic rejected the true model 8–12 percent of the time when the variables were only moderately skewed (skewness < 1.21) but 32 percent of the time when stronger skewness (all variables; skewness $= -2.0$) was present. A similar pattern of rejection rates was found for the GLS estimator, but the ADF estimator had a lower rate of 4 to 12 percent for moderately skewed models and only 8 percent for the more strongly skewed model. The CVM estimator was reported for only the most skewed model and was found to have a zero rejection rate. These results should be compared with an expected rejection rate of 5 percent at the $p = .05$ level.

Boomsma (Chaper 9 in this volume; 1983) reports that the ML LRT statistic appears to behave appropriately with respect to rejection rates for models that have a maximum skewness of 1.0. In models with maximum skewness of 2.0 and of 4.0 the rejection rates ranged from 6 to 19 percent and from 40 to 54 percent, respectively, compared with an expected rejection rate of 5 percent for the normal (zero-skewness) model. He found, however, that a model in which the variables have offsetting skewness (-1.5 to $+1.5$) behaves as expected, with 3 to 6 percent of samples rejecting the model.

The findings of Huba and Harlow (1985) suggest that the ML LRT statistic for models that employ tetrachoric and polychoric correlations as their summary measures of the covariation in the data are considerably larger than the LRT statistics for the estimators based on analyses of product–moment correlations or for the CVM estimator. The clear message of these findings is that the ML LRT statistic is not a reliable guide to model fit when polychoric or tetrachoric correlations are used. However, the provision in LISREL VII of a WLS-estimator-corrected polychoric correlation matrix may substantially change this conclusion.

Overall we can conclude that the LRT statistic for the ML and GLS estimators can probably be trusted in most models with an absolute skewness of 1.0 or less but that they will generally reject the true model too frequently when the skewness of any of the variables is greater than this. There is some evidence that these statistics may be better behaved in models where the skewness of variables offsets one another; that is, when there is an equal preponderance of negative and positive skewness among the variables – a relatively rare occurrence from our experience in real data. When skewness is moderate, the LRT statistic for the ADF estimator also tends to reject the model more often than expected, but it performs better than the ML or GLS estimators in this situation. It has a slightly lower rejection rate and a small variance about the mean estimate of the statistic than the other two estimators. For more strongly skewed data the LRT statistic based on both the ADF and CVM estimators performs well, with few false rejections of the true model.

Other aspects of robustness

Finally we turn to two other aspects of robustness in the interpretation of estimates in structural models. In Chapter 11 Saris, Sattora, and den Ronden show that many of the interpretations of model estimates in studies reported in the literature may not be robust because the power of the test on which they were based is very low. In Chapter 10 Gallini and Casteel investigate the influence of outlier observations on parameter estimates.

Saris et al. put forward a method for assessing the power of tests of the parameters in a model. Their procedure involves testing one model against the hypothesis contained in a specified alternative model. In particular, one of the parameters is specified to take a different value in the alternative model. This procedure thus formalizes the heuristic methods of sensitivity analysis found in the literature (Land & Felson 1978; Kim 1984). The most common test is of the null hypothesis that the parameter is zero in the true population structure. Saris et al. show that the power of model testing depends not only on sample size but also on characteristics of the model, in particular the magnitude of the parameters in the true model, and on the complexity of the model. The power of a test is defined as the probability that an incorrect model will be rejected, that is, $1 - p$(Type II error). This assessment of the power of hypothesis tests rests on estimates of the LRT statistic in alternative models; hence, the preceding discussion of the robustness of this statistic is of prime importance to their method. Clearly, the LRT statistic should be estimated by a method that is robust for the degree of nonnormality present in the data. Once the appropriate estimator has been selected – if in doubt one should use an ADF or CVM estimator – the power of a given hypothesis test can be assessed by the method presented in Chapter 11. Only one parameter at a time can be tested in this way. Hence, given limited resources it will be advantageous to select only those parameters of most interest for investigation in this way. Assessing the power of hypothesis tests is not in itself an issue of robustness against nonnormal data, but rather one of robustness in making inferences from samples about the true structure in the population.

The findings from the study of the influence of outliers on structural model estimates reported by Gallini and Casteel in Chapter 10 show that the effects are greatest in small samples. Essentially, these findings parallel those for regression models, the explanatory power of the model being attenuated by outliers and standard errors being reduced by the removal of outlier observations.

Discussion and concluding comments

Structural modeling employs assumptions of a methodological and a statistical nature in modeling substantive theoretical perspectives of the real world. In this context the grid of relationships in the observed data is employed as a template against which to test competing theoretical models of those relationships in the real world. Thus, the methodological and statistical assumptions may be viewed as aids in linking the substantive model to the data via a procedure for estimating the relationships in the model. The estimates of the relationships in a particular model are then compared against those found in the observed data. If the model adequately describes the data (fits the data), it is accepted as one possible "explanation" of the processes in the population that could have generated the grid of relationships found in the observed data. The methodological and statistical assumptions are brought to bear in both the parameter estimation stage and in the assessment of the fit of the model. The assumptions made in a complex modeling method such as structural equation modeling make relatively strong demands on the functional form of the model and on the statistical properties of the data used to estimate the model. Caveat emptor haunts the literature on applied structural modeling, particularly with respect to the suspected sensitivity of the LRT statistic to violations of these assumptions. The research on robustness that is now available provides us with a fairly detailed map of the sensitivity of various estimators to a range of such violations.

Test statistics and parameter estimates have been found to be robust to moderate departures from normality in terms of the skewness (<2.0) and kurtosis (<2.0) of the univariate distributions of variables in a range of models. The LRT statistic appears to be more sensitive than parameter estimates and estimated standard errors to departures from normality when normal theory estimators (ML, GLS) are employed. The bias in the LRT statistic is serious for models containing variables with more than moderate skewness (>1.0) and kurtosis (>1.0). Recent developments in ADF and CVM estimation methods, however, have provided estimators that appear to be robust and that perform well in simulation studies.

The latter estimators are expensive, but the marginal cost of computer processing time continues to decline by a factor of 2 or more every few years. The LISREL program is now available for microcomputers, and within five years we can expect them to be as powerful in this context as the mainframes of the early eighties. The evaluation of the power of hypothesis tests is also relatively computationally expensive. However, both an ADF estimator and tests of power are now routinely available in the LISREL program (VII and later versions), and ADF estimators are available in other programs (EQS in BMDP, BENWEE). The CVM estimator is available only in Muthén's program (LISCOMP) and in LISREL VII. Both EQS and a preprocessor to LISREL (PRELIS) routinely provide information on the degree of nonnormality of the univariate and multivariate distributions in the data for a model. PRELIS also makes some provision for transforming variables where necessary. However, its major contribution is in making available the weight matrix for computing asymptotically efficient estimates of model parameters from a range of alternative summary measures (covariances, correlations, polychoric correlations) of the covariation in the data. Finally, we stress that the robustness of explanations of the processes that we wish to model are in the end dependent on our ability to replicate them, particularly since we are almost always working with sample data and our objective is to make inferences to the population. Where we are involved in applied research that aims to inform policy and practice, this process of replication can be accomplished by evaluating and testing our own findings with those available from similar studies elsewhere. The pursuit of intellectual theory, however, may proceed on a less time-critical and practice-related path; thus, true replication may be more feasible in that context. If theory is to develop in a linear way, the process of synthesizing and testing models of extant knowledge *before* embarking on the exploratory pursuit of new explanations is essential to any social or behavioral science methodology.

Notes

1. The normal distribution has kurtosis = 0. Distributions that are more peaked (leptokurtosic) have kurtosis values of greater than 0, and those that are flatter (platokurtosic) have kurtosis values of less than 0.
2. See Fox (1984, p. 252) for a discussion of full-information and limited-information estimators.
3. In structural equation modeling, the fit of a model is assessed by its capacity to reproduce the pattern of variances and covariances among the observed models. In regression models these variances and covariances are reproduced exactly because of the just-identified (i.e., saturated) form of the relationships among the observed variables. Because a given structural model imposes constraints on the relationships among the observed variables, based on the specification of the substantive model, it may reproduce the variances and covariances among the observed variables more or less well, depending on whether it is a good or poor explanation of the relationships among the observed variables.
4. Chapters 3 and 6 in Chambers et al. (1983) provide a sound discussion of the interpretation of Q–Q plots.
5. Research reported by Tanaka and Huba (1985) suggests promising lines of inquiry that may yield more information on the behavior of such measures of model fit.
6. This statistic is usually, inappropriately, referred to as the chi-square statistic. Strictly it should be referred to as a likelihood ratio test statistic that has a chi-square distribution, rather than as the chi-square statistic.
7. Boomsma (1983) presents information on the range of skewness typically found in social and behavioral science data.

References

Aitkin, M., & Longford, N. (1986). Statistical modeling issues in school effective-ness studies. *Journal of the Royal Statistical Society A, 149,* 1–42.

Bentler, P. M. (1983a). Some contributions to efficient statistics in structural models: Specification and estimation of moment structures. *Psychometrika, 48,* 493–517.

(1983b). Simultaneous equations as moment structure models: With an intro-duction to latent variable models. *Journal of Econometrics, 22,* 13–42.

(1984). *Theory and Implementation of EQS: A Structural Equations Program.* Los Angeles: BMDP Statistical Software.

Bentler, P. M., & Bonett, D. G. (1980). Significance tests and goodness of fit in the analysis of covariance structures. *Psychological Bulletin, 88,* 588–606.

Boomsma, A. (1983). *On the Robustness of LISREL (Maximum Likelihood Estimation) against Small Sample Size and Non-normality.* Doctoral disserta-tion, University of Groningen, The Netherlands.

Boyd, L. H., & Iverson, G. R. (1979). *Contextual Analysis: Concepts and Statistical Techniques.* Belmont, CA: Wadsworth.

Browne, M. W. (1982). Covariance structures. In D. M. Hawkins (Ed.), *Topics in Applied Multivariate Analysis* (pp. 72–141). Cambridge University Press.

(1984). Asymptotically distribution-free methods for the analysis of covariance structure. *British Journal of Mathematical and Statistical Psychology, 37,* 62–83.

Browne, M. W., & Cudeck, R. (1983). *BENWEE: A Computer Programme for Path Analysis with Latent Variables.* Pretoria: Human Sciences Research Council.

Burstein, L. (1980). The role of levels of analysis in the specification of educational effects. In R. Dreeben & J. A. Thomas (Eds.), *The Analysis of Educational Productivity: Issues in Microanalysis* (pp. 119–90), Cambridge, MA: Ballinger.

Burt, R. S. (1976). Interpretational confounding of unobserved variables in structural equation models. *Sociological Methods and Research, 5,* 3–52.

Chambers, J. M., Cleveland, W. S., Kleiner, B., & Tukey, P. A. (1983). *Graphical Methods for Data Analysis.* Belmont, CA: Wadsworth.

Cliff, N. (1983). Some cautions concerning the application of causal modeling. *Multivariate Behavioral Research, 18,* 115–26.

Cudeck, R., & Browne, M. W. (1983). Cross-validation of covariance structures. *Multivariate Behavioral Research, 18,* 147–67.

Cuttance, P. (1985a). Methodological issues in the statistical analysis of data on the effectiveness of schooling. *British Educational Research Journal, 11*(2), 163–79.

(1985b). A general structural equation modeling framework for the social and behavioral sciences. In R. B. Smith (Ed.), *A Handbook of Social Science Methods* (Vol. 3, pp. 408–65), New York: Praeger.

Fornell, C., & Larcker, D. F. (1981). Evaluating structural equation models with unobservable variables and measurement error. *Journal of Marketing Research, 18*, 39–50.

Fox, J. (1984). *Linear Statistical Models and Related Methods: With Applications to Social Research*. New York: Wiley.

Fuller, E. L., & Hemmerle, W. J. (1966). Robustness of the maximum likelihood estimation procedure in factor analysis. *Psychometrika, 31*, 255–66.

Goldberger, A. S. (1971). Econometrics and psychometrics: A survey of commonalities. *Psychometrika, 36*, 83–107.

Goldberger, A. & Cain, G. (1982). The causal analysis of cognitive outcomes in the Coleman, Hoffer & Kilgore report. *Sociology of Education, 55*, 105–22.

Goldstein, H. (1986). Multilevel mixed linear model analysis using iterative generalised least squares. *Biometrika, 73*, 43–56.

Goldthorpe, J., & Hope, K. (1974). *The Social Grading of Occupations*. New York: Oxford University Press.

Hägglund, G. (1985). *Factor Analysis by Instrumental Variables Methods: The Confirmatory Case*, Research Report 85–2. University of Uppsala, Department of Statistics.

Heckman, J. J. (1976). The common structure of statistical models of truncation, sample selection and limited dependent variables, and a simple estimator for such models. *Annals of Economic and Social Measurement, 5*, 475–92.

Hoelter, J. W. (1983). The analysis of covariance structures: Goodness-of-fit indices. *Sociological Methods and Research, 11*, 325–44.

Holt, D., Smith, T. M. F., & Winter, P. D. (1980). Regression analysis of data from complex surveys. *Journal of the Royal Statistical Society A, 143*, 474–87.

Huba, G. J., & Bentler, P. M. (1983). Test of drug use causal model using asymptotically distribution free methods. *Journal of Drug Education, 13*, 3–17.

Huba, G. J., & Harlow, L. L. (1983). Comparison of maximum likelihood, generalized least squares, ordinary least squares, and asymptotically distribution free parameter estimates in drug abuse latent variable causal models. *Journal of Drug Education, 13*, 387–404.

(1985). Robust estimation for causal models: A comparison of methods in some developmental data sets. In R. M. Lerner & D. L. Featherman (Eds.), *Lifespan Development and Behaviour* (Vol. 6, pp. 69–111). New York: Academic Press.

Huba, G. J., & Tanaka, J. S. (1983). Confirmatory evidence for three daydreaming factors in the short imaginal processes inventory. *Imagination, Cognition, and Personality, 3*, 139–47.

Huba, G. J., Wingard, J. A., & Bentler, P. M. (1981). A comparison of two latent variable causal models for adolescent drug use. *Journal of Personality and Social Psychology, 40*, 180–93.

Johnston, J. (1972). *Econometric Methods* (3rd ed). Tokyo: McGraw-Hill Kogakusha.

Jöreskog, K. G. (1978). Structural analysis of covariance and correlation matrices. *Psychometrika, 43*, 443–77.

Jöreskog, K. G., & Goldberger, A. S. (1972). Factor analysis by generalized least squares. *Psychometrika, 37,* 243–60.

Jöreskog, K. G., & Sörbom, D. (1981). *LISREL: Analysis of Linear Structural Relationships by the Method of Maximum Likelihood.* Chicago: National Educational Resources.

(1985). *PRELIS: A Program for Multivariate Data Screening and Data Summarization, A Preprocessor for Lisrel.* University of Uppsala.

Kendall, M. G., & Stuart, A. (1973). *The Advanced Theory of Statistics* (3rd ed., Vol. 2). London: Griffin.

Kim, J. (1984). An approach to sensitivity analysis in sociological research. *American Sociological Review, 49,* 272–82.

Kim, J., & Ferree, G. D. (1981). Standardization in causal analysis. *Sociological Methods and Research, 10,* 187–210.

Kish, L., & Frankel, M. R. (1974). Inference from complex samples. *Journal of Royal Statistical Society B, 36,* 1–37.

Krane, W. R., & McDonald, R. P. (1978). Scale invariance and the factor analysis of correlation matrices. *British Journal of Mathematical and Statistical Psychology, 31,* 218–28.

Land, K. C., & Felson, M. (1978). Sensitivity analysis of arbitrarily identified simultaneous-equation models. *Sociological Methods and Research, 6,* 283–307.

MacCallum, R. (1985, July). *Some Problems in the Process of Model Modification in Covariance Structure Modeling.* Paper presented to the European Meeting of the Psychometric Society, Cambridge, England.

Maddala, G. S. (1984). *Limited-Dependent and Qualitative Variables in Econometrics.* Cambridge University Press.

Mason, W. M., Wong, G. Y., & Entwistle, B. (1983). Contextual analysis through the multilevel linear model. In S. Leinhart (Ed.), *Sociological Methodology 1983–84* (pp. 72–103). San Francisco: Jossey-Bass.

McDonald, R. P. (1985). *Factor Analysis and Related Methods.* Hillsdale, NJ: Erlbaum.

Mosbäek, E. J., & Wold, H. O. (1970). *Interdependent Systems: Structure and Estimation.* Amsterdam: North Holland.

Muthén, B. (1978) Contributions to factor analysis of dichotomous variables. *Psychometrika, 43,* 551–60.

(1984) A general structural equation model with dichotomous, ordered categorical, and continuous latent variable indicators. *Psychometrika, 49,* 115–32.

Muthén, B., & Kaplan, D. (1985). A comparison of some methodologies for the factor analysis of non-normal Likert variables. *British Journal of Mathematical and Statistical Psychology, 38,* 171–89.

Olsson, U. (1979). On the robustness of factor analysis against crude classification of the observations. *Multivariate Behavioral Research, 14,* 485–500.

Pfeffermann, D., & Smith, T. M. F. (1985) Regression models for grouped populations in cross-section surveys. *International Statistical Review, 53,* 37–59.

Pindyck, R. S., & Rubinfeld, D. L. (1981). *Econometric Models and Economic Forecasts* (2nd ed.) New York: McGraw-Hill.

Raudenbush, S., & Bryk, A. S. (1986). A hierarchical model for studying school effects. *Sociology of Education, 59*, 1–17.

Saris, W., & Stronkhorst, H. (1984). *Causal Modeling in Nonexperimental Research*. Amsterdam: Sociometric Research Foundation.

Scott, A. J., & Holt, D. (1982). The effect of two-stage sampling on ordinary least squares. *Journal of American Statistical Association, 77*, 848–54.

Stewart, A., Prandy, K., & Blackburn, R. M. (1980). *Social Stratification and Occupations*. New York: Macmillan.

Tanaka, J. S. (1982). The evaluation and selection of adequate causal models. *Evaluation and Program Planning, 5*, 11–20.

(1984). *Some Results on the Estimation of Covariance Structure Models*. Unpublished doctoral dissertation, University of California, Los Angeles.

Tanaka, J. S., & Huba, G. J. (1985). A fit index for covariance structure models under arbitrary GLS estimation. *British Journal of Mathematical and Statistical Psychology, 38*, 197–201.

Toulmin, S. (1953). *The Philosophy of Science*. London: Hutchinson's University Library.

Wonnacott, R. H., & Wonnacott, T. H. (1985). *Introductory Statistics for Economists* (4th ed.). New York: Wiley.

Appendix

This appendix contains information on the input for the LISREL program for selected models from Chapters 3 to 8. We assume a reasonable familiarity with the LISREL manual for version V or later. A basic grounding in the relationship between the path diagrams, model equations, matrix formulation of the model, and the LISREL program input is provided in W. E. Saris and L. H. Stronkhorst, *Introduction to Causal Modeling in Non Experimental Research* (Amsterdam: Sociometric Research Foundation 1984). Other introductions are referenced in the first and last chapters of this volume. The formulations of the models provided below are for the LISREL variation of the statistical model underlying structural modeling, and formulations in terms of other structural modeling programs such as EQS and COSAN will vary somewhat, since their parametrization of the model is different from that employed by LISREL.

For standardization purposes we employ the default representations of LISREL matrices that were established in version V of the LISREL program. These defaults are generally upwardly compatible with later versions of the program.

We indicate below the default values of the matrices. Items that may be omitted from the program input are determined by two criteria: Either they are defaults (indicated in bold), or they are not required to describe the parametrization of the model under study. The notational brackets $\langle\!\langle \; \rangle\!\rangle$ indicate these items. Any or all of the items within these brackets may be omitted without causing a program error; for example, any single item or the whole group of items denoted as $\langle\!\langle$ LX = FU, FI LY = FU, FI PH = SY, FR$\rangle\!\rangle$ may be omitted. Single $\langle \; \rangle$ brackets deonote items that must be included but from which one of a set of parameters must be chosen, for example, $\langle$KM or CM or MM or AM$\rangle$.

Program input

Title line: This line may contain any title statement that is less than 80 columns long[1]

DAta[2] $\langle\!\langle$NGroups = #$\rangle\!\rangle$ NInput = # $\langle\!\langle$NObservations = #$\rangle\!\rangle$ $\langle$MA = KM or CM or MM or AM$\rangle$

$\langle$RAwdata $\langle\!\langle$XMissing = # MinValues = # UNit = # REwind FOrmat PP PT$\rangle\!\rangle$ or the following line

$\langle$KM or CM or MM$\rangle$ $\langle$SY or FU$\rangle$ UN = # REwind FOrmat$\rangle$

$\langle\!\langle$LAbels FOrmat REwind UNit = #$\rangle\!\rangle$

[indicate format for reading variable labels on this line, if reading in free format enclose labels between quotes]

[list of variable labels]

《SElection

[list variables in selection order, end list with a slash if not all variables selected》

MOdel 《〈NXvars = ⁑ or NYvars = ⁑〉〈FIxed or 〈NKsi = ⁑ and/or NEta = ⁑〉〉

《 LX=**FU, FI**   LY = **FU, FI**   BE = **ZE, FI**   GA = **FU, FR**
PH = **SY, FR**   PS = **SY, FR**   TD = **DI, FR**   TE = **DI, FR**》

《FIxed list of parameters to be fixed to a particular value, zero or otherwise, among matrices specified with a FRee parameter on MO card.

FRee   list of parameters to be freed in the matrices that are specified with FI parameter on the MO card.

EQual   list of parameters to be constrained to be equal, within a group, or across multiple groups》

VA x.x value to which FIxed parameter is to be constrained.

ST x.x starting value for a FRee or FIxed parameter.

OUtput 〈**ML** or IV or UL or TS or GL〉《PT SE TV PC RS EF VA MR MI FS FD SS TO AM MX = ⁑》

Key to mnemonic abbreviations

DAta description:

NGroups	Number of groups in the model (default = 1)
NInput	Number of variables to be read in the input data
NObservations	Number of cases in the input data
MA	Matrix of moments (sufficient statistics) to be analyzed

May be one of: KM   correlation matrix
CM   covariance matrix
MM   moment matrix of cross products (about origin)
AM   moment matrix augmented with a column of unit values (for estimation of means and intercept values)

RAwdata input:

XMissing	missing value indicator (must be the same for all variables)
MinValues (MV)	minimum number of values for a variable to be treated as continuous
UNit	unit (channel) from which data or other input file is to be read
REwind	rewind UNit to restart next read operation for this UNit at beginning of file
FOrmat	indicates that format follows on the next line, otherwise it is assumed to be a default (free) format, or the format appears as the first line of the file read from UNit = ⁑

PP   print information on polychoric correlations
PT   print technical information on the estimation of polychoric correlations

Matrix data input:
KM   read a correlation matrix
CM   read a covariance matrix
MM   read a matrix of moments about the origin
SY   matrix to be read is symmetric; only diagonal and subdiagonal elements in data
FU   matrix to be read is full; elements both above and below diagonal, plus diagonal, in data

SElection of variables from those input:
SE   select variables by order specified (end with a slash if not all variables selected)

MOdel card and model specification:
NX   number of X variables in the model
NY   number of Y variables in the model
FIxed X variables are to be treated as fixed (i.e., they represent only those values found in the data)
NKsi   number of endogenous (xi, ξ) constructs in the model
NEta   number of exogenous (eta, η) constructs in the model
LX   the lambda-X (λ^x) matrix of loadings for the endogenous constructs
LY   the lambda-Y (λ^y) matrix of loadings for the exogenous constructs
BE   the beta (**B**) matrix of directional relationships between endogenous constructs.
GA   the gamma (Γ) matrix of directional (regression or causal) relationships between exogenous and endogenous constructs
PH   the phi (Φ) matrix of covariances between the endogenous constructs
PS   the psi (Ψ) matrix of covariances and variances between residuals (the latter representing the unexplained variance) among the endogenous constructs in the model
TD   the theta delta (Θ^δ) matrix of error variances and covariances among the X variables.
TE   the theta epsilon (Θ^ϵ) matrix of error variances and covariances among the Y variables
FU   a matrix with elements above, along, and below the main diagonal
SY   a matrix with elements symetric about the main diagonal
DI   denotes that the matrix consists only of a main diagonal, all other elements being zero
ID   the identity matrix, all elements in the diagonal are unity (1s) and zero elsewhere

FI   denotes that the parameters represented by the rows and columns of a matrix are specified to be constrained to a particular value, usually zero

FR   denotes that the parameters represented by the rows and columns of the matrix are to be estimated by the model

EQ   denotes elements of matrices that are to be constrained to be equal to each other

OUtput listing from the run:

OUtput   denotes the end of the model specification and specifies through a series of optional parameters which statistics are to be output, the estimation method to be used, and the format of the output[3]

ML   specifies maximum likelihood estimation (the default)

IV   specifies instrumental variables estimation

UL   specifies unweighted least squares (otherwise known in most situations as ordinary least squares) estimation

TS   specifies two-stage least squares estimation

GL   specifies generalized least squares estimation

Notes

1. See LISREL manual for displaying multiple-line titles and for continuation of commands across lines.
2. Only the upper-case letters of each mnemonic are recognized by the program.
3. See the LISREL manual for the specification of the statistics available and their output format.

Model specifications and program input for selected models from Chapters 3–8

Here we present details of the specification of selected models from four chapters that readers may use to check their understanding of the steps in the formulation and specification of models in the LISREL format. From these chapters we have chosen models that represent different aspects of modeling in the LISREL framework. Those chosen from Chapters 3 and 4 show the application of LISREL to factor and measurement models across multiple groups, and the model from Chapter 8 is an application of a simple structural model for panel data. The models chosen from Chapter 5 demonstrate the application of LISREL to the testing of hypotheses about the hierarchical structure of a particular set of data. Because this is a complex task based on a large number of variables, the reader is referred to the details of the specification of the models presented in the text. The LISREL input is presented here for the full sequence of models tested in the chapter. We present the full specification for the complete set of models, the data, and the LISREL input for each, only for Chapter 7. This enables the reader to follow through and estimate the models for the complete analysis as it is presented in that chapter.

Model 3.7 (Figure A.1)

Specification of the model

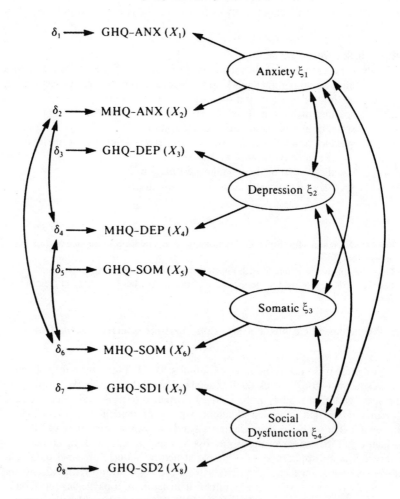

Equations relating the observed measures to the latent constructs:

$$X_1 = \lambda_{11}\xi_1 + \delta_1 \qquad X_5 = \lambda_{53}\xi_3 + \delta_5$$
$$X_2 = \lambda_{21}\xi_1 + \delta_2 \qquad X_6 = \lambda_{63}\xi_3 + \delta_6$$
$$X_3 = \lambda_{32}\xi_2 + \delta_3 \qquad X_7 = \lambda_{74}\xi_4 + \delta_7$$
$$X_4 = \lambda_{42}\xi_2 + \delta_4$$

Figure A.1. (Same as Figure 3.1.) Measurement model for symptom differentiation analysis, Model 3.7.

Equations for the model

$$
\begin{aligned}
x_1 &= \lambda_{11}\xi_1 && + \delta_1 \\
x_2 &= \lambda_{21}\xi_1 && + \delta_2 \\
x_3 &= \lambda_{32}\xi_2 && + \delta_3 \\
x_4 &= \lambda_{42}\xi_2 && + \delta_4 \\
x_5 &= \lambda_{53}\xi_3 && + \delta_5 \\
x_6 &= \lambda_{63}\xi_3 && + \delta_6 \\
x_7 &= \lambda_{74}\xi_4 + \delta_7 \\
x_8 &= \lambda_{84}\delta_4 + \delta_8
\end{aligned}
$$

Matrix format of the equations

$$
\begin{bmatrix} x_1 \\ x_2 \\ x_3 \\ x_4 \\ x_5 \\ x_6 \\ x_7 \\ x_8 \end{bmatrix}
=
\begin{bmatrix}
\lambda_{11} & & & \\
\lambda_{21} & & & \\
& \lambda_{32} & & \\
& \lambda_{42} & & \\
& & \lambda_{53} & \\
& & \lambda_{63} & \\
& & & \lambda_{74} \\
& & & \lambda_{84}
\end{bmatrix}
\begin{bmatrix} \xi_1 \\ \xi_2 \\ \xi_3 \\ \xi_4 \end{bmatrix}
+
\begin{bmatrix} \delta_1 \\ \delta_2 \\ \delta_3 \\ \delta_4 \\ \delta_5 \\ \delta_6 \\ \delta_7 \\ \delta_8 \end{bmatrix}
$$

$$
\mathbf{X} = \mathbf{\Lambda}^x \quad \xi + \delta
$$

LISREL matrices for the model

$$
\mathbf{\Lambda}^x = LX =
\begin{bmatrix}
LX\ 1\ 1 & & & \\
LX\ 2\ 1 & & & \\
& LX\ 3\ 2 & & \\
& LX\ 4\ 2 & & \\
& & LX\ 5\ 3 & \\
& & LX\ 6\ 3 & \\
& & & LX\ 7\ 4 \\
& & & LX\ 8\ 4
\end{bmatrix}
$$

$$
\mathbf{\Theta}_\delta = TD =
\begin{bmatrix}
TD\ 1\ 1 & & & & & & & \\
& TD\ 2\ 2 & & & & & & \\
& & TD\ 3\ 3 & & & & & \\
& TD\ 4\ 2 & & TD\ 4\ 4 & & & & \\
& & & & TD\ 5\ 5 & & & \\
& TD\ 6\ 2 & & TD\ 6\ 4 & & TD\ 6\ 6 & & \\
& & & & & & TD\ 7\ 7 & TD\ 8\ 8
\end{bmatrix}
$$

$$
\mathbf{\Phi} = PH =
\begin{bmatrix}
PH\ 1\ 1 & & & \\
PH\ 2\ 1 & PH\ 2\ 2 & & \\
PH\ 3\ 1 & PH\ 3\ 2 & PH\ 3\ 3 & \\
PH\ 4\ 1 & PH\ 4\ 2 & PH\ 4\ 3 & PH\ 4\ 4
\end{bmatrix}
$$

Data

Correlation matrix for field-independent group

```
1.0000000 0.6505024 0.4808010 0.6195529 0.3772106 0.4324335 0.5748863 0.4879859
0.3407340 0.3001610 0.2947626
0.6505024 1.0000000 0.4855984 0.7108634 0.3259124 0.5590916 0.6594003 0.4978773
0.2343138 0.1934037 0.2173248
0.4808010 0.4855934 1.0000000 0.4445997 0.2727568 0.3218426 0.4294155 0.3017452
0.1549900 0.1738723 0.0864834
0.6195634 0.7108634 0.4445997 1.0000000 0.3127527 0.5155949 0.6576406 0.5288570
0.2676268 0.2171977 0.2523852
0.3772106 0.3259124 0.2727563 0.3127527 1.0000000 0.4830425 0.2482570 0.1467286
0.2983751 0.2314103 0.2934578
8.4324335 0.5590916 0.3218426 0.5155949 0.4830425 1.0000000 0.4906247 0.3234648
0.1723288 0.0931756 0.2093713
0.5748863 0.6594003 0.4294155 0.6576406 0.2432570 0.4906247 1.0000000 0.5630236
0.1784837 0.1739362 0.1356230
0.4879859 0.4978773 0.3017452 0.5288570 0.1467286 0.3234648 0.5630236 1.0000000
0.0668136 0.1195236-0.0104052
0.3407340 0.2343133 0.1549900 0.2676268 0.2983751 0.1723288 0.1784837 0.0668136
1.0000000 0.8834548 0.8566160
0.3001610 0.1934037 0.1788728 0.2171977 0.2314103 0.0981756 0.1739362 0.1195286
0.8384548 1.0000000 0.5242600
0.2947626 0.2173248 0.0864834 0.2523852 0.2934578 0.2093713 0.1356230-0.0104052
0.8566160 0.5242600 1.0000000
```

Correlation matrix for field-dependent group

```
1.0000000 0.7604058 0.6471604 0.6396092 0.6461086 0.5836803 0.5032239 0.4964679
0.5123923 0.5042514 0.4001272
0.7604058 1.0000000 0.6324643 0.7565407 0.5648491 0.6411440 0.6037718 0.5901142
0.5147620 0.5177481 0.3878404
0.6471604 0.6324643 1.0000000 0.5432632 0.4658157 0.5101629 0.3543079 0.4004101
0.4727217 0.4291029 0.4148707
0.6396092 0.7565407 0.5432632 1.0000000 0.4161682 0.5947570 0.5881391 0.4687943
0.4634032 0.4584156 0.3538641
0.6461086 0.5648491 0.4658157 0.4161682 1.0000000 0.5507690 0.4418440 0.2964725
0.4625410 0.4364939 0.3843688
0.5886303 0.6411440 0.5101629 0.5947570 0.5507690 1.0000000 0.3120730 0.3142236
0.4720327 0.4333905 0.3385014
0.5082239 0.6037713 0.3543079 0.5881391 0.4418440 0.3120730 1.0000000 0.5546625
0.3366259 0.2941223 0.3099194
0.4964679 0.5901142 0.4004101 0.4687943 0.2964725 0.3142238 0.5546625 1.0000000
0.2895594 0.2804612 0.2318121
0.5123923 0.5147620 0.4727217 0.4634032 0.4625410 0.4720827 0.3366259 0.2895594
1.0000000 0.9179433 0.8646796
0.5042514 0.5177431 0.4291029 0.4584156 0.4364989 0.4833908 0.2941223 0.2804612
0.9179488 1.0000000 0.5944605
0.4001272 0.3878404 0.4148707 0.3538641 0.3848688 0.3385014 0.3099194 0.2318121
0.8646796 0.5944605 1.0000000
```

Labels file

```
'  GQA  ' '  MHQA  ' '  GQD  ' '  MHQD  ' '  GQS  ' '  MQS  ' '  XXXX  '
'  YYYY  ' '  ZZZZ  ' '  GQY1  ' '  GQY2  '
```

LISREL input

Model 3.1

LISREL 6 (LISTING = OUT 1, WORKSPACE = 500)
SYNDROME DIFFERENTIATION ANALYSIS − FI GROUP
DA   NG = 2   NI = 11   NO = 120   MA = KM

```
LA    UN = 8   RE
KM    FU   UN = 11   FO
(8F10.7)
SE
1   2   3   4   5   6   10   11/
MO   NX = 8   NK = 4   PH = SY, FR   TD = SY, FI
FI   PH (1,1)   PH (2,2)   PH (3,3)   PH (4,4)
VA   1.0   PH (1,1)   PH (2,2)   PH (3,3)   PH (4,4)
FR   LX (1,1)   LX (2,1)   LX (3,2)   LX (4,2)
FR   LX (7,4)   LX (8,4)
FR   LX (5,3)   LX (6,3)
FR   TD (1,1)   TD (2,2)   TD (3,3)   TD (4,4)
FR   TD (5,5)   TD (6,6)
FR   TD (7,7)
FR   TD (8,8)
OU   TV   MI   RS
SYNDROME DIFFERENTIATION ANALYSIS – FD GROUP
DA   NO = 98
LA   UN = 8
KM   FU   UN = 12   FO
(8F10.7)
SE
1   2   3   4   5   6   10   11/
MO   PH = SP   LX = SP   TD = SP
FI   PH (1,1)   PH (2,2)   PH (3,3)
VA   1.0   PH (1,1)   PH (2,2)   PH (3,3)
FI PH (4,4)
VA   1.0   PH (4,4)
OU   SE   MI   RS
```

Model 3.7

```
LISREL 6 (LISTING = OUT 7, WORKSPACE = 500)
SYNDROME DIFFERENTIATION ANALYSIS – FI GROUP
DA   NG = 2 NI = 11   NO = 120   MA = KM
LA   UN = 8   RE
KM   FU   UN = 11   FO
(8F10.7)
SE
1   2   3   4   5   6   10   11/
MO   NX = 8   NK = 4   PH = SY, FR   TD = SY, FI
FI   PH (1,1)   PH (2,2)   PH (3,3)   PH (4,4)
VA   1.0   PH (1,1)   PH (2,2)   PH (3,3)   PH (4,4)
FR   LX (1,1)   LX (2,1)   LX (3,2)   LX (4,2)
FR   LX (7,4)   LX (8,4)
```

```
FR   LX  (5,3)   LX  (6,3)
EQ   LX  (1,1)   LX  (2,1)
EQ   LX  (4,2)   LX  (3,2)
EQ   LX  (5,3)   LX  (6,3)
EQ   LX  (7,4)   LX  (8,4)
FR   TD  (1,1)   TD  (2,2)   TD  (3,3)   TD  (4,4)
FR   TD  (5,5)   TD  (6,6)
FR   TD  (7,7)
FR   TD  (8,8)
EQ   TD  (1,1)   TD  (2,2)
EQ   TD  (3,3)   TD  (4,4)
EQ   TD  (5,5)   TD  (6,6)
EQ   TD  (7,7)   TD  (8,8)
FR   TD  (4,2)   TD  (6,2)   TD  (6,4)
OU   TV  MI   RS
SYNDROME DIFFERENTIATION ANALYSIS − FD GROUP
DA   NO = 98
LA   UN = 8
KM   FU   UN = 12   FO
(8F10.7)
SE
1  2  3  4  5  6  10  11/
MO   PH = SP   LX = IN   TD = IN
FI   PH  (1,1)   PH  (2,2)   PH  (3,3)
VA   1.0   PH  (1,1)   PH  (2,2)   PH  (3,3)
FI PH  (4,4)
VA   1.0   PH  (4,4)
OU   SE   MI   RS
```

Model 4.5 (Figure A.2)

Specification of the model

Equations for the model

$$
\begin{aligned}
x_1 &= \lambda_{11}\xi_1 && + \delta_1 \\
x_2 &= \lambda_{21}\xi_1 && + \delta_2 \\
x_3 &= \quad\quad \lambda_{32}\xi_2 && + \delta_3 \\
x_4 &= \quad\quad \lambda_{42}\xi_2 && + \delta_4 \\
x_5 &= \quad\quad\quad\quad \lambda_{53}\xi_3 && + \delta_5 \\
x_6 &= \quad\quad\quad\quad \lambda_{63}\xi_3 && + \delta_6
\end{aligned}
$$

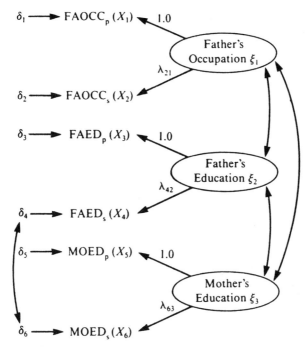

Figure A.2. (Same as Figure 4.1.) Measurement model of report of parental socioeconomic status. Variables are described in Table 4.1

Matrix format of the equations

$$
\begin{bmatrix} x_1 \\ x_2 \\ x_3 \\ x_4 \\ x_5 \\ x_6 \end{bmatrix}
=
\begin{bmatrix} \lambda_{11} \\ \lambda_{21} \\ & \lambda_{32} \\ & \lambda_{42} \\ & & \lambda_{53} \\ & & \lambda_{63} \end{bmatrix}
\begin{bmatrix} \xi_1 \\ \xi_2 \\ \xi_3 \\ \xi_4 \end{bmatrix}
+
\begin{bmatrix} \delta_1 \\ \delta_2 \\ \delta_3 \\ \delta_4 \\ \delta_5 \\ \delta_6 \end{bmatrix}
$$

$$\mathbf{X} \quad = \quad \mathbf{\Lambda}^x \qquad \xi \quad + \quad \delta$$

LISREL matrices for the model

$$
\mathbf{\Lambda}^x = LX =
\begin{bmatrix}
LX\ 1\ 1 & & \\
LX\ 2\ 1 & & \\
& LX\ 3\ 2 & \\
& LX\ 4\ 2 & \\
& & LX\ 5\ 3 \\
& & LX\ 6\ 3
\end{bmatrix}
$$

$$\Theta_\delta = TD = \begin{bmatrix} TD\ 1\ 1 & & & & & \\ & TD\ 2\ 2 & & & & \\ & & TD\ 3\ 3 & & & \\ & & & TD\ 4\ 4 & & \\ & & & & TD\ 5\ 5 & \\ & & & TD\ 6\ 4 & & TD\ 6\ 6 \end{bmatrix}$$

$$\Phi = PH = \begin{bmatrix} PH\ 1\ 1 & & \\ PH\ 2\ 1 & PH\ 2\ 2 & \\ PH\ 3\ 1 & PH\ 3\ 2 & PH\ 3\ 3 \end{bmatrix}$$

LISREL input

Seniors' reports of parental status: whites (Model 4.5)

```
DA NG=2 NI=6 NO=1502 MA=CM
LA
'PFASEI' 'FASEI' 'PFAED' 'FAED' 'PMAED' 'MAED'
KM SY
 1.0000000
 0.7101643  1.0000000
 0.5801628  0.6174708  1.0000000
 0.5717937  0.6137355  0.9085483  1.0000000
 0.4111465  0.4401737  0.6042968  0.5861159  1.0000000
 0.4152458  0.4520828  0.5918648  0.5990632  0.8738597  1.0000000
SD
   22.4990    22.0093    2.2067    2.2632    1.7599    1.8563
MO NX=6 NK=3 LX=FU,FI TD=SY,FI PH=SY,FR
LK
'TRUEFAOC' 'TRUEFAED' 'TRUEMAED'
EQ LX(5,3) LX(6,3)
FREE TD(1,1)  TD(3,3) TD(4,4) TD(5,5) TD(6,6)
EQ TD(1,1) TD(2,2)
FREE TD(6,4)
EQ LX(1,1) LX(2,1)
EQ LX(3,2) LX(4,2)
ST 1.0 LX(1,1) LX(3,2) LX(5,3)
OU SE TV RS FD SS TO
SENIORS' REPORTS OF PARENTAL STATUS: BLACKS (MODEL 5)
DA NO=99
LA
'PFASEI' 'FASEI' 'PFAED' 'FAED' 'PMAED' 'MAED'
KM SY
 1.0000000
 0.5778486  1.0000000
 0.6693734  0.6250294  1.0000000
 0.5590930  0.5760426  0.8302376  1.0000000
 0.4396363  0.4342983  0.6346900  0.5595682  1.0000000
 0.4511116  0.4052264  0.5933101  0.6154144  0.8277926  1.0000000
SD
   22.5915    24.3283    2.1415    2.1978    1.8309    2.0368
MO NX=6 NK=3 LX=SS TD=SS PH=IN
LK
'TRUEFAOC' 'TRUEFAED' 'TRUEMAED'
FREE TD(6,4)
EQ LX(1,1) LX(2,1)
EQ LX(3,2) LX(4,2)
EQ LX(5,3) LX(6,3)
FREE TD(2,2) TD(4,4)
EQ TD(1,3,3) TD(3,3)
EQ TD(1,1,1) TD(1,1)
EQ TD(1,5,5) TD(5,5)
FREE TD(6,6)
OU SE TV RS FD SS TO
```

Chapter 5 model LISREL inputs

Full details of the model specifications, plus the figures, are available in the text of Chapter 5 and are not repeated here. We leave it as an exercise for the reader to formulate the specification of the models in equation and matrix notation. The LISREL inputs for the full sequence of tests presented in Tables 5.3 and 5.8 are presented below.

Data for Models 5.1.1–5.4.2 reported in Table 5.3

```
'KN' 'CO' 'AP' 'AN' 'SY' 'EV'
1 .514 1 .496. .712 1 .358 .648 .632 1 .412 .415 .450
.371 1 .386 .355 .348. .294 .426 1
```

LISREL input for models reported in Table 5.3

Kropp and Stoker data for atomic structure: Model 5.1.1
```
DA   NI = 6   MA = KM   NO = 5057
LA   UN = 8   RE
KM   UN = 8   RE
MO   NY = 6   NE = 1   LY = FU, FR   TE = DI, FR
FI   TE (1,1)
FI   LY (1,1)
ST  1.0 LY (1,1)
OU
```

Kropp and Stoker data for atomic structure: Model 5.2.1
```
DA   NI = 6   MA = KM   NO = 5057
LA   UN = 8   RE
KM   UN = 8   RE
MO   NY = 6   NE = 6   LY = ID   BE = FU, FI   TE = DI, FR
PS = DI, FR
FR   BE (2,1)   BE (3,2)   BE (4,3)   BE (5,4)   BE (6,5)
FI   TE (1)   TE (6)
OU   SE   RS   MI   FD   SS
```

Kropp and Stoker data for atomic structure: Model 5.2.2
```
DA   NI = 6   MA = KM   NO = 5057
LA   UN = 8   RE
KM   UN = 8   RE
MO   NY = 6   NE = 6   LY = ID   BE = FU, FI   TE = DI, FR
PS = DI, FR
FR   BE (2,1)   BE (3,2)   BE (4,3)   BE (5,4)   BE (6,5)
FR   BE (5,1)
FI   TE (1)   TE (6)
OU   SE   RS   MI   FD   SS
```

Kropp and Stoker data for atomic structure: Model 5.3.1
DA   NI = 6   MA = KM   NO = 5057
LA   UN = 8   RE
KM   UN = 8   RE
SE
2,3,4,5,6/
MO   NY = 5   NE = 1   LY = FU, FR   TE = DI, FR
FI   TE (1,1)
FI   LY (1,1)
ST 1.0 LY (1,1)
OU

Kropp and Stoker data for atomic structure: Model 5.4.1
DA   NI = 6   MA = KM   NO = 5057
LA   UN = 8   RE
KM   UN = 8   RE
SE
2,3,4,5,6/
MO   NY = 5   NE = 5   LY = ID   BE = FU, FI   TE = DI, FR
PS = DI, FR
FR   BE   (2,1)   BE (3,2)   BE (4,3)   BE (5,4)
FI   TE (1)   TE (5)
OU   SE   RS   MI   FD   SS

Kropp and Stoker data for atomic structure: Model 5.4.2
DA   NI = 6   MA = KM   NO = 5057
LA   UN = 8   RE
KM   UN = 8   RE
SE
2,3,4,5,6/
MO   NY = 5   NE = 5   LY = ID   BE = FU, FI   TE = DI, FR
PS = DI, FR
FR   BE   (2,1)   BE (3,2)   BE (4,3)   BE (5,4)
FI   TE (1)   TE (5)   PS(3)
OU   SE   RS   MI   FD   SS

Data for Models 5.5.1–5.7.1 reported in Table 5.8

'A KN' 'A CO' 'A AP' 'A AN' 'A SY' 'A EV' 'G KN' 'G CO' 'G AP' 'G AN' 'G SY'

'G EV' 'L KN' 'L CO' 'L AP' 'L AN' 'L SY' 'L EV' 'S KN' 'S CO' 'S AP' 'S AN'
'S SY' 'S EV'

```
1    .514 1    .496 .712 1    .358 .648 .632 1    .412 .415
.450 .371 1    .386 .355 .348 .294 .426 1    .582 .381 .400
.289 .331 .317 1    .475 .516 .540 .462 .400 .311 .481 1
.474 .490 .537 .432 .396 .323 .513 .698 1    .346 .404 .436
.364 .294 .227 .351 .608 .614 1    .284 .301 .324 .276 .361
.215 .298 .372 .411 .331 1    .389 .368 .372 .305 .373 .467
.409 .382 .394 .295 .277 1    .531 .381 .377 .285 .326 .312 .603
.445 .459 .333 .284 .364 1    .490 .493 .501 .416 .395 .336
.497 .586 .583 .461 .356 .389 .577 1    .501 .481 .483 .403
.410 .362 .491 .574 .602 .472 .370 .378 .564 .719 1
.456 .463 .479 .412 .428 .359 .436 .533 .546 .430 .340
.372 .498 .675 .684 1    .469 .458 .460 .401 .534 .400 .448
.481 .483 .365 .392 .420 .486 .551 .562 .558 1    .379
.380 .360 .328 .390 .420 .334 .356 .337 .249 .234 .450
.340 .379 .369 .376 .453 1.572 .353 .355 .261 .327 .329
.595 .391 .386 .235 .193 .384 .497 .417 .417 .385 .414 .340 1
.490 .537 .557 .488 .417 .342 .479 .605 .603 .477 .338
.410 .467 .598 .588 .584 .522 .393 .512 1    .494 .522
.525 .444 .404 .347 .495 .584 .587 .459 .338 .401 .472
.573 .589 .558 .510 .384 .508 .753 1    .348 .475 .488 .437
.339 .283 .350 .516 .525 .419 .283 .319 .353 .530 .504
.509 .446 .327 .337 .680 .619 1    .369 .401 .419 .368
.459 .342 .377 .442 .418 .314 .334 .380 .353 .439 .436
.452 .549 .375 .385 .509 .497 .425 1    .358 .383 .406
.358 .378 .377 .340 .400 .426 .292 .263 .411 .333
.406 .413 .417 .449 .397 .353 .472 .455 .397 .409 1
```

LISREL input for models reported in Table 5.8

Kropp and Stoker data, all tests: Model 5.5.1

```
DA NI=24 MA=KM NO=3850

LA UN=8 RE

KM-UN=8 RE
MO NY=24 NE=6 BE=FU,FI TE=DI,FI PS=DI,FR
FR BE(2,1) BE(3,2) BE(4,3) BE(5,4) BE(6,5)
MA LY
*
.741 6*0 .668 6*0 .670 6*0 .599 6*0 .678 6*0 .653
.811 6*0 .770 6*0 .785 6*0 .598 6*0 .502 6*0 .702
.718 6*0 .753 6*0 .758 6*0 .706 6*0 .792 6*0 .649
.734 6*0 .793 6*0 .766 6*0 .718 6*0 .685 6*0 .591
MA TE
*
.451 .553 .551 .641 .540 .574 .343 .407 .384 .642
.748 .507 .485 .432 .426 .501 .372 .579 .461 .372
.413 .485 .531 .651
OU SE RS MI FD SS
```

Kropp and Stoker data, all tests: Model 5.5.2

```
DA NI=24 MA=KM NO=3850
LA UN=8  RE

KM UN=8  RE
MO NY=24 NE=6 BE=FU,FI TE=SY     PS=DI,FR
FR BE(2,1) BE(3,2) BE(4,3) BE(5,4) BE(6,5)
PA TE
*
1
1 1
1 1 1
1 1 1 1
1 1 1 1 1
1 1 1 1 1 1
0 0 0 0 0 0 1
0 0 0 0 0 0 1 1
0 0 0 0 0 0 1 1 1
0 0 0 0 0 0 1 1 1 1
0 0 0 0 0 0 1 1 1 1 1
0 0 0 0 0 0 1 1 1 1 1 1
0 0 0 0 0 0 0 0 0 0 0 1
0 0 0 0 0 0 0 0 0 0 0 1 1
0 0 0 0 0 0 0 0 0 0 0 1 1 1
0 0 0 0 0 0 0 0 0 0 0 1 1 1 1
0 0 0 0 0 0 0 0 0 0 0 1 1 1 1 1
0 0 0 0 0 0 0 0 0 0 0 1 1 1 1 1 1
0 0 0 0 0 0 0 0 0 0 0 0 0 0 0 0 0 1
0 0 0 0 0 0 0 0 0 0 0 0 0 0 0 0 0 1 1
0 0 0 0 0 0 0 0 0 0 0 0 0 0 0 0 0 1 1 1
0 0 0 0 0 0 0 0 0 0 0 0 0 0 0 0 0 1 1 1 1
0 0 0 0 0 0 0 0 0 0 0 0 0 0 0 0 0 1 1 1 1 1
0 0 0 0 0 0 0 0 0 0 0 0 0 0 0 0 0 1 1 1 1 1 1
MA LY
*
.741 6*0 .668 6*0 .670 6*0 .599 6*0 .678 6*0 .653
.811 6*0 .770 6*0 .785 6*0 .598 6*0 .502 6*0 .702
.718 6*0 .753 6*0 .758 6*0 .706 6*0 .792 6*0 .649
.734 6*0 .793 6*0 .766 6*0 .718 6*0 .685 6*0 .591
MA TE
*
.451
0 .553
0 0 .551
```

```
0 0 0 .641
0 0 0 0 .540
0 0 0 0 0 .574
0 0 0 0 0 0 .343
0 0 0 0 0 0 0 .407
0 0 0 0 0 0 0 0 .384
0 0 0 0 0 0 0 0 0 .642
0 0 0 0 0 0 0 0 0 0 .748
0 0 0 0 0 0 0 0 0 0 0 .507
0 0 0 0 0 0 0 0 0 0 0 0 .485
0 0 0 0 0 0 0 0 0 0 0 0 0 .432
0 0 0 0 0 0 0 0 0 0 0 0 0 0 .426
0 0 0 0 0 0 0 0 0 0 0 0 0 0 0 .501
0 0 0 0 0 0 0 0 0 0 0 0 0 0 0 0 .372
0 0 0 0 0 0 0 0 0 0 0 0 0 0 0 0 0 .579
0 0 0 0 0 0 0 0 0 0 0 0 0 0 0 0 0 0 .461
0 0 0 0 0 0 0 0 0 0 0 0 0 0 0 0 0 0 0 .372
0 0 0 0 0 0 0 0 0 0 0 0 0 0 0 0 0 0 0 0 .413
0 0 0 0 0 0 0 0 0 0 0 0 0 0 0 0 0 0 0 0 0 .485
0 0 0 0 0 0 0 0 0 0 0 0 0 0 0 0 0 0 0 0 0 0 .531
0 0 0 0 0 0 0 0 0 0 0 0 0 0 0 0 0 0 0 0 0 0 0 .651
OU SE RS MI FD SS
```

Kropp and Stoker data, all tests: Model 5.6.1

```
DA NI=24 MA=KM NO=3850
LA UN=8 RE
KM UN=8 RE
SE
2,3,4,5,6,8,9,10,11,12,14,15,16,17,18,20,21,22,23,24/
MO NY=20 NE=5 BE=FU,FI TE=DI,FI PS=DI,FR
FR BE(2,1) BE(3,2) BE(4,3) BE(5,4)
MA LY
*
.668 5*0 .670 5*0 .599 5*0 .678 5*0 .653
.770 5*0 .785 5*0 .598 5*0 .502 5*0 .702
.753 5*0 .758 5*0 .706 5*0 .792 5*0 .649
.793 5*0 .766 5*0 .718 5*0 .685 5*0 .591
MA TE
*
.553 .551 .641 .540 .574 .407 .384 .642
.748 .507 .432 .426 .501 .372 .579 .372
.413 .485 .531 .651
OU SE RS MI FD SS
```

Kropp and Stoker data, all tests: Model 5.6.2

```
DA NI=24 MA=KM NO=3850
SE
2,3,4,5,6,8,9,10,11,12,14,15,16,17,18,20,21,22,23,24/
MO NY=20 NE=5 BE=FU,FI TE=SY    PS=DI,FR
FR BE(2,1) BE(3,2) BE(4,3) BE(5,4)
PA TE
*
1
1 1
1 1 1
1 1 1 1
1 1 1 1 1
0 0 0 0 0 1
0 0 0 0 0 1 1
0 0 0 0 0 1 1 1
0 0 0 0 0 1 1 1 1
0 0 0 0 0 1 1 1 1
0 0 0 0 0 0 0 0 0 1
0 0 0 0 0 0 0 0 0 1 1
0 0 0 0 0 0 0 0 0 1 1 1
0 0 0 0 0 0 0 0 0 1 1 1 1
0 0 0 0 0 0 0 0 0 1 1 1 1 1
0 0 0 0 0 0 0 0 0 0 0 0 0 0 1
0 0 0 0 0 0 0 0 0 0 0 0 0 0 1 1
0 0 0 0 0 0 0 0 0 0 0 0 0 0 1 1 1
0 0 0 0 0 0 0 0 0 0 0 0 0 0 1 1 1 1
0 0 0 0 0 0 0 0 0 0 0 0 0 0 1 1 1 1 1
MA LY
*
.668 5*0 .670 5*0 .599 5*0 .678 5*0 .653
.770 5*0 .785 5*0 .598 5*0 .502 5*0 .702
.753 5*0 .758 5*0 .706 5*0 .792 5*0 .649
.793 5*0 .766 5*0 .718 5*0 .685 5*0 .591
MA TE
*
.553
0 .551
0 0 .641
0 0 0 .540
0 0 0 0 .574
0 0 0 0 0 .407
0 0 0 0 0 0 .384
0 0 0 0 0 0 0 .642
```

```
0 0 0 0 0 0 0 .748
0 0 0 0 0 0 0 0 .507
0 0 0 0 0 0 0 0 0 .432
0 0 0 0 0 0 0 0 0 0 .426
0 0 0 0 0 0 0 0 0 0 0 .501
0 0 0 0 0 0 0 0 0 0 0 0 .372
0 0 0 0 0 0 0 0 0 0 0 0 0 .579
0 0 0 0 0 0 0 0 0 0 0 0 0 0 .372
0 0 0 0 0 0 0 0 0 0 0 0 0 0 0 .413
0 0 0 0 0 0 0 0 0 0 0 0 0 0 0 0 .485
0 0 0 0 0 0 0 0 0 0 0 0 0 0 0 0 0 .531
0 0 0 0 0 0 0 0 0 0 0 0 0 0 0 0 0 0 .651
OU SE RS MI FD SS
```

Kropp and Stoker data, all tests: Model 5.6.3

```
DA NI=24 MA=KM NO=3850
LA UN=8

KM UN=8

SE
2,3,4,5,6,8,9,10,11,12,14,15,16,17,18,20,21,22,23,24/
MO NY=20 NE=9 BE=FU,FI TE=DI,FR PS=DI,FI
FR BE(2,1) BE(3,2) BE(4,3) BE(5,4)
FR PS(1)-PS(5)
PA LY
*
0 0 0 0 0 1 0 0 0
0 0 0 0 0 1 0 0 0
0 0 0 0 0 1 0 0 0
0 0 0 0 0 1 0 0 0
0 0 0 0 0 1 0 0 0
1 0 0 0 0 0 1 0 0
0 1 0 0 0 0 1 0 0
0 0 1 0 0 0 1 0 0
0 0 0 1 0 0 1 0 0
0 0 0 0 1 0 1 0 0
1 0 0 0 0 0 0 1 0
0 1 0 0 0 0 0 1 0
0 0 1 0 0 0 0 1 0
0 0 0 1 0 0 0 1 0
0 0 0 0 1 0 0 1 0
1 0 0 0 0 0 0 0 1
0 1 0 0 0 0 0 0 1
0 0 1 0 0 0 0 0 1
```

```
0 0 0 1 0 0 0 0 1
0 0 0 0 1 0 0 0 1
ST 1.0 LY(1,1) LY(2,2) LY(3,3) LY(4,4) LY(5,5)
ST 1.0 PS(6)-PS(9)
OU SE RS MI FD SS
```

Model 7.1 (Figure A.3)

Specification of the model

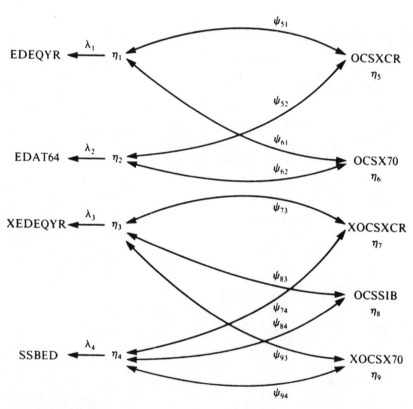

Figure A.3. (Same as Figure 7.1.) Structural equation model for testing homogeneity within and between siblings in regressions of occupational status on educational attainment. The model includes all covariances among $\eta_1 \ldots \eta_9$, but only those subject to constraints are shown and labeled.

Equations for Model 7.1.1

$$
\begin{aligned}
Y_1 &= 4.39\eta_1 & & & & & & & & + \varepsilon_1 \\
Y_2 &= & 3.35\eta_2 & & & & & & & + \varepsilon_2 \\
Y_3 &= & & 5.17\eta_3 & & & & & & + \varepsilon_3 \\
Y_4 &= & & & 4.94\eta_4 & & & & & + \varepsilon_4 \\
Y_5 &= & & & & \eta_5 & & & & + \varepsilon_5 \\
Y_6 &= & & & & & \eta_6 & & & + \varepsilon_6 \\
Y_7 &= & & & & & & \eta_7 & & + \varepsilon_7 \\
Y_8 &= & & & & & & & \eta_8 & + \varepsilon_8 \\
Y_9 &= & & & & & & & & \eta_9 + \varepsilon_9
\end{aligned}
$$

Matrix format of the equations for the model

$$
\begin{bmatrix} Y_1 \\ Y_2 \\ Y_3 \\ Y_4 \\ Y_5 \\ Y_6 \\ Y_7 \\ Y_8 \\ Y_9 \end{bmatrix}
=
\begin{bmatrix}
4.39 & 0 & 0 & 0 & 0 & 0 & 0 & 0 & 0 \\
0 & 3.35 & 0 & 0 & 0 & 0 & 0 & 0 & 0 \\
0 & 0 & 5.17 & 0 & 0 & 0 & 0 & 0 & 0 \\
0 & 0 & 0 & 4.94 & 0 & 0 & 0 & 0 & 0 \\
0 & 0 & 0 & 0 & 1.0 & 0 & 0 & 0 & 0 \\
0 & 0 & 0 & 0 & 0 & 1.0 & 0 & 0 & 0 \\
0 & 0 & 0 & 0 & 0 & 0 & 1.0 & 0 & 0 \\
0 & 0 & 0 & 0 & 0 & 0 & 0 & 1.0 & 0 \\
0 & 0 & 0 & 0 & 0 & 0 & 0 & 0 & 1.0
\end{bmatrix}
\begin{bmatrix} \eta_1 \\ \eta_2 \\ \eta_3 \\ \eta_4 \\ \eta_5 \\ \eta_6 \\ \eta_7 \\ \eta_8 \\ \eta_9 \end{bmatrix}
$$

$$
\mathbf{Y} \quad = \qquad\qquad\qquad\qquad\qquad \mathbf{\Lambda}^y \qquad\qquad\qquad\qquad\qquad\qquad \mathbf{\eta}
$$

LISREL matrices for the model

$$
\mathbf{\Lambda}^y = \mathbf{LY} =
\begin{bmatrix}
4.39 & 0 & 0 & 0 & 0 & 0 & 0 & 0 & 0 \\
0 & 3.35 & 0 & 0 & 0 & 0 & 0 & 0 & 0 \\
0 & 0 & 5.17 & 0 & 0 & 0 & 0 & 0 & 0 \\
0 & 0 & 0 & 4.94 & 0 & 0 & 0 & 0 & 0 \\
0 & 0 & 0 & 0 & 1.0 & 0 & 0 & 0 & 0 \\
0 & 0 & 0 & 0 & 0 & 1.0 & 0 & 0 & 0 \\
0 & 0 & 0 & 0 & 0 & 0 & 1.0 & 0 & 0 \\
0 & 0 & 0 & 0 & 0 & 0 & 0 & 1.0 & 0 \\
0 & 0 & 0 & 0 & 0 & 0 & 0 & 0 & 1.0
\end{bmatrix}
$$

$$
\mathbf{\Psi} = \mathbf{PS} =
\begin{bmatrix}
\text{PS 1 1} \\
\text{PS 2 1} & \text{PS 2 2} \\
\text{PS 3 1} & \text{PS 3 2} & \text{PS 3 3} \\
\text{PS 4 1} & \text{PS 4 2} & \text{PS 4 3} & \text{PS 4 4} \\
\text{PS 5 1} & \text{PS 5 1} & \text{PS 5 3} & \text{PS 5 4} & \text{PS 5 5} \\
\text{PS 5 1} & \text{PS 5 1} & \text{PS 6 3} & \text{PS 6 4} & \text{PS 6 5} & \text{PS 6 6} \\
\text{PS 7 1} & \text{PS 7 2} & \text{PS 7 3} & \text{PS 7 4} & \text{PS 7 5} & \text{PS 7 6} & \text{PS 7 7} \\
\text{PS 8 1} & \text{PS 8 2} & \text{PS 8 3} & \text{PS 8 4} & \text{PS 8 5} & \text{PS 8 6} & \text{PS 8 7} & \text{PS 8 8} \\
\text{PS 9 1} & \text{PS 9 2} & \text{PS 9 3} & \text{PS 9 4} & \text{PS 9 5} & \text{PS 9 6} & \text{PS 9 7} & \text{PS 9 8} & \text{PS 9 9}
\end{bmatrix}
$$

LISREL input for Models 7.1.1–7.1.4

Regressions with equal reduced form slopes

```
DA NI=9 NOBS=518 MA=CM
LA
*
'XEDEQYR' 'SSBED' 'EDEQYR' 'EDAT64' 'XOCSXCR' 'OCSSIB' 'XOCSX70'
'OCSXCR' 'OCSX70'
CM
(4D20.13)
 0.5167008954243D+01  0.4679783126592D+01  0.4938070842326D+01  0.1922921816539D+01
 0.1949806949807D+01  0.4386996557209D+01  0.1815463432485D+01  0.1827591614826D+01
 0.3471849025041D+01  0.3345914579957D+01  0.3627641502926D+01  0.3238972071952D+01
 0.2166210542348D+01  0.1139875075252D+01  0.6582034415362D+01  0.3569933505328D+01
 0.3302070018432D+01  0.1140821946633D+01  0.1122999127123D+01  0.5235668842959D+01
 0.6274622362490D+01  0.3621744780335D+01  0.3242735052857D+01  0.1210572885314D+01
 0.1194227627373D+01  0.5336248715763D+01  0.4963113333139D+01  0.6446553035743D+01
 0.1391681952781D+01  0.1364161548669D+01  0.2822630647346D+01  0.2344899377790D+01
 0.1651115593313D+01  0.1620192034477D+01  0.1532529966490D+01  0.5951538627534D+01
 0.1638921681630D+01  0.1577077688878D+01  0.2975257164254D+01  0.2472673949769D+01
 0.1941411027899D+01  0.1848463228034D+01  0.1678794058818D+01  0.4802423584718D+01
 0.5787209952562D+01
SE
3 4 1 2 8 9 5 6 7
MO NX=0 NY=9 NE=9 NK=0 BE=ZE TE=ZE PS=SY,FR LY=FU,FI TD=ZE
ST 1.0 LY(5,5) LY(6,6) LY(7,7) LY(8,8) LY(9,9)
ST 4.38700 LY(1,1)
ST 3.34591 LY(2,2)
ST 5.16701 LY(3,3)
ST 4.93807 LY(4,4)
ST 0.5 PS(1,1)-PS(9,9)
ST 2.0 PS(1,1) PS(2,2) PS(3,3) PS(4,4) PS(5,5) PS(6,6) PS(7,7) PS(8,8) PS(9,9)
[EQ PS(5,1) PS(6,1) PS(5,2) PS(6,2)]/ADD FOR MODELS 1.1, 1.3, AND 1.4
[EQ PS(7,3) PS(8,3) PS(9,3) PS(7,4) PS(8,4) PS(9,4)]/ADD FOR MODELS 1.2-1.4
[EQ PS(6,2) PS(7,3)]/ADD FOR MODEL 1.4
OU SS ND=5 TO SE
```

Model 7.2 (Figure A.4)

Specification of the model

Equations for Model 7.2.1

Measurement model

$$
\begin{aligned}
Y_1 &= \eta_1 + \eta_2 \\
Y_2 &= \quad\;\; \eta_2 + \eta_3 \\
X_1 &= \xi_1 + \xi_2 \\
X_2 &= \quad\;\; \xi_2 + \xi_3
\end{aligned}
$$

Structural model

$$
\begin{aligned}
\eta_1 &= y_{11}\xi_1 &&+ \zeta_1 \\
\eta_2 &= \quad\; y_{22}\xi_2 &&+ \zeta_2 \\
\eta_3 &= \quad\quad\quad y_{33}\xi_3 &&+ \zeta_3
\end{aligned}
$$

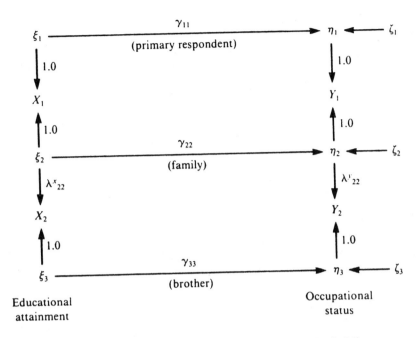

Figure A.4. (Same as Figure 7.2.) Structural equation model of sibling resemblance in educational attainment and occupational status.

Matrix format of the equations for the model

$$\begin{bmatrix} Y_1 \\ Y_2 \end{bmatrix} = \begin{bmatrix} 1.0 & 1.0 & 0 \\ 0 & 1.0 & 1.0 \end{bmatrix} \begin{bmatrix} \eta_1 \\ \eta_2 \\ \eta_3 \end{bmatrix}$$

$$\mathbf{Y} \quad = \quad \boldsymbol{\Lambda}^y \quad\quad\quad \boldsymbol{\eta}$$

$$\begin{bmatrix} X_1 \\ X_2 \end{bmatrix} = \begin{bmatrix} 1.0 & 1.0 & 0 \\ 0 & 1.0 & 1.0 \end{bmatrix} \begin{bmatrix} \xi_1 \\ \xi_2 \\ \xi_3 \end{bmatrix}$$

$$\mathbf{X} \quad = \quad \boldsymbol{\Lambda}^x \quad\quad\quad \boldsymbol{\xi}$$

$$\begin{bmatrix} \eta_1 \\ \eta_2 \\ \eta_3 \end{bmatrix} = \begin{bmatrix} \gamma_{11} & 0 & 0 \\ 0 & \gamma_{22} & 0 \\ 0 & 0 & \gamma_{33} \end{bmatrix} \begin{bmatrix} \xi_1 \\ \xi_2 \\ \xi_3 \end{bmatrix} + \begin{bmatrix} \zeta_1 \\ \zeta_2 \\ \zeta_3 \end{bmatrix}$$

$$\boldsymbol{\eta} \quad = \quad \boldsymbol{\Gamma} \quad\quad\quad \boldsymbol{\xi} \quad + \quad \boldsymbol{\zeta}$$

LISREL matrices for the model

$$\Lambda^y = \mathrm{LY} = \begin{bmatrix} 1.0 & 1.0 & 0 \\ 0 & 1.0 & 1.0 \end{bmatrix}$$

$$\Lambda^x = \mathrm{LX} = \begin{bmatrix} 1.0 & 1.0 & 0 \\ 0 & 1.0 & 1.0 \end{bmatrix}$$

$$\Gamma = \mathrm{GA} = \begin{bmatrix} \mathrm{GA}\,1\,1 & 0 & 0 \\ 0 & \mathrm{GA}\,2\,2 & 0 \\ 0 & 0 & \mathrm{GA}\,3\,3 \end{bmatrix}$$

$$\Phi = \mathrm{PH} = [\mathrm{PH}\,1\,1 \quad \mathrm{PH}\,2\,2 \quad \mathrm{PH}\,3\,3]$$

$$\Psi = \mathrm{PS} = [\mathrm{PS}\,1\,1 \quad \mathrm{PS}\,2\,2 \quad \mathrm{PS}\,3\,3]$$

LISREL input for Models 7.2.1–7.2.5

Family model in observables

```
DA NI=9 NOBS=518 MA=CM
LA
*
'XEDEQYR' 'SSBED' 'EDEQYR' 'EDAT64' 'XOCSXCR' 'OCSSIB' 'XOCSX70'
'OCSXCR' 'OCSX70'
CM
(4D20.13)
 0.5167008954243D+01 0.4679783126592D+01 0.4938070842326D+01 0.1922921816539D+01
 0.1949806949807D+01 0.4386996557209D+01 0.1815463432485D+01 0.1827591614826D+01
 0.5471849025041D+01 0.3345914579957D+01 0.3627641502926D+01 0.3238972071952D+01
 0.1166210542348D+01 0.1139875075252D+01 0.6582034415362D+01 0.3569933505328D+01
 0.3302070018432D+01 0.1140821946633D+01 0.1122999127123D+01 0.5235668842959D+01
 0.6274622362490D+01 0.3621744780335D+01 0.3242735052857D+01 0.1210572885314D+01
 0.1194227627373D+01 0.5336248715763D+01 0.4963113333139D+01 0.6446553035743D+01
 0.1391681952781D+01 0.1364161548669D+01 0.2822630647346D+01 0.2344899377790D+01
 0.1651115593313D+01 0.1620192034477D+01 0.1532529966490D+01 0.5951538627534D+01
 0.1638921681630D+01 0.1577077688878D+01 0.2975257164254D+01 0.2472673949769D+01
 0.1941411027899D+01 0.1848463228034D+01 0.1678794058818D+01 0.4802423584718D+01
 0.5787209952562D+01
SE
 8 5 3 1/
MO NX=2 NY=2 NE=3 NK=3 BE=ZE GA=FU,FI TE=ZE PS=DI,FR LY=FU,FI TD=ZE C
PH=DI,FR LX=FU,FI
 FR GA(1,1) GA(2,2) GA(3,3)
 ST .7 GA(1,1) GA(2,2) GA(3,3)
 ST 2.0 PS(1,1) PS(2,2) PS(3,3)
 ST 2.0 PH(1,1) PH(2,2) PH(3,3)
 ST 1.0 LY(1,1) LY(1,2) LY(2,3) LY(2,2)
 ST 1.0 LX(1,1) LX(1,2) LX(2,3) LX(2,2)
[EQ GA(1,1) GA(3,3)]/ADD FOR MODEL 2.2
[EQ GA(1,1) GA(2,2) GA(3,3)]/ADD FOR MODELS 2.3-2.5
[EQ PS(1,1) PS(3,3)]/ADD FOR MODELS 2.4-2.5
[EQ PH(1,1) PH(3,3)]/ADD FOR MODEL 2.5
OU SS ND=5 TO SE
```

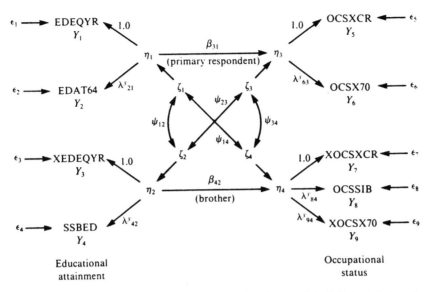

Figure A.5. (Same as Figure 7.3.) Structural equation model of distinct fraternal regressions of occupational status on educational attainment with errors in variables but no family factors. See Table 7.6 for specifications of error covariances.

Model 7.3 (Figure A.5)

Specification of the model

Equation for Model 7.3.1

Measurement model

$$
\begin{aligned}
Y_1 &= \eta_1 & &+ \varepsilon_1 \\
Y_2 &= \lambda^y_{21}\eta_1 & &+ \varepsilon_2 \\
Y_3 &= \eta_2 & &+ \varepsilon_3 \\
Y_4 &= \lambda^y_{42}\eta_2 & &+ \varepsilon_4 \\
Y_5 &= \eta_3 & &+ \varepsilon_5 \\
Y_6 &= \lambda^y_{63}\eta_3 & &+ \varepsilon_6 \\
Y_7 &= \eta_4 & &+ \varepsilon_7 \\
Y_8 &= \lambda^y_{84}\eta_4 & &+ \varepsilon_8 \\
Y_9 &= \lambda^y_{94}\eta_4 & &+ \varepsilon_9
\end{aligned}
$$

Structural model

$$
\begin{aligned}
\eta_1 &= & &+ \zeta_1 \\
\eta_2 &= & &+ \zeta_2 \\
\eta_3 &= \beta_{31}\eta_1 & &+ \zeta_3 \\
\eta_4 &= & \beta_{42}\eta_2 &+ \zeta_4
\end{aligned}
$$

Matrix format of the equations for the model

$$
\begin{bmatrix} Y_1 \\ Y_2 \\ Y_3 \\ Y_4 \\ Y_5 \\ Y_6 \\ Y_7 \\ Y_8 \\ Y_9 \end{bmatrix}
=
\begin{bmatrix}
1.0 & 0 & 0 & 0 \\
\lambda_{21}^y & 0 & 0 & 0 \\
0 & 1.0 & 0 & 0 \\
0 & \lambda_{42}^y & 0 & 0 \\
0 & 0 & 1.0 & 0 \\
0 & 0 & \lambda_{63}^y & 0 \\
0 & 0 & 0 & 1.0 \\
0 & 0 & 0 & \lambda_{84}^y \\
0 & 0 & 0 & \lambda_{94}^y
\end{bmatrix}
\begin{bmatrix} \eta_1 \\ \eta_2 \\ \eta_3 \\ \eta_4 \end{bmatrix}
+
\begin{bmatrix} \varepsilon_1 \\ \varepsilon_2 \\ \varepsilon_3 \\ \varepsilon_4 \\ \varepsilon_5 \\ \varepsilon_6 \\ \varepsilon_7 \\ \varepsilon_8 \\ \varepsilon_9 \end{bmatrix}
$$

$$\mathbf{Y} = \mathbf{\Lambda}^y \quad \mathbf{\eta} + \mathbf{\varepsilon}$$

$$
\begin{bmatrix} \eta_1 \\ \eta_2 \\ \eta_3 \\ \eta_4 \end{bmatrix}
=
\begin{bmatrix}
0 & 0 & 0 & 0 \\
0 & 0 & 0 & 0 \\
\beta_{31} & 0 & 0 & 0 \\
0 & \beta_{42} & 0 & 0
\end{bmatrix}
\begin{bmatrix} \eta_1 \\ \eta_2 \\ \eta_3 \\ \eta_4 \end{bmatrix}
+
\begin{bmatrix} \zeta_1 \\ \zeta_2 \\ \zeta_3 \\ \zeta_4 \end{bmatrix}
$$

$$\mathbf{\eta} = \mathbf{B} \quad \mathbf{\eta} + \mathbf{\zeta}$$

LISREL matrices for the model

$$
\mathbf{M}^y = \mathbf{LY} =
\begin{bmatrix}
1.0 & 0 & 0 & 0 \\
\text{LY } 2\,2 & 0 & 0 & 0 \\
0 & 1.0 & 0 & 0 \\
0 & \text{LY } 4\,2 & 0 & 0 \\
0 & 0 & 1.0 & 0 \\
0 & 0 & \text{LY } 6\,3 & 0 \\
0 & 0 & 0 & 1.0 \\
0 & 0 & 0 & \text{LY } 8\,4 \\
0 & 0 & 0 & \text{LY } 9\,4
\end{bmatrix}
$$

$$
\mathbf{B} = \mathbf{BE} =
\begin{bmatrix}
0 & 0 & 0 & 0 \\
0 & 0 & 0 & 0 \\
\text{BE } 3\,1 & 0 & 0 & 0 \\
0 & \text{BE } 4\,2 & 0 & 0
\end{bmatrix}
$$

$$
\mathbf{\Psi} = \mathbf{PS} =
\begin{bmatrix}
\text{PS } 1\,1 & & & \\
\text{PS } 2\,1 & \text{PS } 2\,2 & & \\
0 & \text{PS } 3\,2 & \text{PS } 3\,3 & \\
\text{PS } 4\,1 & 0 & \text{PS } 4\,3 & \text{PS } 4\,4
\end{bmatrix}
$$

$$\Theta_\varepsilon = TE = \begin{bmatrix} TE\ 1\ 1 & & & & & & & & \\ 0 & TE\ 2\ 2 & & & & & & & \\ 0 & 0 & TE\ 3\ 3 & & & & & & \\ TE\ 4\ 1 & 0 & 0 & TE\ 4\ 4 & & & & & \\ TE\ 5\ 1 & 0 & 0 & TE\ 5\ 4 & TE\ 5\ 5 & & & & \\ TE\ 6\ 1 & 0 & 0 & TE\ 6\ 4 & TE\ 6\ 5 & TE\ 6\ 6 & & & \\ 0 & 0 & TE\ 7\ 3 & 0 & 0 & 0 & TE\ 7\ 7 & & \\ TE\ 8\ 1 & 0 & 0 & TE\ 8\ 4 & TE\ 8\ 5 & TE\ 8\ 6 & 0 & TE\ 8\ 8 & \\ 0 & 0 & TE\ 9\ 3 & 0 & 0 & 0 & TE\ 6\ 5 & 0 & TE\ 9\ 9 \end{bmatrix}$$

LISREL input for Models 7.3.1–7.3.9

Measurement model in Y

```
DA NI=9 NOBS=518 MA=CM
LA
*
'XEDEQYR' 'SSBED' 'EDEQYR' 'EDAT64' 'XOCSXCR' 'OCSSIB' 'XOCSX70'
'OCSXCR' 'OCSX70'
CM
(4D20.13)
  0.5167008954243D+01 0.4679783126592D+01 0.4938070842326D+01 0.1922921816539D+01
  0.1949806949807D+01 0.4386996557209D+01 0.1815463432485D+01 0.1827591614826D+01
  0.3471849025041D+01 0.3345914579957D+01 0.3627641502926D+01 0.3238972071952D+01
  0.1166210542348D+01 0.1139875075252D+01 0.6582034415362D+01 0.3569933505328D+01
  0.3302070018432D+01 0.1140821946633D+01 0.1122999127123D+01 0.5235668842959D+01
  0.6274622362490D+01 0.3621744780335D+01 0.3242735052857D+01 0.1210572885314D+01
  0.1194227627373D+01 0.5336248715763D+01 0.4963113333139D+01 0.6446553035743D+01
  0.1391681952781D+01 0.1364161548669D+01 0.2822630647346D+01 0.2344899377790D+01
  0.1651115593313D+01 0.1620192034477D+01 0.1532529966490D+01 0.5951538627534D+01
  0.1638921681630D+01 0.1577077688878D+01 0.2975257164254D+01 0.2472673949769D+01
  0.1941411027899D+01 0.1848463228034D+01 0.1678794058818D+01 0.4802423584718D+01
  0.5787209952562D+01
SE
3 4 1 2 8 9 5 6 7
MO NX=0 NY=9 NE=4 NK=0 BE=FU,FI TE=SY,FI PS=SY,FR LY=FU,FI TD=ZE
START 1.0 LY (1,1) LY(3,2) LY(5,3) LY(7,4)
FREE LY(2,1) LY (4,2) LY (6,3) LY(8,4) LY(9,4)
FREE TE(1,1) TE (2,2) TE(3,3) TE(4,4) TE(5,5) TE(6,6) TE(7,7)
FREE TE(8,8) TE(9,9)
FREE TE (5,1) TE (7,3) TE(3,9) TE(1,6) TE(4,8) TE(7,9) TE(5,6)
EQUAL TE(7,9) TE(5,6)
[FR TE(4,1) TE(8,1) TE(5,4) TE(6,4) TE(8,5) TE(8,6)]/ADD FOR MODEL 3.1
START .70 ALL
START .20 TE (5,1) TE(7,3) TE(3,9) TE(1,6) TE(7,9) TE(5,6)
START -.20 TE(4,8)
START 3.0 PS(1,1) PS(2,2) PS(3,3) PS(4,4)
FREE BE(3,1) BE(4,2)
[EQ BE(3,1) BE(4,2)]/ADD FOR MODELS 3.1B-3.9B
START 0.7 BE(3,1) BE(4,2)
FIX PS(3,1) PS(4,2)
ST 0 PS(3,1) PS(4,2)
[EQ TE(1,5) TE(1,6) TE(3,7) TE(3,9)]/ADD FOR MODELS 3.3-3.9
[FI LY(2,1) LY(4,2) LY(6,3) LY(8,4) LY(9,4)]/ADD FOR MODELS 3.4-3.9
[ST 1.0 LY(2,1) LY(4,2) LY(6,3) LY(8,4) LY(9,4)]/ADD FOR MODELS 3.4-3.9
[FR LY(2,1)]/ADD FOR MODELS 3.5-3.9
[EQ TE(1,1) TE(3,3)]/ADD FOR MODELS 3.6-3.9
[EQ TE(5,5) TE(7,7)]/ADD FOR MODELS 3.6-3.9
[EQ TE(6,6) TE(9,9)]/ADD FOR MODEL 3.6
[EQ PS(3,3) PS(4,4)]/ADD FOR MODELS 3.8-3.9
[EQ PS(1,1) PS(2,2)]/ADD FOR MODEL 3.9
OU SS ND=5 TO SE
```

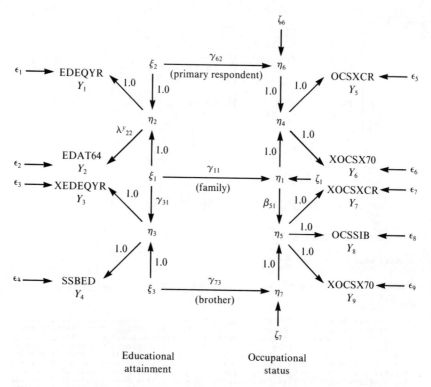

Figure A.6. (Same as Figure 7.4.) Structural equation model of sibling resemblance in educational attainment and occupational status with errors in variables and latent family factors.

Model 7.4 (Figure A.6)

Specification of the model

Equations for Model 7.4.1

Measurement model

$$
\begin{aligned}
Y_1 &= && \eta_2 && && && + \varepsilon_1 \\
Y_2 &= \lambda_{22}^y\eta_2 && && && && + \varepsilon_2 \\
Y_3 &= && && \eta_3 && && + \varepsilon_3 \\
Y_4 &= && && \eta_3 && && + \varepsilon_4 \\
Y_5 &= && && && \eta_4 && + \varepsilon_5 \\
Y_6 &= && && && \eta_4 && + \varepsilon_6 \\
Y_7 &= && && && && \eta_5 + \varepsilon_7 \\
Y_8 &= && && && && \eta_5 + \varepsilon_8 \\
Y_9 &= && && && && \eta_5 + \varepsilon_9
\end{aligned}
$$

Structural model

$$
\begin{aligned}
\eta_1 &= y_{11}\xi_1 && && && + \zeta_1 \\
\eta_2 &= \xi_1 + \xi_2 \\
\eta_3 &= \xi_1 && + \xi_3 \\
\eta_4 &= && && \eta_1 + \eta_6 \\
\eta_5 &= && && \eta_1 && + \eta_7 \\
\eta_6 &= && y_{62}\xi_2 && && + \zeta_6 \\
\eta_7 &= && && y_{73}\xi_3 && + \zeta_7
\end{aligned}
$$

Matrix format of the equations for the model

$$
\begin{bmatrix} Y_1 \\ Y_2 \\ Y_3 \\ Y_4 \\ Y_5 \\ Y_6 \\ Y_7 \\ Y_8 \\ Y_9 \end{bmatrix}
=
\begin{bmatrix}
0 & 1.0 & 0 & 0 & 0 & 0 & 0 \\
0 & \lambda^y_{22} & 0 & 0 & 0 & 0 & 0 \\
0 & 0 & 1.0 & 0 & 0 & 0 & 0 \\
0 & 0 & 1.0 & 0 & 0 & 0 & 0 \\
0 & 0 & 0 & 1.0 & 0 & 0 & 0 \\
0 & 0 & 0 & 1.0 & 0 & 0 & 0 \\
0 & 0 & 0 & 0 & 1.0 & 0 & 0 \\
0 & 0 & 0 & 0 & 1.0 & 0 & 0 \\
0 & 0 & 0 & 0 & 1.0 & 0 & 0
\end{bmatrix}
\begin{bmatrix} \eta_1 \\ \eta_2 \\ \eta_3 \\ \eta_4 \\ \eta_5 \\ \eta_6 \\ \eta_7 \end{bmatrix}
+
\begin{bmatrix} \varepsilon_1 \\ \varepsilon_2 \\ \varepsilon_3 \\ \varepsilon_4 \\ \varepsilon_5 \\ \varepsilon_6 \\ \varepsilon_7 \\ \eta_8 \\ \varepsilon_9 \end{bmatrix}
$$

$$
\mathbf{Y} \qquad = \qquad\qquad\qquad \mathbf{\Lambda}^y \qquad\qquad\qquad\qquad\qquad \mathbf{\eta} \quad + \quad \mathbf{\varepsilon}
$$

$$
\begin{bmatrix} \eta_1 \\ \eta_2 \\ \eta_3 \\ \eta_4 \\ \eta_5 \\ \eta_6 \\ \eta_7 \end{bmatrix}
=
\begin{bmatrix}
\gamma_{11} & 0 & 0 \\
1.0 & 1.0 & 0 \\
1.0 & 0 & 1.0 \\
0 & 0 & 0 \\
0 & 0 & 0 \\
0 & \gamma_{62} & 0 \\
0 & 0 & \gamma_{73}
\end{bmatrix}
\begin{bmatrix} \zeta_1 \\ \zeta_2 \\ \zeta_3 \end{bmatrix}
+
\begin{bmatrix}
0 & 0 & 0 & 0 & 0 & 0 & 0 \\
0 & 0 & 0 & 0 & 0 & 0 & 0 \\
0 & 0 & 0 & 0 & 0 & 0 & 0 \\
1.0 & 0 & 0 & 0 & 0 & 1.0 & 0 \\
1.0 & 0 & 0 & 0 & 0 & 0 & 1.0 \\
0 & 0 & 0 & 0 & 0 & 0 & 0 \\
0 & 0 & 0 & 0 & 0 & 0 & 0
\end{bmatrix}
\begin{bmatrix} \eta_1 \\ \eta_2 \\ \eta_3 \\ \eta_4 \\ \eta_5 \\ \eta_6 \\ \eta_7 \end{bmatrix}
+
\begin{bmatrix} \zeta_1 \\ 0 \\ 0 \\ 0 \\ 0 \\ \zeta_6 \\ \zeta_7 \end{bmatrix}
$$

$$
\mathbf{\eta} \quad = \quad \mathbf{\Gamma} \qquad\quad \mathbf{\xi} \quad + \qquad\qquad\qquad \mathbf{B} \qquad\qquad\qquad\qquad \mathbf{\eta} \; + \; \mathbf{\zeta}
$$

LISREL matrices for the model

$$
\mathbf{\Lambda}^y = \mathbf{LY} =
\begin{bmatrix}
0 & 1.0 & 0 & 0 & 0 & 0 & 0 \\
0 & LY\,2\,2 & 0 & 0 & 0 & 0 & 0 \\
0 & 0 & 1.0 & 0 & 0 & 0 & 0 \\
0 & 0 & 1.0 & 0 & 0 & 0 & 0 \\
0 & 0 & 0 & 1.0 & 0 & 0 & 0 \\
0 & 0 & 0 & 1.0 & 0 & 0 & 0 \\
0 & 0 & 0 & 0 & 1.0 & 0 & 0 \\
0 & 0 & 0 & 0 & 1.0 & 0 & 0 \\
0 & 0 & 0 & 0 & 1.0 & 0 & 0
\end{bmatrix}
$$

$$
\mathbf{B} = \mathbf{BE} =
\begin{bmatrix}
0 & 0 & 0 & 0 & 0 & 0 & 0 \\
0 & 0 & 0 & 0 & 0 & 0 & 0 \\
0 & 0 & 0 & 0 & 0 & 0 & 0 \\
1.0 & 0 & 0 & 0 & 0 & 1.0 & 0 \\
1.0 & 0 & 0 & 0 & 0 & 0 & 1.0 \\
0 & 0 & 0 & 0 & 0 & 0 & 0 \\
0 & 0 & 0 & 0 & 0 & 0 & 0
\end{bmatrix}
$$

$$\Gamma = GA = \begin{bmatrix} GA\ 1\ 1 & 0 & 0 \\ 1.0 & 1.0 & 0 \\ 1.0 & 0 & 1.0 \\ 0 & 0 & 0 \\ 0 & 0 & 0 \\ 0 & GA\ 6\ 2 & 0 \\ 0 & 0 & GA\ 7\ 3 \end{bmatrix}$$

$$\Phi = PH = [PH\ 1\ 1 \quad PH\ 2\ 2 \quad PH\ 3\ 3]$$

$$\Psi = PS = [PS\ 1\ 1 \quad 0 \quad 0 \quad 0 \quad 0 \quad PS\ 6\ 6 \quad PS\ 7\ 7]$$

$$\Theta_\varepsilon = TE = \begin{bmatrix} TE\ 1\ 1 \\ 0 & TE\ 2\ 2 \\ 0 & 0 & TE\ 1\ 1 \\ 0 & 0 & 0 & TE\ 4\ 4 \\ TE\ 1\ 5 & 0 & 0 & 0 & TE\ 5\ 5 \\ TE\ 1\ 5 & 0 & 0 & 0 & TE\ 6\ 5 & TE\ 6\ 6 \\ 0 & 0 & TE\ 1\ 5 & 0 & 0 & 0 & TE\ 5\ 5 \\ 0 & 0 & 0 & TE\ 8\ 4 & 0 & 0 & 0 & TE\ 8\ 8 \\ 0 & 0 & TE\ 1\ 5 & 0 & 0 & 0 & TE\ 6\ 5 & 0 & TE\ 9\ 9 \end{bmatrix}$$

LISREL input for Models 7.4.1–7.4.9

Full sib model – Constrained measurement and just-identified structure

```
DA NI=9 NOBS=518 MA=CM
LA
*
'XEDEQYR' 'SSBED' 'EDEQYR' 'EDAT64' 'XOCSXCR' 'OCSSIB' 'XOCSX70'
'OCSXCR' 'OCSX70'
CM
(4D20.13)
 0.5167008954243D+01 0.4679783126592D+01 0.4938070842326D+01 0.1922921816539D+01
 0.1949806949807D+01 0.4386996557209D+01 0.1815463432485D+01 0.1827591614826D+01
 0.3471849025041D+01 0.3345914579957D+01 0.3627641502926D+01 0.3238972071952D+01
 0.1166210542348D+01 0.1139875075252D+01 0.6582034415362D+00 0.3569933505328D+01
 0.3302070018432D+01 0.1140821946633D+01 0.1122999127123D+01 0.5235668842959D+01
 0.6274622362490D+01 0.3621744780335D+01 0.3242735052857D+01 0.1210572885314D+01
 0.1194227627373D+01 0.5336248715763D+01 0.4963113333139D+01 0.6446553035743D+01
 0.1391681952781D+01 0.1364161548669D+01 0.2822630647346D+01 0.2344899377790D+01
 0.1651115593313D+01 0.1620192034477D+01 0.1532529966490D+01 0.5951538627534D+01
 0.1638921681630D+01 0.1577077688878D+01 0.2975257164254D+01 0.2472673949769D+01
 0.1941411027899D+01 0.1848463228034D+01 0.1678794058818D+01 0.4802423584718D+01
 0.5787209952562D+01
SE
3 4 1 2 8 9 5 6 7
MO NX=0 NY=9 NE=7 NK=3 BE=FU,FI TE=SY,FI PS=DI,FR LY=FU,FI TD=ZE C
GA=FU,FI PH=DI,FR LX=FU,FI
FR BE(5,1)
FR GA(1,1) GA (6,2) GA(7,3) GA(3,1)
ST 1.0 GA(2,1) GA(2,2) GA(3,3)
FREE LY(2,2) LY (4,3) LY (6,4) LY(8,5) LY(9,5)
FIX PS(2,2) PS(3,3) PS (4,4) PS (5,5)
ST 0 PS(2,2) PS (3,3) PS (4,4) PS (5,5)
FREE TE(1,1) TE (2,2) TE(3,3) TE(4,4) TE(5,5) TE(6,6) TE(7,7)
FREE TE(8,8) TE(9,9)
FREE TE (5,1) TE (7,3) TE(3,9) TE(1,6) TE(4,8) TE(7,9) TE(5,6)
EQUAL TE(7,9) TE(5,6)
START .70 ALL
START .20 TE (5,1) TE(7,3) TE(3,9) TE(1,6) TE(7,9) TE(5,6)
START -.20 TE(4,8)
START 1.0 BE(4,6) BE(4,1) BE(5,7)
```

```
START 1.0 LY (1,2) LY(3,3) LY(5,4) LY(7,5)
EQ TE(1,5) TE(1,6) TE(3,7) TE(3,9)
FI LY(4,3) LY(6,4) LY(8,5) LY(9,5)
ST 1.0 LY(4,3) LY(6,4) LY(8,5) LY(9,5)
EQ TE(1,1) TE(3,3)
EQ TE(5,5) TE(7,7)
FI BE(5,1)
ST 1.0 BE(5,1)
FI GA(3,1)
ST 1.0 GA(3,1)
[EQ GA(6,2) GA(7,3)]/ADD FOR MODEL 4.2
[EQ GA(6,2) GA(7,3) GA(1,1)]/ADD FOR MODELS 4.3-4.5
[EQ PS(6,6) PS(7,7)]/ADD FOR MODELS 4.4-4.5
[EQ PH(2,2) PH(3,3)]/ADD FOR MODEL 4.5
OU TV SS ND=5 TO MR SE
```

Chapter 8, final model (Figure A.7)

Specification of the model

Equations for the model

Measurement model

$$
\begin{aligned}
y_1 &= \lambda^y_{11}\eta_1 &&&&&&+ \varepsilon_1 \\
y_2 &= &\lambda^y_{22}\eta_2 &&&&&+ \varepsilon_2 \\
y_3 &= &\lambda^y_{32}\eta_2 &&&&&+ \varepsilon_3 \\
y_4 &= &\lambda^y_{42}\eta_2 &&&&&+ \varepsilon_4 \\
y_5 &= &&\lambda^y_{53}\eta_3 &&&&+ \varepsilon_5 \\
y_6 &= &&&\lambda^y_{64}\eta_4 &&&+ \varepsilon_6 \\
y_7 &= &&&\lambda^y_{74}\eta_4 &&&+ \varepsilon_7 \\
y_8 &= &&&\lambda^y_{84}\eta_4 &&&+ \varepsilon_8 \\
y_9 &= &&&&\lambda^y_{95}\eta_5 &&+ \varepsilon_9 \\
y_{10} &= &&&&&\lambda^y_{10,6}\eta_6 &+ \varepsilon_{10} \\
y_{11} &= &&&&&\lambda^y_{11,6}\eta_6 &+ \varepsilon_{11} \\
y_{12} &= &&&&&\lambda^y_{12,6}\eta_6 &+ \varepsilon_{12}
\end{aligned}
$$

Structural model

$$
\begin{aligned}
\eta_1 &= \beta_{13}\eta_3 + \beta_{14}\eta_4 + \beta_{15}\eta_5 &&+ \zeta_1 \\
\eta_2 &= \beta_{23}\eta_3 + \beta_{24}\eta_4 &+ \beta_{26}\eta_6 &+ \zeta_2 \\
\eta_3 &= &\beta_{35}\eta_5 + \beta_{36}\eta_6 &+ \zeta_3 \\
\eta_4 &= &\beta_{45}\eta_5 + \beta_{46}\eta_6 &+ \zeta_4 \\
\eta_5 &= &&+ \zeta_5 \\
\eta_6 &= &&+ \zeta_6
\end{aligned}
$$

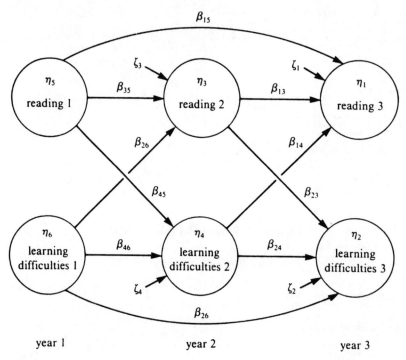

Figure A.7. (Same as Figure 8.4.) Three-wave analysis: basic structural model.

Matrix format of the equations

$$
\begin{bmatrix}
y_1 \\
y_2 \\
y_3 \\
y_4 \\
y_5 \\
y_6 \\
y_7 \\
y_8 \\
y_9 \\
y_{10} \\
y_{11} \\
y_{12}
\end{bmatrix}
=
\begin{bmatrix}
\lambda_{11} & & & & & \\
& \lambda_{22} & & & & \\
& \lambda_{32} & & & & \\
& \lambda_{42} & & & & \\
& & \lambda_{53} & & & \\
& & & \lambda_{64} & & \\
& & & \lambda_{74} & & \\
& & & \lambda_{84} & & \\
& & & & \lambda_{95} & \\
& & & & & \lambda_{10,6} \\
& & & & & \lambda_{11,6} \\
& & & & & \lambda_{12,6}
\end{bmatrix}
\begin{bmatrix}
\eta_1 \\
\eta_2 \\
\eta_3 \\
\eta_4 \\
\eta_5 \\
\eta_6
\end{bmatrix}
+
\begin{bmatrix}
\varepsilon_1 \\
\varepsilon_2 \\
\varepsilon_3 \\
\varepsilon_4 \\
\varepsilon_5 \\
\varepsilon_6 \\
\varepsilon_7 \\
\varepsilon_8 \\
\varepsilon_9 \\
\varepsilon_{10} \\
\varepsilon_{11} \\
\varepsilon_{12}
\end{bmatrix}
$$

$$
\mathbf{Y} \quad = \quad \mathbf{\Lambda}^y \quad \quad \quad \boldsymbol{\eta} \quad + \quad \boldsymbol{\varepsilon}
$$

$$
\begin{bmatrix} \eta_1 \\ \eta_2 \\ \eta_3 \\ \eta_4 \\ \eta_5 \\ \eta_6 \end{bmatrix} = \begin{bmatrix} & & \beta_{13} & \beta_{14} & \beta_{15} & \\ & & \beta_{23} & \beta_{24} & & \beta_{26} \\ & & & & \beta_{35} & \beta_{46} \\ & & & & \beta_{45} & \beta_{46} \\ & & & & & \\ & & & & & \end{bmatrix} \begin{bmatrix} \eta_1 \\ \eta_2 \\ \eta_3 \\ \eta_4 \\ \eta_5 \\ \eta_6 \end{bmatrix} + \begin{bmatrix} \zeta_1 \\ \zeta_2 \\ \zeta_3 \\ \zeta_4 \\ \zeta_5 \\ \zeta_6 \end{bmatrix}
$$

$$\eta = \beta \qquad \eta + \zeta$$

LISREL input

Three-wave model (Final version)

```
DA   NI = 12   NOBS = 1317   MA = CM
LA
*
'ERTRW3'  'YR3AITM4'  'YR3AITM5'  'YR3AITM6'  'ERTRW2'  'YR2AITM4'
'YR2AITM5'  'YR2AITM6'  'ERTRW'  'YR1AITM4'  'YR1AITM5'  'YR1AITM6'
CM


  1.000
 -0.479    1.000
 -0.441    0.664    1.000
 -0.483    0.772    0.697    1.000
  0.762   -0.458   -0.406   -0.430    1.000
 -0.472    0.512    0.399    0.506   -0.461    1.000
 -0.462    0.430    0.438    0.465   -0.458    0.592    1.000
 -0.461    0.468    0.437    0.497   -0.452    0.730    0.723    1.000
  0.770   -0.449   -0.402   -0.424    0.815   -0.453   -0.440   -0.440    1.000
 -0.478    0.490    0.405    0.472   -0.495    0.516    0.440    0.490   -0.508    1.000
 -0.452    0.406    0.394    0.402   -0.468    0.424    0.464    0.435   -0.497    0.660    1.000
 -0.495    0.462    0.407    0.479   -0.503    0.497    0.439    0.517   -0.509    0.755    0.714    1.000

MO  NX=O        NK=O       NY=12  NE=6    LX=FU, FI  LY=FU, FI  BE=SD, FI  PS=SY, FI
       TD=DI, FR  TE=DI, FR
FR     BE 1 3      BE 1 4      BE 1 5      BE 2 3      BE 2 4      BE 2 6     BE 3 5     BE 3 6
       BE 4 5      BE 4 6
       LY 3 2      LY 4 2      LY 7 4      LY 8 4      LY 11 6     LY 12 6
       TE 6 2      TE 7 3      TE 8 4      TE 10 6     TE 11 7     TE 12 8    TE 10 2    TE 11 3
       TE 12 4
       PS 1 1      PS 2 1      PS 2 2      PS 3 3      PS 4 3      PS 4 4     PS 5 5     PS 6 5
       PS 6 6

ST 1.0    LY 2 2   LY 6 4   LY 10 6  LY 1 1   LY 5 3   LY 9 5
ST 1.0    TE 2 2   TE 3 3   TE 4 4   TE 6 6   TE 7 7   TE 8 8
          TE 10 10  TE 11 11  TE 12 12
ST 0.054  TE 5 5   TE 9 9
ST 0.039  TE 1 1

OU  SE  TV  PC  RS
```

Glossary

Attenuation Term referring to a relationship between two or more variables when one or more of them is *measured with error*. In a regression model the estimate of the regression coefficient is reduced or attenuated when an explanatory variable is measured with error.

Chi-square statistic A statistic indicating the goodness-of-fit of a model to the data; distributed asymptotically according to the chi-square distribution. Often employed to test hypotheses about the likelihood ratio statistic for model fit.

Common factor A latent construct that models the common variation between a set of observed variables.

Correlation A measure of the degree of linear relationship between two variables, taking a maximum value of 1 when the variables are perfectly related to each other. A normalized measure of covariation.

Covariance A measure of the degree of linear association between two variables. Related to the correlation coefficient by the following formula: correlation r between two variables X & Y = covariance between X & Y/(square root of the variance of X × square root of the variance of Y).

Degrees of freedom A measure of the degree of overidentification in a structural model.

Distribution The variation among observations on a random variable. Many estimation procedures assume that the distribution of the continuous variables in a model is *normal*.

Distribution free A method of *robust* estimation that does not require particular assumptions about the distributional form of the variables in the model.

Endogenous A term referring to variables or constructs whose variation is modeled as determined wholly or in part by other variables in the model.

Errors of measurement Latent constructs are modeled by observed variables that are assumed to measure the latent construct with some degree of error. Similarly,

312

observed values of test scores typically contain some error of measurement, defined as the difference between the true score and the observed score.

Exogenous A term referring to constructs whose variation is assumed to be determined by variables external to the model.

Factor analysis A form of multivariate analysis in which the variation among observed variables is modeled in terms of a lower number of factors that describes the pattern of covariation between them. *See also* Latent construct.

First derivative The rate of change in the minimization function employed to estimate the parameters of a model. In maximum likelihood estimation of structural equation models, the first derivative of the likelihood function with respect to a *fixed* parameter indicates the extent to which, if freed, the fit of the model to the data would be improved – hence its use and implementation in LISREL as a diagnostic indicator of the goodness of fit of individual elements of a model to the data.

Fit (of model to data) A measure of the overall congruence between the observed covariance matrix and that implied by the estimates of the model parameters. In structural equation models, an assessment of the fit of a model to the data is made from inspection of a range of indicators (see Chapter 12).

Fixed parameter A term used in LISREL to denote a parameter that takes a fixed or given value. The value is usually zero, but in principle any value is possible. The purpose of fixing parameters to a particular value varies according to the situation. An example is the case in which the loading of one indicator on a latent construct is set equal to a nonzero value (usually 1) in order to define the scale of measurement for the construct. Parameters representing relationships between latent constructs may be set to particular fixed values on the basis of theoretical considerations or knowledge from other sources.

Free parameter A term used in LISREL to denote a parameter that is estimated from the data for the model. *See also* Fixed parameter.

Generalized least squares A method of estimation that allows for heterogeneity of variances and covariances. An option available for estimating models in LISREL; it has theoretical large-sample properties that are similar to those of maximum likelihood.

Goodness-of-fit *See* Fit.

Hierarchical models A set of models each of which is related to those immediately above or below it in the hierarchy by the property that it can be transformed into those models by the deletion or addition of a small number of parameters (often one). The difference in fit between models related in this way can be tested by a comparison of their chi-squared goodness-of-fit test statistics. The difference between the values of the chi-square fit statistic for any pair of models itself has a chi-square distribution, with degrees of freedom equal to the difference in degrees of freedom between the two models.

Identified A model is identified if unique estimates of parameter values can be obtained. A model is overidentified if the values of one or more of the parameters can be obtained from more than one unique combination of the variances and covariances for the observed variables in the model. A just-identified model is one in which the estimates of each parameter can be obtained from only one unique combination of the variances and covariances. Such models have a perfect fit to the data and include the set of models that do not involve latent constructs (e.g., regression models). An underidentified model is one in which some parameters are not uniquely estimable from the variances and covariances. For such models the goodness-of-fit of the model to the data is indeterminate.

Indicator An observed variable that measures or indicates a *latent construct*.

Latent construct (or latent variable) An unobserved or hypothetical variable that is modeled as a linear combination of the observed variables plus parameters that may allow for measurement error in these observed variables. *Factors* (in factor analysis) and *true scores* (in test theory) are examples of latent constructs.

Leptokurtic A statistical term describing distributions that have longer tails (and are more peaked) than the normal distribution.

LISREL An acronym for "linear structural relations," an implementation of structural equation modeling or covariance structures due to Karl Jöreskog and Dag Sörbom.

Loading (of an indicator on a latent construct) A parameter that represents the relationship of a latent construct to each of its constituent observed variables.

Maximum likelihood A method of estimation that maximizes the likelihood function for the parameters of a particular model, given the data. Estimates of parameters obtained from maximum likelihood may not be robust in small samples (see Chapter 12).

Measurement error *See* Errors of measurement.

Measurement model That part of the structural equation model that relates the observed variables to the latent constructs.

Model (modeling) A representation of the relationships between constructs and variables. The specification of a model may derive from either theoretical or empirical procedures. In *structural modeling* the term is used to refer to the specific path diagram and the set of equations relating variables and the constructs that they imply.

Modification index A diagnostic indicator of the fit of individual parameters in a structural model (*see also* First derivatives). Employed specifically to measure the improvement in the chi-squared measure of goodness-of-fit statistic associated with a *fixed* parameter in a model.

Multiple-group analysis Within LISREL, a form of simultaneous analysis of a number of variance–covariance matrices (or moment matrices), each corresponding to a separate group of observations, allowing constraints to be imposed on the parameters across groups.

Multivariate normality a distributional assumption of normality in the multivariate space spanned by the parameters in a model.

Normalized residuals Residuals that are transformed to have unit variance.

Normality A distributional characteristic of an observed variable. Widely assumed in the application of structural equation modeling through the use of a variance–covariance matrix to summarize the information in the data.

Outlier An observation that may have come from a distribution that is different from that of the remainder of the data. Such observations may be the product of gross errors of measurement, data coding, etc., but they may also be genuine observations from a distribution that is different from the other values in the sample. If not recognized, they may exert undue influence on the determination of the estimates of a model. *Robust* methods of estimation often seek to alleviate the problems caused by the failure to notice outliers in the data.

Parallel measures Alternative forms of the same measure having the same relationship (loading) to the latent construct that they jointly represent and the same measurement error variance. The correlation between two parallel measures is equal to the (common) reliability of the measures.

Parameter Each of the relationships in a model is represented by a parameter. Parameters may also represent a characteristic of a single variable, such as a mean.

Path analysis A form of regression analysis between the observed variables in a model.

Random variable A variable that is observed randomly with respect to its values. For example, the social status of an individual is observed at random in a survey in which sample members are chosen randomly. This is to be contrasted with the case in which the observations on a variable are observed in accordance with some pattern related to those values, say, the highest 5 percent of the known values in that population. Thus, the observations on a race variable are not random if the survey is of one race only. But the values of other variables will be observed randomly if the sample members are chosen at random. In more general terms, a random variable is defined as a numerical quantity whose value is determined by the outcome of a chance experiment.

Reliability A property of measurement. The capacity of a measure to provide the same reading of a given event on many occasions. Variation in test scores, for example, is composed of a component that is due to the *true score* and another that is referred to as *measurement error*. The reliability of the test is then defined as the ratio of the variance component due to the true score to the total variance of the observed scores on the test.

Robust estimation A method of estimation that is not dependent on the distributional form of the variables involved, and in particular one that is not heavily influenced by the presence of *outliers*.

Skewness A measure of asymmetry in the distribution of the observations on a variable.

Specification error An error in the specification of the relationships between the variables in a model.

Standard deviation A measure of the dispersion of a *random variable*, equal to the square root of its *variance*.

Standardized solution The estimates for a model in which all the latent constructs are constrained to have unit variance.

Variance A measure of the dispersion or variability in a *random variable*. The square of the standard deviation.

Variance–covariance matrix The set of *variances* of, and *covariances* between, a number of *variables*.

Index

additive relationships, 16–17
aggregated data, 132
assumptions
  factor model, 11–14
  measurement, 16–17
  normality, 16, 18–20
  regression model, 9–11
  structural equation models, 14–21
  violation of, *see* robustness
asymptotic estimates, 186
autocorrelation, 93

BENWEE, 262
beta, 282
binary variables, 12

categorical variables, 12
chi square, *see* fit of models
classical test score theory, *see*
  measurement model
confirmatory methods, *see* structural
  modeling
constraints
  inequality constraints, 221–39
  restrictions, 221
  see also fixed parameters
contextual effects models, 109
continuous variables, 12, 246
convergence problems, 172–3
correlation, 247
correlation matrix, 162–3, 169, 171
COSAN, 6, 238
covariance, 14, 246
  see also covariation
covariation, 246–9
  attenuation of measures of covariation,
  248
  canonical correlation, 248
  censored distributions, 249
  linearity, 16–17
  polychoric correlation, 1, 249
  robustness of measures, 266–8

tetrachoric correlation, 12
truncated distributions, 249
cross product, 246
cross validation, 244–5

degrees of freedom, 233
delta, 282
dependent variable, 9–10
disturbance terms, 150
disturbances, *see* residuals

empirical underidentification, 99
endogenous variables, 11
epsilon, 282
EQS, 6
error variance, 123–7
  correlated errors, 80
  negative estimates, 74, 81
  see also Heywood cases
estimation
  asymptotically distribution-free
    estimator (ADF), 253
  categorical variable method (CVM),
    253–4
  efficiency of estimation, 93
  generalized least squares (GLS), 252–4
  instrumental variables method (IV), 252
  maximum likelihood (ML), 82, 160–86,
    252–5
  ordinary least squares (OLS), 252
  two-stage least squares (2SLS), 252
  unweighted least squares (ULS), 252
  weighted least squares (WLS), 254
eta, 282
exploratory methods
  significance tests, 243–4
  see also structural modeling

fallible measurement, *see* measurement
  error
fit of models, 30–4, 56, 70–81, 97–103,
  115–32, 148, 172, 181–2, 189, 193,

317